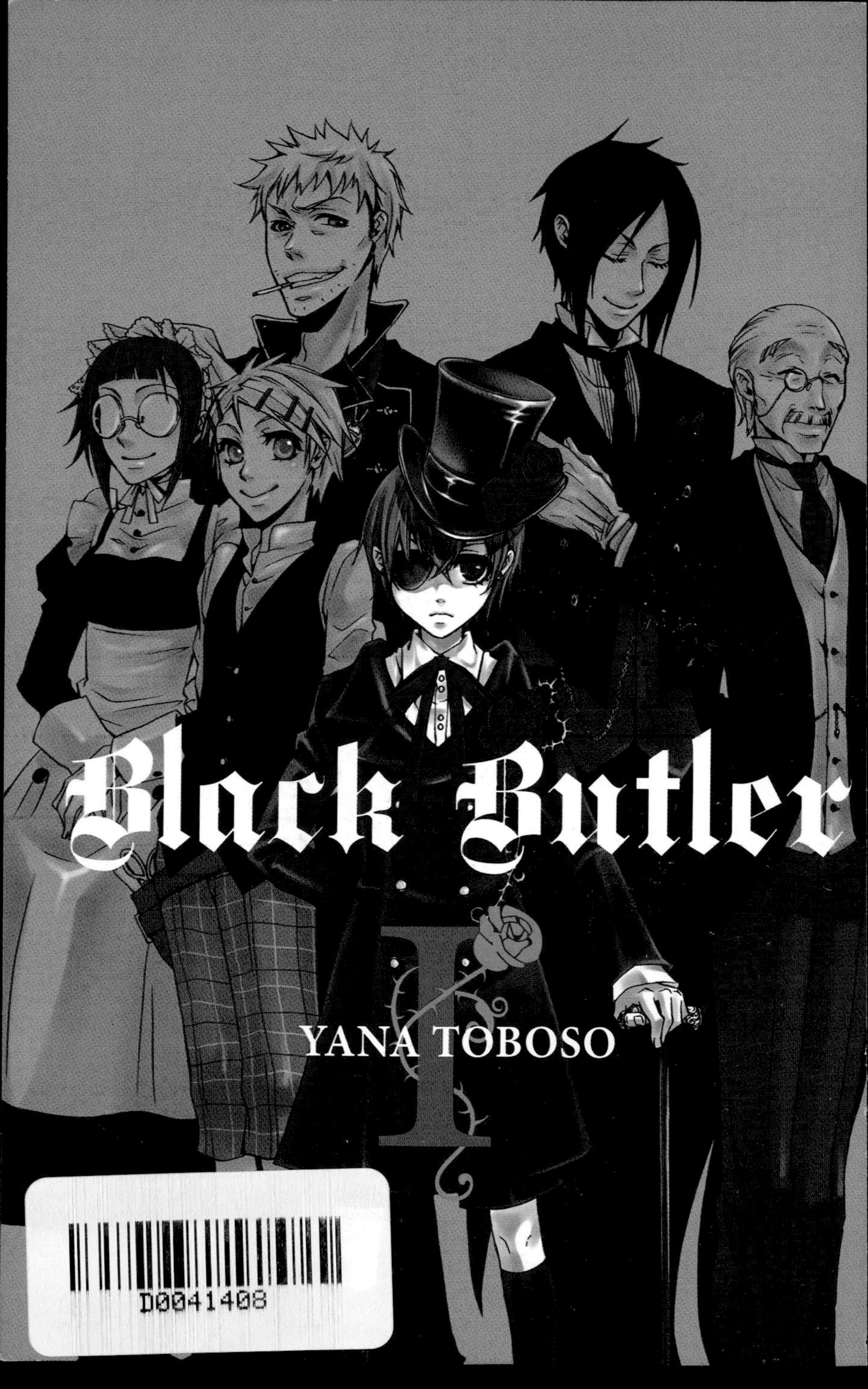
Black Butler
I
YANA TOBOSO

# Contents

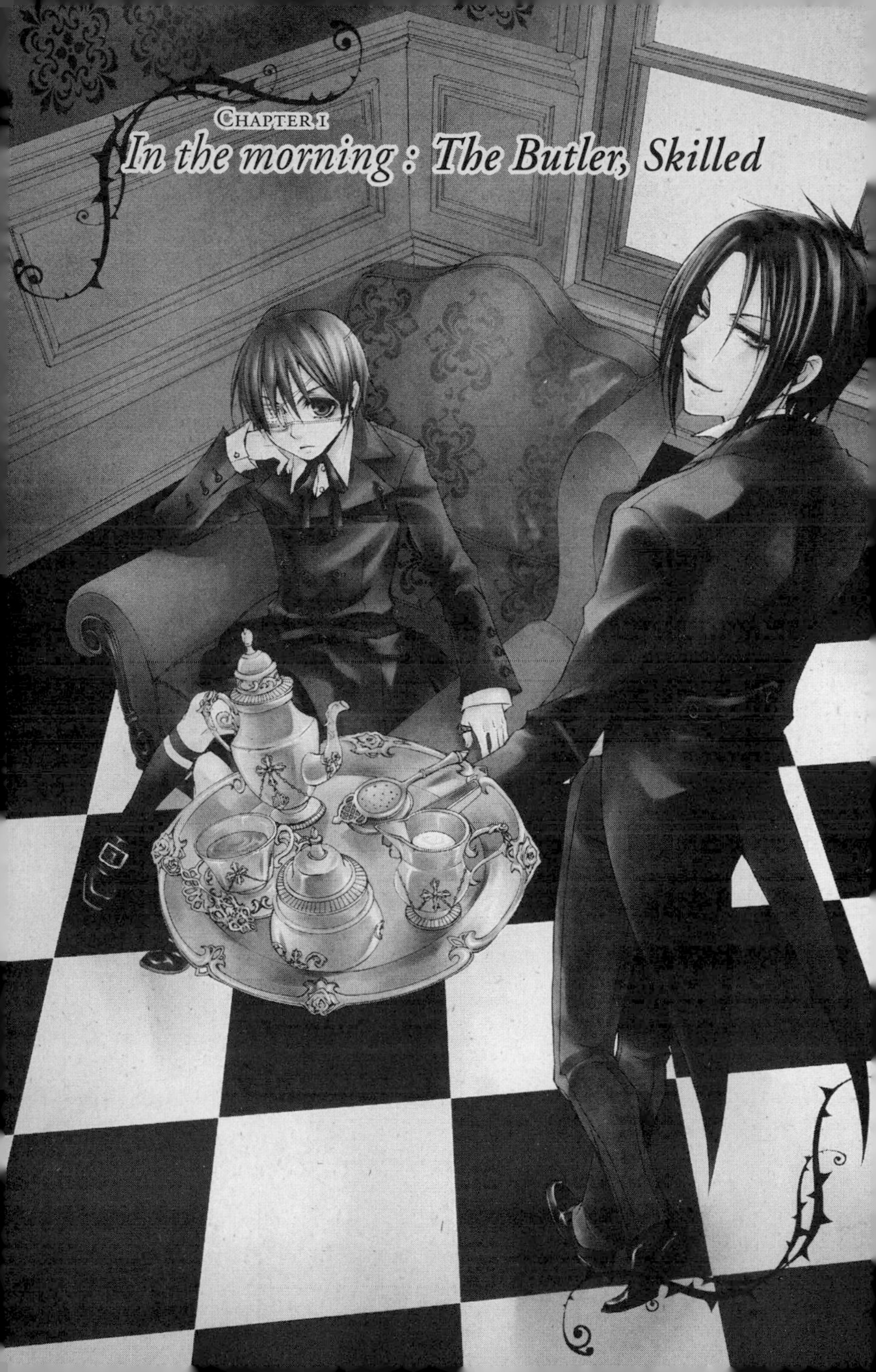
Chapter 1
In the morning : The Butler, Skilled

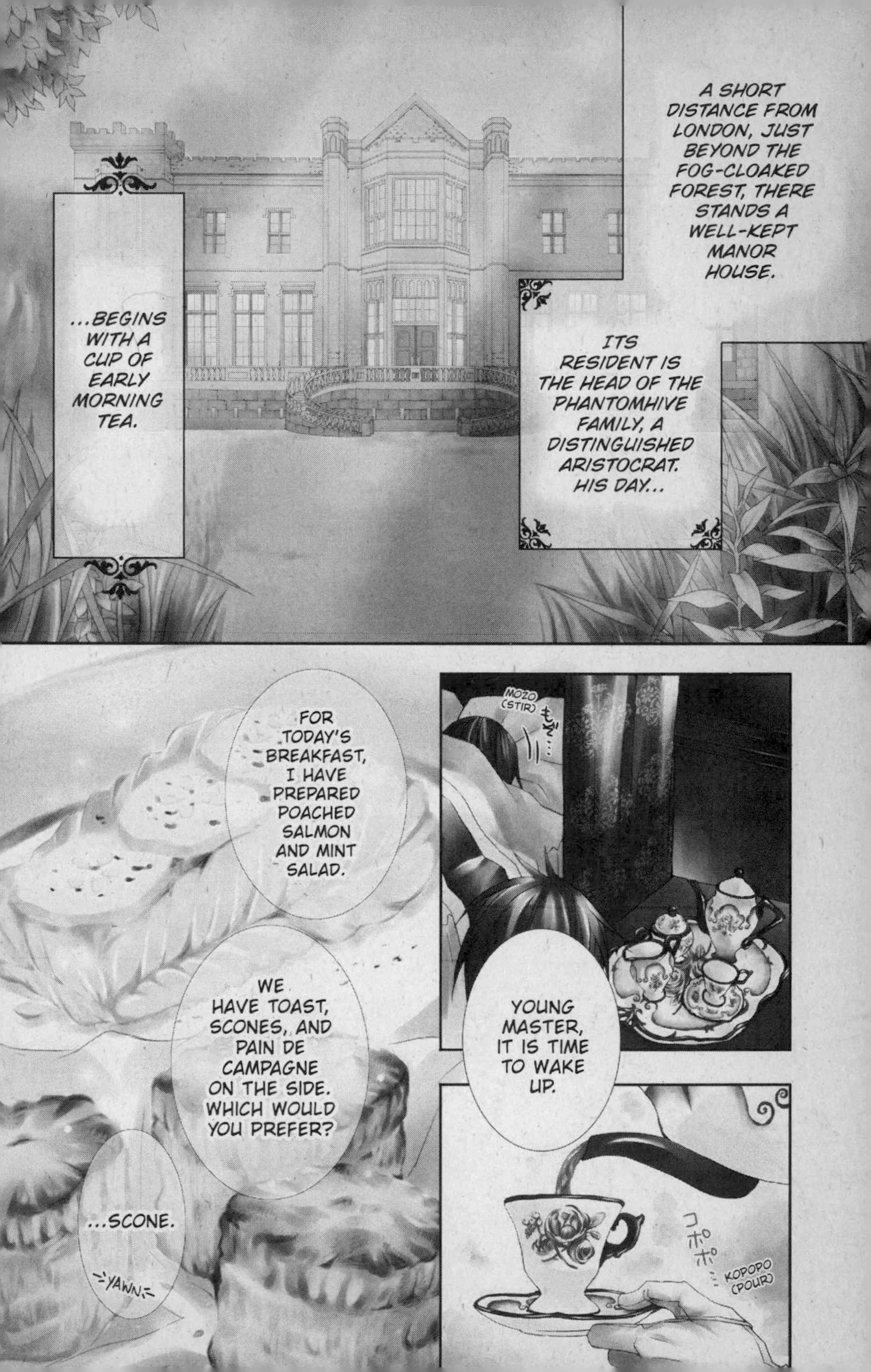
A SHORT DISTANCE FROM LONDON, JUST BEYOND THE FOG-CLOAKED FOREST, THERE STANDS A WELL-KEPT MANOR HOUSE.
ITS RESIDENT IS THE HEAD OF THE PHANTOMHIVE FAMILY, A DISTINGUISHED ARISTOCRAT. HIS DAY...
...BEGINS WITH A CUP OF EARLY MORNING TEA.
MOZO (STIR) もぞ…
YOUNG MASTER, IT IS TIME TO WAKE UP.
コポポ KOPOPO (POUR)
FOR TODAY'S BREAKFAST, I HAVE PREPARED POACHED SALMON AND MINT SALAD.
WE HAVE TOAST, SCONES, AND PAIN DE CAMPAGNE ON THE SIDE. WHICH WOULD YOU PREFER?
...SCONE.
YAWN

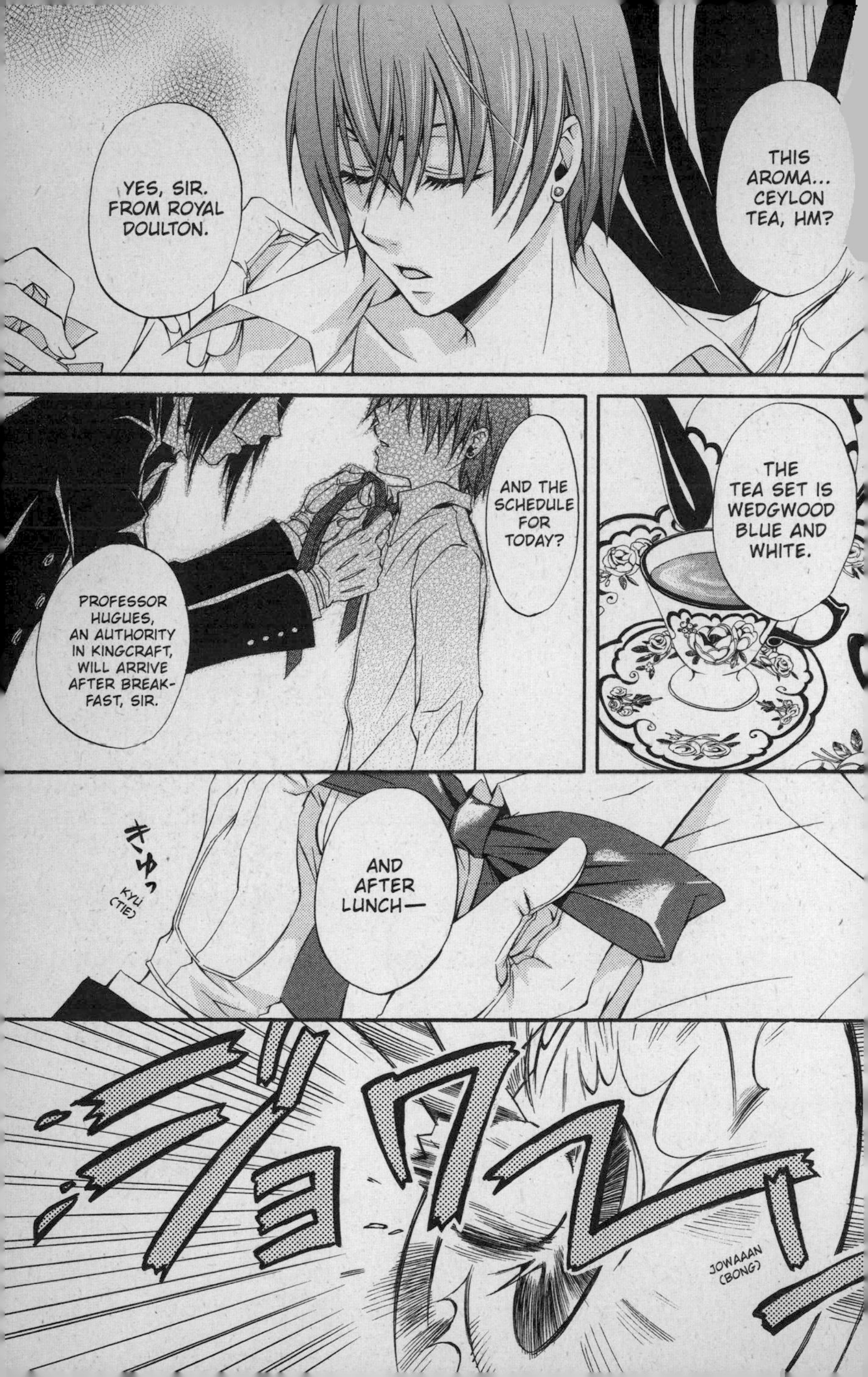
THIS AROMA... CEYLON TEA, HM?
YES, SIR. FROM ROYAL DOULTON.
THE TEA SET IS WEDGWOOD BLUE AND WHITE.
AND THE SCHEDULE FOR TODAY?
PROFESSOR HUGUES, AN AUTHORITY IN KINGCRAFT, WILL ARRIVE AFTER BREAK-FAST, SIR.
AND AFTER LUNCH—
きゅっ
KYU (TIE)
JOWAAAN (BONG)

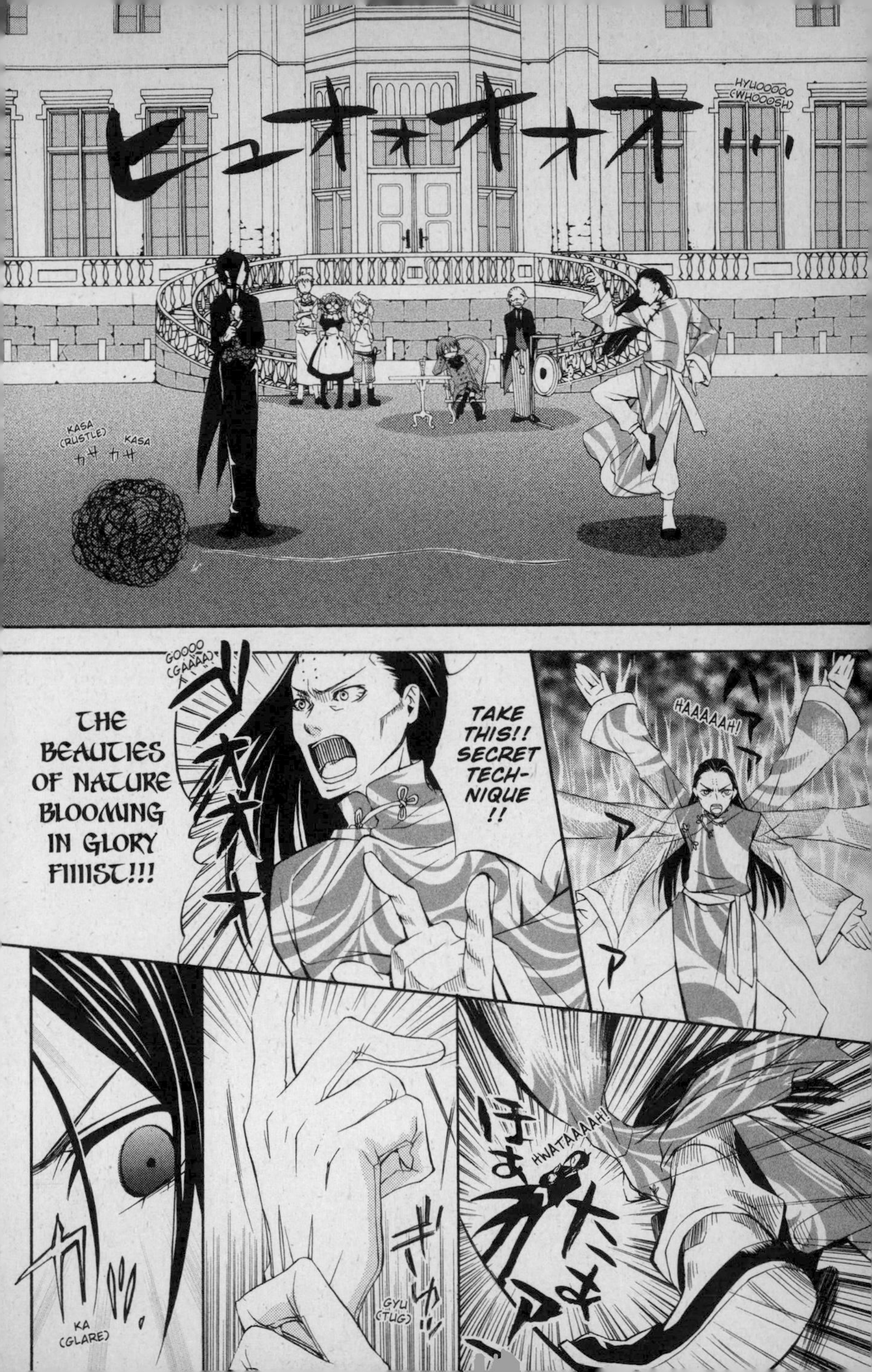
HYUOOOOO (WHOOOSH)
KASA (RUSTLE) KASA
HAAAAAH!
TAKE THIS!! SECRET TECH-NIQUE!!
GOOOO (GAAAA)
THE BEAUTIES OF NATURE BLOOMING IN GLORY FIIIIST!!!
HWATAAAAH!
GYU (TUG)
KA (GLARE)

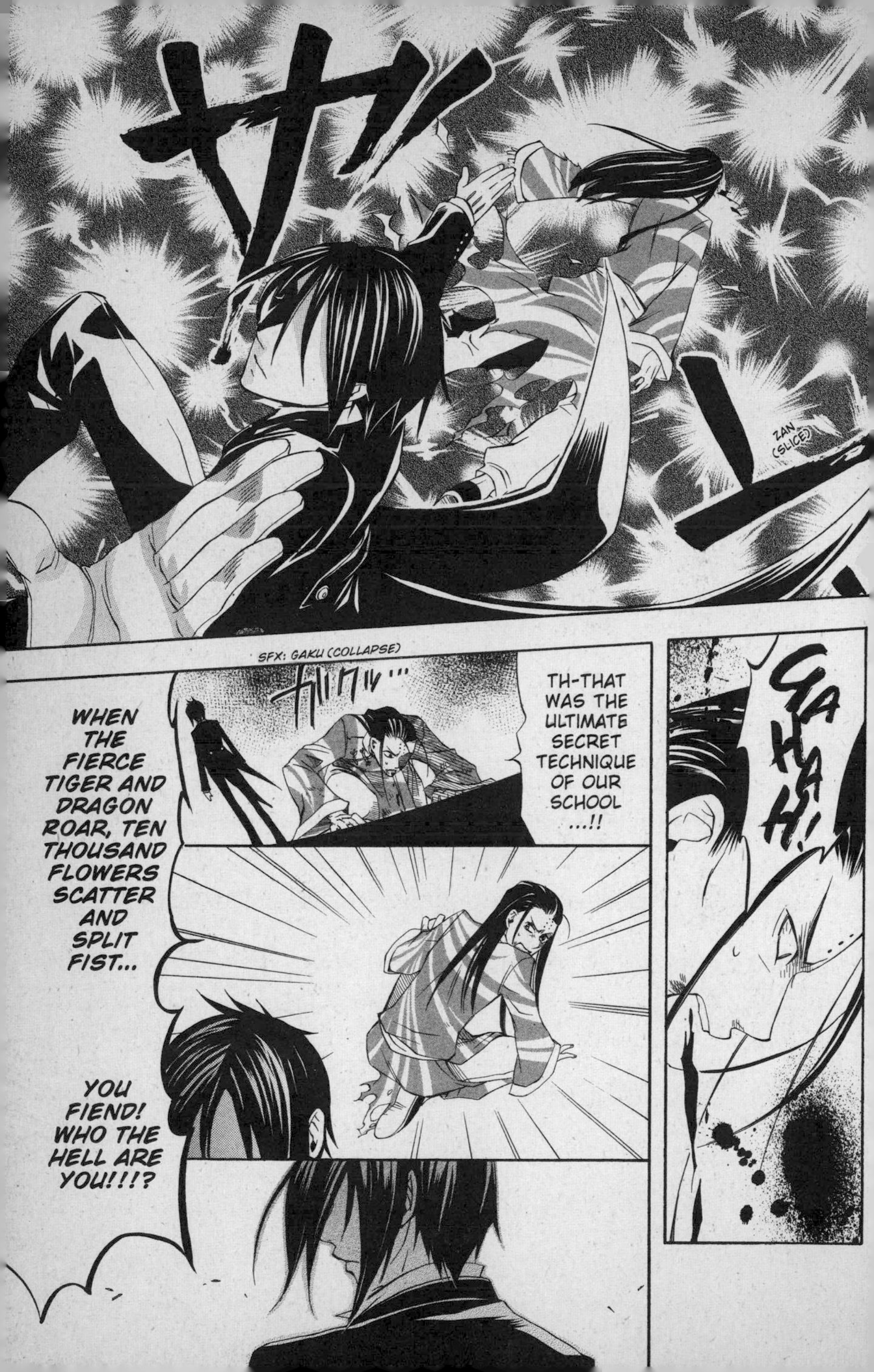
ZAN (SLICE)
GAHAH!
SFX: GAKU (COLLAPSE)
TH-THAT WAS THE ULTIMATE SECRET TECHNIQUE OF OUR SCHOOL ...!!
WHEN THE FIERCE TIGER AND DRAGON ROAR, TEN THOUSAND FLOWERS SCATTER AND SPLIT FIST...
YOU FIEND! WHO THE HELL ARE YOU!!!?

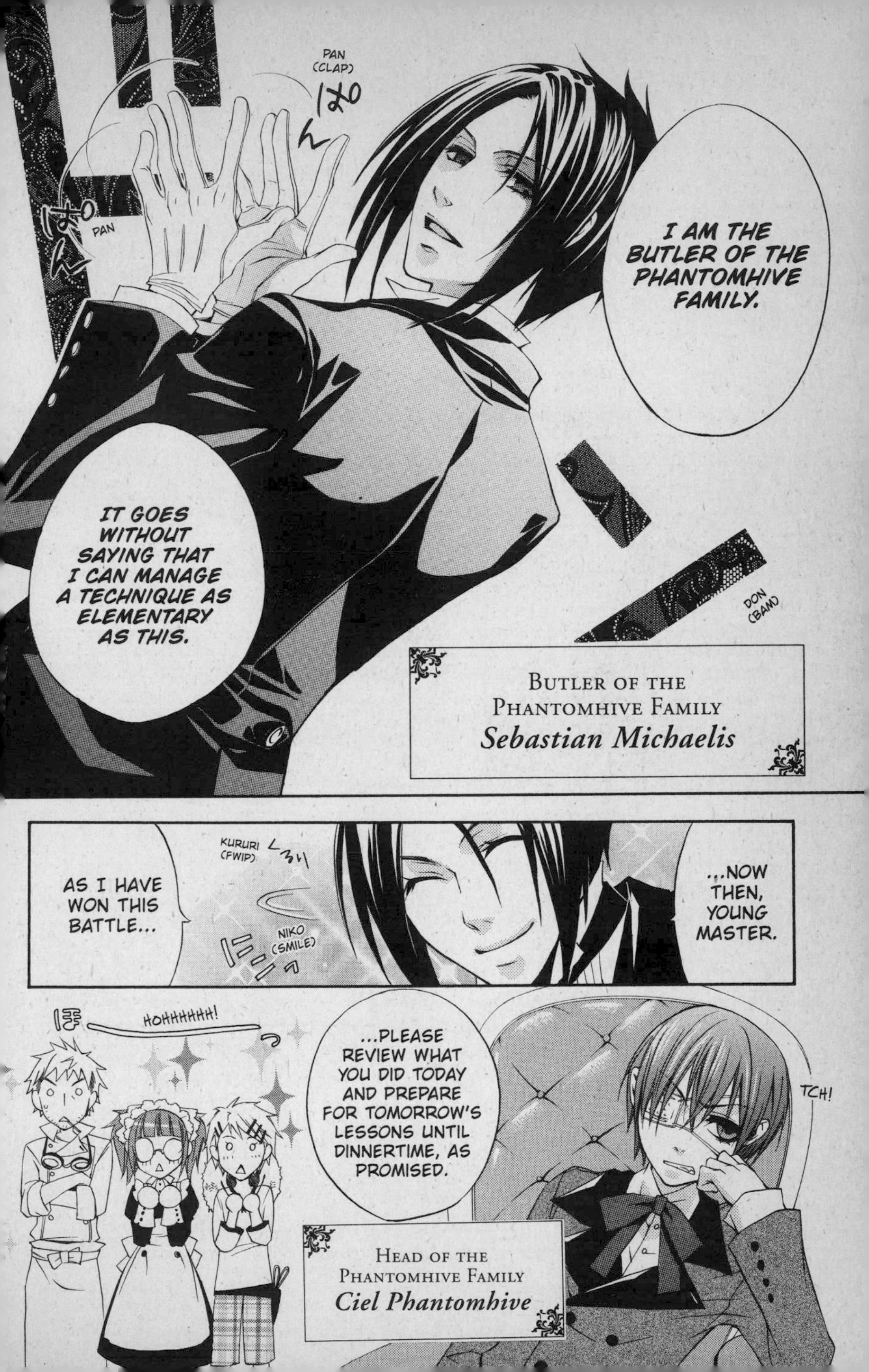
I AM THE BUTLER OF THE PHANTOMHIVE FAMILY.
ぱん
PAN (CLAP)
ぱん
PAN
IT GOES WITHOUT SAYING THAT I CAN MANAGE A TECHNIQUE AS ELEMENTARY AS THIS.
DON (BAM)
BUTLER OF THE PHANTOMHIVE FAMILY
*Sebastian Michaelis*
...NOW THEN, YOUNG MASTER.
くるり
KURURI (FWIP)
にこっ
NIKO (SMILE)
AS I HAVE WON THIS BATTLE...
TCH!
...PLEASE REVIEW WHAT YOU DID TODAY AND PREPARE FOR TOMORROW'S LESSONS UNTIL DINNERTIME, AS PROMISED.
HEAD OF THE PHANTOMHIVE FAMILY
*Ciel Phantomhive*
ほっ
HOHHHHHH!

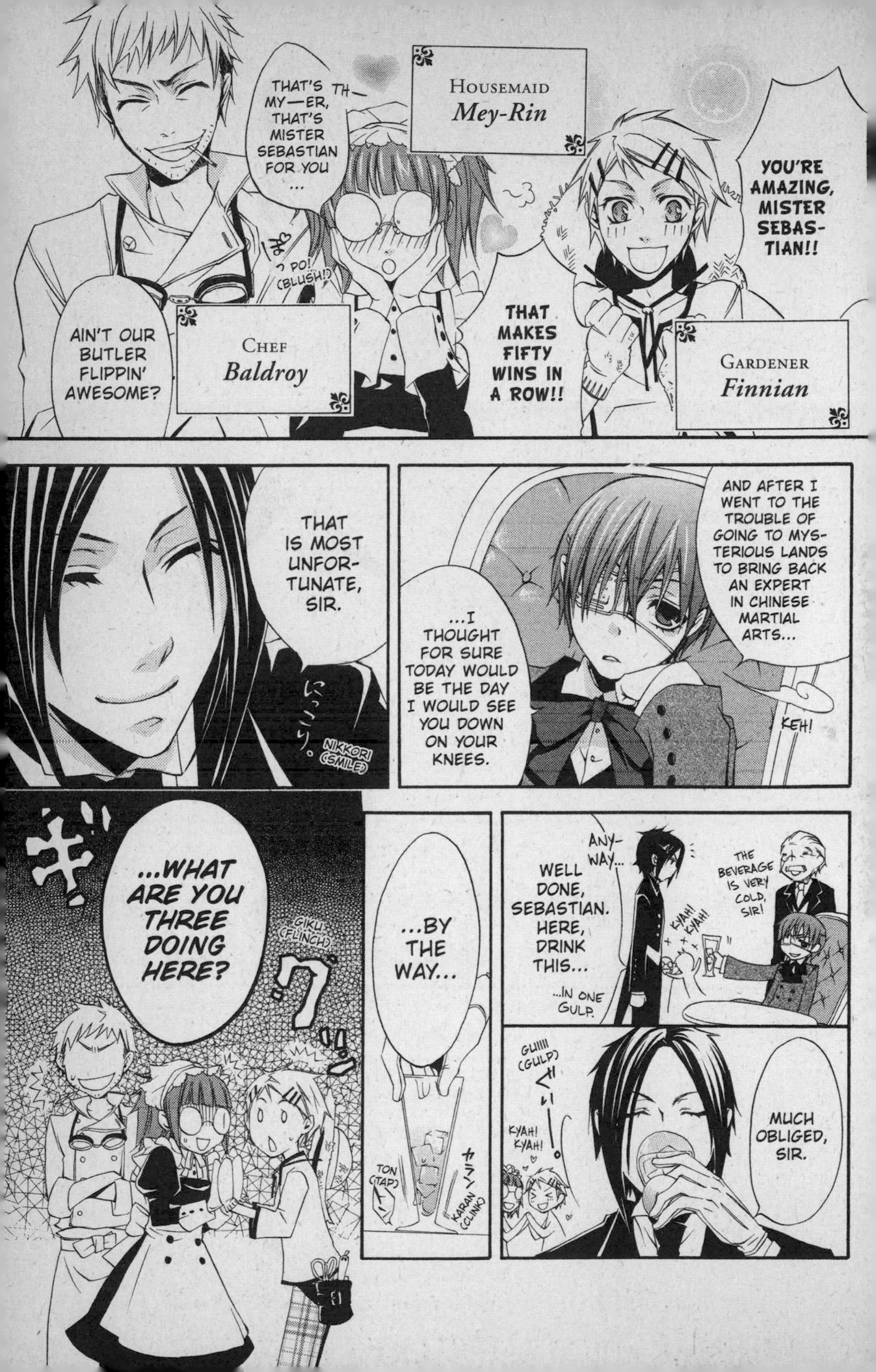
YOU'RE AMAZING, MISTER SEBASTIAN!!
GARDENER
Finnian
THAT MAKES FIFTY WINS IN A ROW!!
HOUSEMAID
Mey-Rin
TH—
THAT'S MY—ER, THAT'S MISTER SEBASTIAN FOR YOU ...
PO! (BLUSH!)
CHEF
Baldroy
AIN'T OUR BUTLER FLIPPIN' AWESOME?
AND AFTER I WENT TO THE TROUBLE OF GOING TO MYSTERIOUS LANDS TO BRING BACK AN EXPERT IN CHINESE MARTIAL ARTS...
KEH!
...I THOUGHT FOR SURE TODAY WOULD BE THE DAY I WOULD SEE YOU DOWN ON YOUR KNEES.
THAT IS MOST UNFORTUNATE, SIR.
NIKKORI (SMILE)
THE BEVERAGE IS VERY COLD, SIR!
KYAH! KYAH!
ANY-WAY...
WELL DONE, SEBASTIAN. HERE, DRINK THIS...
...IN ONE GULP.
MUCH OBLIGED, SIR.
GUIIII (GULP)
KYAH! KYAH!
...BY THE WAY...
KARAN (CLINK)
TON (TAP)
...WHAT ARE YOU THREE DOING HERE?
GIKU (FLINCH)

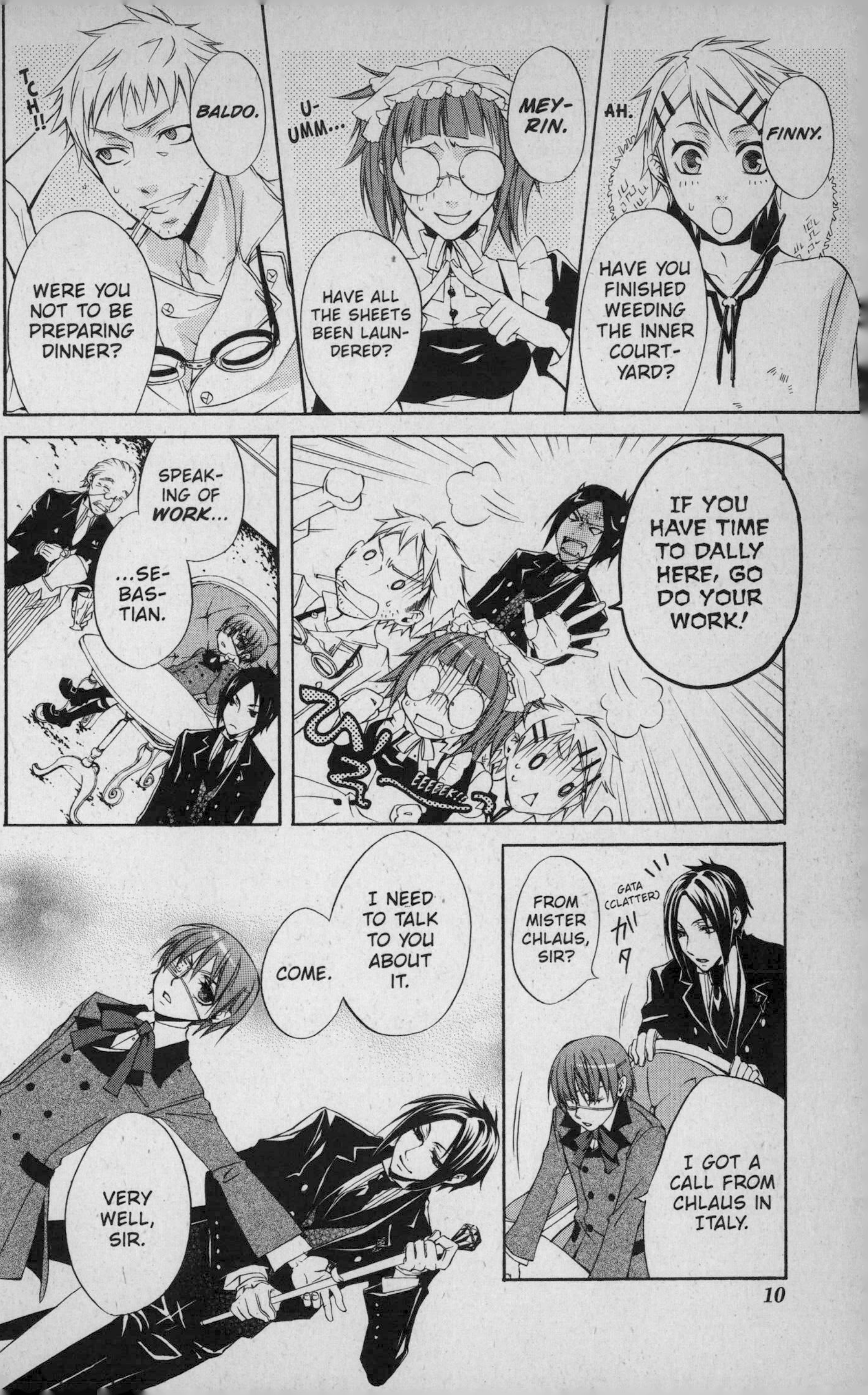
FINNY.
AH.
HAVE YOU FINISHED WEEDING THE INNER COURTYARD?
MEYRIN.
U-UMM...
HAVE ALL THE SHEETS BEEN LAUNDERED?
BALDO.
TCH!!
WERE YOU NOT TO BE PREPARING DINNER?
IF YOU HAVE TIME TO DALLY HERE, GO DO YOUR WORK!
EEEEEK!!
SPEAKING OF WORK...
...SEBASTIAN.
GATA (CLATTER)
FROM MISTER CHLAUS, SIR?
I GOT A CALL FROM CHLAUS IN ITALY.
I NEED TO TALK TO YOU ABOUT IT.
COME.
VERY WELL, SIR.

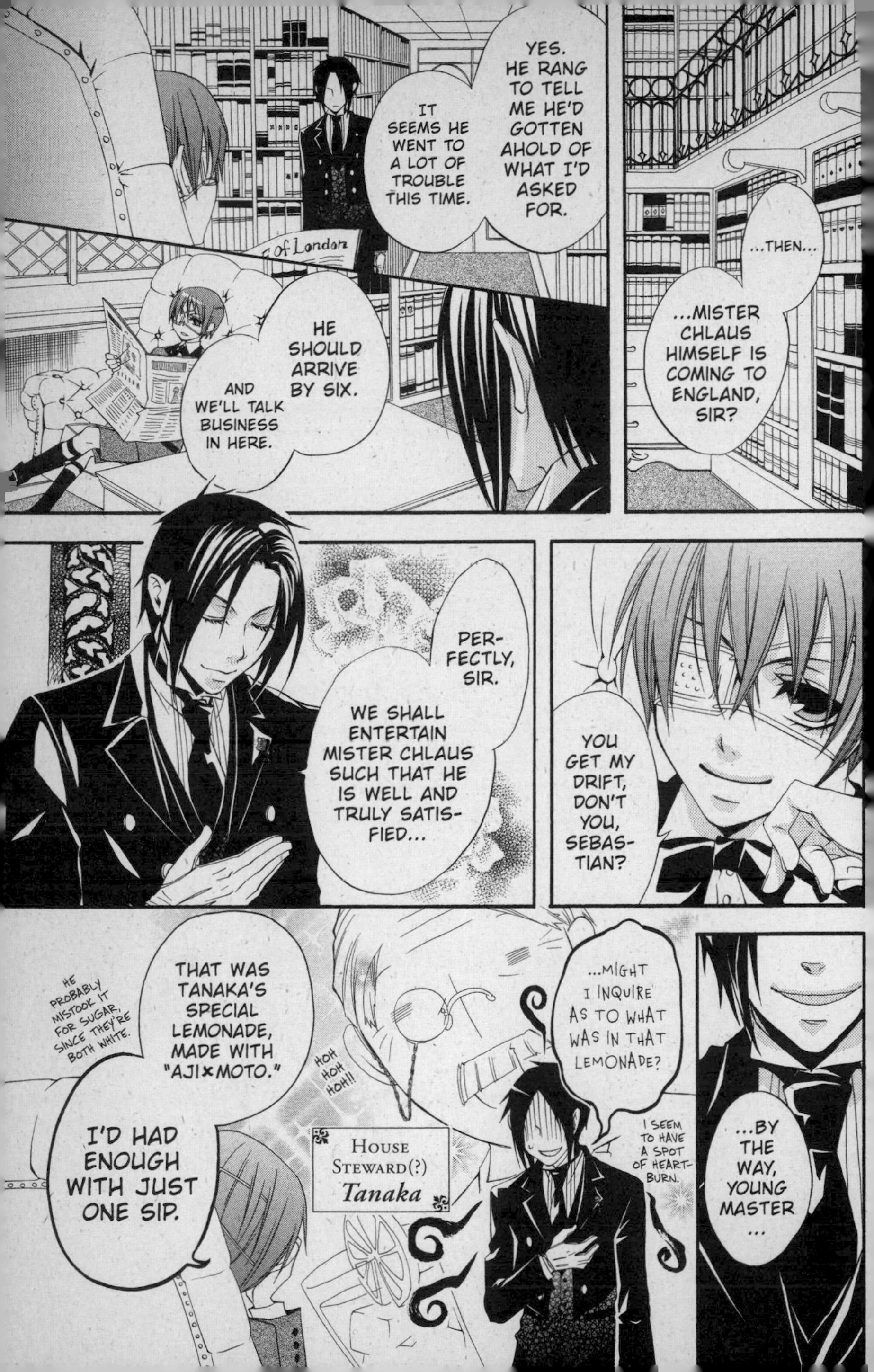
...THEN...
...MISTER CHLAUS HIMSELF IS COMING TO ENGLAND, SIR?
YES. HE RANG TO TELL ME HE'D GOTTEN AHOLD OF WHAT I'D ASKED FOR.
IT SEEMS HE WENT TO A LOT OF TROUBLE THIS TIME.
of London
HE SHOULD ARRIVE BY SIX.
AND WE'LL TALK BUSINESS IN HERE.
YOU GET MY DRIFT, DON'T YOU, SEBAS-TIAN?
PER-FECTLY, SIR.
WE SHALL ENTERTAIN MISTER CHLAUS SUCH THAT HE IS WELL AND TRULY SATIS-FIED...
...BY THE WAY, YOUNG MASTER...
...MIGHT I INQUIRE AS TO WHAT WAS IN THAT LEMONADE?
I SEEM TO HAVE A SPOT OF HEART-BURN.
HOH HOH HOH!!
THAT WAS TANAKA'S SPECIAL LEMONADE, MADE WITH "AJI×MOTO."
HE PROBABLY MISTOOK IT FOR SUGAR, SINCE THEY'RE BOTH WHITE.
I'D HAD ENOUGH WITH JUST ONE SIP.
HOUSE STEWARD(?) Tanaka

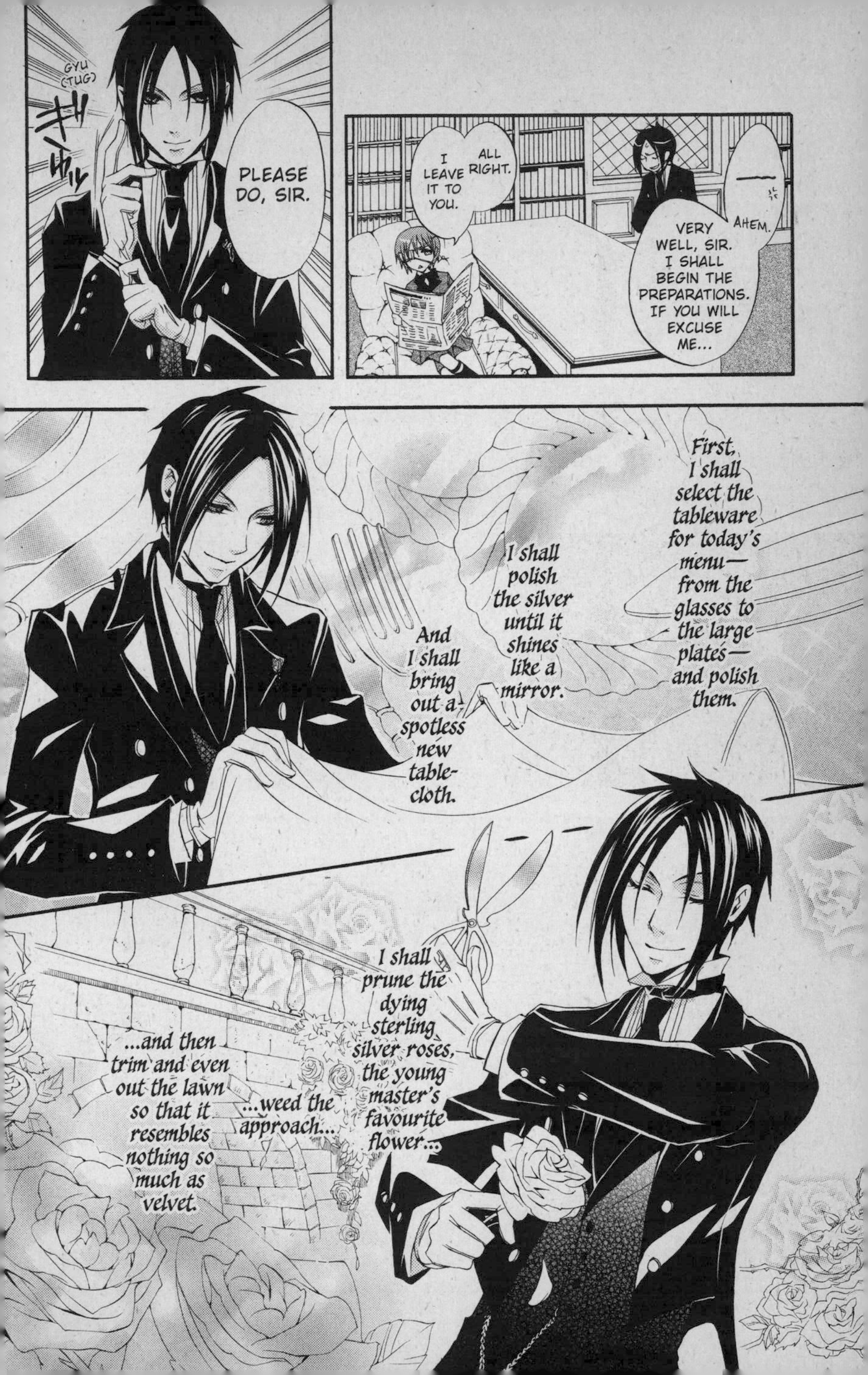
ALL RIGHT.
I LEAVE IT TO YOU.
———
AHEM.
VERY WELL, SIR. I SHALL BEGIN THE PREPARATIONS. IF YOU WILL EXCUSE ME...
GYU (TUG)
PLEASE DO, SIR.
First, I shall select the tableware for today's menu—from the glasses to the large plates—and polish them.
I shall polish the silver until it shines like a mirror.
And I shall bring out a spotless new table-cloth.
— —
I shall prune the dying sterling silver roses, the young master's favourite flower...
...weed the approach...
...and then trim and even out the lawn so that it resembles nothing so much as velvet.

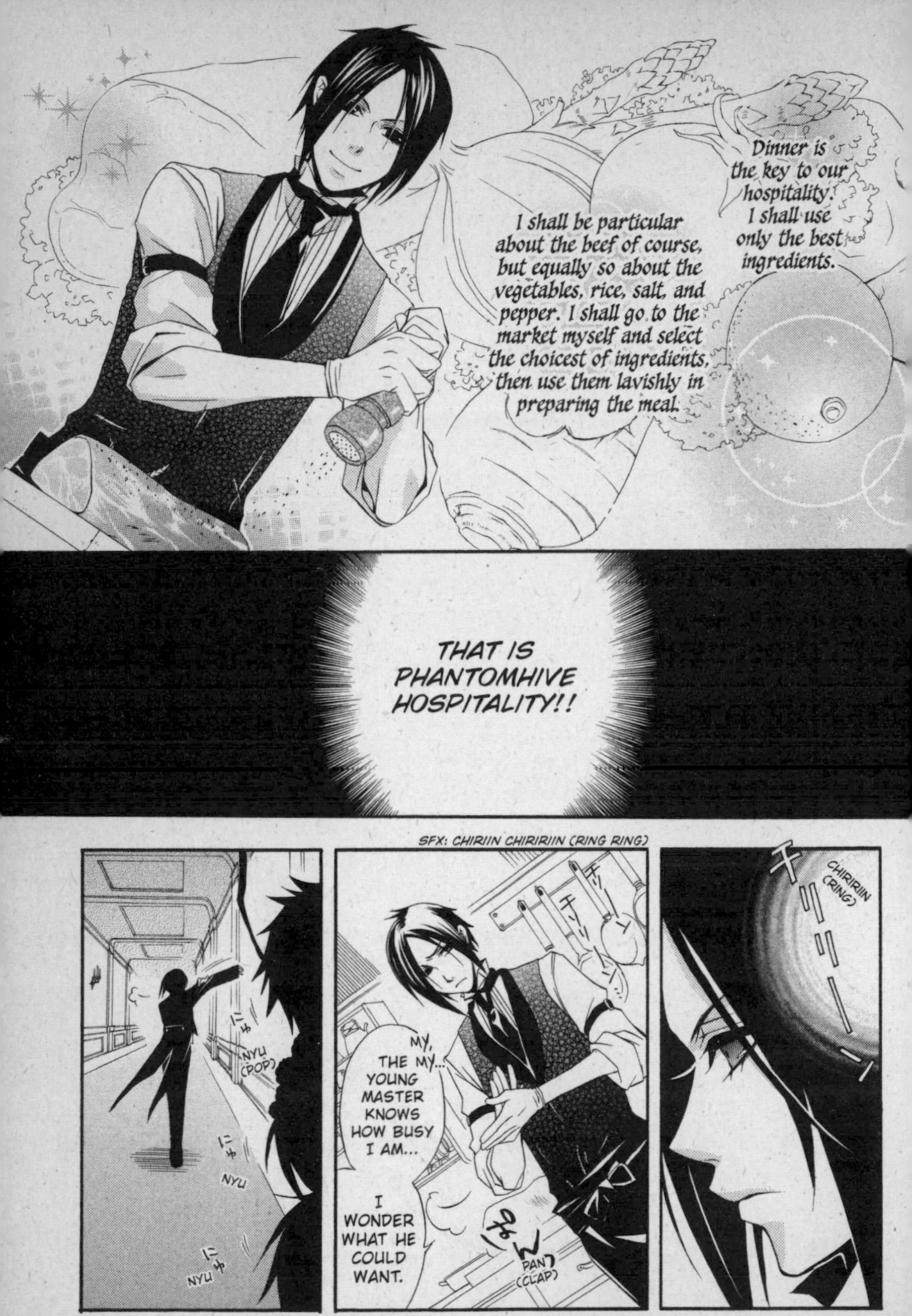
Dinner is the key to our hospitality. I shall use only the best ingredients.
I shall be particular about the beef of course, but equally so about the vegetables, rice, salt, and pepper. I shall go to the market myself and select the choicest of ingredients, then use them lavishly in preparing the meal.
THAT IS PHANTOMHIVE HOSPITALITY!!
CHIRIIN (RING)
SFX: CHIRIIN CHIRIRIIN (RING RING)
MY, THE MY...
YOUNG MASTER KNOWS HOW BUSY I AM...
I WONDER WHAT HE COULD WANT.
PAN (CLAP)
NYU (POP)
NYU
NYU

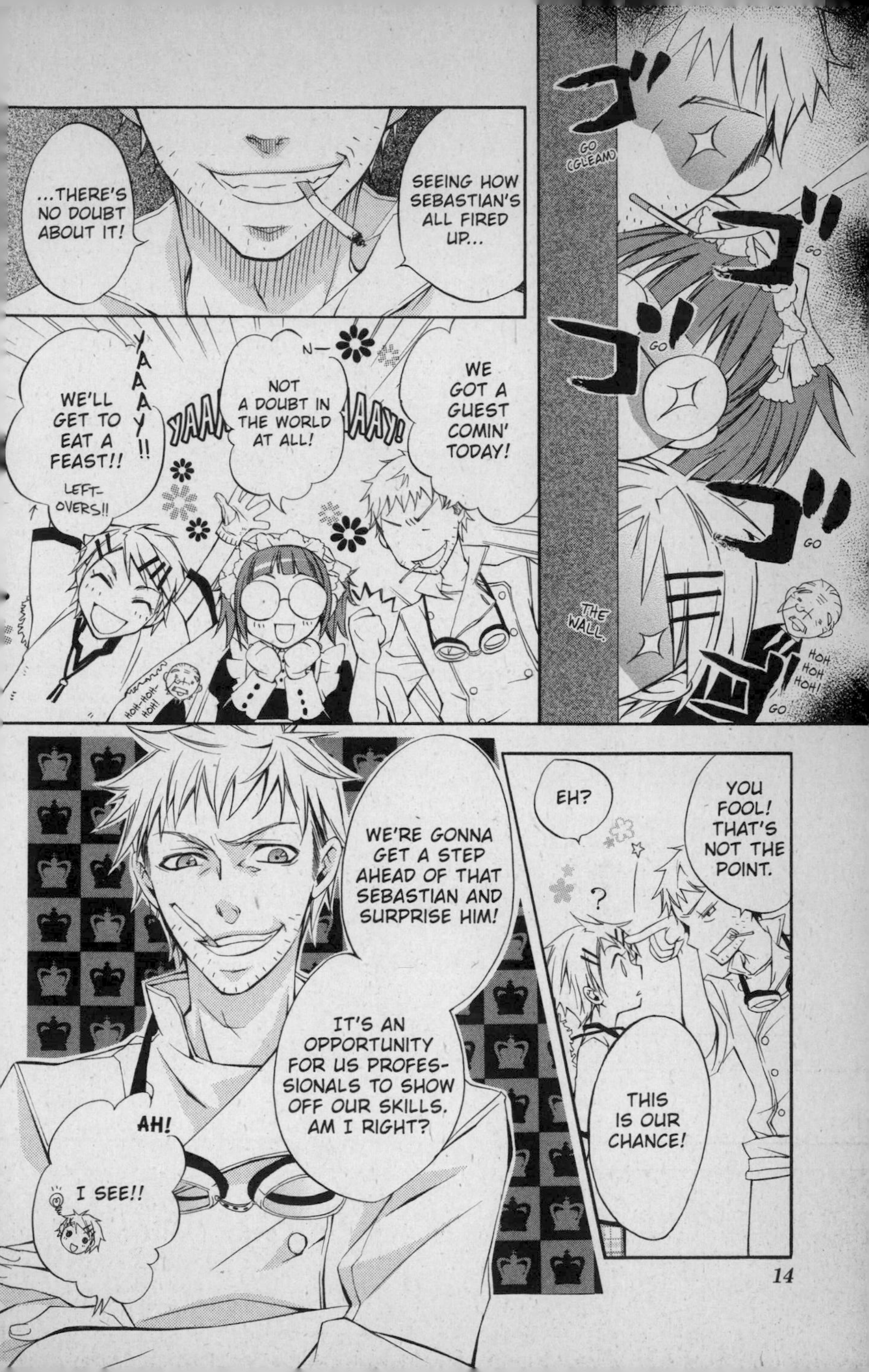
GO (GLEAM)
GO
GO
GO
THE WALL.
HOH HOH HOH!
GO
SEEING HOW SEBASTIAN'S ALL FIRED UP...
...THERE'S NO DOUBT ABOUT IT!
WE GOT A GUEST COMIN' TODAY!
N—
NOT A DOUBT IN THE WORLD AT ALL!
YAAAAY!!
WE'LL GET TO EAT A FEAST!!
LEFT-OVERS!!
HOH-HOH-HOH!
YOU FOOL! THAT'S NOT THE POINT.
EH?
?
THIS IS OUR CHANCE!
WE'RE GONNA GET A STEP AHEAD OF THAT SEBASTIAN AND SURPRISE HIM!
IT'S AN OPPORTUNITY FOR US PROFES-SIONALS TO SHOW OFF OUR SKILLS. AM I RIGHT?
AH!
I SEE!!

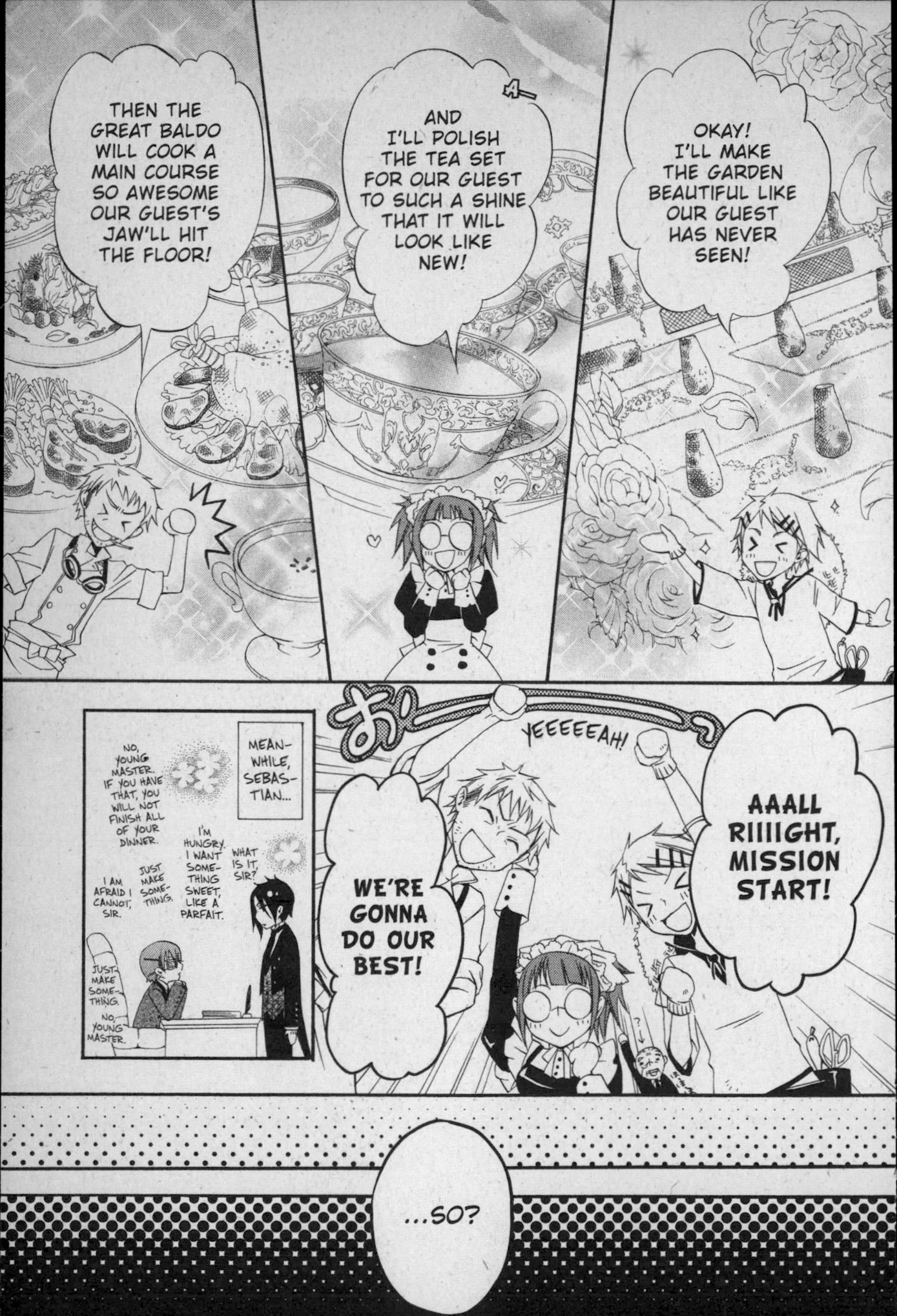
OKAY! I'LL MAKE THE GARDEN BEAUTIFUL LIKE OUR GUEST HAS NEVER SEEN!
AND I'LL POLISH THE TEA SET FOR OUR GUEST TO SUCH A SHINE THAT IT WILL LOOK LIKE NEW!
THEN THE GREAT BALDO WILL COOK A MAIN COURSE SO AWESOME OUR GUEST'S JAW'LL HIT THE FLOOR!
AAALL RIIIIGHT, MISSION START!
YEEEEEAH!
お
WE'RE GONNA DO OUR BEST!
MEAN-WHILE, SEBAS-TIAN...
WHAT IS IT, SIR?
I'M HUNGRY. I WANT SOME-THING SWEET, LIKE A PARFAIT.
NO, YOUNG MASTER. IF YOU HAVE THAT, YOU WILL NOT FINISH ALL OF YOUR DINNER.
JUST MAKE SOME-THING.
I AM AFRAID I CANNOT, SIR.
JUST MAKE SOME-THING.
NO, YOUNG MASTER.
...SO?

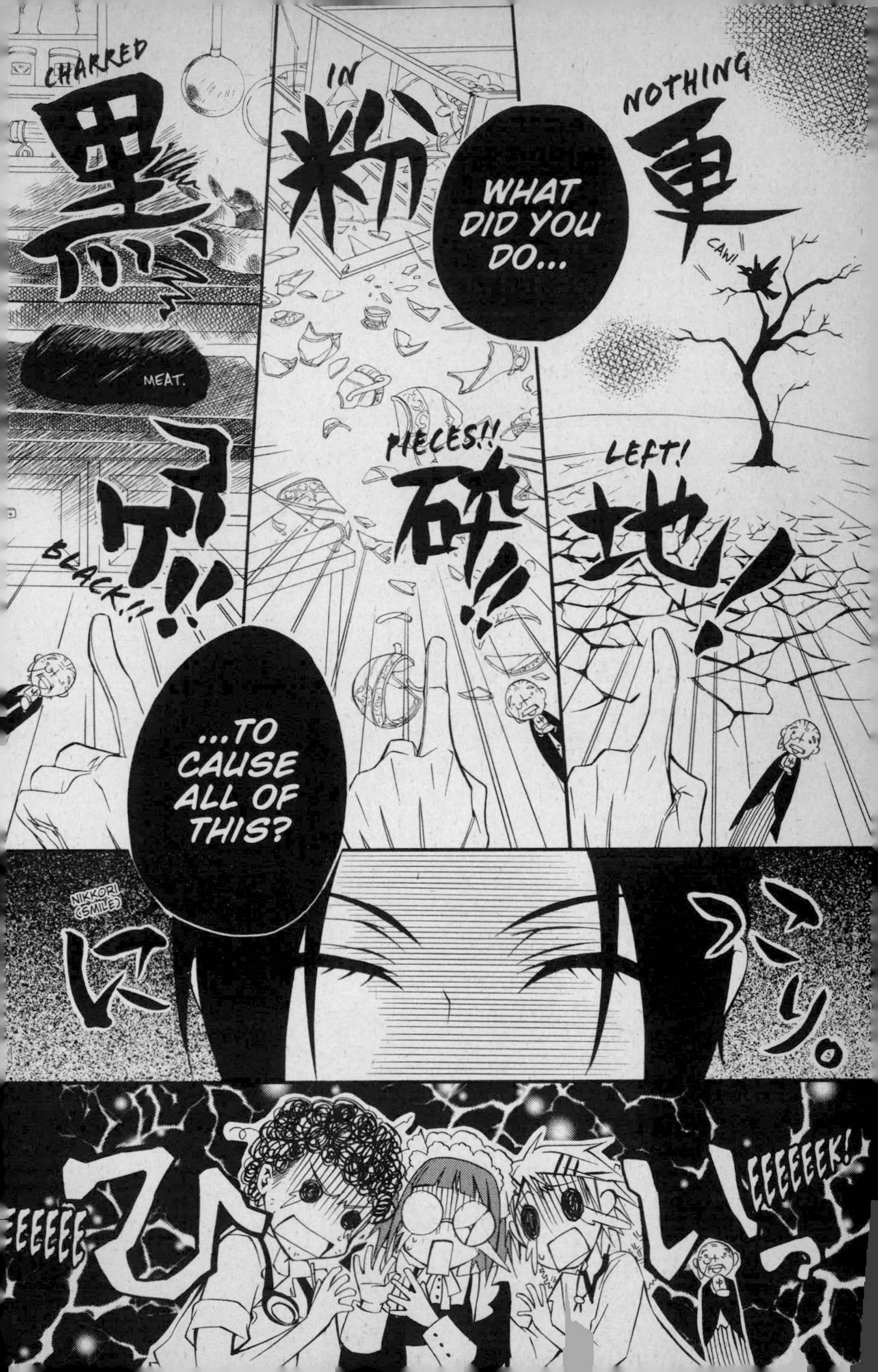
WHAT DID YOU DO...
NOTHING
CAW!
LEFT!
IN
PIECES!!
CHARRED
MEAT.
BLACK!!
...TO CAUSE ALL OF THIS?
NIKKORI (SMILE)
EEEEEEK!
EEEEEE

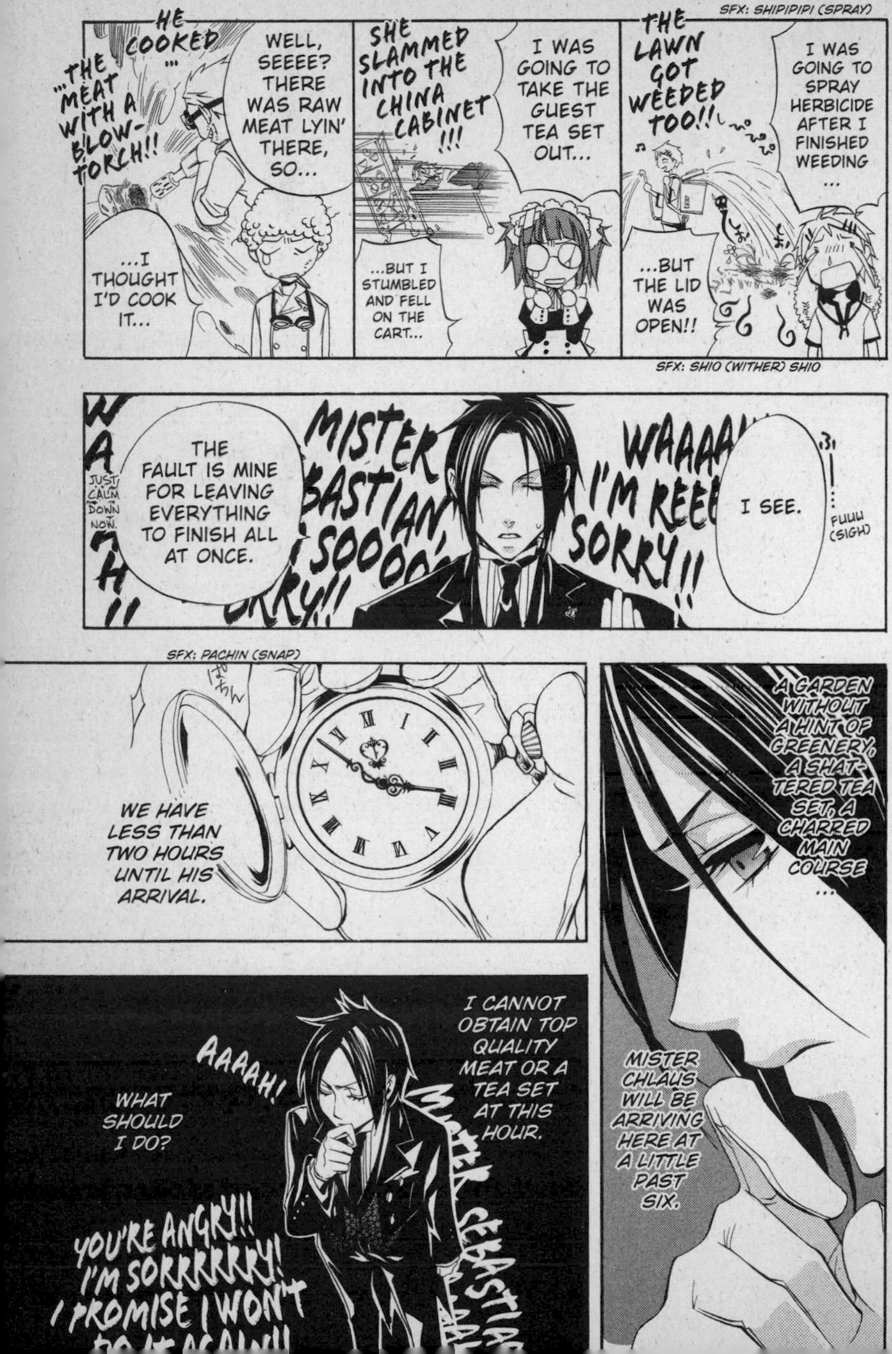
SFX: SHIPIPIPI (SPRAY)
I WAS GOING TO SPRAY HERBICIDE AFTER I FINISHED WEEDING ...
THE LAWN GOT WEEDED TOO!!
...BUT THE LID WAS OPEN!!
SFX: SHIO (WITHER) SHIO
I WAS GOING TO TAKE THE GUEST TEA SET OUT...
SHE SLAMMED INTO THE CHINA CABINET!!!
...BUT I STUMBLED AND FELL ON THE CART...
WELL, SEEEE? THERE WAS RAW MEAT LYIN' THERE, SO...
HE COOKED ...
...THE MEAT WITH A BLOW-TORCH!!
...I THOUGHT I'D COOK IT...
I SEE.
FUUU (SIGH)
I'M REEE SORRY!!
MISTER BASTIAN, SOOOO
THE FAULT IS MINE FOR LEAVING EVERYTHING TO FINISH ALL AT ONCE.
JUST CALM DOWN NOW.
A GARDEN WITHOUT A HINT OF GREENERY, A SHATTERED TEA SET, A CHARRED MAIN COURSE ...
MISTER CHLAUS WILL BE ARRIVING HERE AT A LITTLE PAST SIX.
SFX: PACHIN (SNAP)
WE HAVE LESS THAN TWO HOURS UNTIL HIS ARRIVAL.
I CANNOT OBTAIN TOP QUALITY MEAT OR A TEA SET AT THIS HOUR.
AAAAH!
WHAT SHOULD I DO?
YOU'RE ANGRY!! I'M SORRRRRY! I PROMISE I WON'T

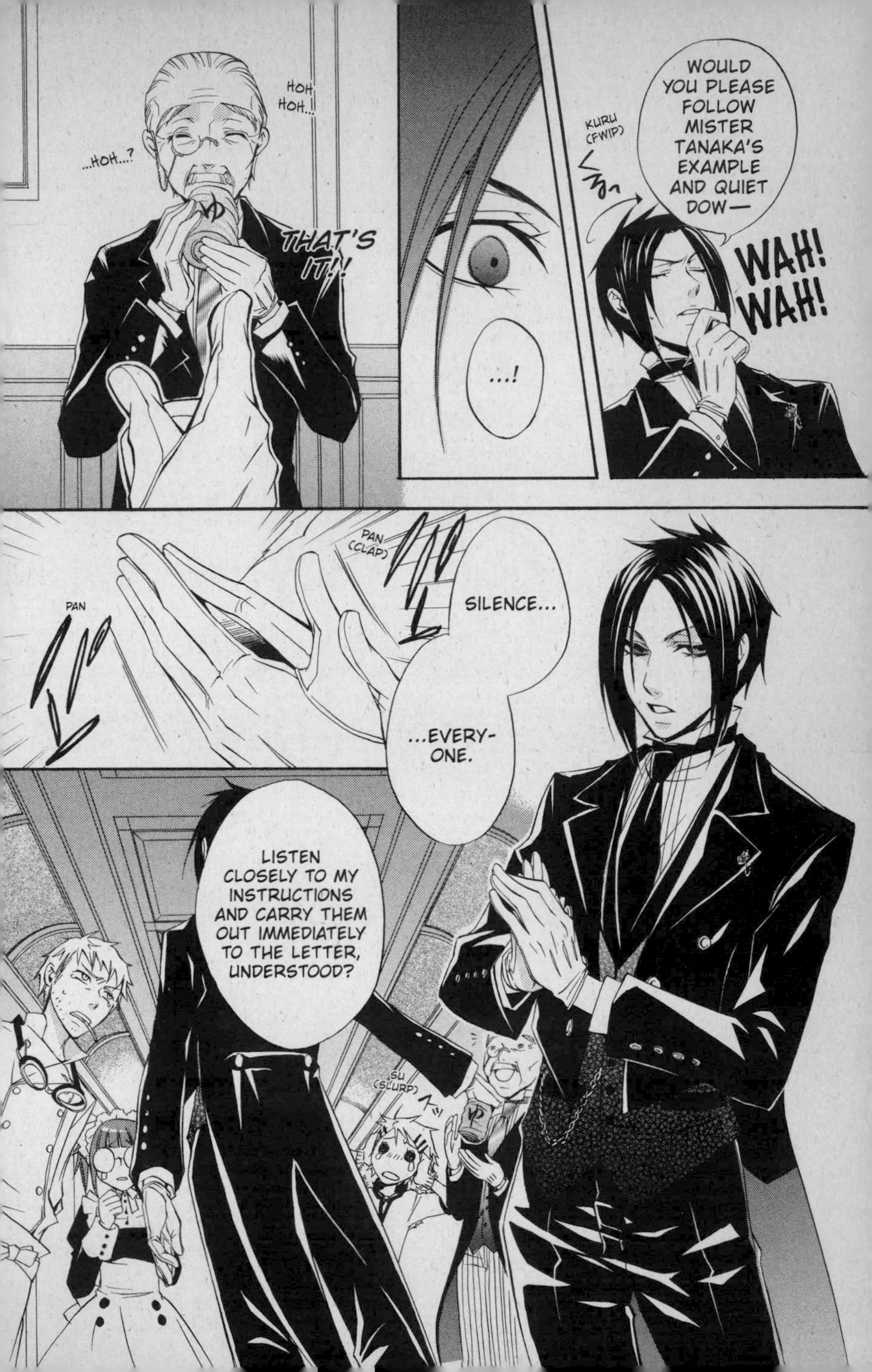
KURU (FWIP)
WOULD YOU PLEASE FOLLOW MISTER TANAKA'S EXAMPLE AND QUIET DOW—
WAH! WAH!
...!
HOH HOH..!
...HOH...?
THAT'S IT!!
PAN (CLAP)
SILENCE...
PAN
...EVERY-ONE.
LISTEN CLOSELY TO MY INSTRUCTIONS AND CARRY THEM OUT IMMEDIATELY TO THE LETTER, UNDERSTOOD?
SU (SLURP)

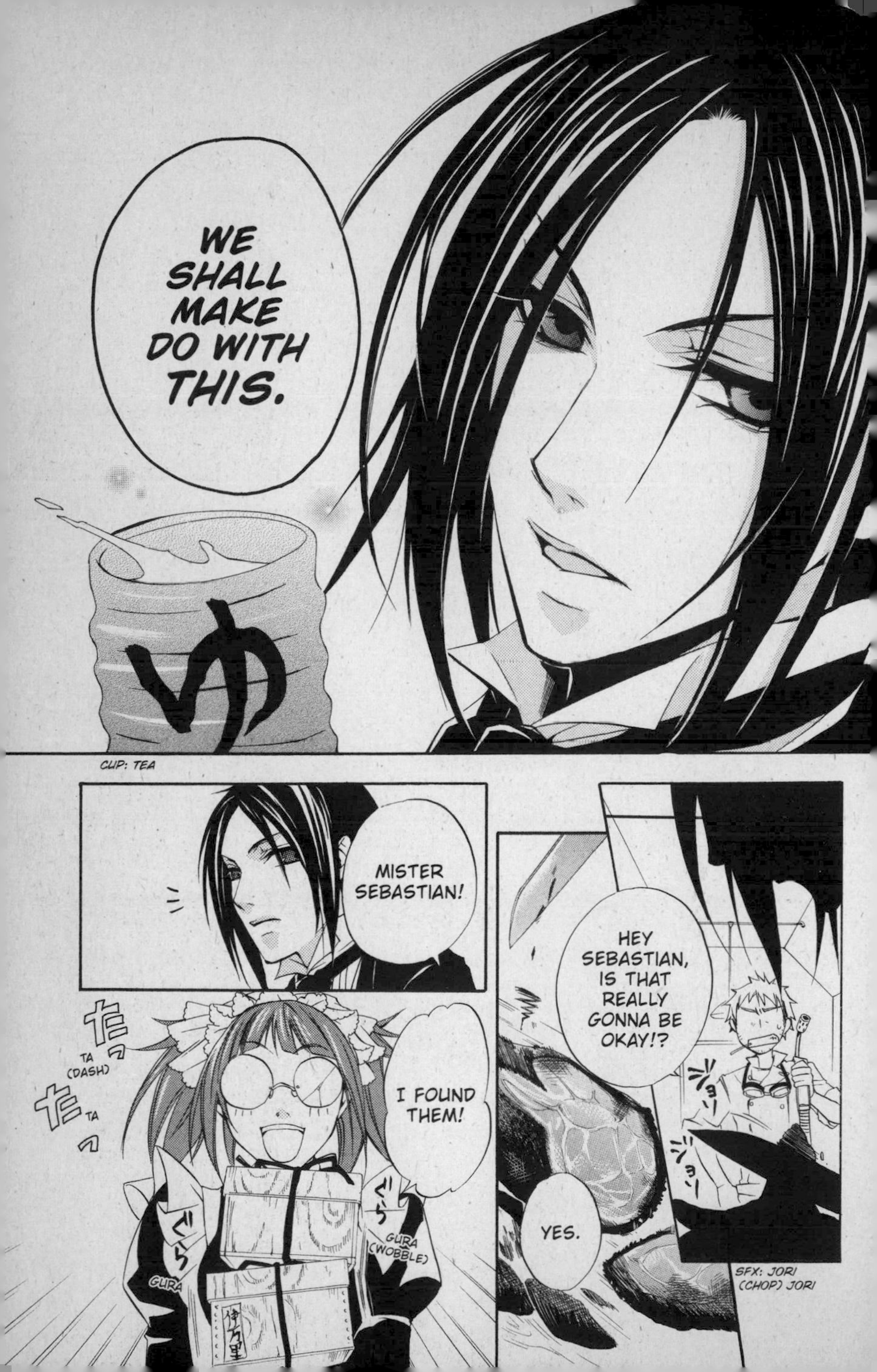
WE SHALL MAKE DO WITH THIS.
CUP: TEA
HEY SEBASTIAN, IS THAT REALLY GONNA BE OKAY!?
YES.
SFX: JORI (CHOP) JORI
MISTER SEBASTIAN!
I FOUND THEM!
TA (DASH) TA
GURA (WOBBLE) GURA

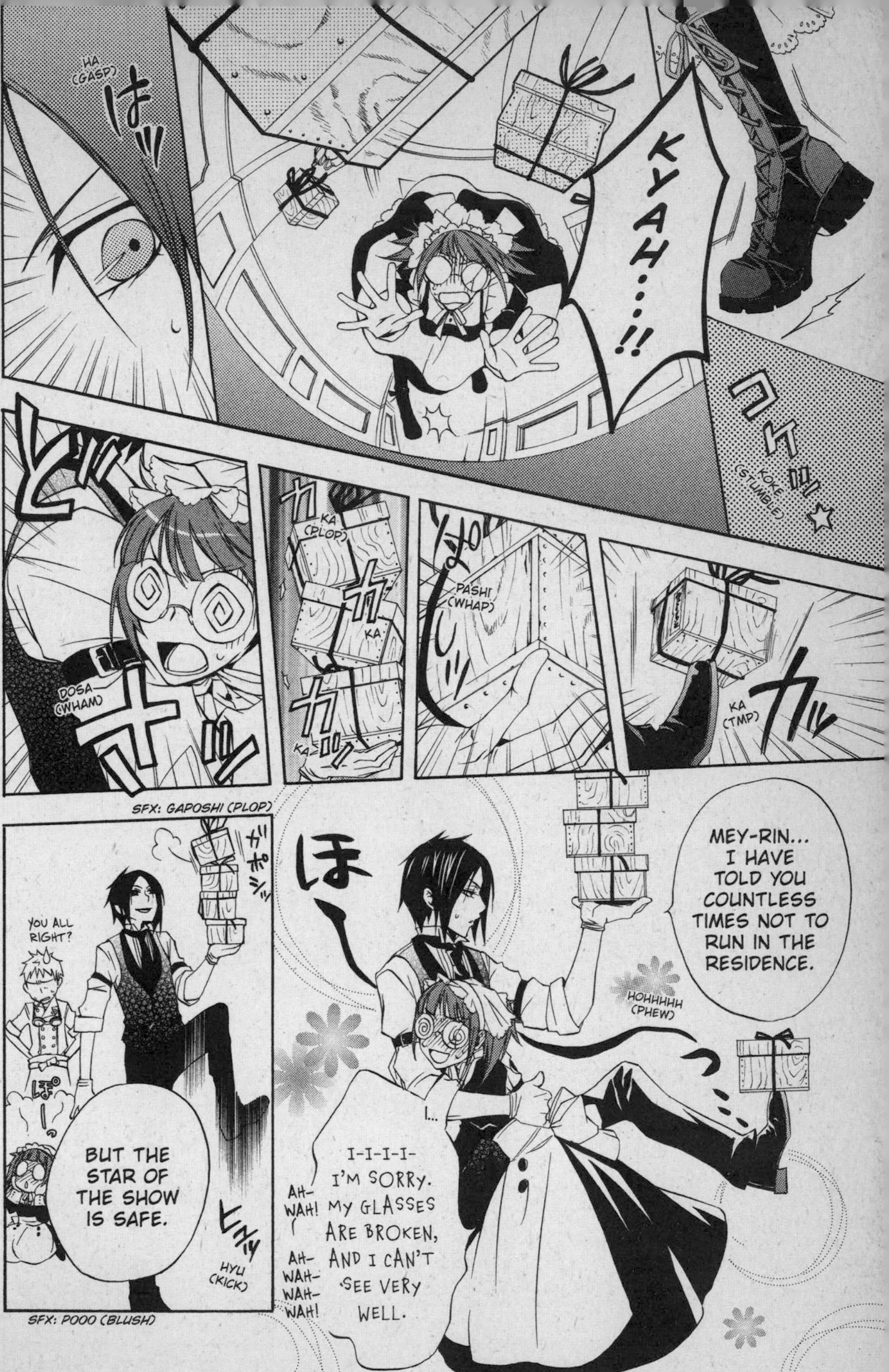
KOKE (STUMBLE)
KYAH...!!
HA (GASP)
KA (TMP)
PASHI (WHAP)
KA (PLOP)
KA
KA
DOSA (WHAM)
SFX: GAPOSHI (PLOP)
MEY-RIN... I HAVE TOLD YOU COUNTLESS TIMES NOT TO RUN IN THE RESIDENCE.
HOHHHHH (PHEW)
I...
I-I-I-I- I'M SORRY. MY GLASSES ARE BROKEN, AND I CAN'T SEE VERY WELL.
AH-WAH!
AH-WAH-WAH-WAH!
YOU ALL RIGHT?
BUT THE STAR OF THE SHOW IS SAFE.
HYU (KICK)
SFX: POOO (BLUSH)

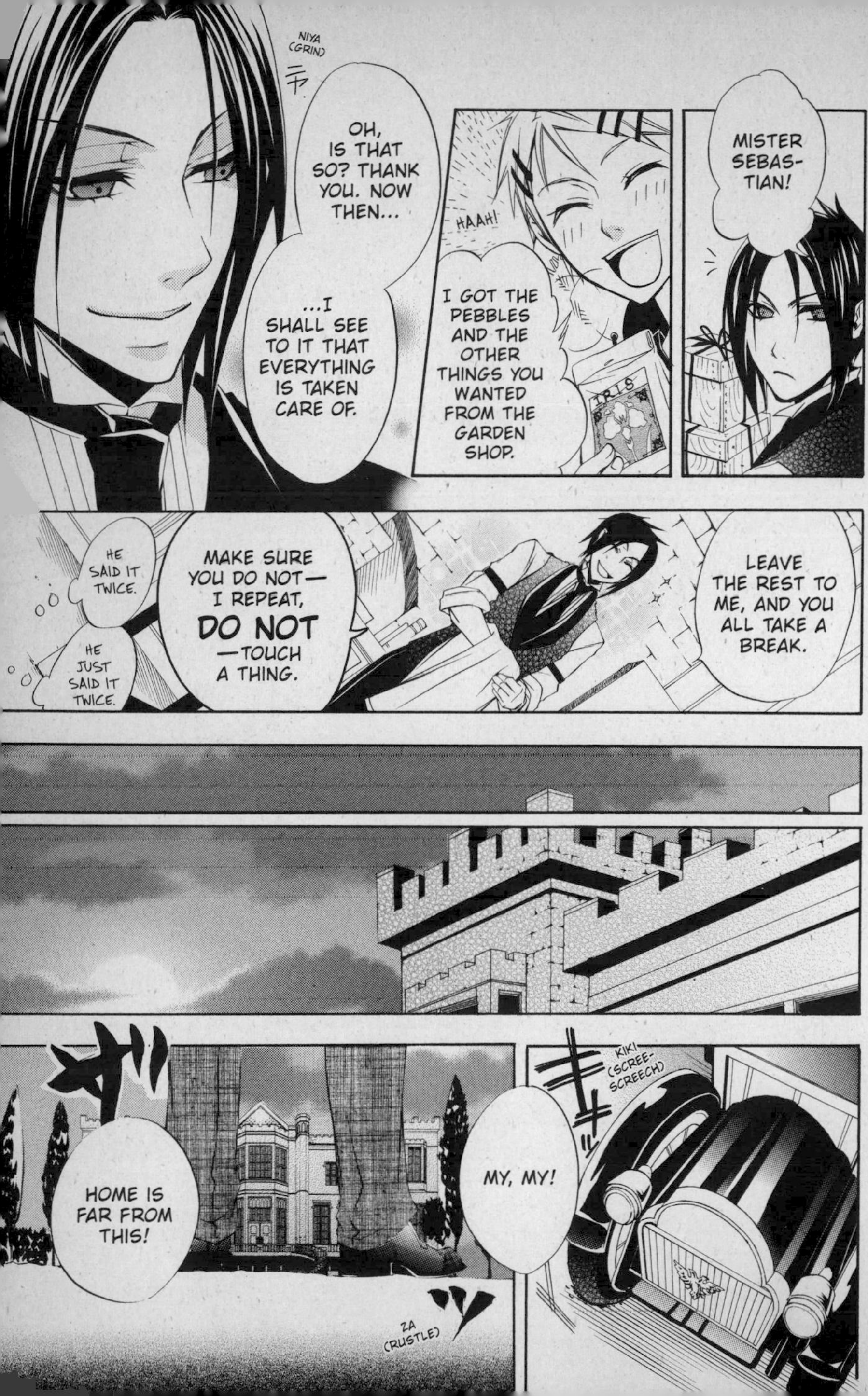
MISTER SEBASTIAN!
HAAH!
I GOT THE PEBBLES AND THE OTHER THINGS YOU WANTED FROM THE GARDEN SHOP.
IRIS
NIYA (GRIN)
OH, IS THAT SO? THANK YOU. NOW THEN...
...I SHALL SEE TO IT THAT EVERYTHING IS TAKEN CARE OF.
LEAVE THE REST TO ME, AND YOU ALL TAKE A BREAK.
MAKE SURE YOU DO NOT—I REPEAT, DO NOT—TOUCH A THING.
HE SAID IT TWICE.
HE JUST SAID IT TWICE.
KIKI (SCREE-SCREECH)
MY, MY!
HOME IS FAR FROM THIS!
ZA (RUSTLE)

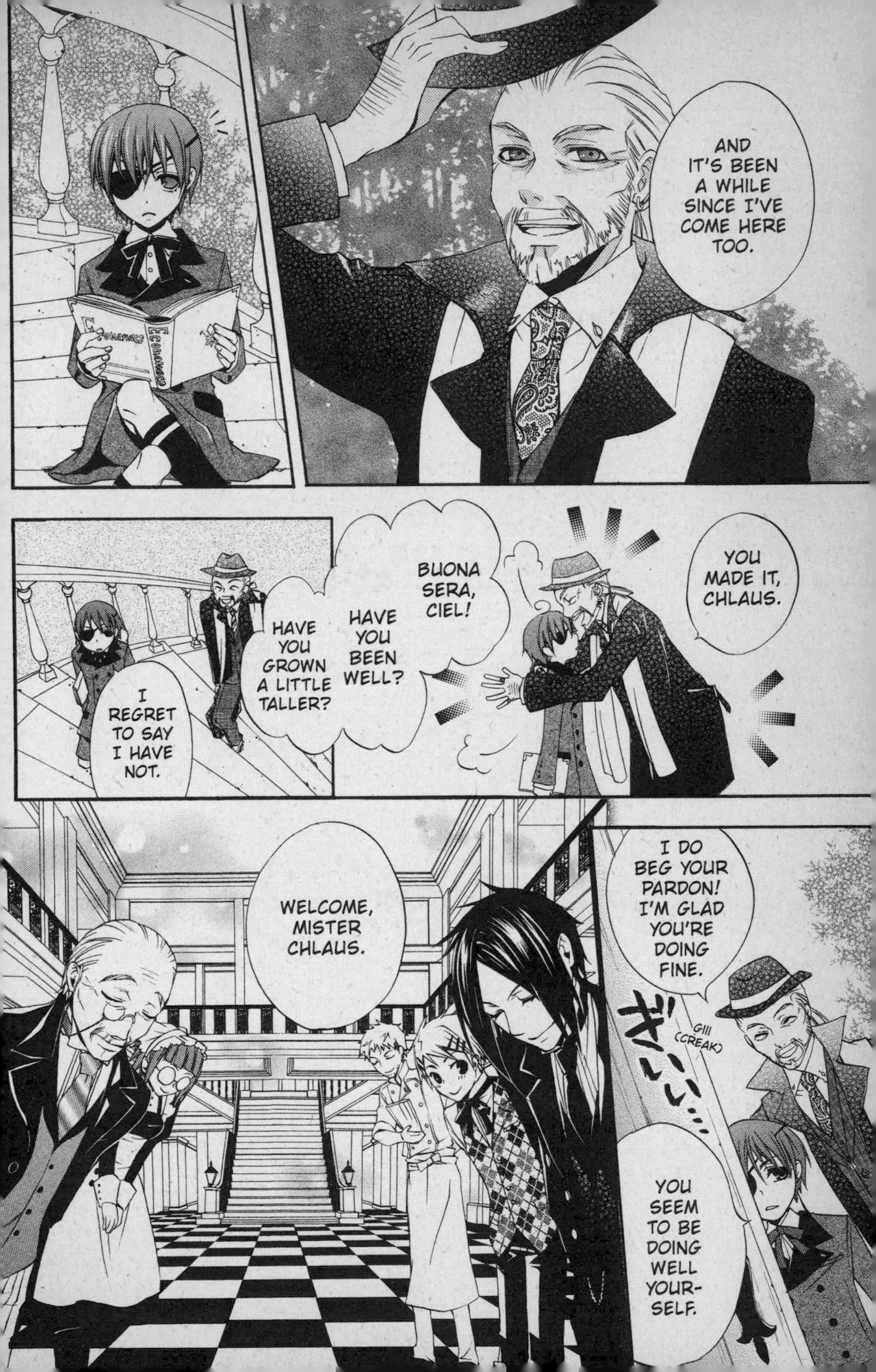
AND IT'S BEEN A WHILE SINCE I'VE COME HERE TOO.
YOU MADE IT, CHLAUS.
BUONA SERA, CIEL!
HAVE YOU BEEN WELL?
HAVE YOU GROWN A LITTLE TALLER?
I REGRET TO SAY I HAVE NOT.
I DO BEG YOUR PARDON! I'M GLAD YOU'RE DOING FINE.
ぎぃぃ…
GIII (CREAK)
YOU SEEM TO BE DOING WELL YOUR-SELF.
WELCOME, MISTER CHLAUS.

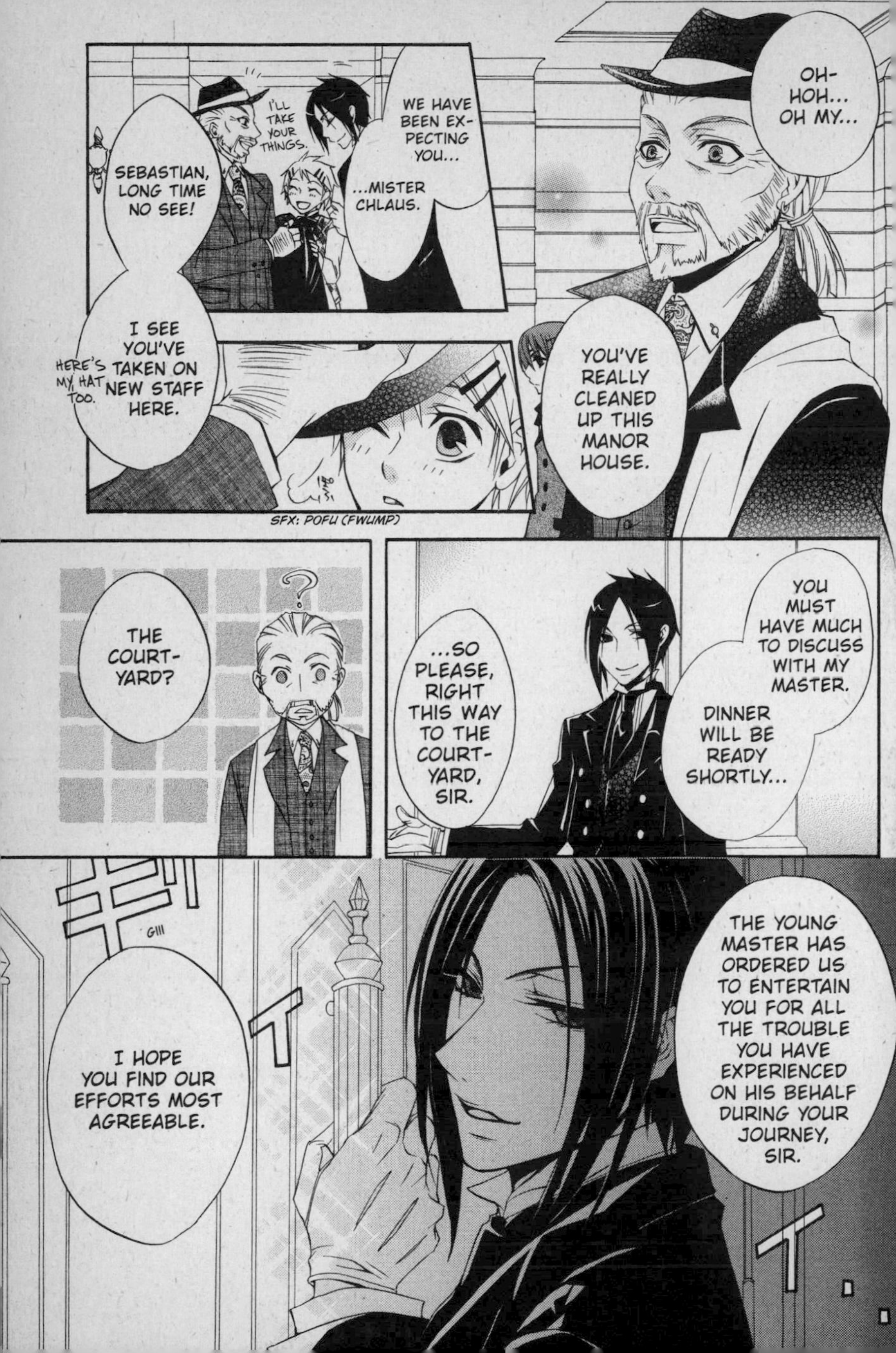
OH-HOH... OH MY...
YOU'VE REALLY CLEANED UP THIS MANOR HOUSE.
WE HAVE BEEN EXPECTING YOU...
...MISTER CHLAUS.
I'LL TAKE YOUR THINGS.
SEBASTIAN, LONG TIME NO SEE!
I SEE YOU'VE TAKEN ON NEW STAFF HERE.
HERE'S MY HAT TOO.
SFX: POFU (FWUMP)
YOU MUST HAVE MUCH TO DISCUSS WITH MY MASTER.
DINNER WILL BE READY SHORTLY...
...SO PLEASE, RIGHT THIS WAY TO THE COURTYARD, SIR.
THE COURTYARD?
THE YOUNG MASTER HAS ORDERED US TO ENTERTAIN YOU FOR ALL THE TROUBLE YOU HAVE EXPERIENCED ON HIS BEHALF DURING YOUR JOURNEY, SIR.
I HOPE YOU FIND OUR EFFORTS MOST AGREEABLE.
GIII

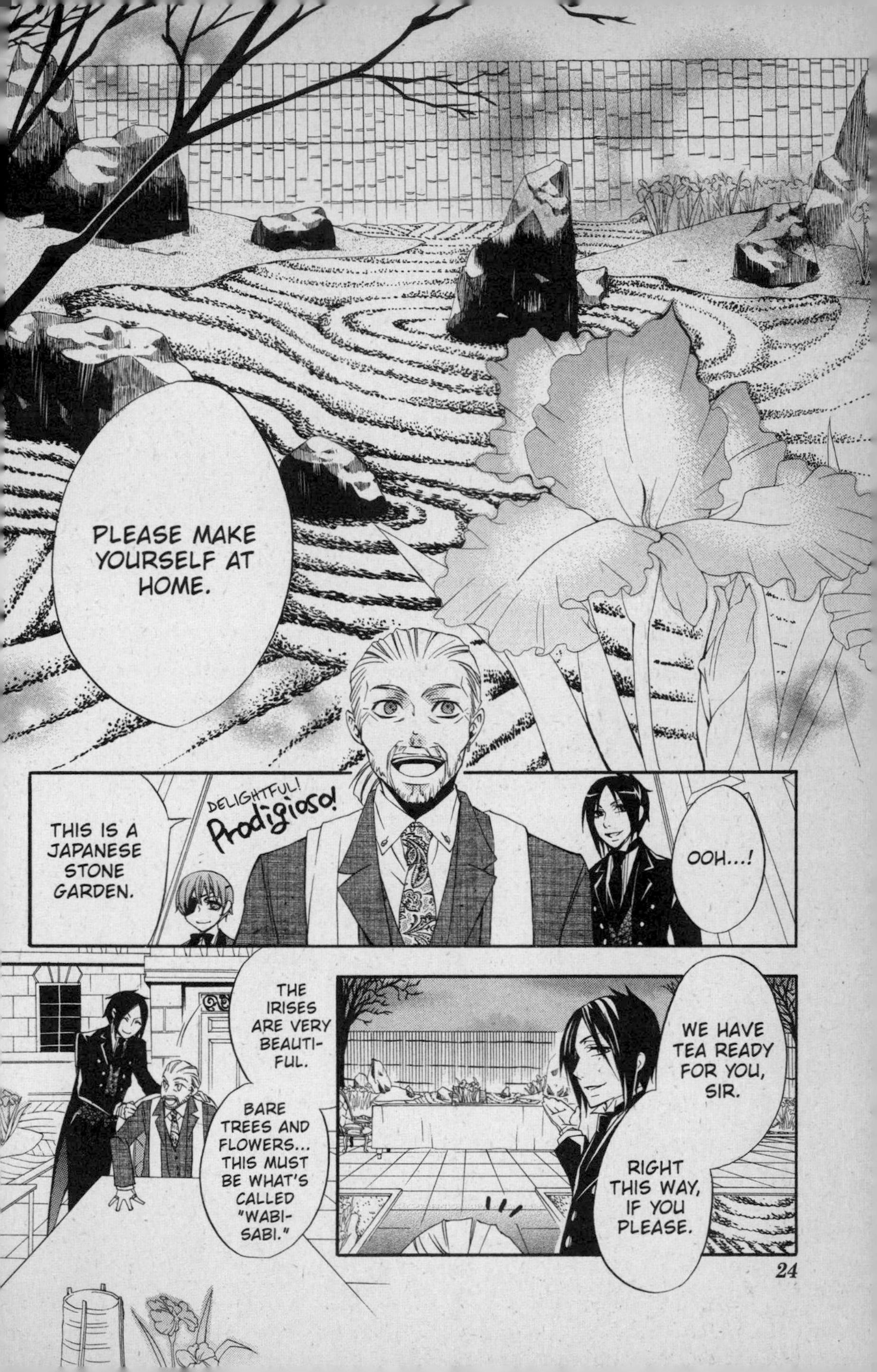
PLEASE MAKE YOURSELF AT HOME.
OOH...!
DELIGHTFUL!
Prodigioso!
THIS IS A JAPANESE STONE GARDEN.
WE HAVE TEA READY FOR YOU, SIR.
RIGHT THIS WAY, IF YOU PLEASE.
THE IRISES ARE VERY BEAUTIFUL.
BARE TREES AND FLOWERS... THIS MUST BE WHAT'S CALLED "WABI-SABI."

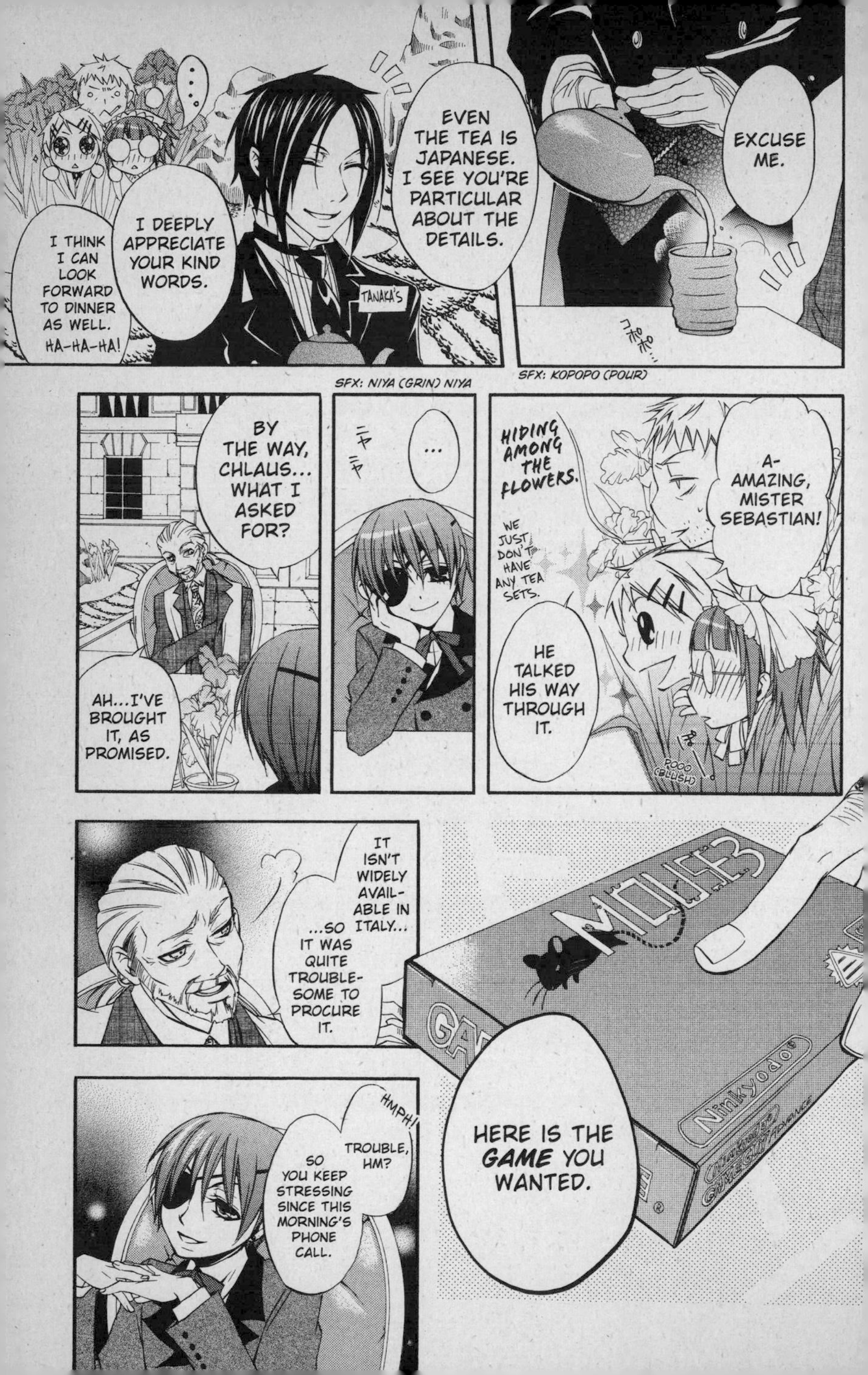
EXCUSE ME.
コポポ…
SFX: KOPOPO (POUR)
…
EVEN THE TEA IS JAPANESE. I SEE YOU'RE PARTICULAR ABOUT THE DETAILS.
I DEEPLY APPRECIATE YOUR KIND WORDS.
TANAKA'S
I THINK I CAN LOOK FORWARD TO DINNER AS WELL. HA-HA-HA!
SFX: NIYA (GRIN) NIYA
HIDING AMONG THE FLOWERS.
A-AMAZING, MISTER SEBASTIAN!
WE JUST DON'T HAVE ANY TEA SETS.
HE TALKED HIS WAY THROUGH IT.
POOO (BLUSH)
ニヤ ニヤ
…
BY THE WAY, CHLAUS… WHAT I ASKED FOR?
AH…I'VE BROUGHT IT, AS PROMISED.
Ninkyodo
HERE IS THE *GAME* YOU WANTED.
IT ISN'T WIDELY AVAIL-ABLE IN ITALY…
…SO IT WAS QUITE TROUBLE-SOME TO PROCURE IT.
HMPH!
TROUBLE, HM?
SO YOU KEEP STRESSING SINCE THIS MORNING'S PHONE CALL.

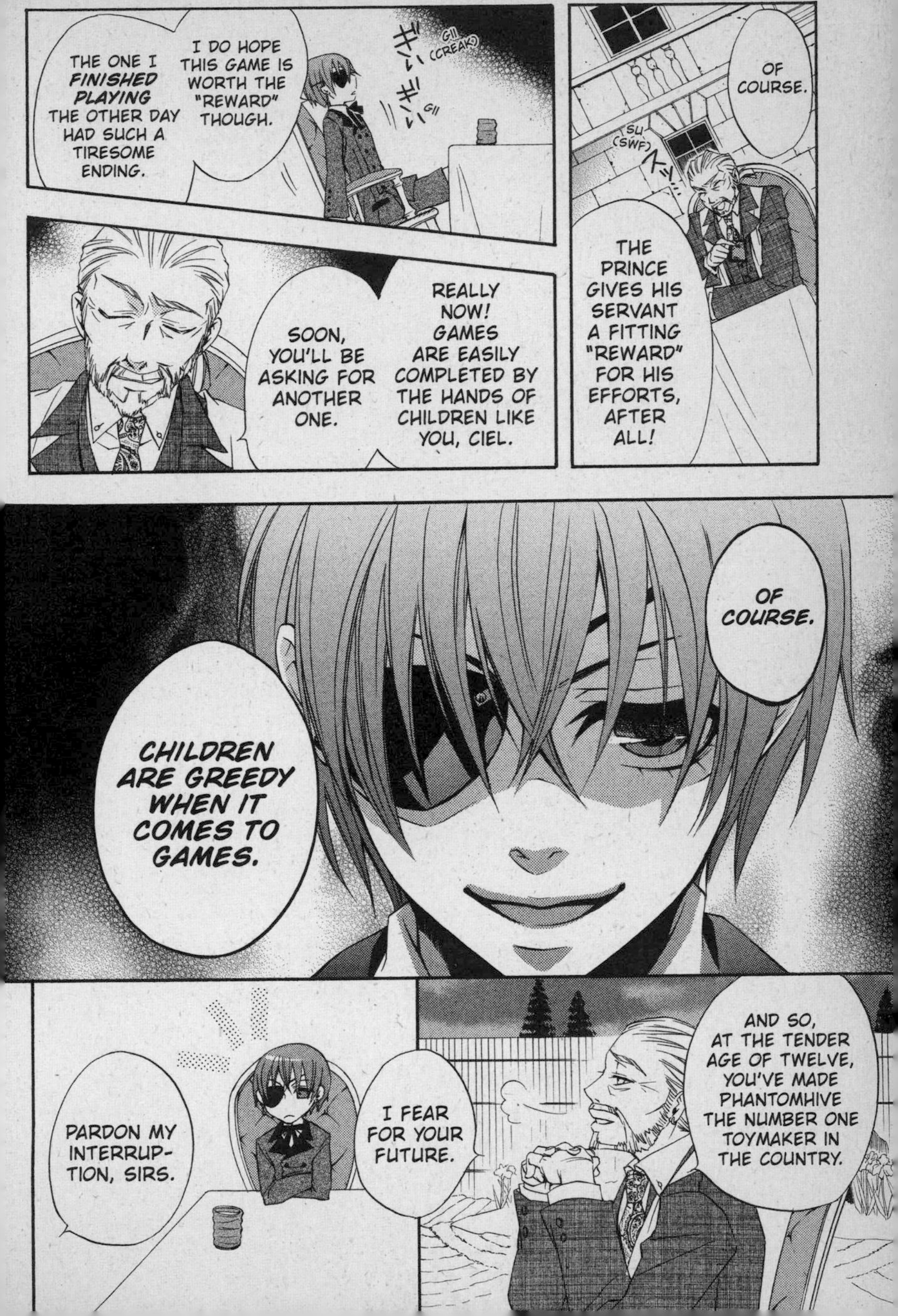
OF COURSE.
SU (SWF)
THE PRINCE GIVES HIS SERVANT A FITTING "REWARD" FOR HIS EFFORTS, AFTER ALL!
GII (CREAK)
GII
I DO HOPE THIS GAME IS WORTH THE "REWARD" THOUGH.
THE ONE I *FINISHED PLAYING* THE OTHER DAY HAD SUCH A TIRESOME ENDING.
REALLY NOW! GAMES ARE EASILY COMPLETED BY THE HANDS OF CHILDREN LIKE YOU, CIEL.
SOON, YOU'LL BE ASKING FOR ANOTHER ONE.
OF COURSE.
CHILDREN ARE GREEDY WHEN IT COMES TO GAMES.
AND SO, AT THE TENDER AGE OF TWELVE, YOU'VE MADE PHANTOMHIVE THE NUMBER ONE TOYMAKER IN THE COUNTRY.
I FEAR FOR YOUR FUTURE.
PARDON MY INTERRUP-TION, SIRS.

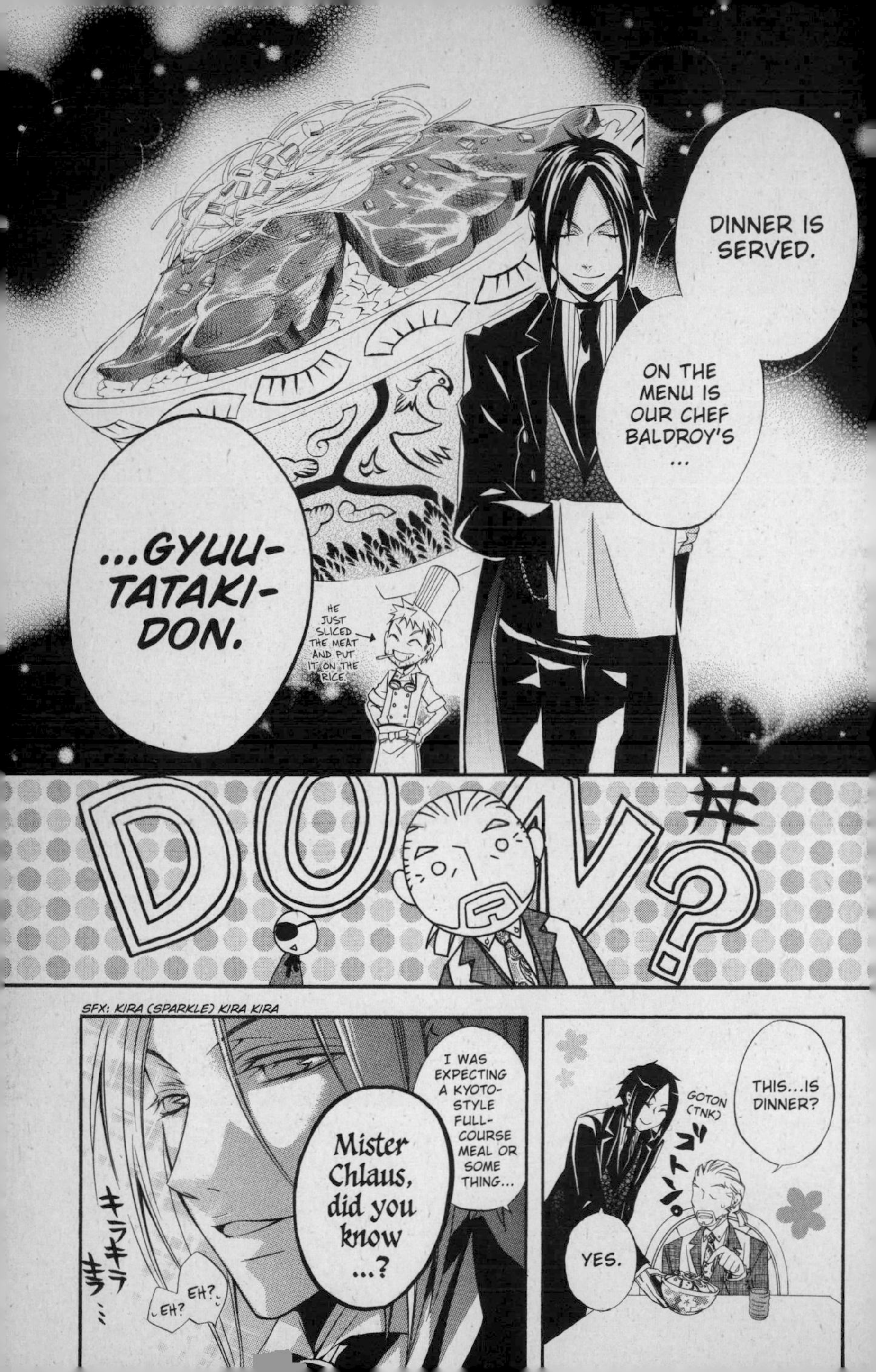
DINNER IS SERVED.
ON THE MENU IS OUR CHEF BALDROY'S ...
...GYUU-TATAKI-DON.
HE JUST SLICED THE MEAT AND PUT IT ON THE RICE.
DON?
THIS...IS DINNER?
GOTON (TNK)
YES.
SFX: KIRA (SPARKLE) KIRA KIRA
I WAS EXPECTING A KYOTO-STYLE FULL-COURSE MEAL OR SOME THING...
Mister Chlaus, did you know ...?
EH?
EH?

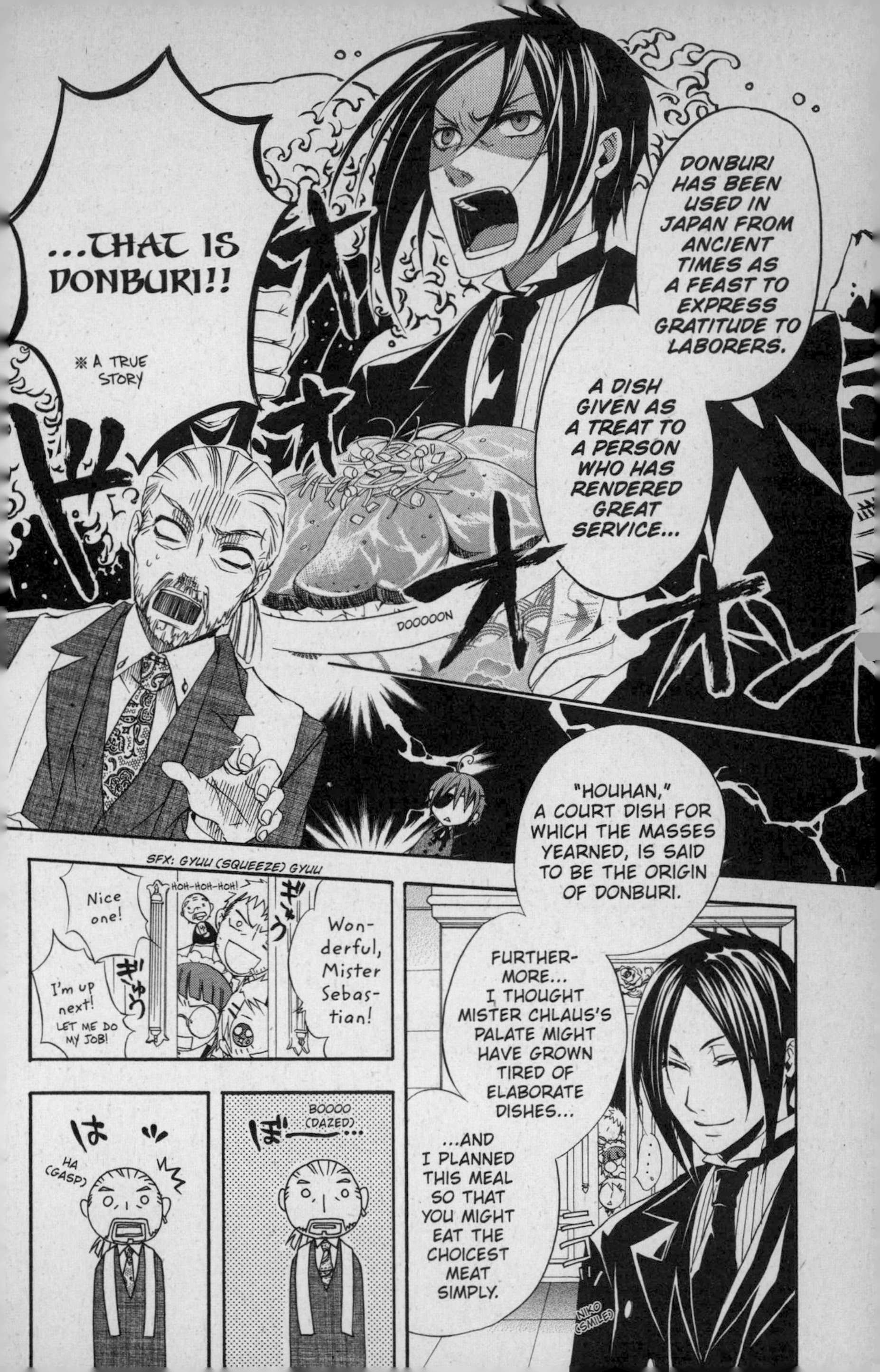
DONBURI HAS BEEN USED IN JAPAN FROM ANCIENT TIMES AS A FEAST TO EXPRESS GRATITUDE TO LABORERS.
A DISH GIVEN AS A TREAT TO A PERSON WHO HAS RENDERED GREAT SERVICE...
...THAT IS DONBURI!!
※ A TRUE STORY
DOOOOON
"HOUHAN," A COURT DISH FOR WHICH THE MASSES YEARNED, IS SAID TO BE THE ORIGIN OF DONBURI.
FURTHERMORE... I THOUGHT MISTER CHLAUS'S PALATE MIGHT HAVE GROWN TIRED OF ELABORATE DISHES...
...AND I PLANNED THIS MEAL SO THAT YOU MIGHT EAT THE CHOICEST MEAT SIMPLY.
NIKO (SMILE)
SFX: GYUU (SQUEEZE) GYUU
Won-derful, Mister Sebas-tian!
HOH-HOH-HOH!
Nice one!
I'm up next!
LET ME DO MY JOB!
BOOOO (DAZED)
HA (GASP)

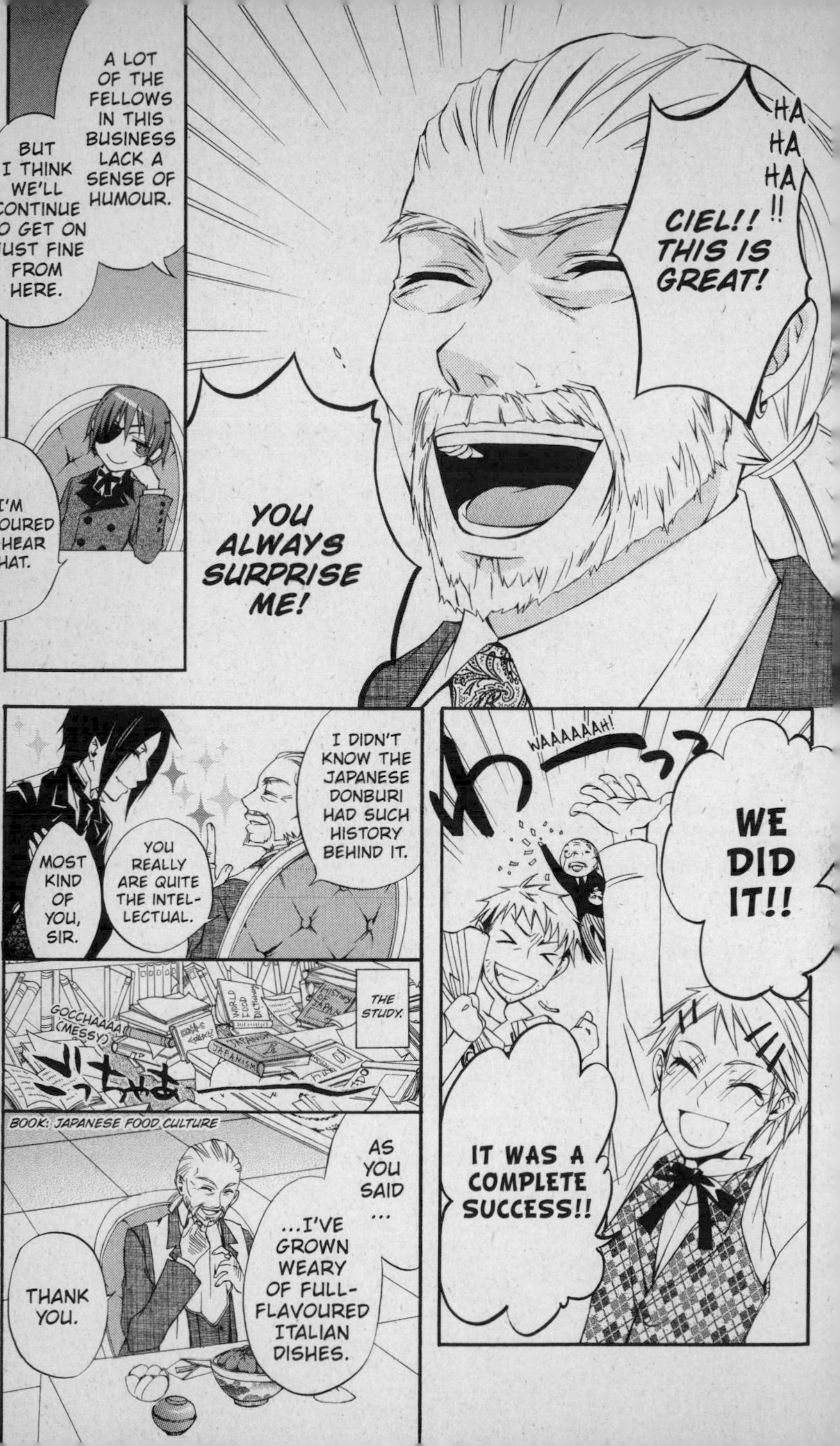
HA HA HA!!
CIEL!! THIS IS GREAT!
YOU ALWAYS SURPRISE ME!
A LOT OF THE FELLOWS IN THIS BUSINESS LACK A SENSE OF HUMOUR.
BUT I THINK WE'LL CONTINUE TO GET ON JUST FINE FROM HERE.
I'M HONOURED TO HEAR THAT.
WAAAAAAH!
WE DID IT!!
IT WAS A COMPLETE SUCCESS!!
I DIDN'T KNOW THE JAPANESE DONBURI HAD SUCH HISTORY BEHIND IT.
YOU REALLY ARE QUITE THE INTEL-LECTUAL.
MOST KIND OF YOU, SIR.
THE STUDY.
WORLD FOOD DICTIONARY
HISTORY OF JAPAN
JAPANISM
GOCCHAAAA (MESSY)
BOOK: JAPANESE FOOD CULTURE
AS YOU SAID...
...I'VE GROWN WEARY OF FULL-FLAVOURED ITALIAN DISHES.
THANK YOU.

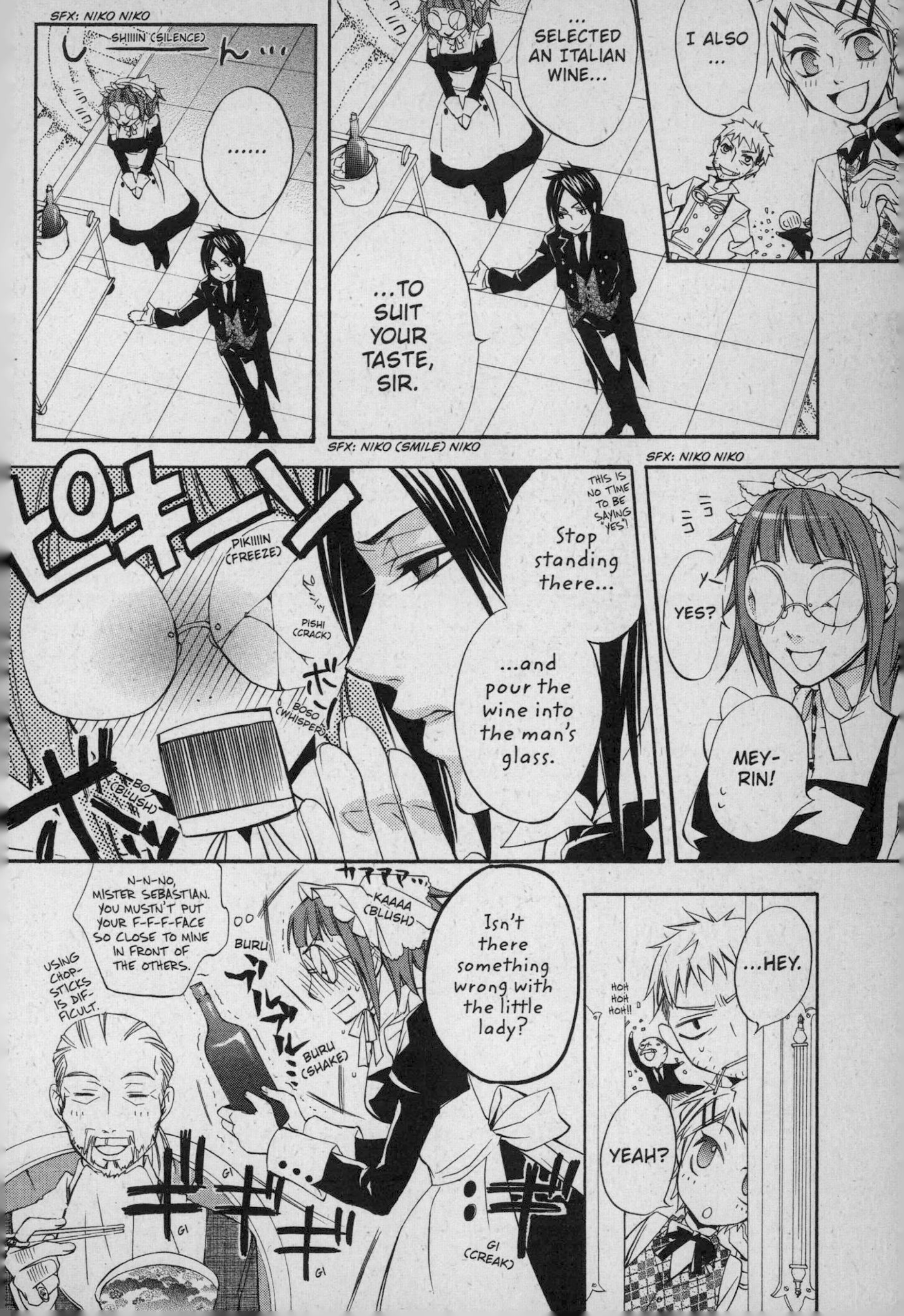
I ALSO ...
... SELECTED AN ITALIAN WINE...
...TO SUIT YOUR TASTE, SIR.
SFX: NIKO (SMILE) NIKO
SFX: NIKO NIKO
SHIIIIN (SILENCE)
......
SFX: NIKO NIKO
YES?
MEY-RIN!
THIS IS NO TIME TO BE SAYING "YES"!
Stop standing there...
...and pour the wine into the man's glass.
PIKIIIIN (FREEZE)
PISHI (CRACK)
BOSO (WHISPER)
BO (BLUSH)
...HEY.
HOH HOH HOH!!
YEAH?
Isn't there something wrong with the little lady?
KAAAA (BLUSH)
N-N-NO, MISTER SEBASTIAN. YOU MUSTN'T PUT YOUR F-F-F-FACE SO CLOSE TO MINE IN FRONT OF THE OTHERS.
BURU
BURU (SHAKE)
USING CHOP-STICKS IS DIF-FICULT.
...
GI
GI
GI
GI (CREAK)

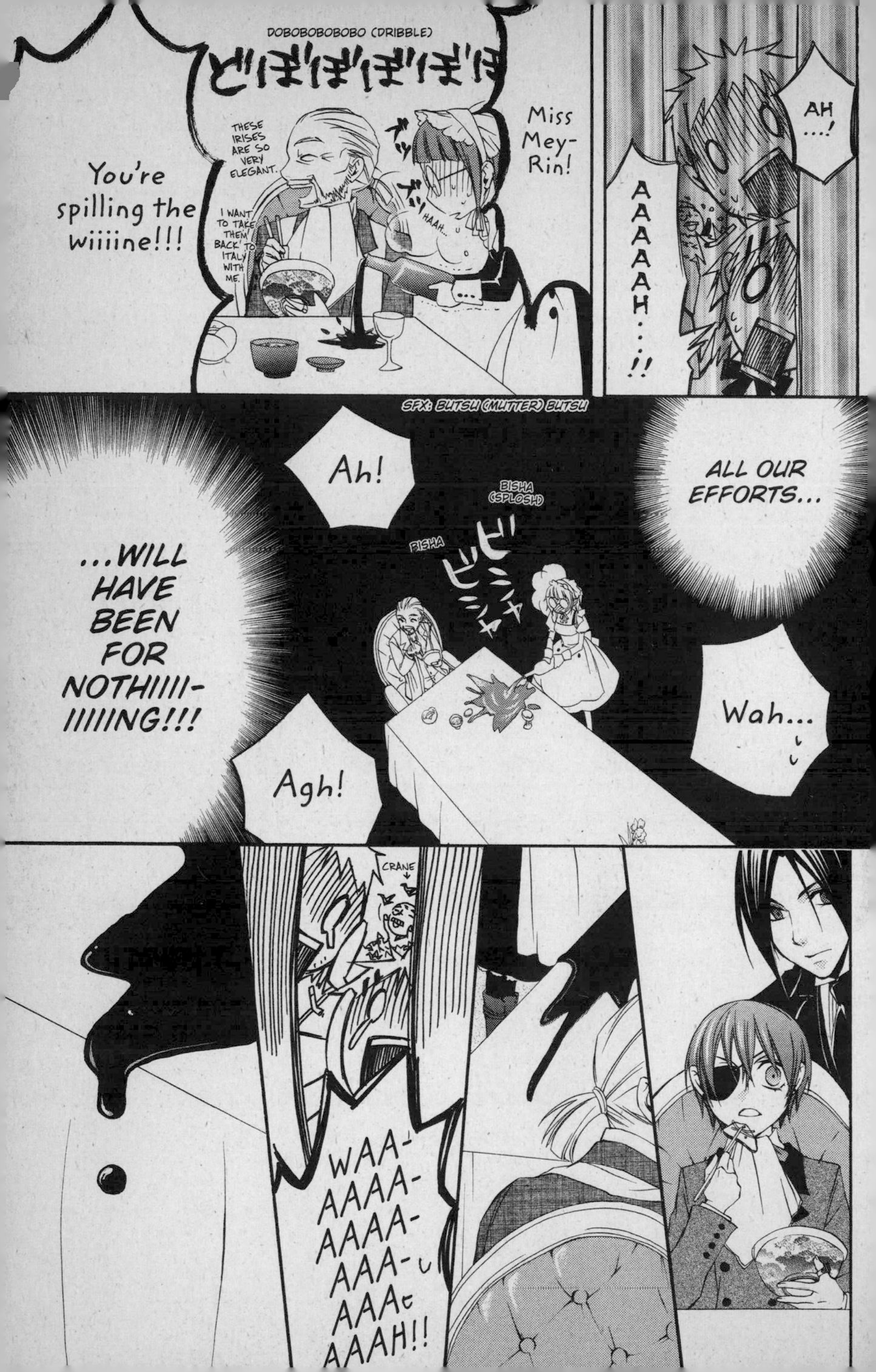
AH...!
AAAAAH...!!
どぼぼぼぼぼ
DOBOBOBOBOBO (DRIBBLE)
Miss Mey-Rin!
THESE IRISES ARE SO VERY ELEGANT.
I WANT TO TAKE THEM BACK TO ITALY WITH ME.
You're spilling the wiiiine!!!
HAAH...
...
SFX: BUTSU (MUTTER) BUTSU
ALL OUR EFFORTS...
Ah!
BISHA (SPLOSH)
BISHA
...WILL HAVE BEEN FOR NOTHIIIII-IIIIING!!!
Wah...
Agh!
CRANE
WAA-AAAA-AAAA-AAA-AAAt AAAH!!

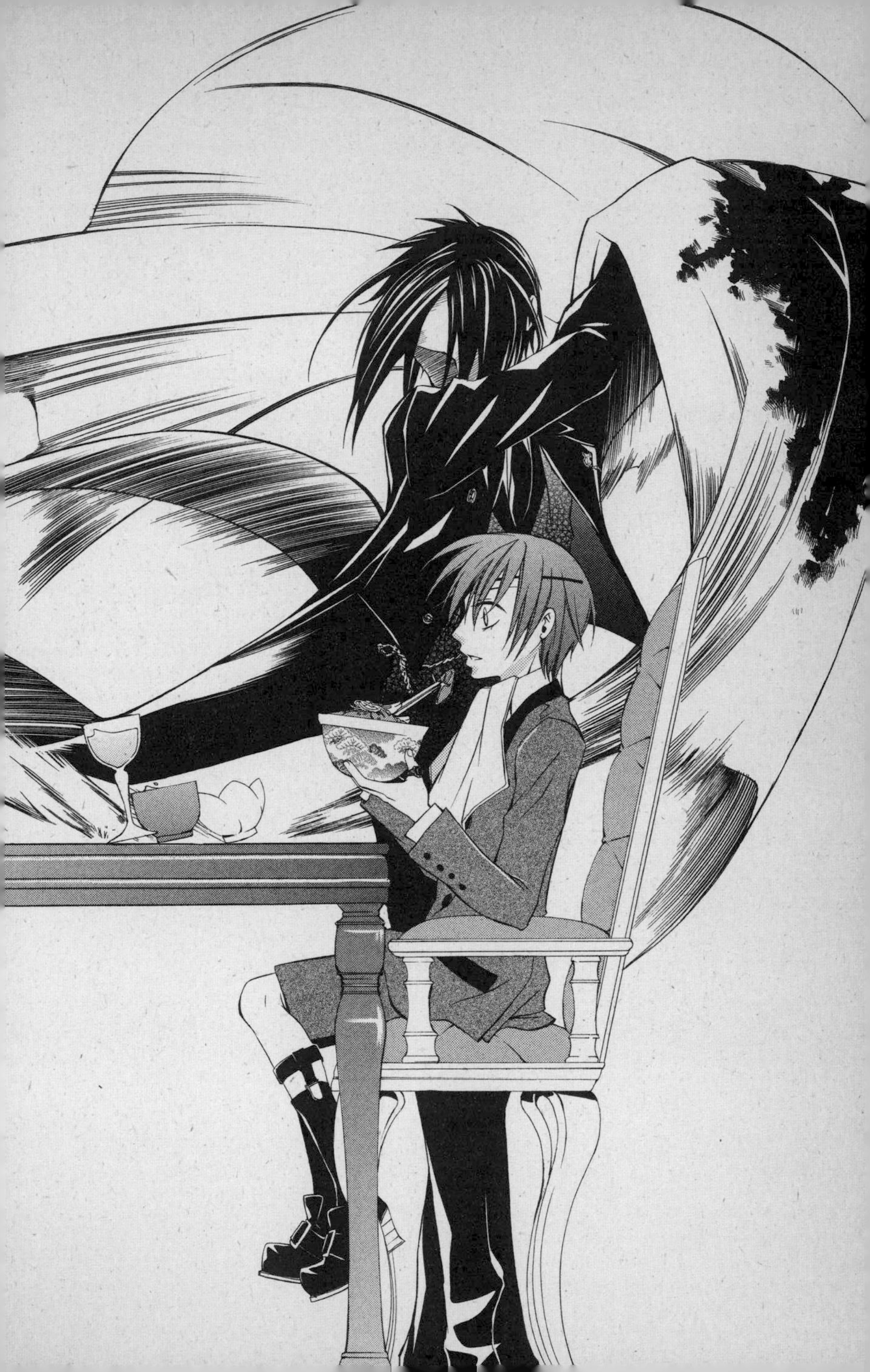

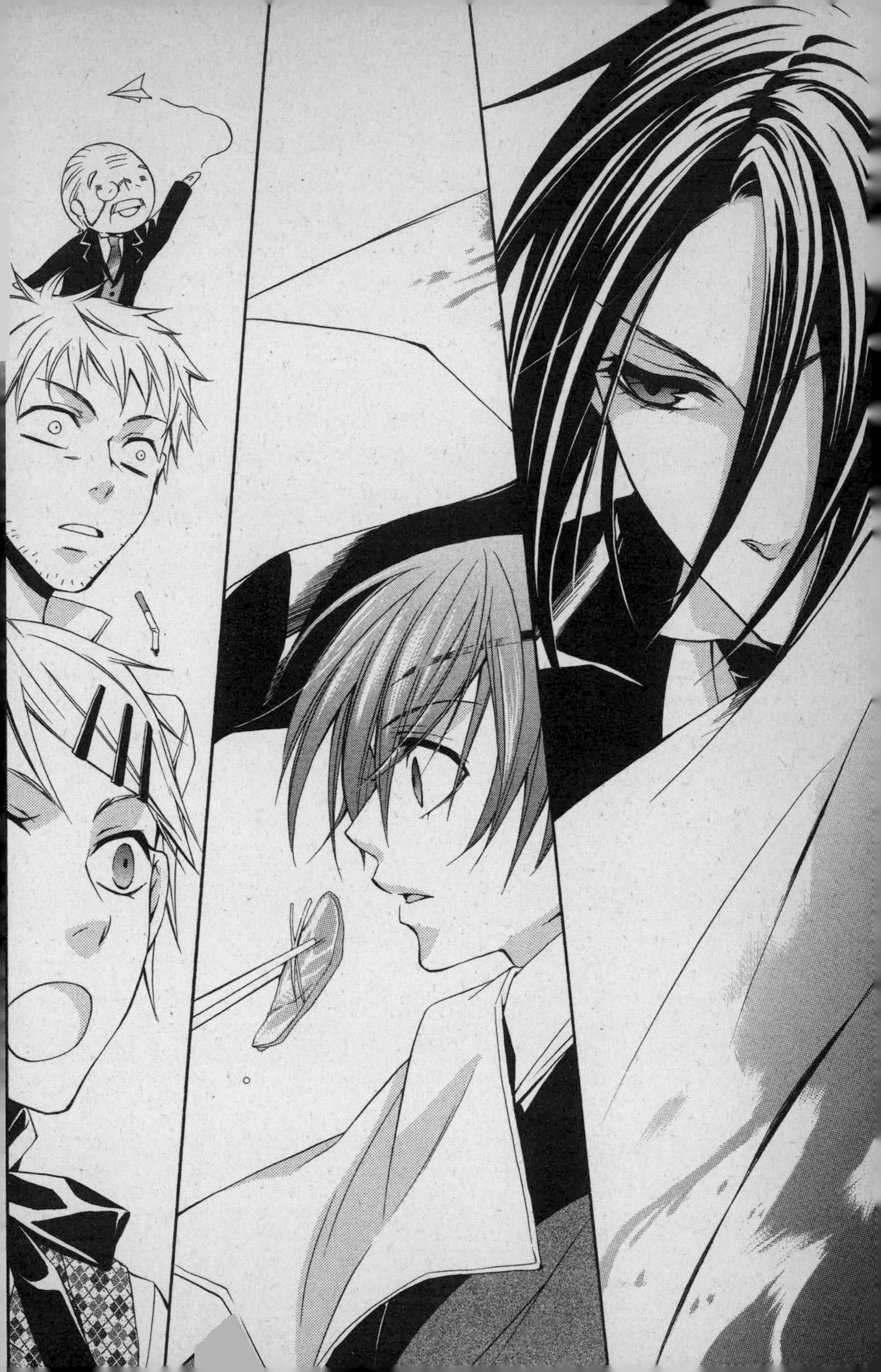

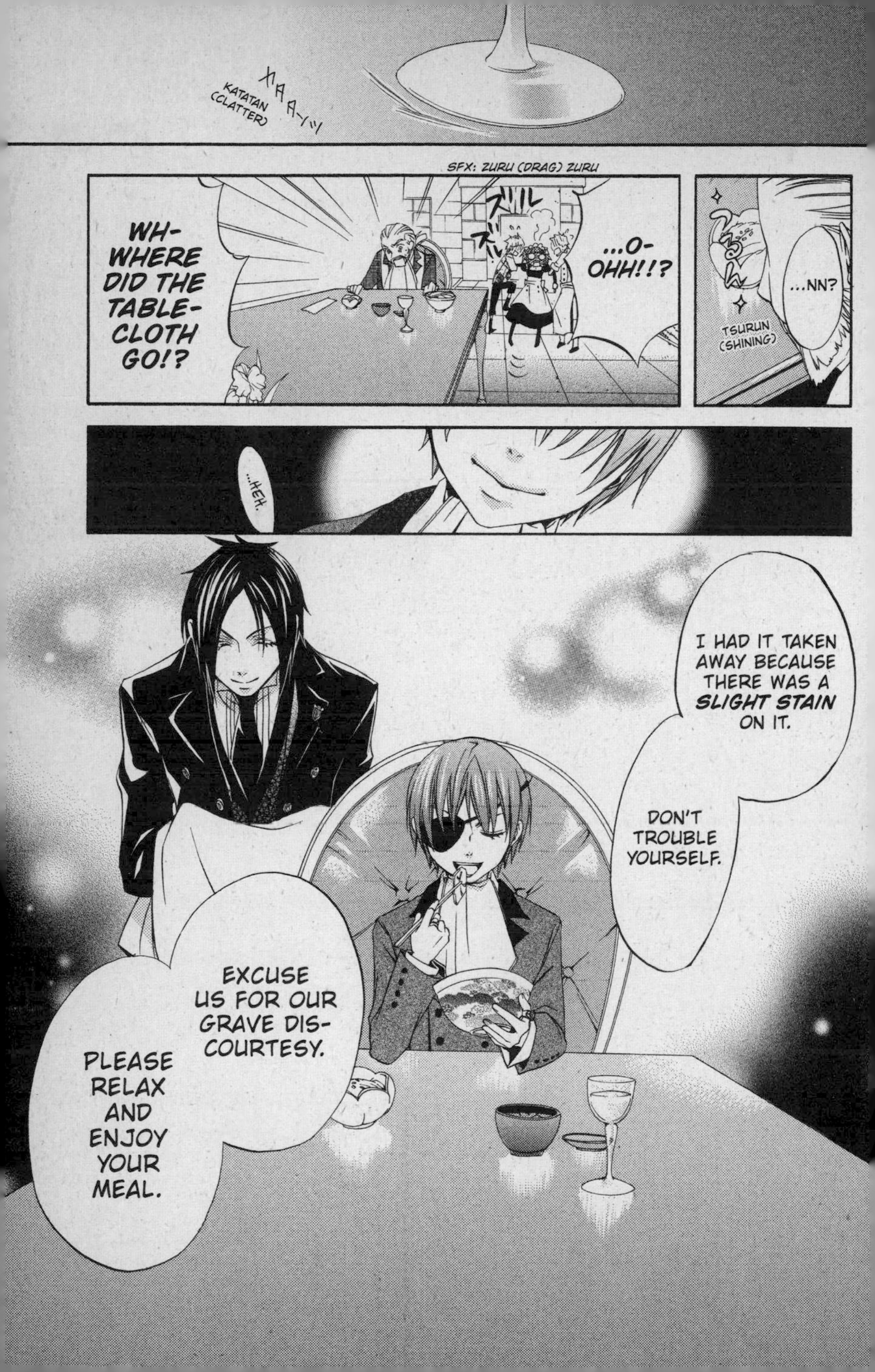

KATATAN (CLATTER)
TSURUN (SHINING)
...NN?
SFX: ZURU (DRAG) ZURU
ズル ズル
...O-OHH!!?
WH-WHERE DID THE TABLE-CLOTH GO!?
...HEH.
I HAD IT TAKEN AWAY BECAUSE THERE WAS A ***SLIGHT STAIN*** ON IT.
DON'T TROUBLE YOURSELF.
EXCUSE US FOR OUR GRAVE DIS-COURTESY.
PLEASE RELAX AND ENJOY YOUR MEAL.

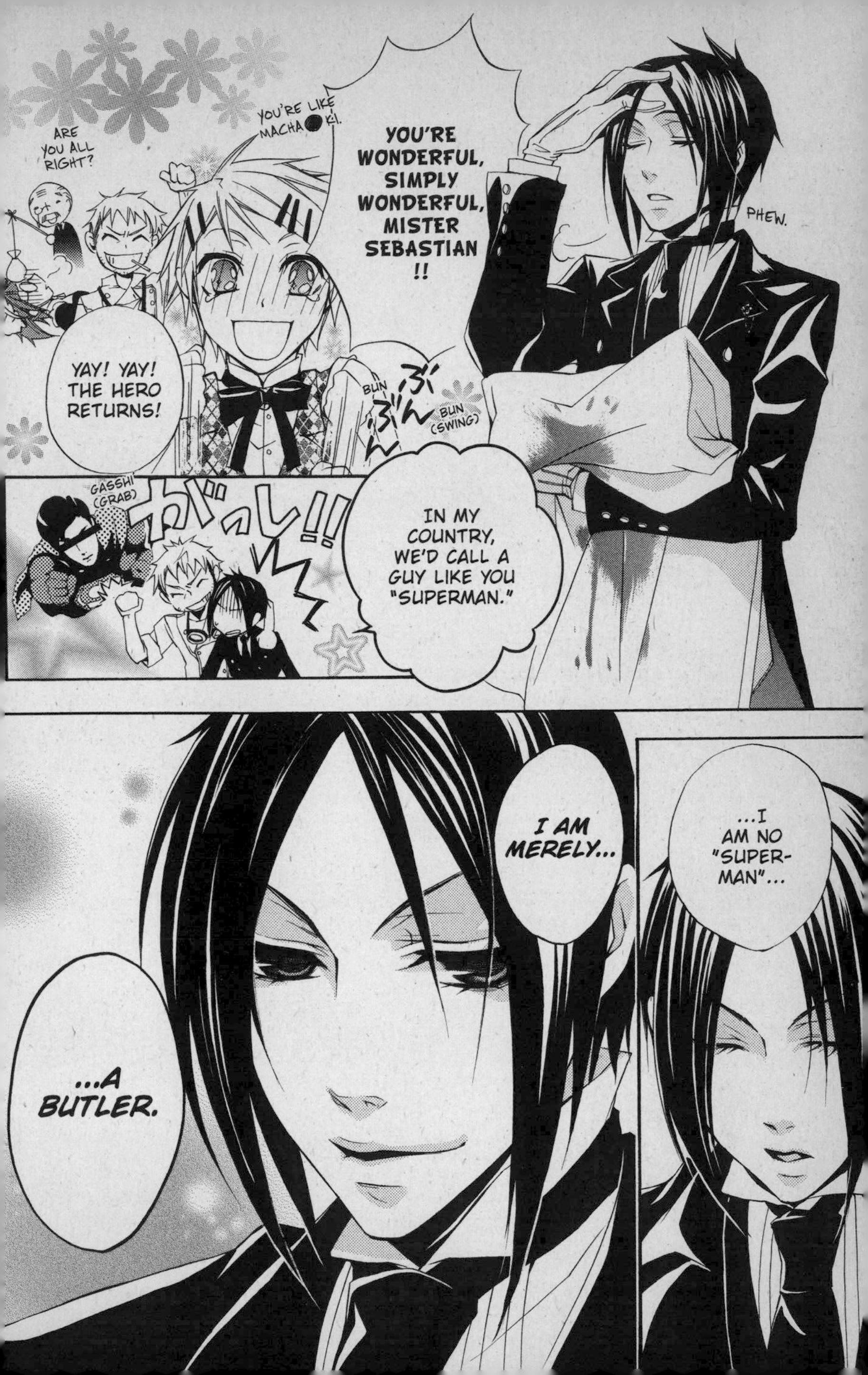
PHEW.
YOU'RE WONDERFUL, SIMPLY WONDERFUL, MISTER SEBASTIAN!!
YOU'RE LIKE MACHA●KI.
ARE YOU ALL RIGHT?
YAY! YAY! THE HERO RETURNS!
ぶんぶん
BUN BUN (SWING)
IN MY COUNTRY, WE'D CALL A GUY LIKE YOU "SUPERMAN."
がっし!!
GASSHI (GRAB)
...I AM NO "SUPER-MAN"...
I AM MERELY...
...A BUTLER.

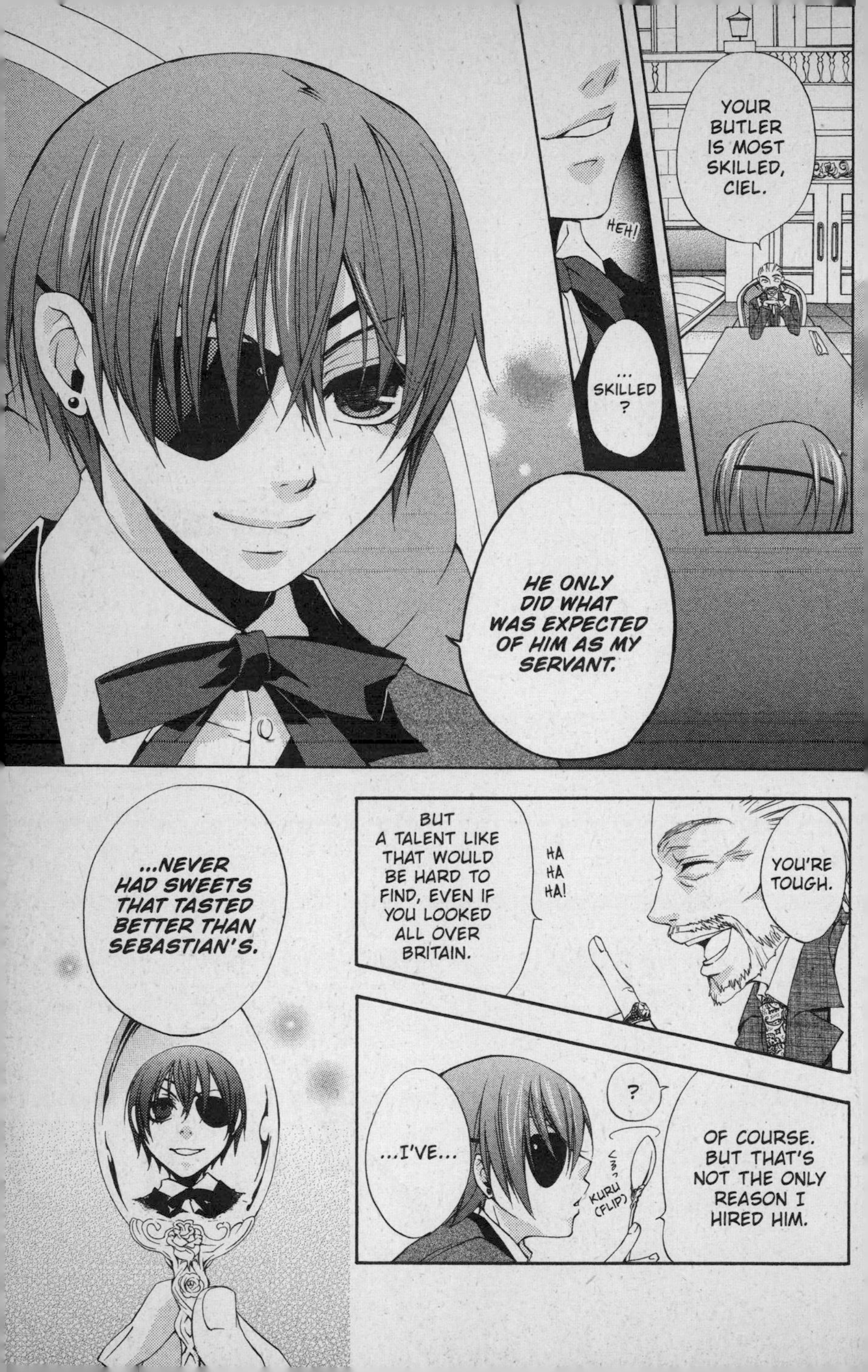
YOUR BUTLER IS MOST SKILLED, CIEL.
HEH!
...SKILLED?
HE ONLY DID WHAT WAS EXPECTED OF HIM AS MY SERVANT.
YOU'RE TOUGH.
HA HA HA!
BUT A TALENT LIKE THAT WOULD BE HARD TO FIND, EVEN IF YOU LOOKED ALL OVER BRITAIN.
OF COURSE. BUT THAT'S NOT THE ONLY REASON I HIRED HIM.
?
KURU (FLIP)
...I'VE...
...NEVER HAD SWEETS THAT TASTED BETTER THAN SEBASTIAN'S.

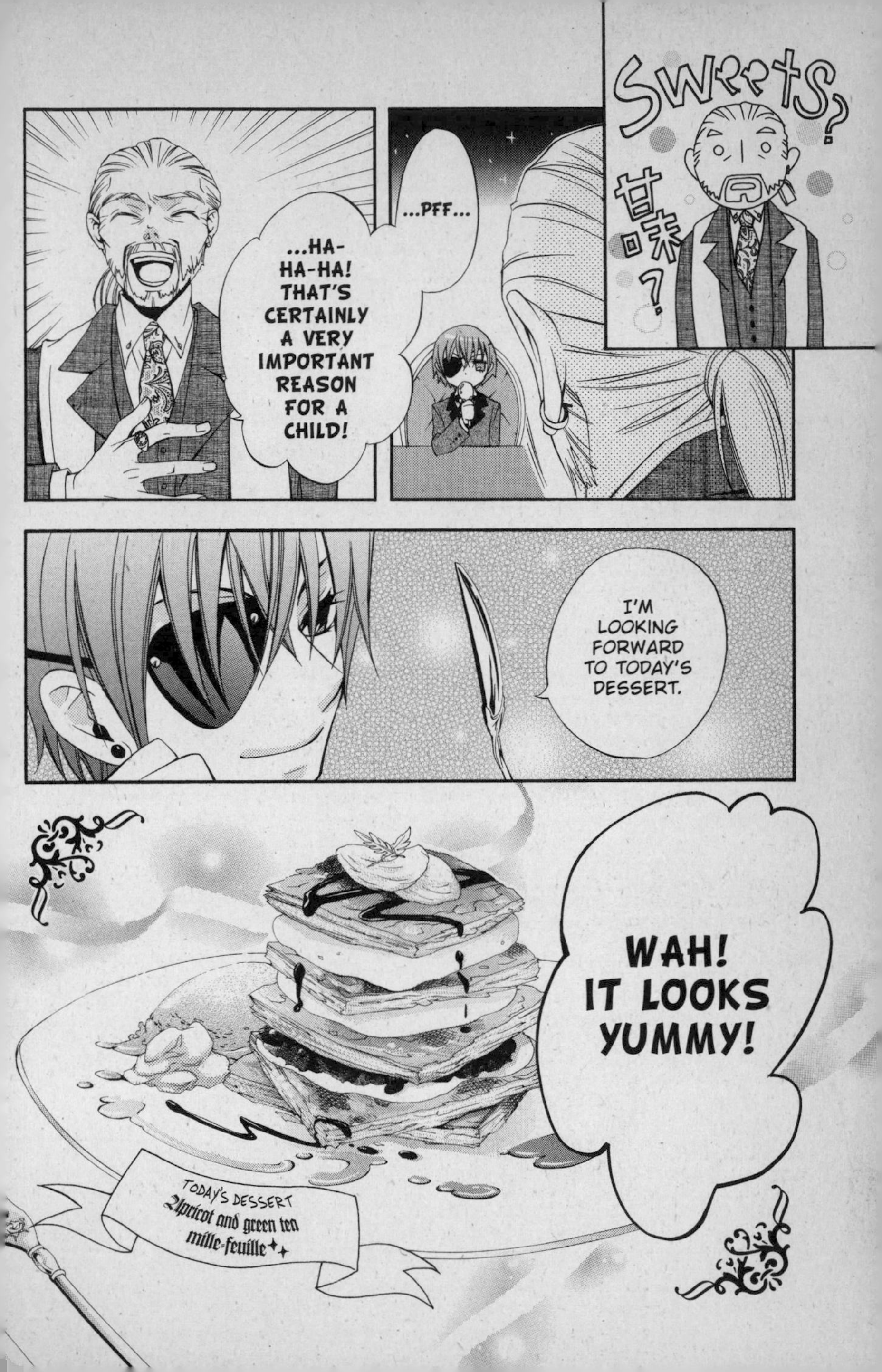
Sweets?
甘味?
...PFF...
...HA-HA-HA! THAT'S CERTAINLY A VERY IMPORTANT REASON FOR A CHILD!
I'M LOOKING FORWARD TO TODAY'S DESSERT.
WAH! IT LOOKS YUMMY!
TODAY'S DESSERT
Apricot and green tea mille-feuille

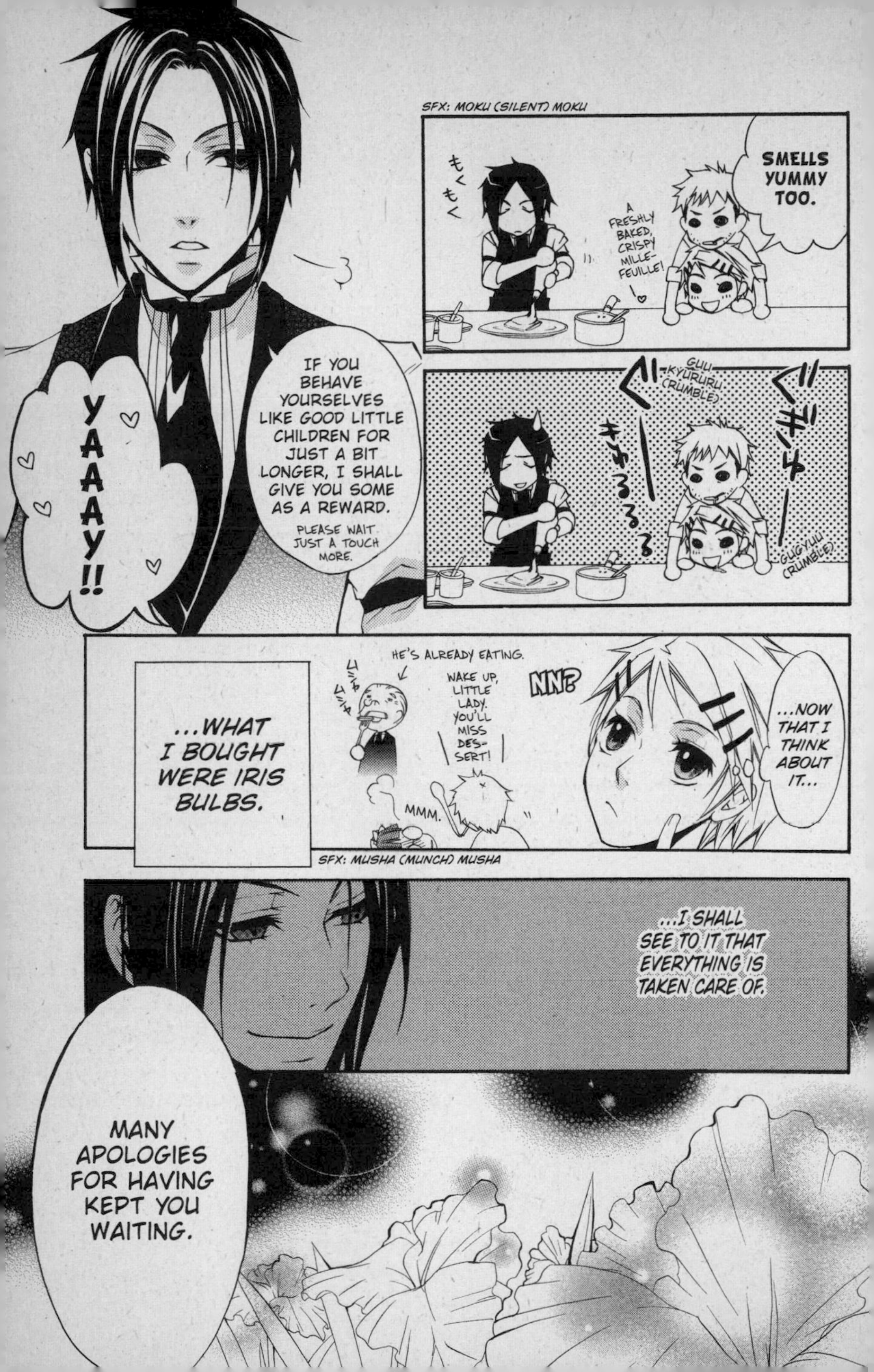
SFX: MOKU (SILENT) MOKU
もく もく
A FRESHLY BAKED, CRISPY MILLE-FEUILLE!
SMELLS YUMMY TOO.
GUU KYURURU (RUMBLE)
GUGYUU (RUMBLE)
IF YOU BEHAVE YOURSELVES LIKE GOOD LITTLE CHILDREN FOR JUST A BIT LONGER, I SHALL GIVE YOU SOME AS A REWARD.
PLEASE WAIT JUST A TOUCH MORE.
YAAAAY!!
...NOW THAT I THINK ABOUT IT...
NN?
WAKE UP, LITTLE LADY. YOU'LL MISS DES-SERT!
HE'S ALREADY EATING.
MMM.
SFX: MUSHA (MUNCH) MUSHA
...WHAT I BOUGHT WERE IRIS BULBS.
...I SHALL SEE TO IT THAT EVERYTHING IS TAKEN CARE OF.
MANY APOLOGIES FOR HAVING KEPT YOU WAITING.

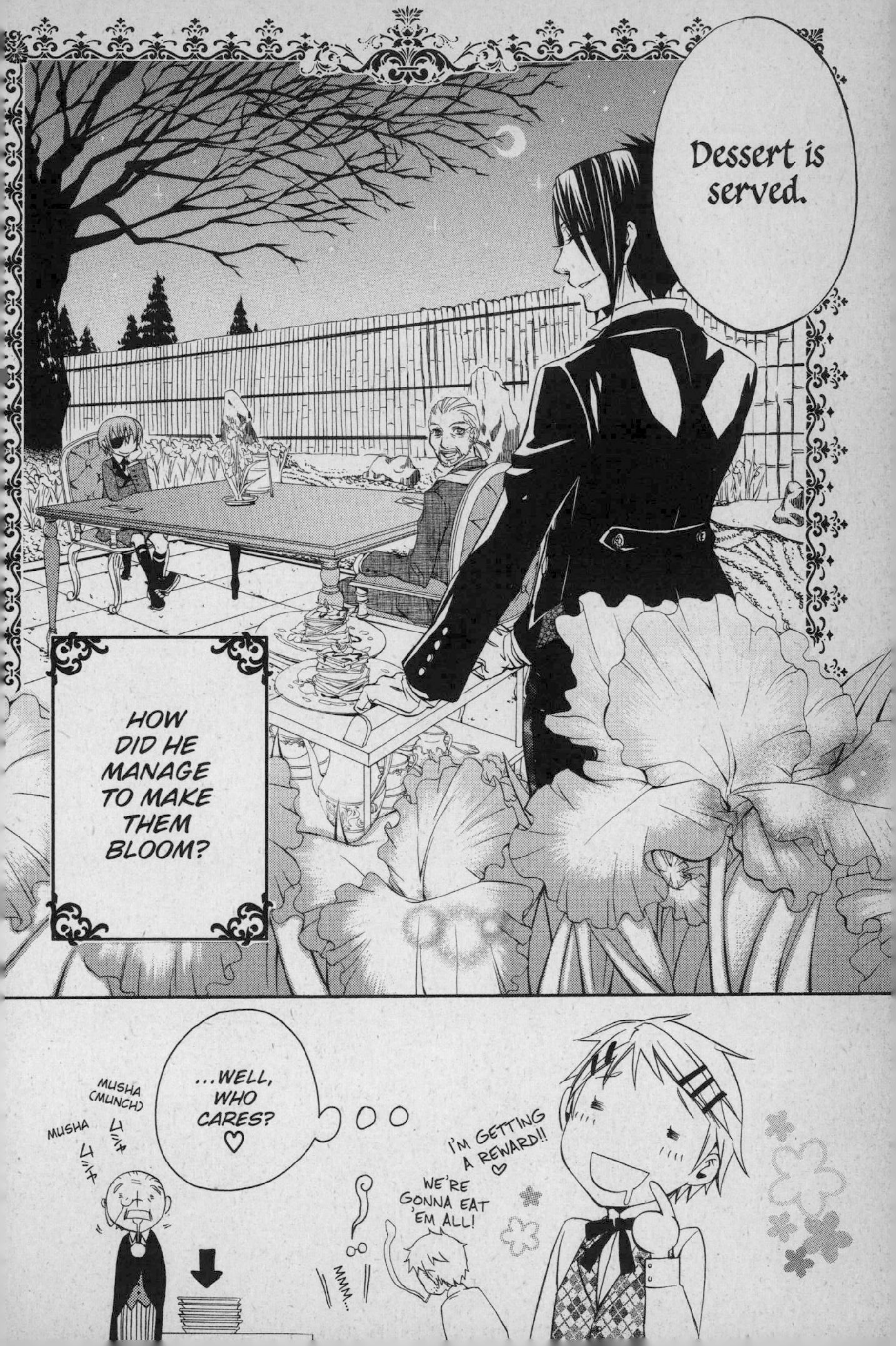
Dessert is served.
HOW DID HE MANAGE TO MAKE THEM BLOOM?
I'M GETTING A REWARD!! ♡
WE'RE GONNA EAT 'EM ALL!
MMM...
...WELL, WHO CARES? ♡
MUSHA (MUNCH)
ムシャ
MUSHA
ムシャ

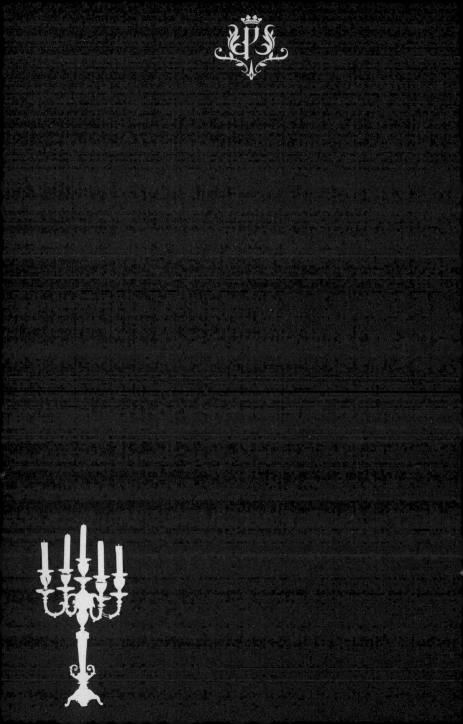

Black Butler

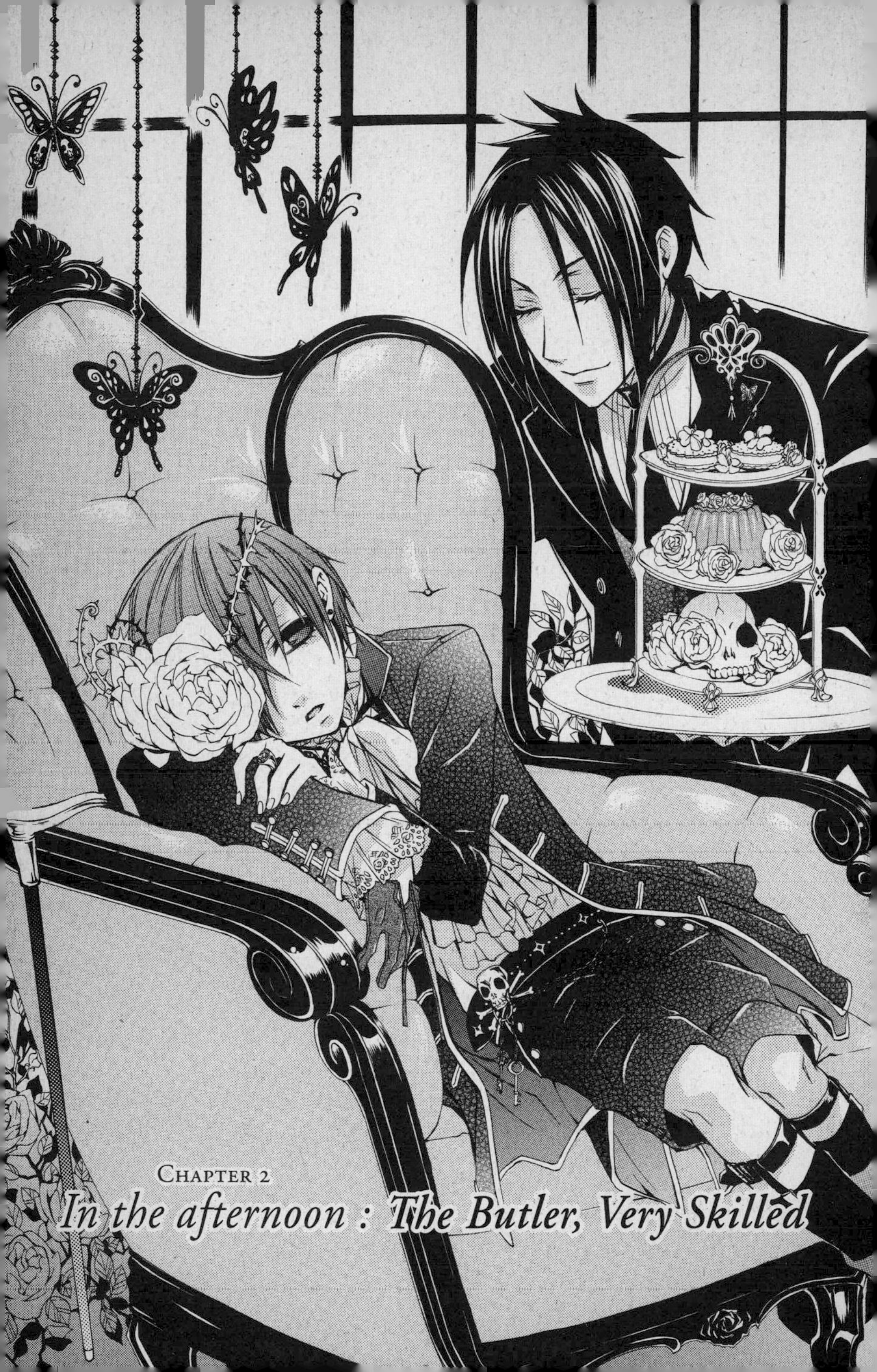

## Chapter 2
# In the afternoon : The Butler, Very Skilled

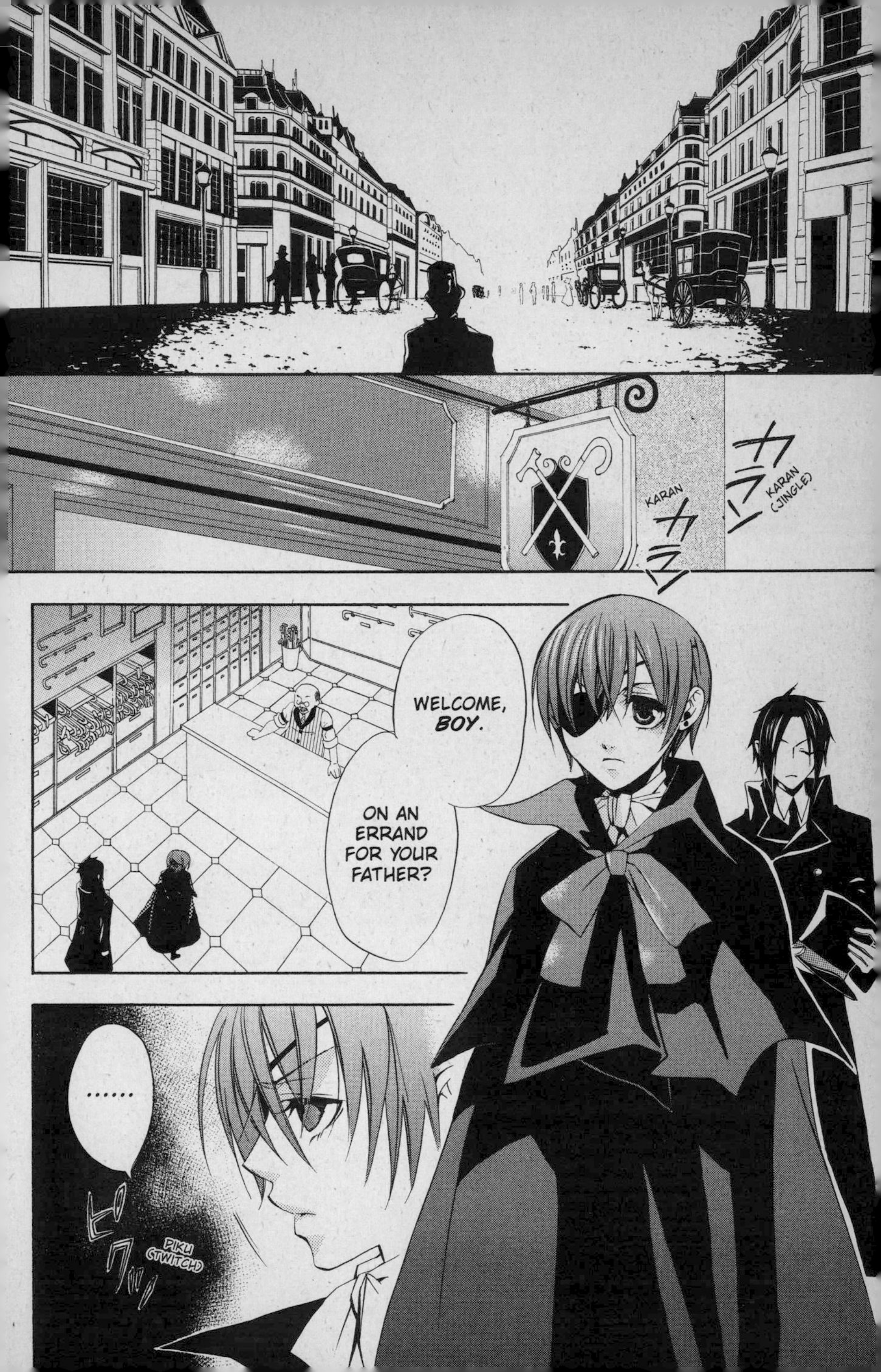
KARAN (JINGLE)
KARAN
WELCOME, BOY.
ON AN ERRAND FOR YOUR FATHER?
......
PIKU (TWITCH)

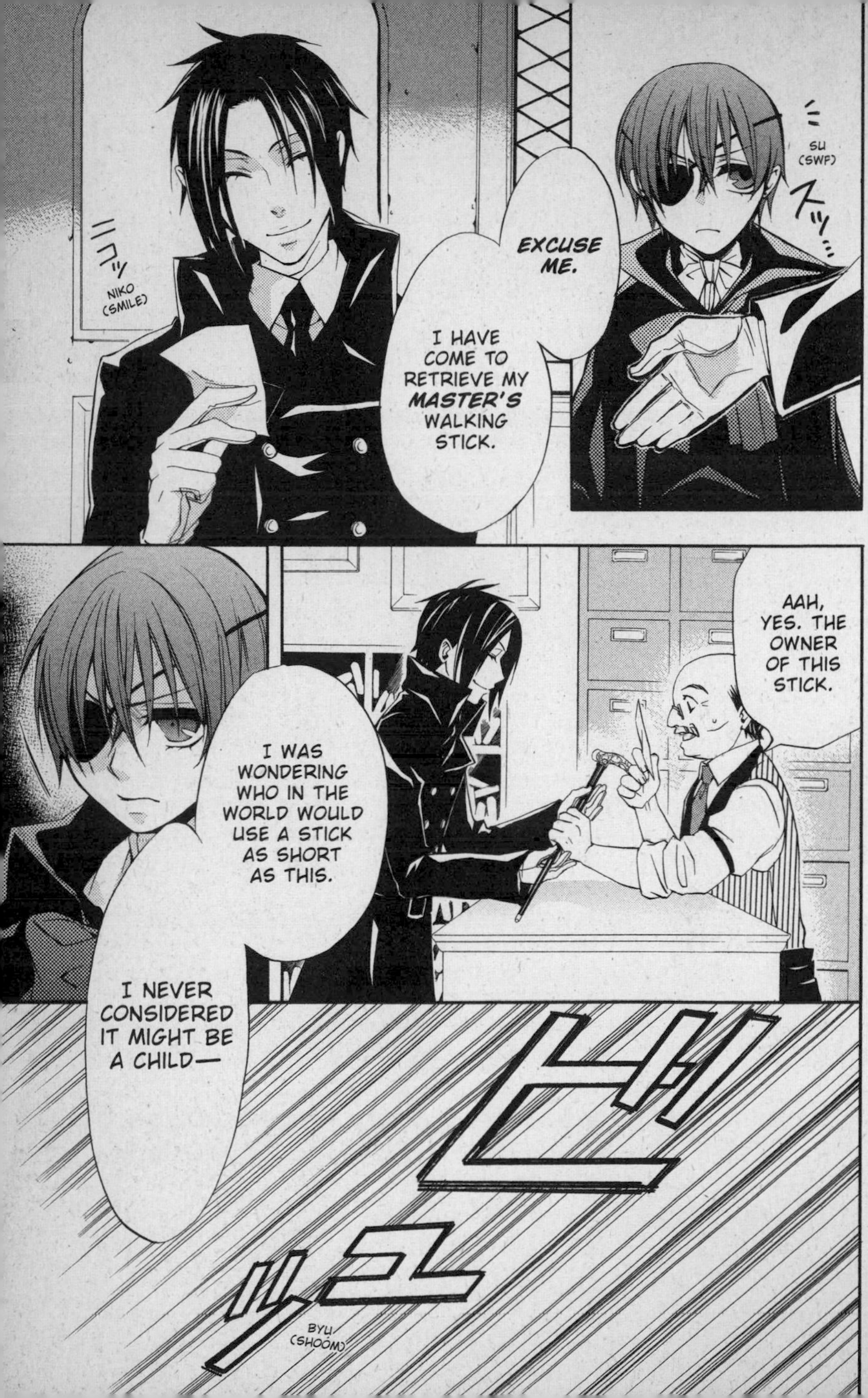
SU (SWF)
EXCUSE ME.
I HAVE COME TO RETRIEVE MY MASTER'S WALKING STICK.
NIKO (SMILE)
AAH, YES. THE OWNER OF THIS STICK.
I WAS WONDERING WHO IN THE WORLD WOULD USE A STICK AS SHORT AS THIS.
I NEVER CONSIDERED IT MIGHT BE A CHILD—
BYU (SHOOM)

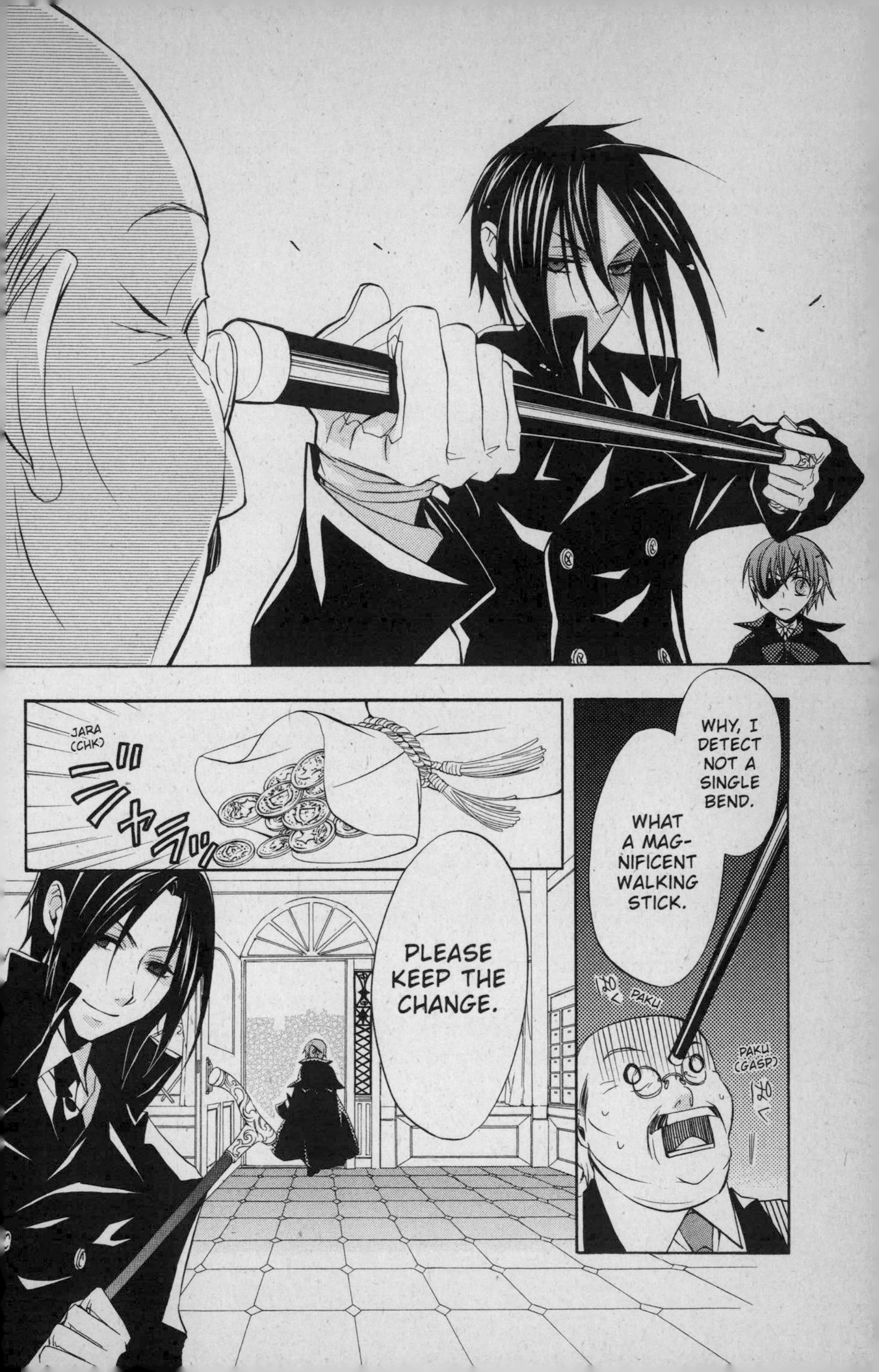
WHY, I DETECT NOT A SINGLE BEND.
WHAT A MAGNIFICENT WALKING STICK.
PAKU
PAKU (GASP)
JARA (CHK)
PLEASE KEEP THE CHANGE.

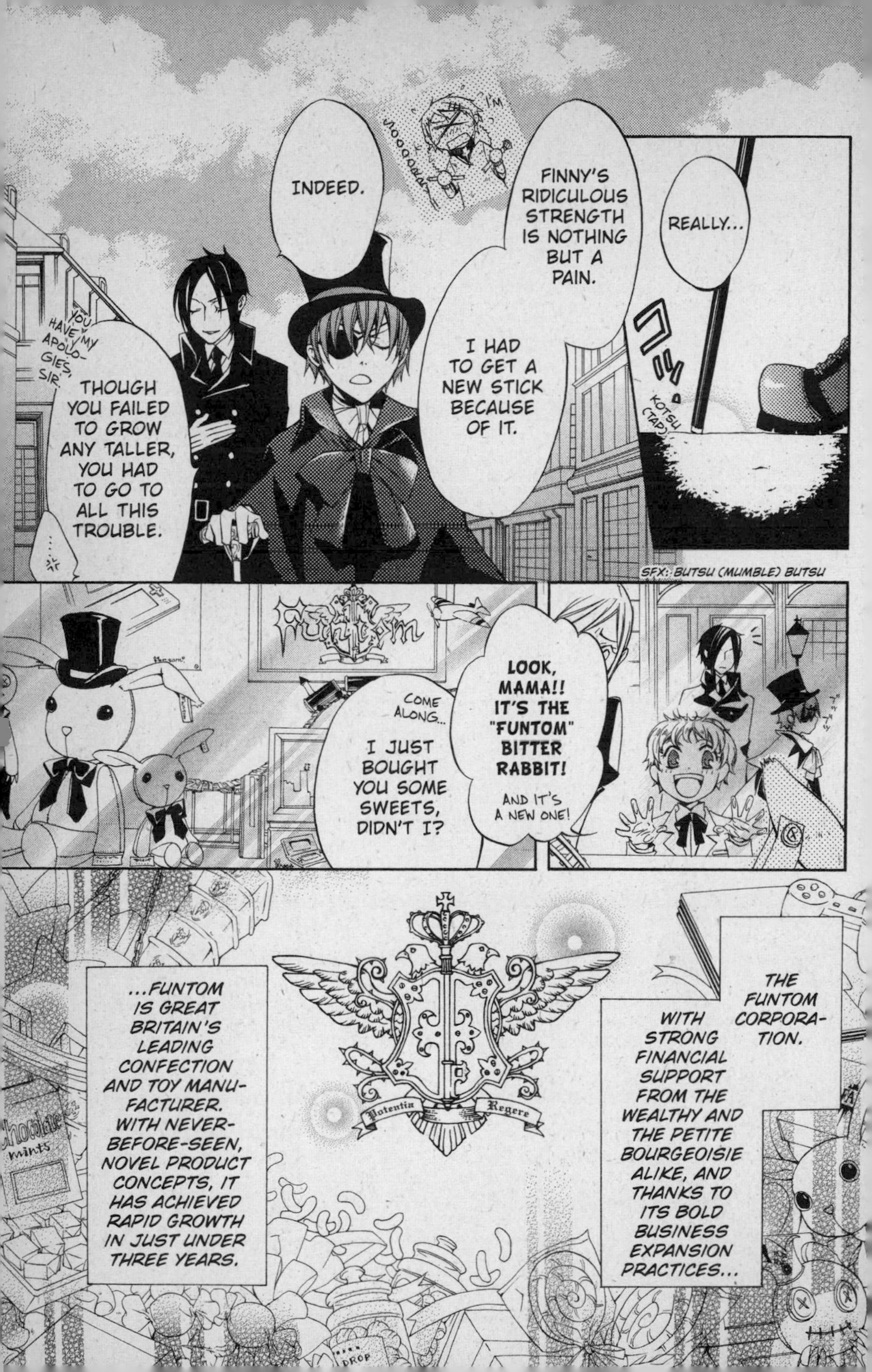
REALLY...
KOTSU (TAP)
FINNY'S RIDICULOUS STRENGTH IS NOTHING BUT A PAIN.
I'M SOOOOORRY
INDEED.
I HAD TO GET A NEW STICK BECAUSE OF IT.
YOU HAVE MY APOLOGIES, SIR.
THOUGH YOU FAILED TO GROW ANY TALLER, YOU HAD TO GO TO ALL THIS TROUBLE.
...!
SFX: BUTSU (MUMBLE) BUTSU
LOOK, MAMA!! IT'S THE "FUNTOM" BITTER RABBIT!
AND IT'S A NEW ONE!
COME ALONG...
I JUST BOUGHT YOU SOME SWEETS, DIDN'T I?
Funtom
THE FUNTOM CORPORATION.
WITH STRONG FINANCIAL SUPPORT FROM THE WEALTHY AND THE PETITE BOURGEOISIE ALIKE, AND THANKS TO ITS BOLD BUSINESS EXPANSION PRACTICES...
Potentia Regere
...FUNTOM IS GREAT BRITAIN'S LEADING CONFECTION AND TOY MANUFACTURER. WITH NEVER-BEFORE-SEEN, NOVEL PRODUCT CONCEPTS, IT HAS ACHIEVED RAPID GROWTH IN JUST UNDER THREE YEARS.
Chocolate mints
DROP

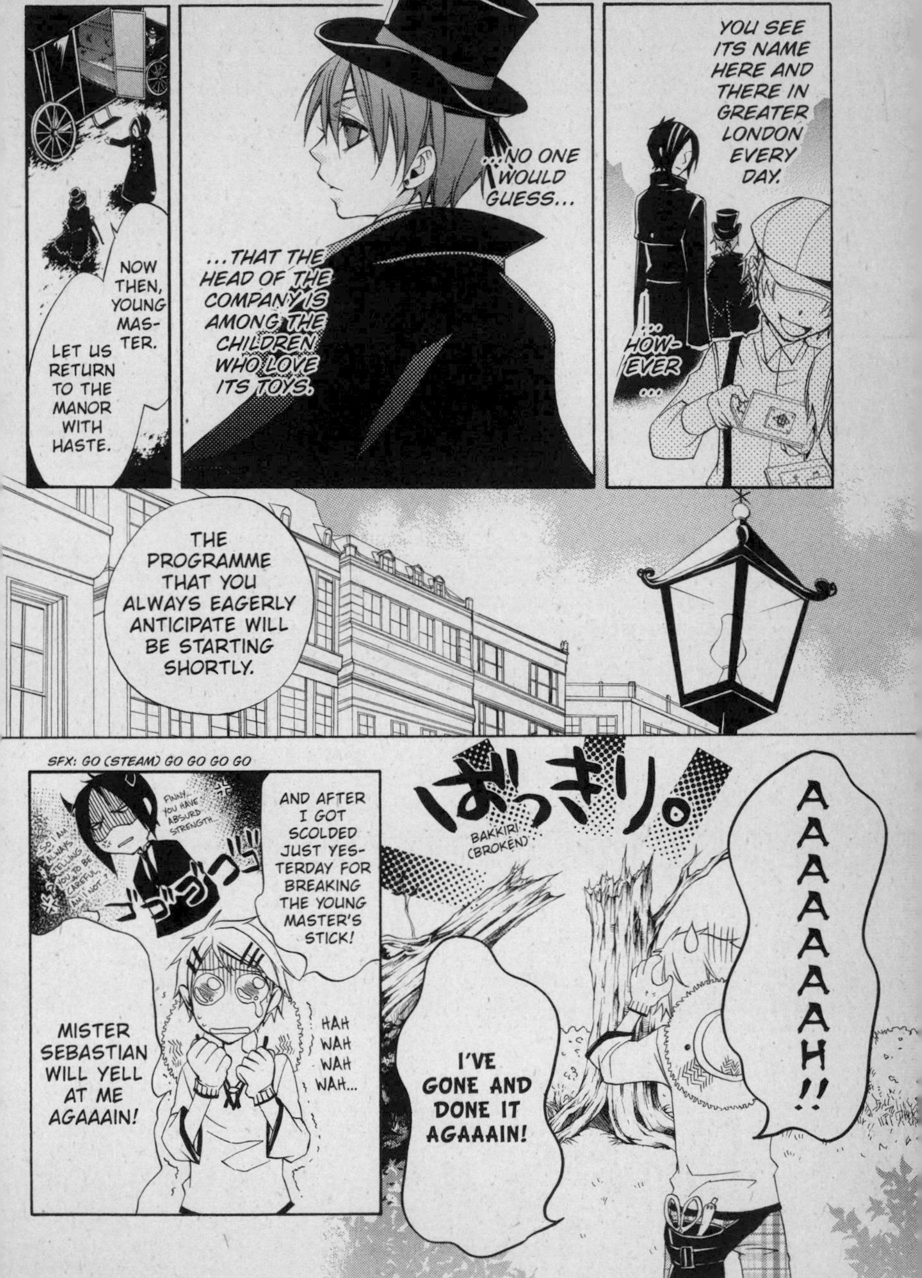
YOU SEE ITS NAME HERE AND THERE IN GREATER LONDON EVERY DAY.
...HOWEVER...
...NO ONE WOULD GUESS...
...THAT THE HEAD OF THE COMPANY IS AMONG THE CHILDREN WHO LOVE ITS TOYS.
NOW THEN, YOUNG MASTER.
LET US RETURN TO THE MANOR WITH HASTE.
THE PROGRAMME THAT YOU ALWAYS EAGERLY ANTICIPATE WILL BE STARTING SHORTLY.
AAAAAAAH!!
BAKKIRI (BROKEN)
I'VE GONE AND DONE IT AGAAAIN!
AND AFTER I GOT SCOLDED JUST YESTERDAY FOR BREAKING THE YOUNG MASTER'S STICK!
FINNY... YOU HAVE ABSURD STRENGTH...
SO I AM ALWAYS TELLING YOU TO BE CAREFUL, AM I NOT...?
SFX: GO (STEAM) GO GO GO GO
HAH WAH WAH WAH...
MISTER SEBASTIAN WILL YELL AT ME AGAAAIN!

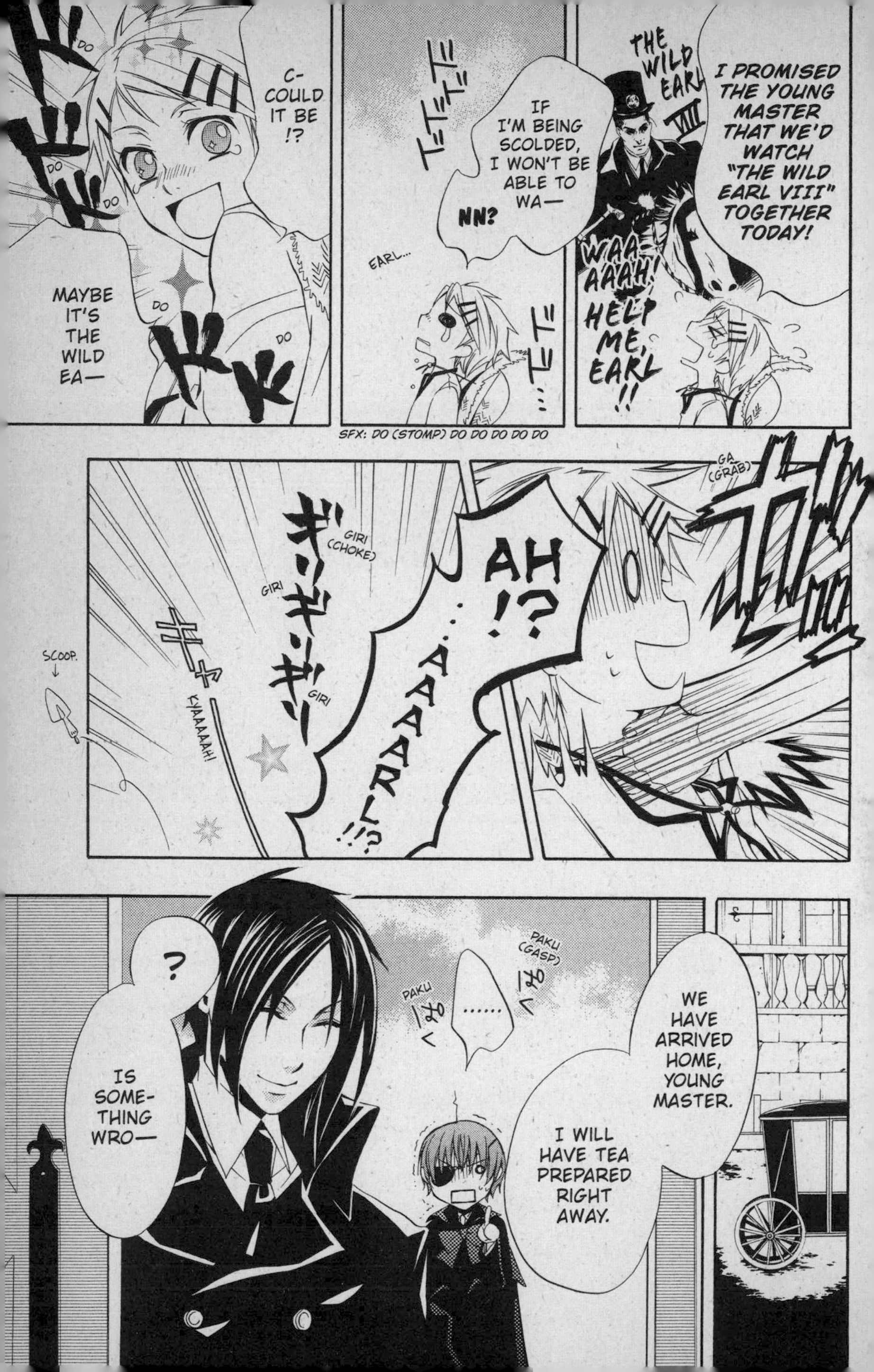

I PROMISED THE YOUNG MASTER THAT WE'D WATCH "THE WILD EARL VIII" TOGETHER TODAY!
THE WILD EARL VIII
WAAAAAH! HELP ME, EARL!!
IF I'M BEING SCOLDED, I WON'T BE ABLE TO WA—
NN?
EARL...
C-COULD IT BE!?
DO
DO
DO
DO
DO
MAYBE IT'S THE WILD EA—
SFX: DO (STOMP) DO DO DO DO DO
GA (GRAB)
AH!? ...AAAAARL!!?
GIRI (CHOKE)
GIRI
GIRI
KYAAAAAAH!
SCOOP.
WE HAVE ARRIVED HOME, YOUNG MASTER.
I WILL HAVE TEA PREPARED RIGHT AWAY.
......
PAKU (GASP)
PAKU
?
IS SOMETHING WRO—

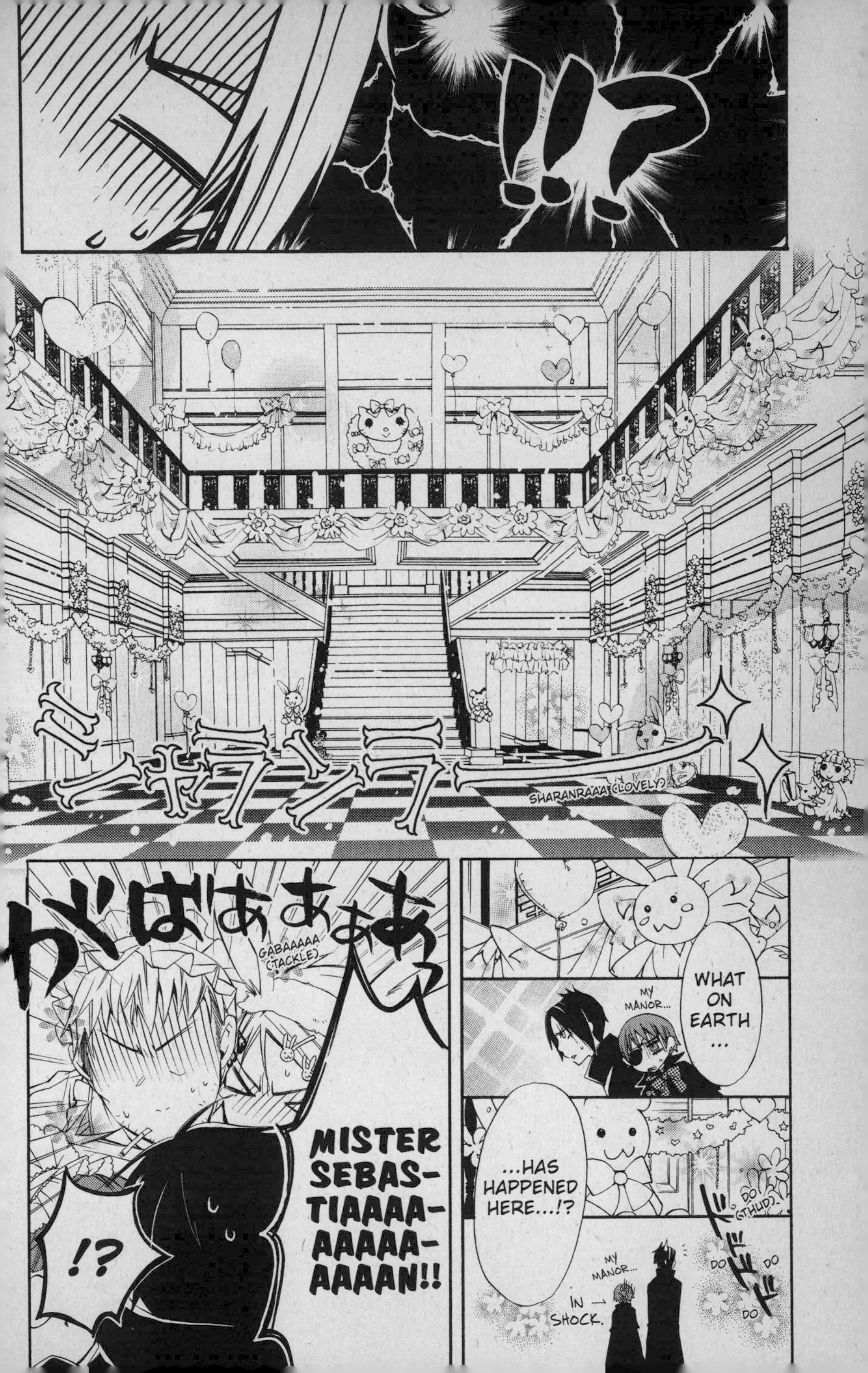
!!
SHARANRAAA (LOVELY)
WHAT ON EARTH ...
MY MANOR...
...HAS HAPPENED HERE...!?
DO (THUD)
DO DO DO
MY MANOR...
IN → SHOCK.
GABAAAAA (TACKLE)
MISTER SEBAS-TIAAAA-AAAAA-AAAAN!!
!?

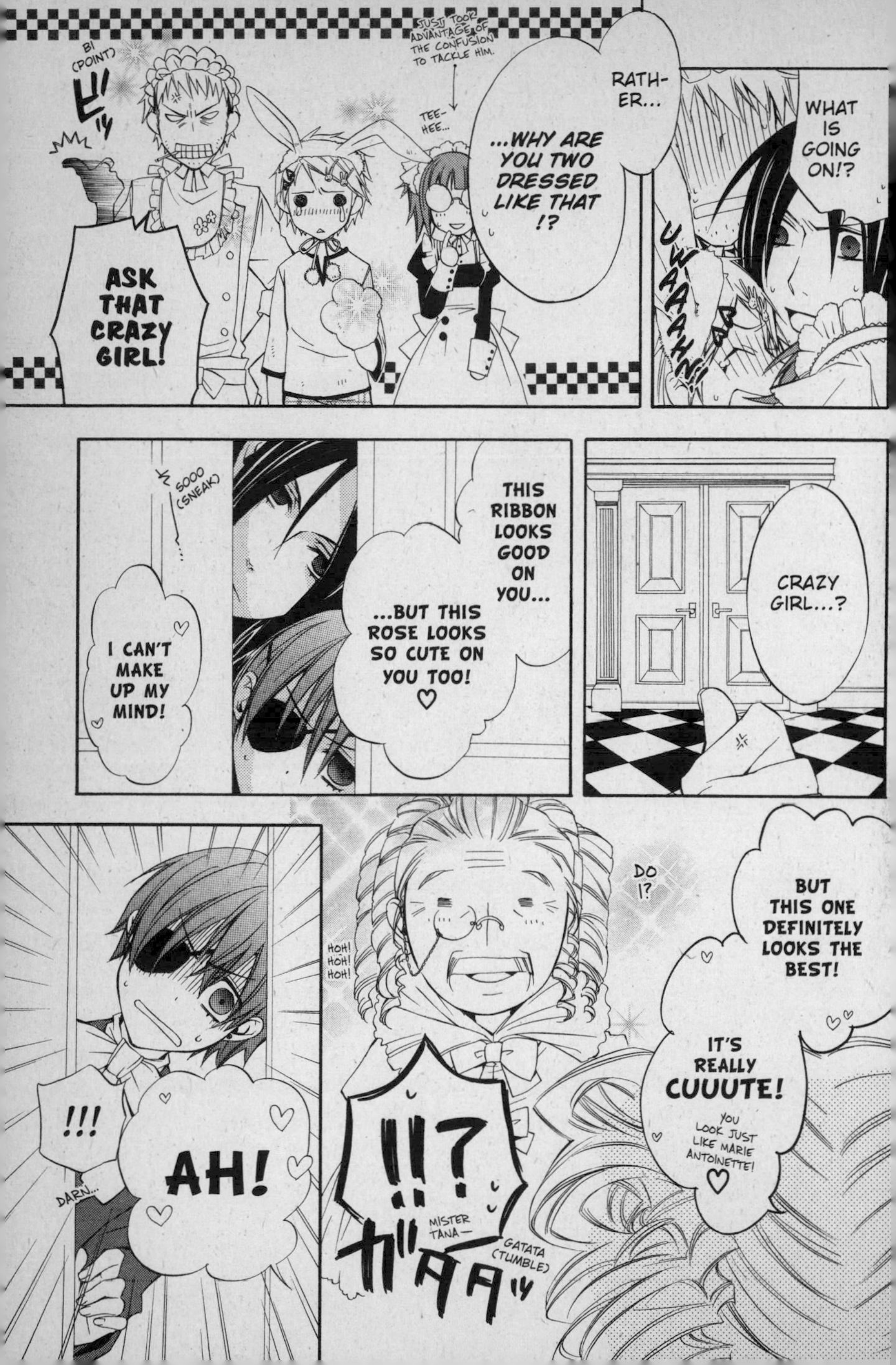
WHAT IS GOING ON!?
UWAAAAHN!!
RATHER...
...WHY ARE YOU TWO DRESSED LIKE THAT!?
JUST TOOK ADVANTAGE OF THE CONFUSION TO TACKLE HIM.
TEE-HEE...
BI (POINT)
ASK THAT CRAZY GIRL!
CRAZY GIRL...?
THIS RIBBON LOOKS GOOD ON YOU...
...BUT THIS ROSE LOOKS SO CUTE ON YOU TOO! ♡
SOOO (SNEAK)
I CAN'T MAKE UP MY MIND!
BUT THIS ONE DEFINITELY LOOKS THE BEST!
DO I?
IT'S REALLY CUUUTE!
YOU LOOK JUST LIKE MARIE ANTOINETTE! ♡
HOH! HOH! HOH!
!!?
MISTER TANA—
GATATA (TUMBLE)
!!!
AH!
DARN...

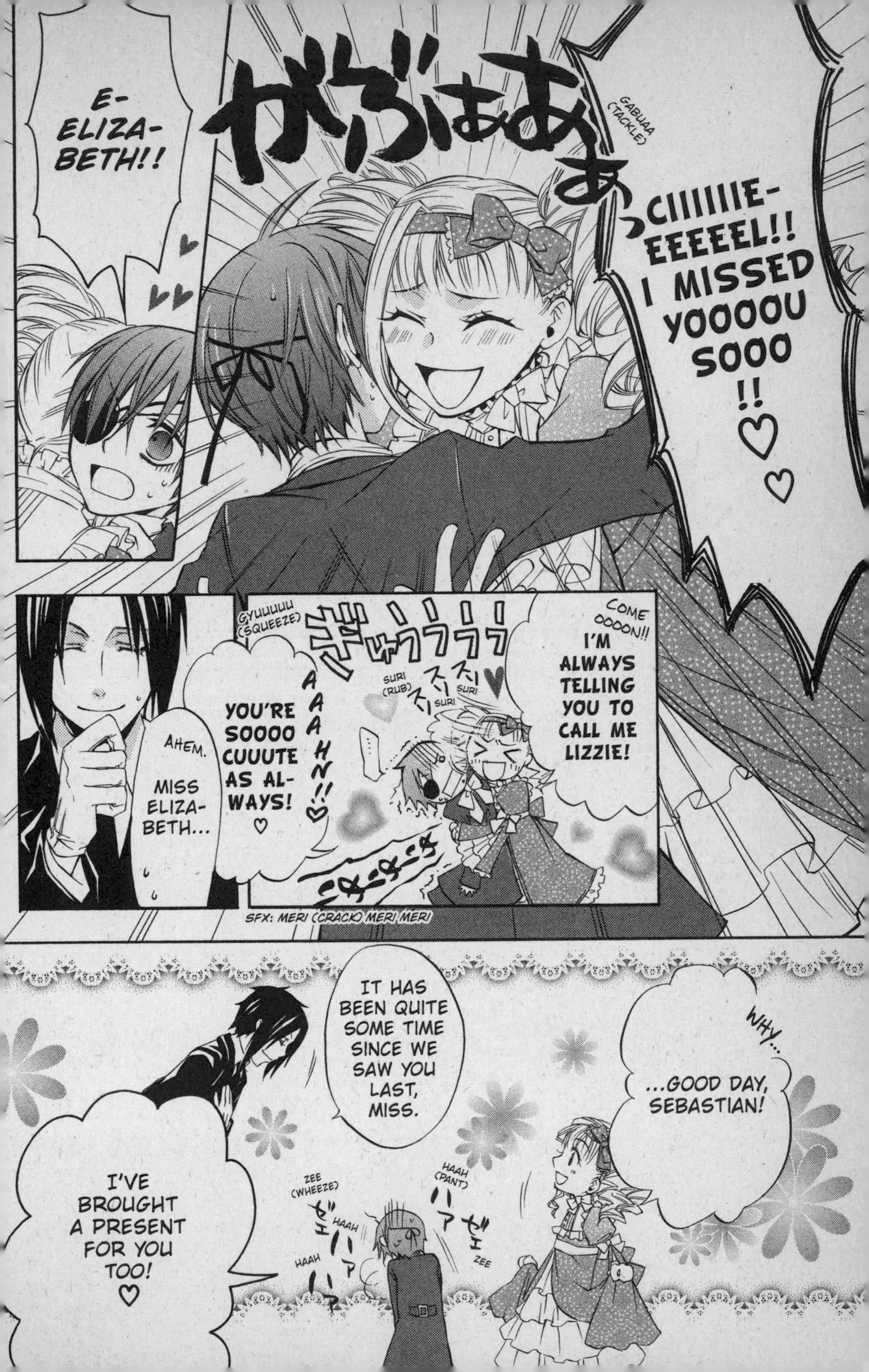
GABUAA (TACKLE)
CIIIIIIE-EEEEEL!! I MISSED YOOOOU SOOO!! ♡ ♡
E-ELIZA-BETH!!
COME OOOON!!
I'M ALWAYS TELLING YOU TO CALL ME LIZZIE!
GYUUUUUU (SQUEEZE)
SURI (RUB) SURI SURI
AAAHN!! ♡
YOU'RE SOOOO CUUUTE AS AL-WAYS! ♡
AHEM.
MISS ELIZA-BETH...
SFX: MERI (CRACK) MERI MERI
WHY...
...GOOD DAY, SEBASTIAN!
IT HAS BEEN QUITE SOME TIME SINCE WE SAW YOU LAST, MISS.
HAAH (PANT)
ZEE (WHEEZE)
HAAH
HAAH
ZEE
I'VE BROUGHT A PRESENT FOR YOU TOO! ♡

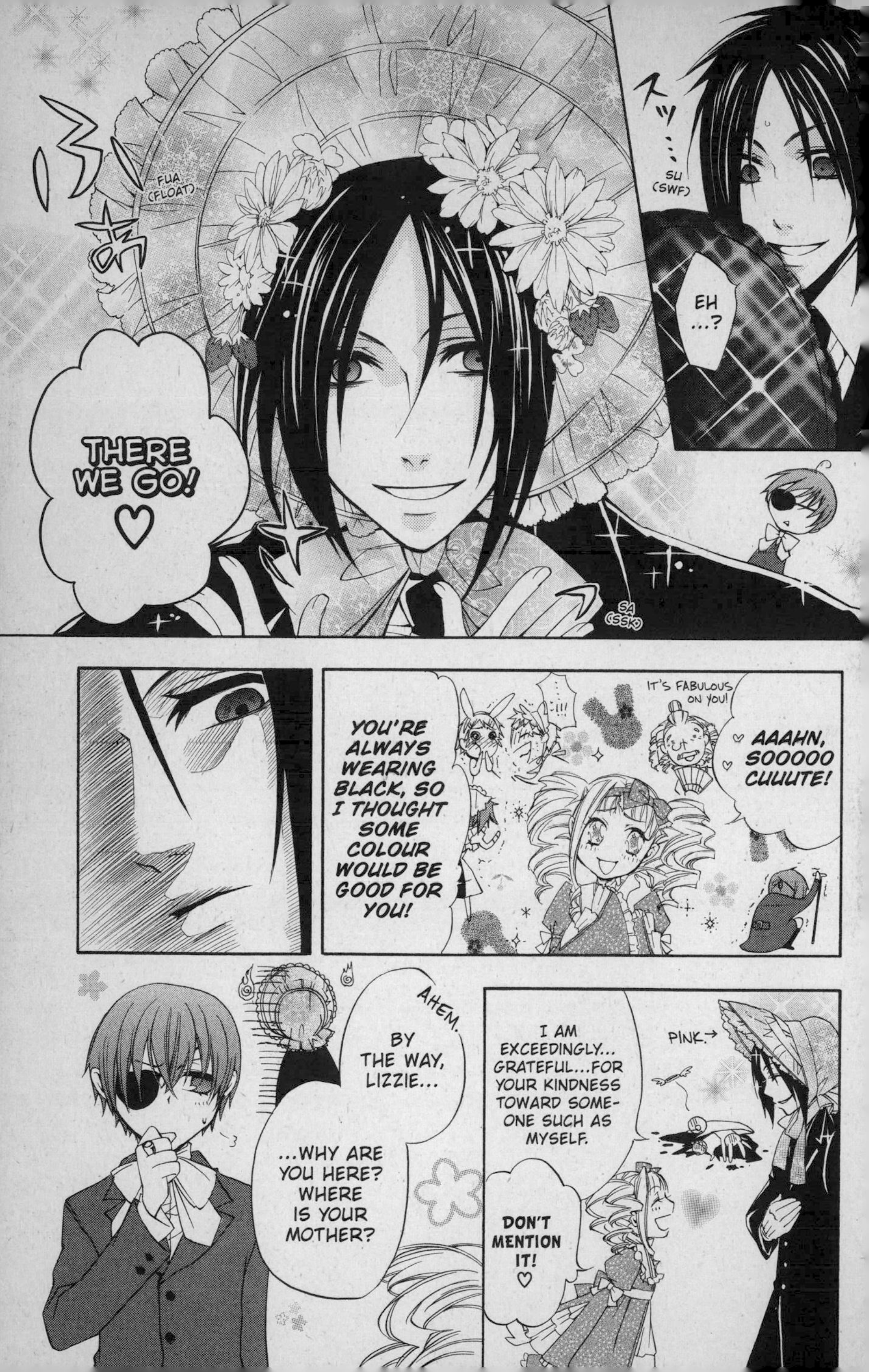
SU (SWF)
EH ...?
FUA (FLOAT)
THERE WE GO! ♡
SA (SSK)
IT'S FABULOUS ON YOU!
AAAHN, SOOOOO CUUUTE!
YOU'RE ALWAYS WEARING BLACK, SO I THOUGHT SOME COLOUR WOULD BE GOOD FOR YOU!
PINK.→
I AM EXCEEDINGLY... GRATEFUL...FOR YOUR KINDNESS TOWARD SOME-ONE SUCH AS MYSELF.
DON'T MENTION IT! ♡
AHEM.
BY THE WAY, LIZZIE...
...WHY ARE YOU HERE? WHERE IS YOUR MOTHER?

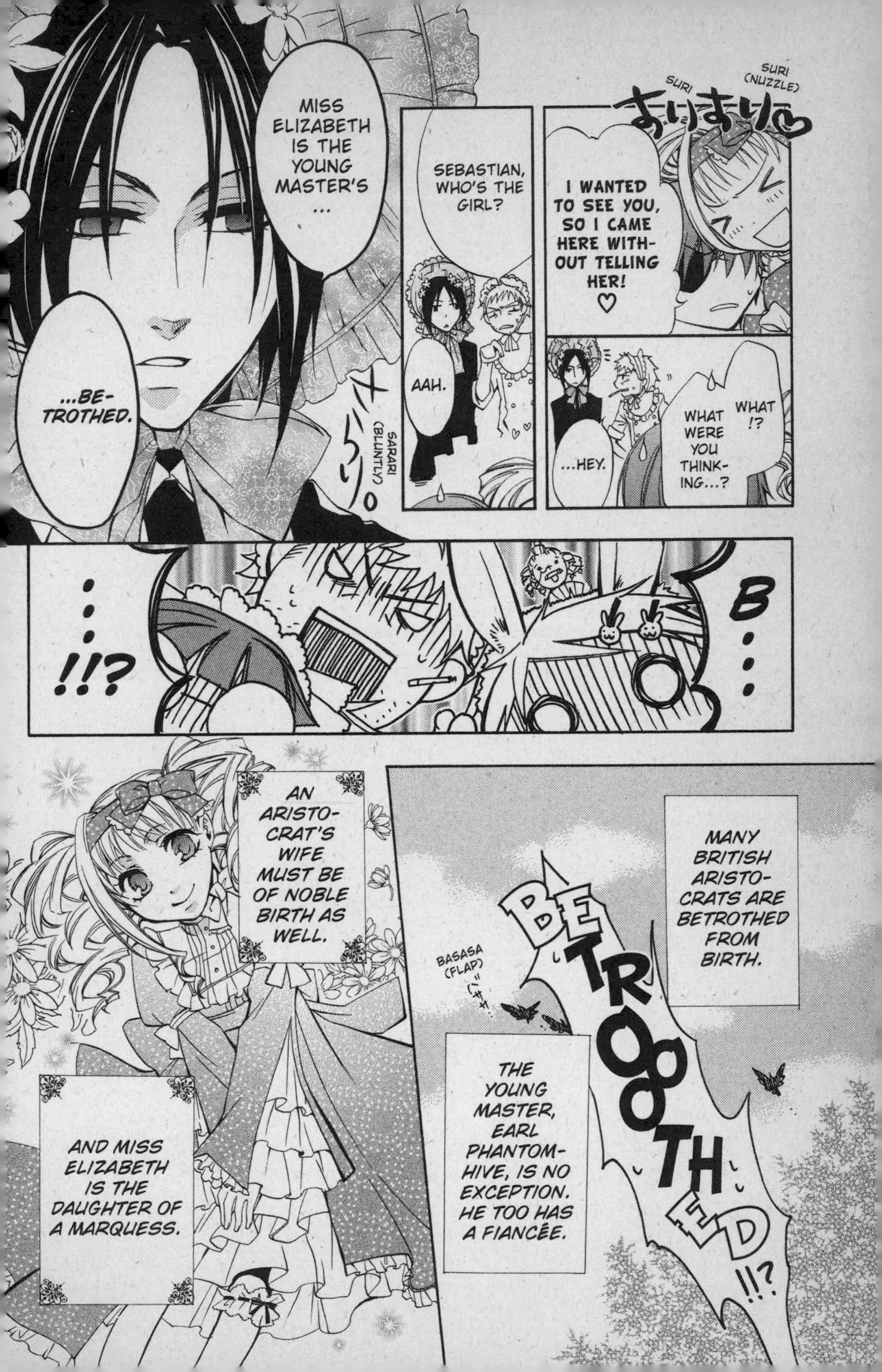
SURI SURI (NUZZLE)
I WANTED TO SEE YOU, SO I CAME HERE WITH-OUT TELLING HER! ♡
WHAT !?
WHAT WERE YOU THINK-ING...?
...HEY.
SEBASTIAN, WHO'S THE GIRL?
AAH.
MISS ELIZABETH IS THE YOUNG MASTER'S ...
SARARI (BLUNTLY)
...BE-TROTHED.
B...
...!!?
MANY BRITISH ARISTO-CRATS ARE BETROTHED FROM BIRTH.
BETROOOTHED!!?
BASASA (FLAP)
THE YOUNG MASTER, EARL PHANTOM-HIVE, IS NO EXCEPTION. HE TOO HAS A FIANCÉE.
AN ARISTO-CRAT'S WIFE MUST BE OF NOBLE BIRTH AS WELL.
AND MISS ELIZABETH IS THE DAUGHTER OF A MARQUESS.

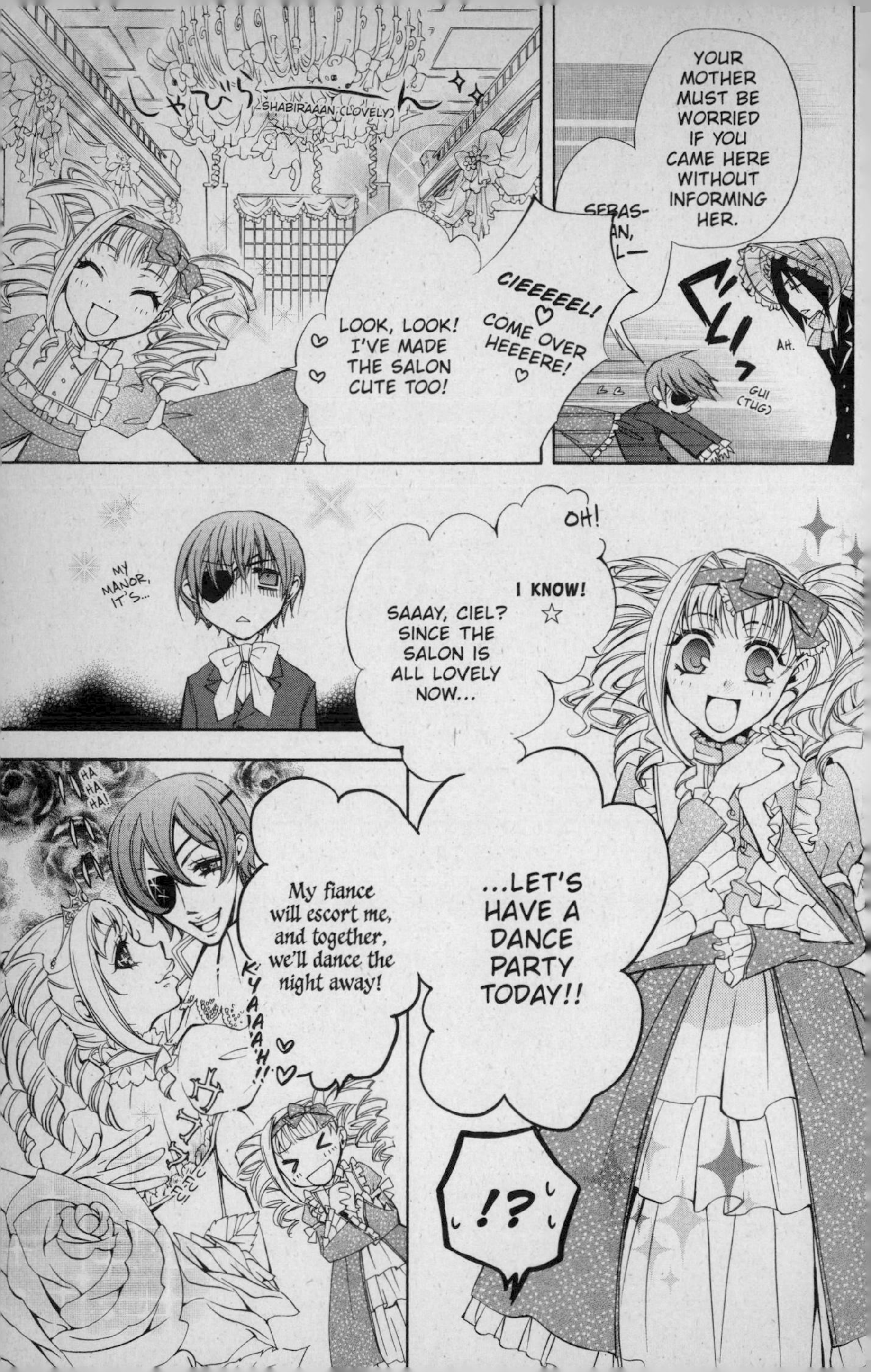
YOUR MOTHER MUST BE WORRIED IF YOU CAME HERE WITHOUT INFORMING HER.
SEBAS-AN, L—
GUI (TUG)
AH.
SHABIRAAAN (LOVELY)
CIEEEEEL! COME OVER HEEEERE!
LOOK, LOOK! I'VE MADE THE SALON CUTE TOO!
OH!
I KNOW!
SAAAY, CIEL? SINCE THE SALON IS ALL LOVELY NOW...
MY MANOR, IT'S...
...LET'S HAVE A DANCE PARTY TODAY!!
!?
My fiance will escort me, and together, we'll dance the night away!
KYAAAAAH!!
HA HA HA!
FU FU FU

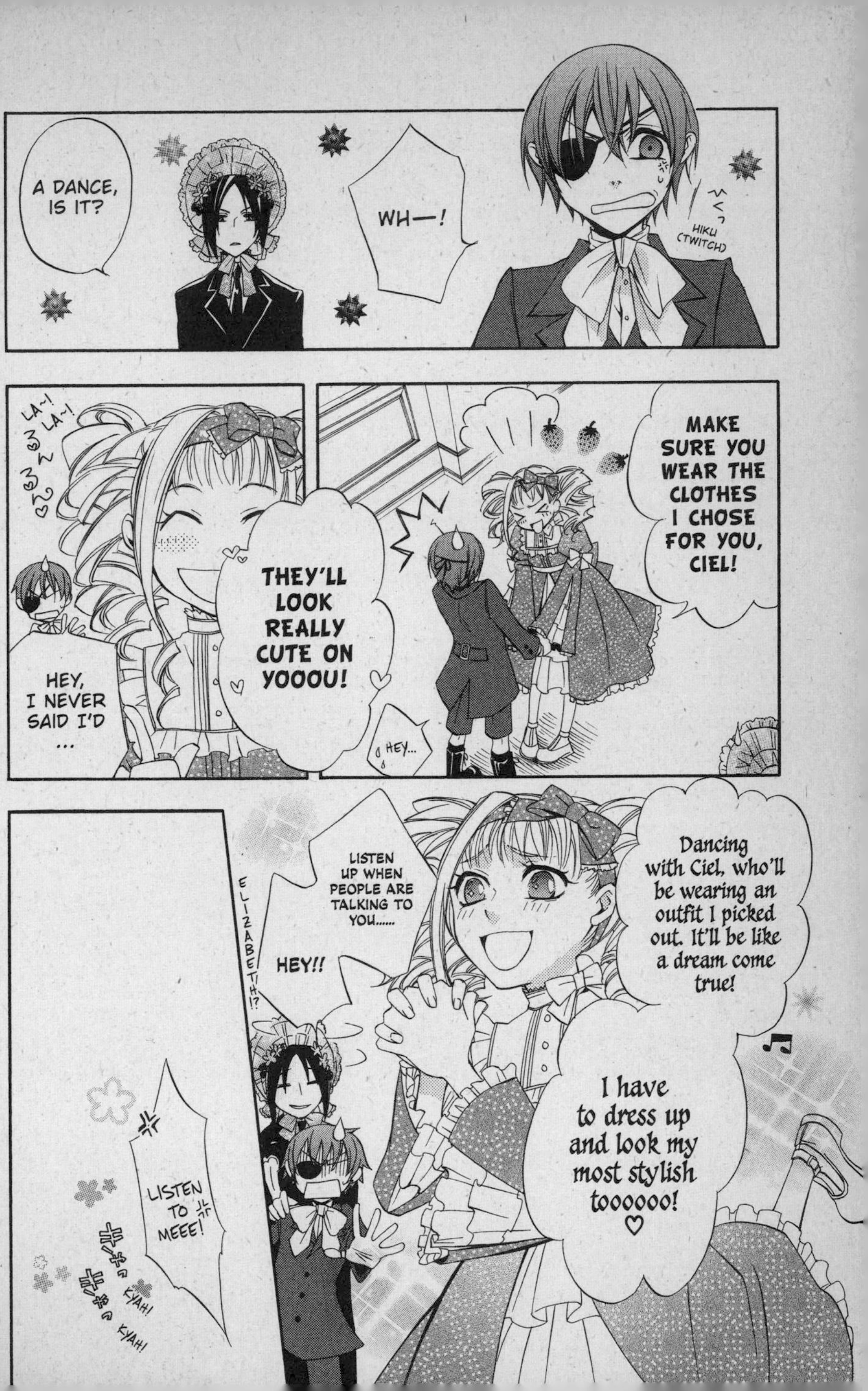
WH—!
HIKU (TWITCH)
A DANCE, IS IT?
MAKE SURE YOU WEAR THE CLOTHES I CHOSE FOR YOU, CIEL!
HEY...
THEY'LL LOOK REALLY CUTE ON YOOOU!
LA~! LA~!
HEY, I NEVER SAID I'D ...
Dancing with Ciel, who'll be wearing an outfit I picked out. It'll be like a dream come true!
I have to dress up and look my most stylish toooooo!
LISTEN UP WHEN PEOPLE ARE TALKING TO YOU......
HEY!!
ELIZABETH!?
LISTEN TO MEEE!
KYAH!
KYAH!

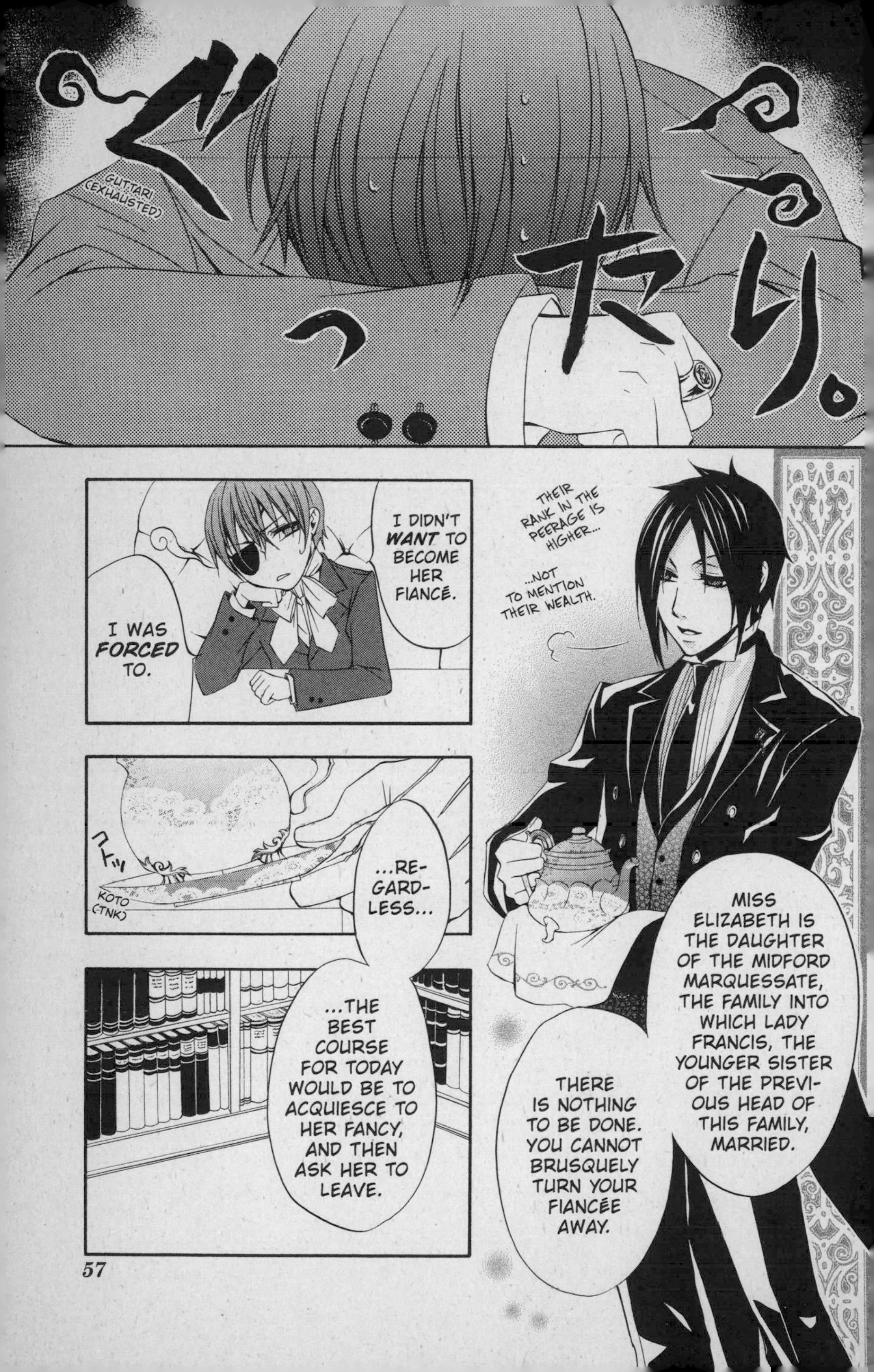
ぐったり。
GUTTARI (EXHAUSTED)
THEIR RANK IN THE PEERAGE IS HIGHER...
...NOT TO MENTION THEIR WEALTH.
MISS ELIZABETH IS THE DAUGHTER OF THE MIDFORD MARQUESSATE, THE FAMILY INTO WHICH LADY FRANCIS, THE YOUNGER SISTER OF THE PREVIOUS HEAD OF THIS FAMILY, MARRIED.
THERE IS NOTHING TO BE DONE. YOU CANNOT BRUSQUELY TURN YOUR FIANCÉE AWAY.
I DIDN'T ***WANT*** TO BECOME HER FIANCÉ.
I WAS ***FORCED*** TO.
...REGARDLESS...
KOTO (TNK)
...THE BEST COURSE FOR TODAY WOULD BE TO ACQUIESCE TO HER FANCY, AND THEN ASK HER TO LEAVE.

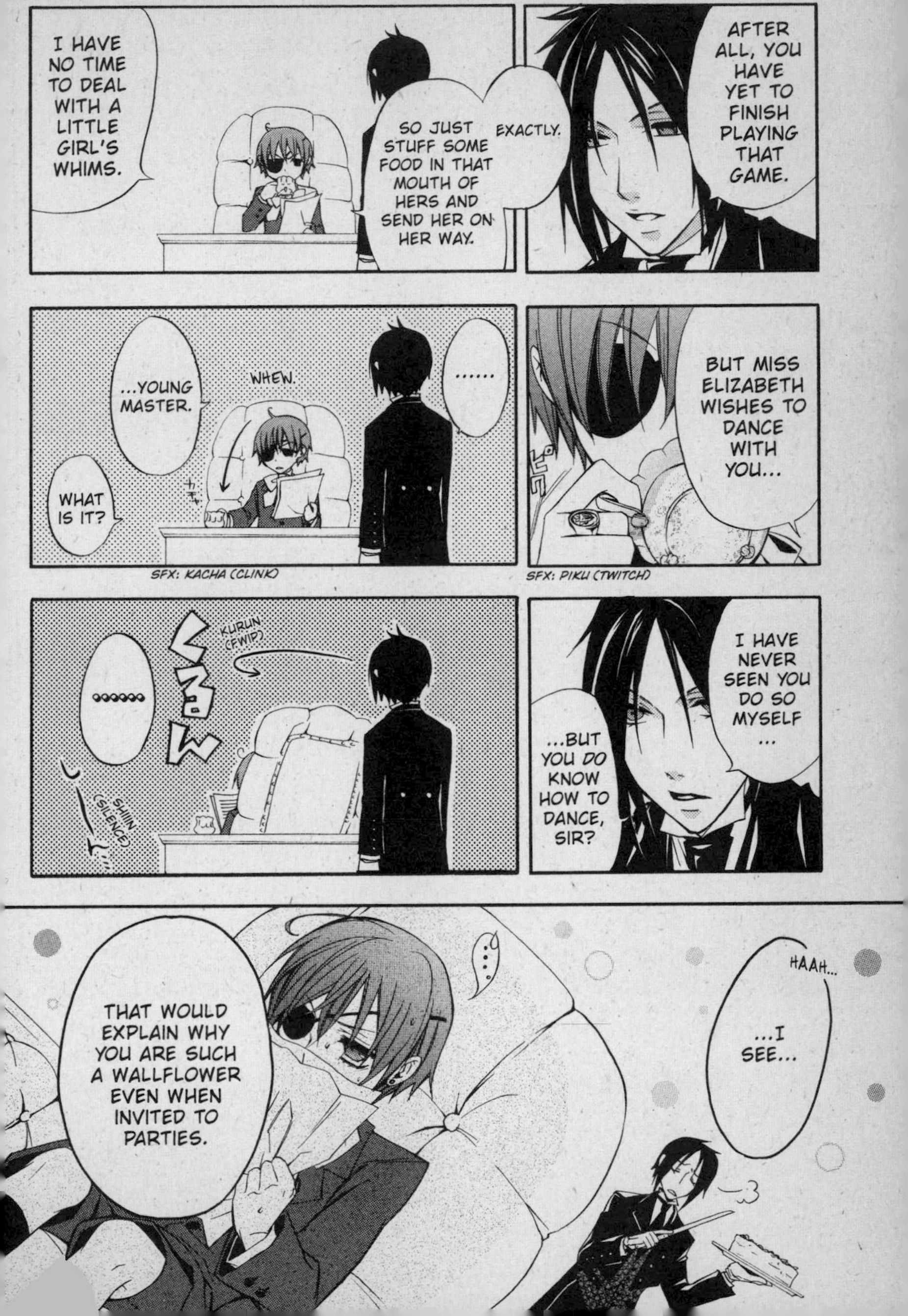
I HAVE NO TIME TO DEAL WITH A LITTLE GIRL'S WHIMS.
SO JUST STUFF SOME FOOD IN THAT MOUTH OF HERS AND SEND HER ON HER WAY.
EXACTLY.
AFTER ALL, YOU HAVE YET TO FINISH PLAYING THAT GAME.
WHEW.
...YOUNG MASTER.
WHAT IS IT?
......
SFX: KACHA (CLINK)
BUT MISS ELIZABETH WISHES TO DANCE WITH YOU...
SFX: PIKU (TWITCH)
......
KURUN (FWIP)
SHIIN (SILENCE)
I HAVE NEVER SEEN YOU DO SO MYSELF ...
...BUT YOU DO KNOW HOW TO DANCE, SIR?
...
HAAH...
...I SEE...
THAT WOULD EXPLAIN WHY YOU ARE SUCH A WALLFLOWER EVEN WHEN INVITED TO PARTIES.

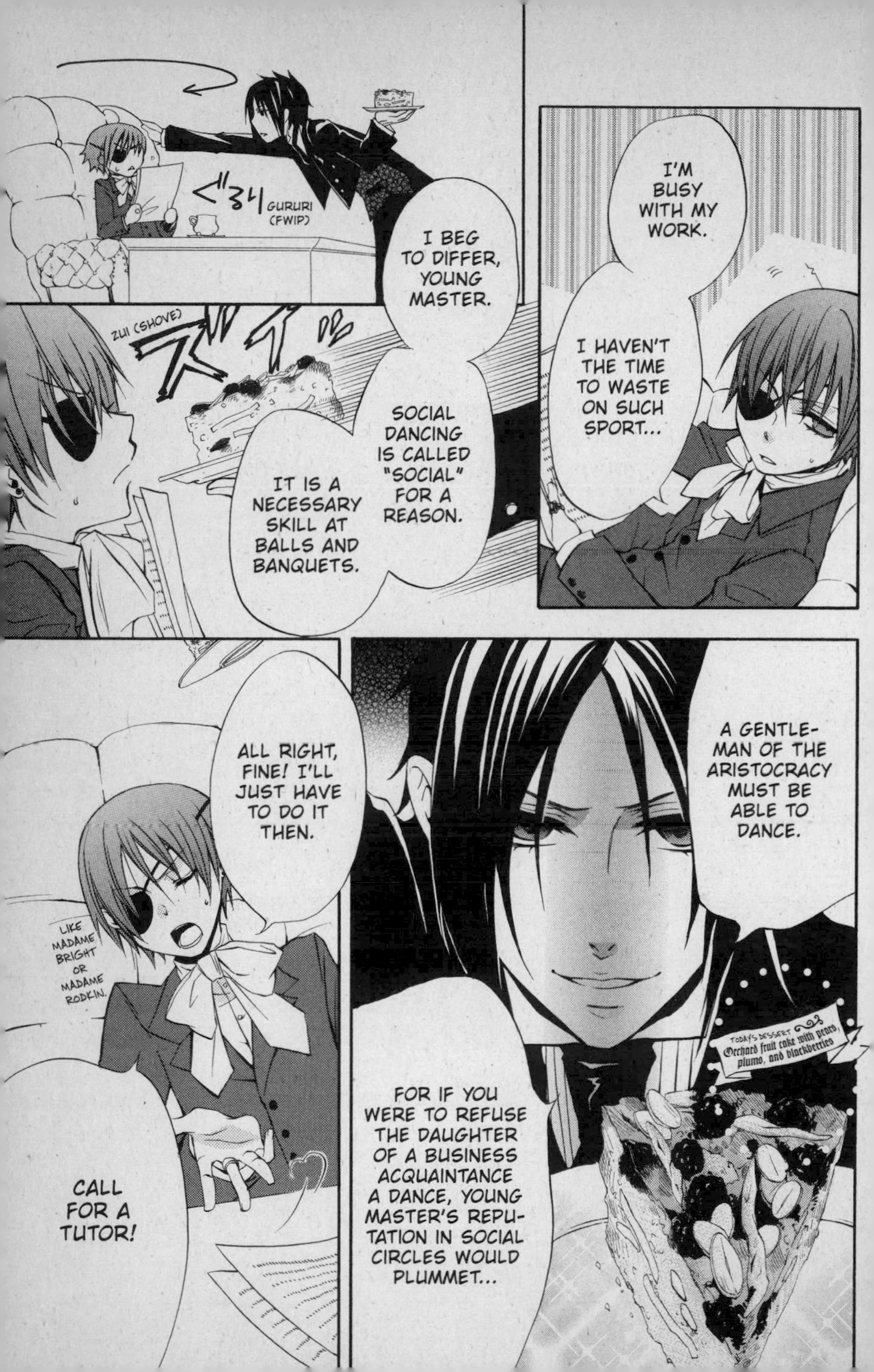
I'M BUSY WITH MY WORK.
I HAVEN'T THE TIME TO WASTE ON SUCH SPORT...
I BEG TO DIFFER, YOUNG MASTER.
ぐるり
GURURI (FWIP)
ZUI (SHOVE)
SOCIAL DANCING IS CALLED "SOCIAL" FOR A REASON.
IT IS A NECESSARY SKILL AT BALLS AND BANQUETS.
A GENTLE-MAN OF THE ARISTOCRACY MUST BE ABLE TO DANCE.
TODAY'S DESSERT Orchard fruit cake with pears, plums, and blackberries
FOR IF YOU WERE TO REFUSE THE DAUGHTER OF A BUSINESS ACQUAINTANCE A DANCE, YOUNG MASTER'S REPU-TATION IN SOCIAL CIRCLES WOULD PLUMMET...
ALL RIGHT, FINE! I'LL JUST HAVE TO DO IT THEN.
LIKE MADAME BRIGHT OR MADAME RODKIN.
CALL FOR A TUTOR!

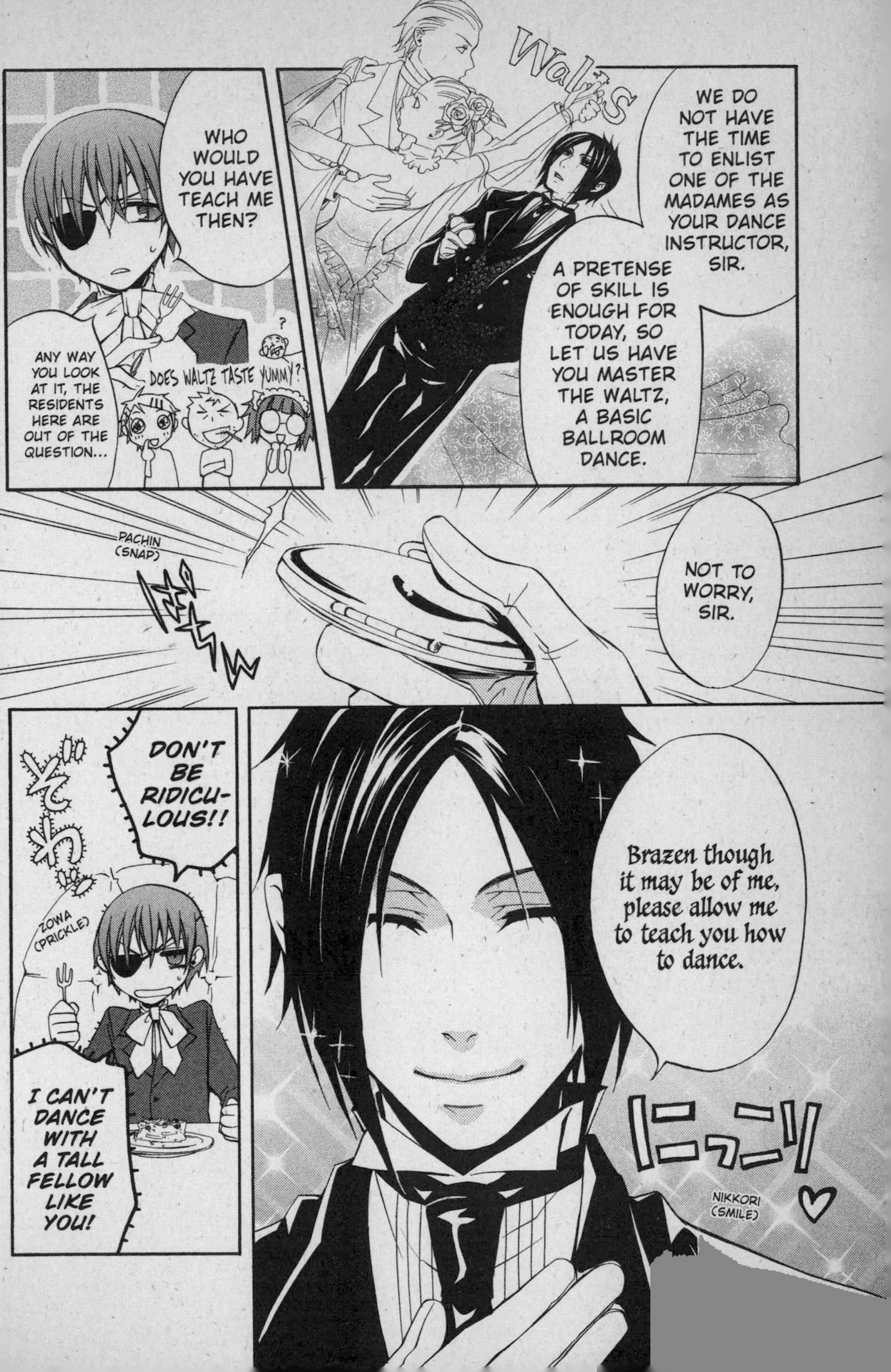
Waltz
WE DO NOT HAVE THE TIME TO ENLIST ONE OF THE MADAMES AS YOUR DANCE INSTRUCTOR, SIR.
A PRETENSE OF SKILL IS ENOUGH FOR TODAY, SO LET US HAVE YOU MASTER THE WALTZ, A BASIC BALLROOM DANCE.
WHO WOULD YOU HAVE TEACH ME THEN?
?
DOES WALTZ TASTE YUMMY?
ANY WAY YOU LOOK AT IT, THE RESIDENTS HERE ARE OUT OF THE QUESTION...
NOT TO WORRY, SIR.
PACHIN (SNAP)
Brazen though it may be of me, please allow me to teach you how to dance.
NIKKORI (SMILE)
DON'T BE RIDICULOUS!!
ZOWA (PRICKLE)
I CAN'T DANCE WITH A TALL FELLOW LIKE YOU!

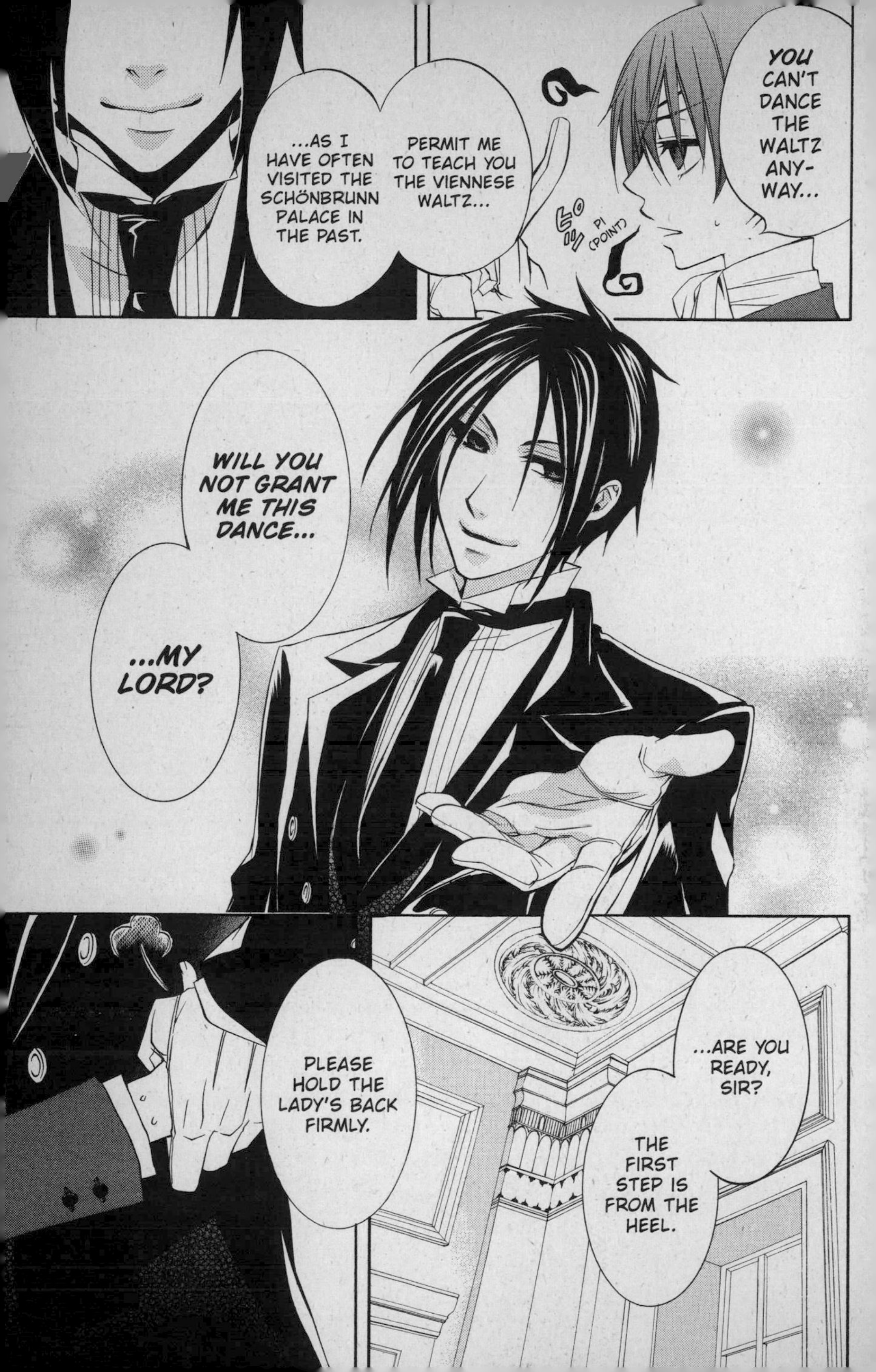
YOU CAN'T DANCE THE WALTZ ANY-WAY...
PI (POINT)
PERMIT ME TO TEACH YOU THE VIENNESE WALTZ...
...AS I HAVE OFTEN VISITED THE SCHÖNBRUNN PALACE IN THE PAST.
WILL YOU NOT GRANT ME THIS DANCE...
...MY LORD?
...ARE YOU READY, SIR?
THE FIRST STEP IS FROM THE HEEL.
PLEASE HOLD THE LADY'S BACK FIRMLY.

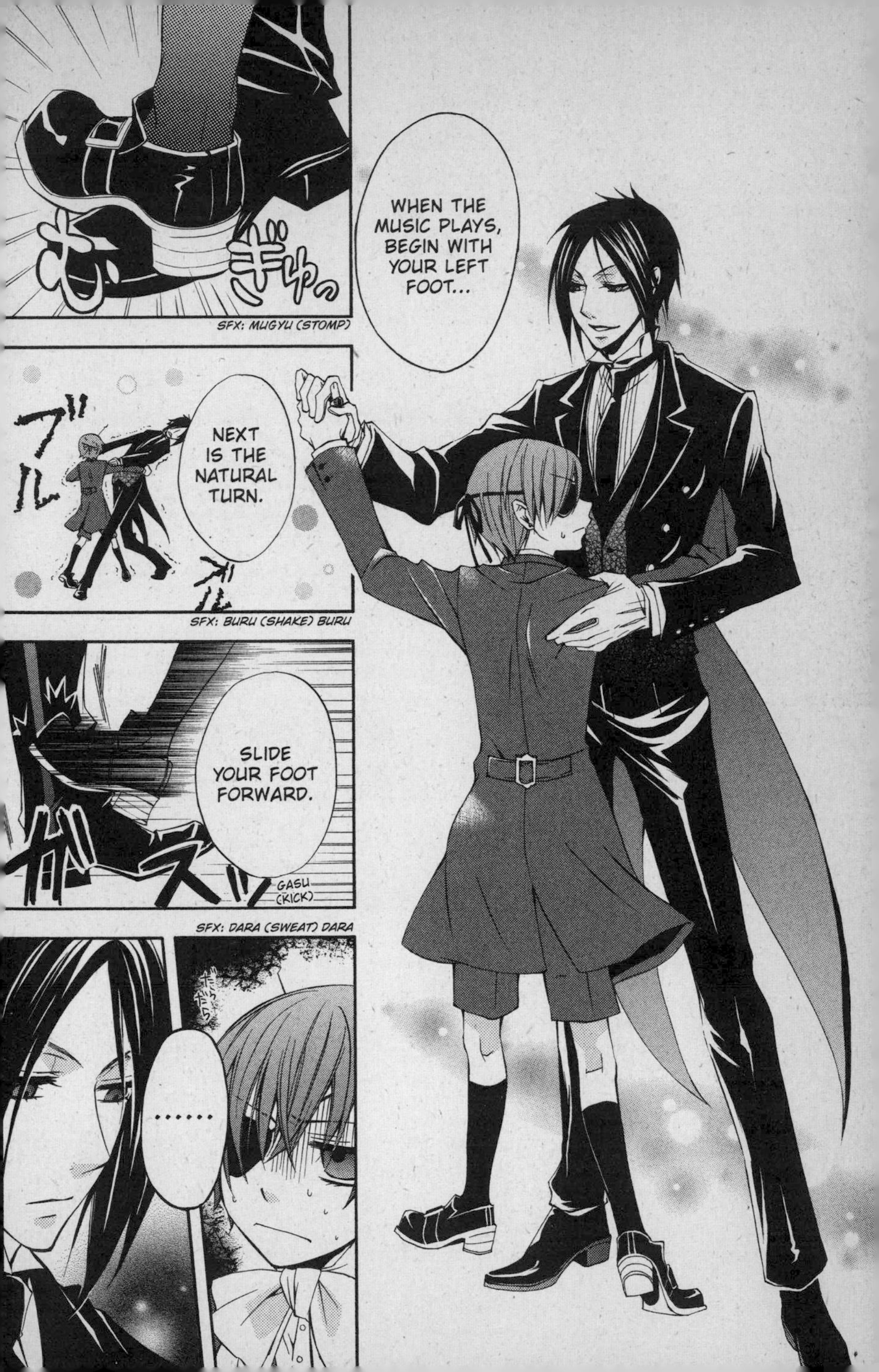
WHEN THE MUSIC PLAYS, BEGIN WITH YOUR LEFT FOOT...
SFX: MUGYU (STOMP)
NEXT IS THE NATURAL TURN.
SFX: BURU (SHAKE) BURU
SLIDE YOUR FOOT FORWARD.
GASU (KICK)
SFX: DARA (SWEAT) DARA
......

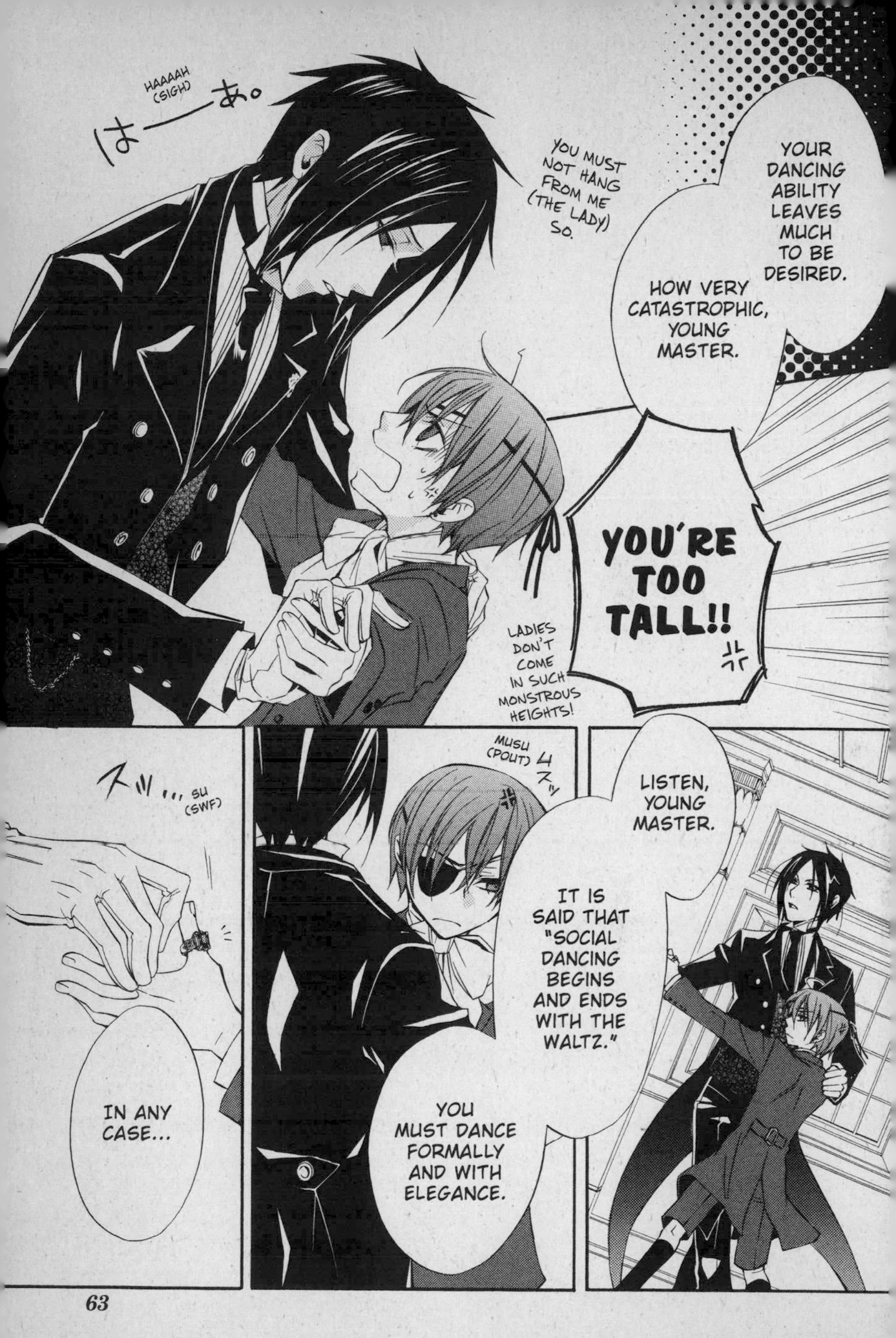

YOUR DANCING ABILITY LEAVES MUCH TO BE DESIRED.
HOW VERY CATASTROPHIC, YOUNG MASTER.
YOU MUST NOT HANG FROM ME (THE LADY) SO.
はーあ。
HAAAAH (SIGH)
YOU'RE TOO TALL!!
LADIES DON'T COME IN SUCH MONSTROUS HEIGHTS!
LISTEN, YOUNG MASTER.
ムスッ
MUSU (POUT)
IT IS SAID THAT "SOCIAL DANCING BEGINS AND ENDS WITH THE WALTZ."
YOU MUST DANCE FORMALLY AND WITH ELEGANCE.
スッ...
SU (SWF)
IN ANY CASE...

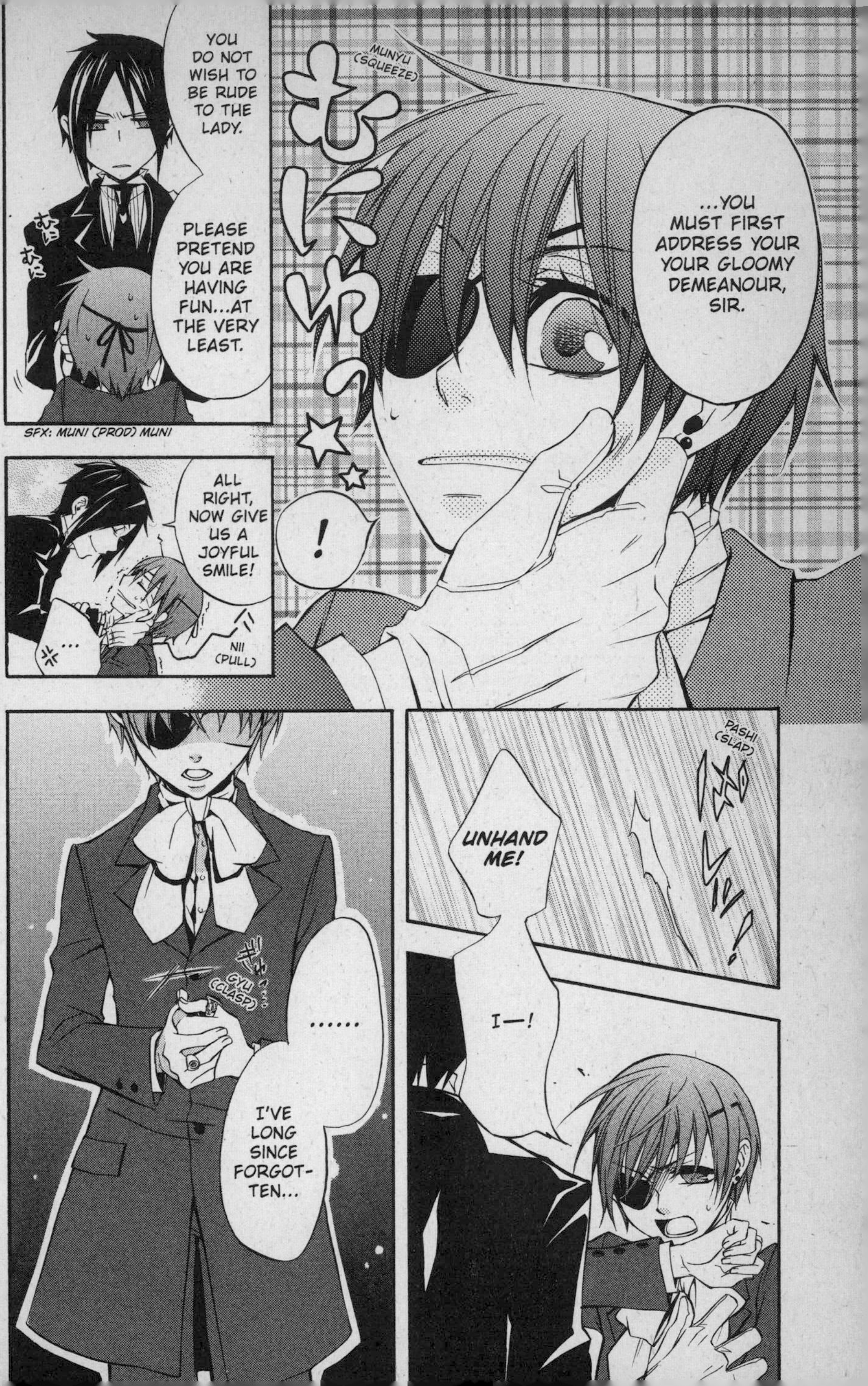
MUNYU (SQUEEZE)
...YOU MUST FIRST ADDRESS YOUR YOUR GLOOMY DEMEANOUR, SIR.
!
YOU DO NOT WISH TO BE RUDE TO THE LADY.
PLEASE PRETEND YOU ARE HAVING FUN...AT THE VERY LEAST.
SFX: MUNI (PROD) MUNI
ALL RIGHT, NOW GIVE US A JOYFUL SMILE!
NII (PULL)
...
PASHI (SLAP)
UNHAND ME!
I—!
GYU (CLASP)
......
I'VE LONG SINCE FORGOT-TEN...

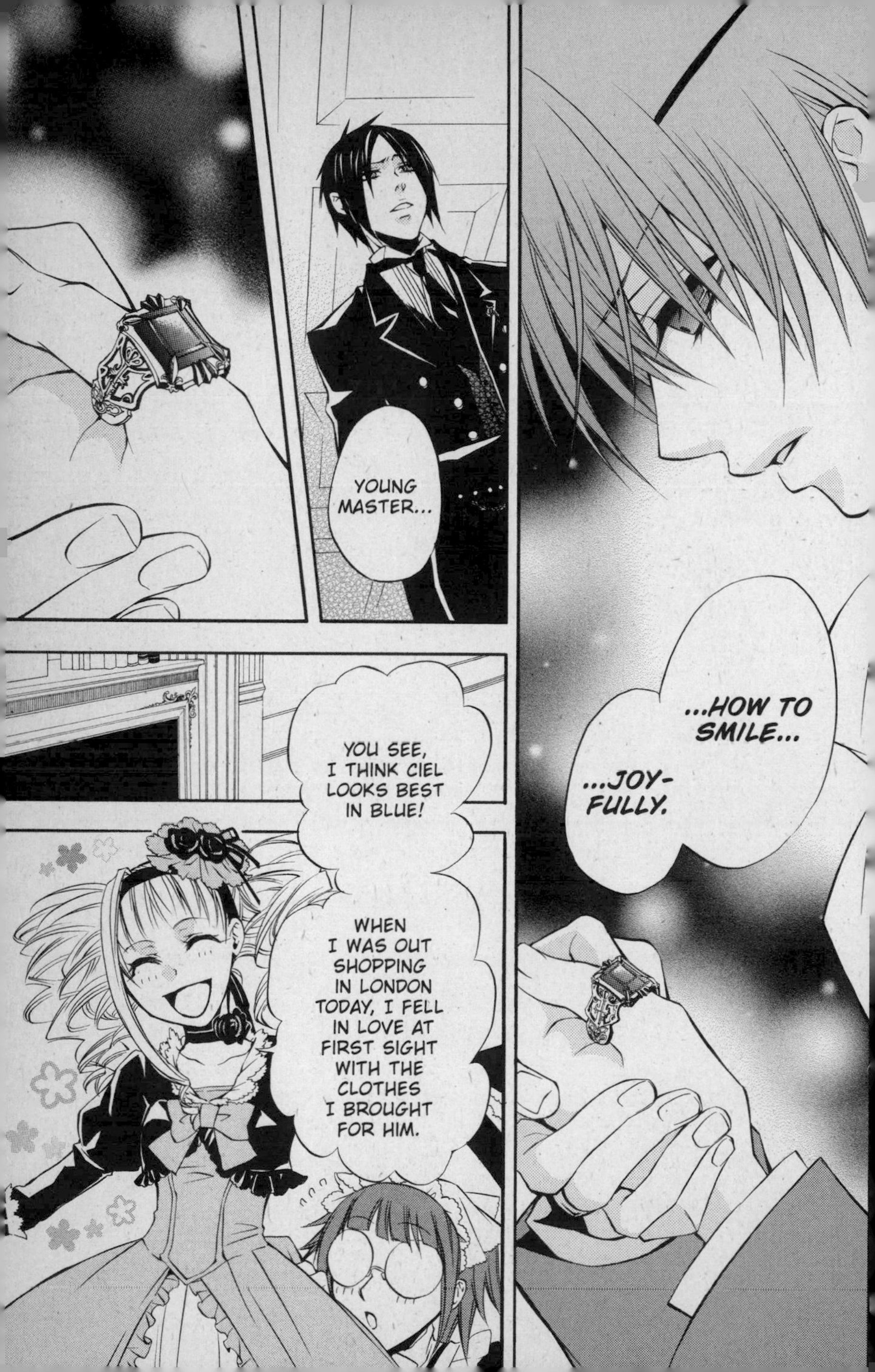
...HOW TO SMILE...
...JOY-FULLY.
YOUNG MASTER...
YOU SEE, I THINK CIEL LOOKS BEST IN BLUE!
WHEN I WAS OUT SHOPPING IN LONDON TODAY, I FELL IN LOVE AT FIRST SIGHT WITH THE CLOTHES I BROUGHT FOR HIM.

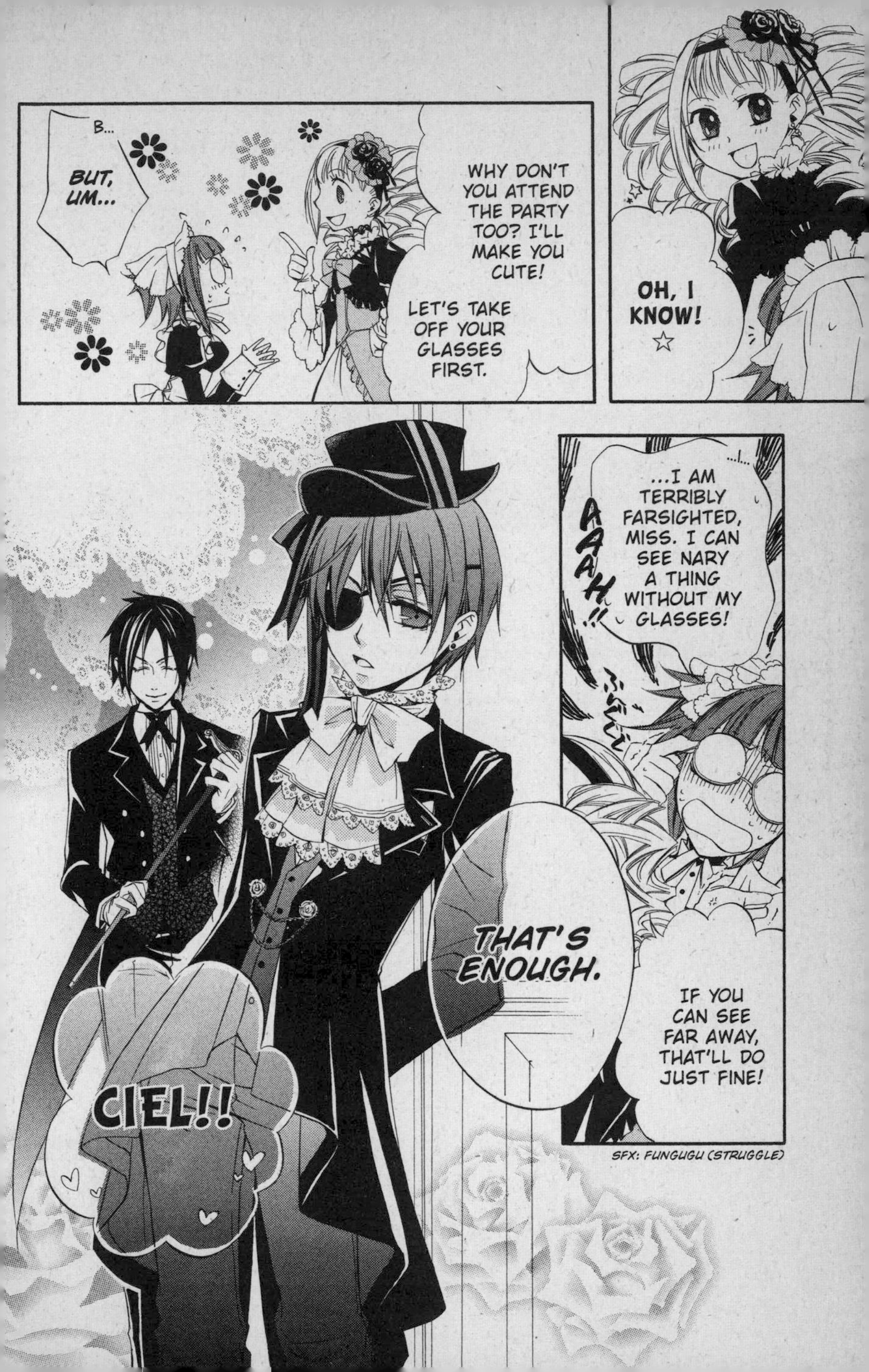
OH, I KNOW! ☆
WHY DON'T YOU ATTEND THE PARTY TOO? I'LL MAKE YOU CUTE!
LET'S TAKE OFF YOUR GLASSES FIRST.
B...
BUT, UM...
...I...
...I AM TERRIBLY FARSIGHTED, MISS. I CAN SEE NARY A THING WITHOUT MY GLASSES!
AAAH!!
IF YOU CAN SEE FAR AWAY, THAT'LL DO JUST FINE!
THAT'S ENOUGH.
CIEL!!
SFX: FUNGUGU (STRUGGLE)

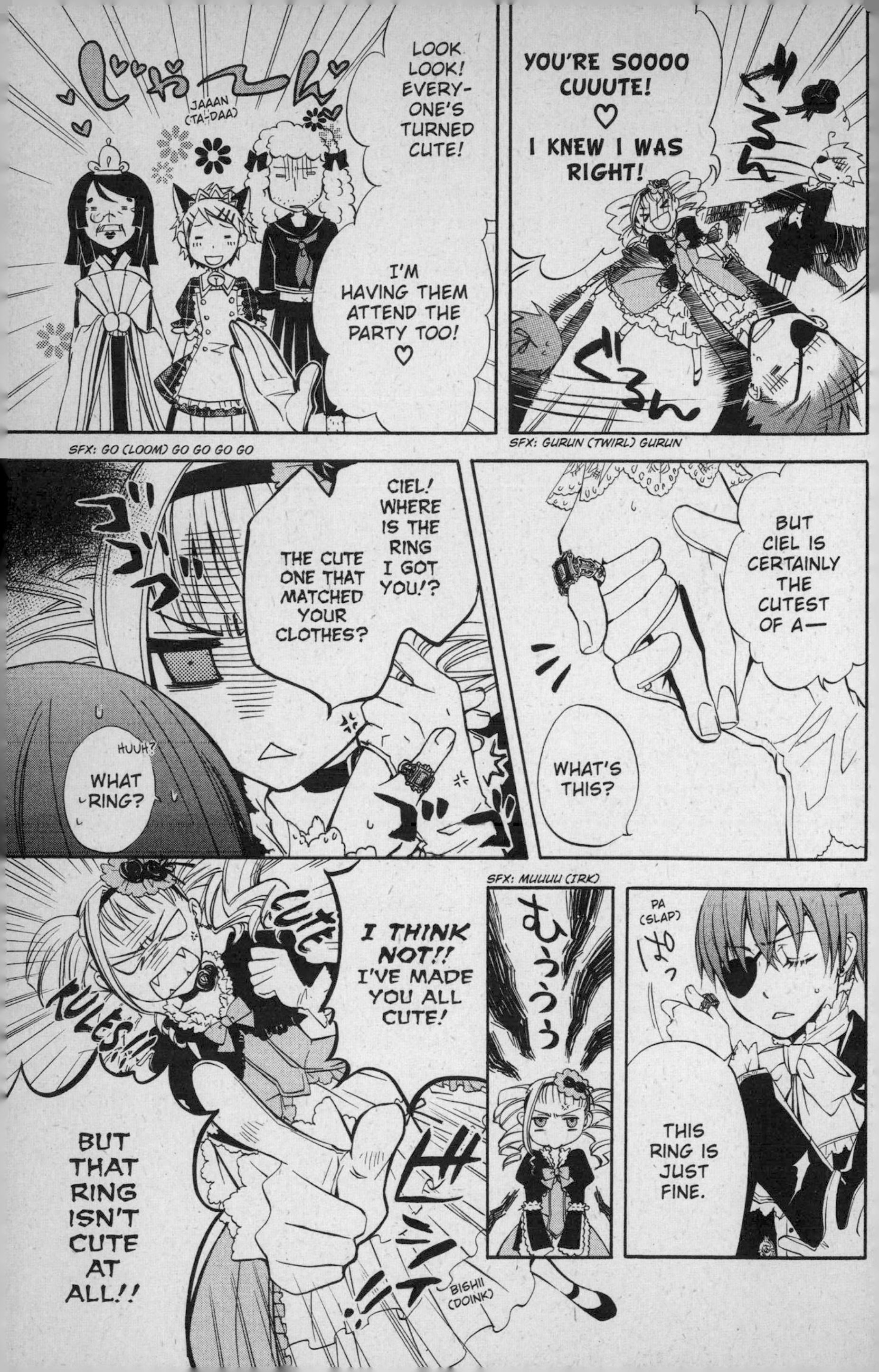
YOU'RE SOOOO CUUUTE! ♡ I KNEW I WAS RIGHT!
SFX: GURUN (TWIRL) GURUN
LOOK LOOK! EVERY-ONE'S TURNED CUTE!
JAAAN (TA-DAA)
I'M HAVING THEM ATTEND THE PARTY TOO! ♡
SFX: GO (LOOM) GO GO GO GO
BUT CIEL IS CERTAINLY THE CUTEST OF A—
WHAT'S THIS?
CIEL! WHERE IS THE RING I GOT YOU!?
THE CUTE ONE THAT MATCHED YOUR CLOTHES?
HUUH?
WHAT RING?
PA (SLAP)
THIS RING IS JUST FINE.
SFX: MUUUU (IRK)
I THINK NOT!! I'VE MADE YOU ALL CUTE!
CUTE RULES!!
BUT THAT RING ISN'T CUTE AT ALL!!
BISHII (DOINK)

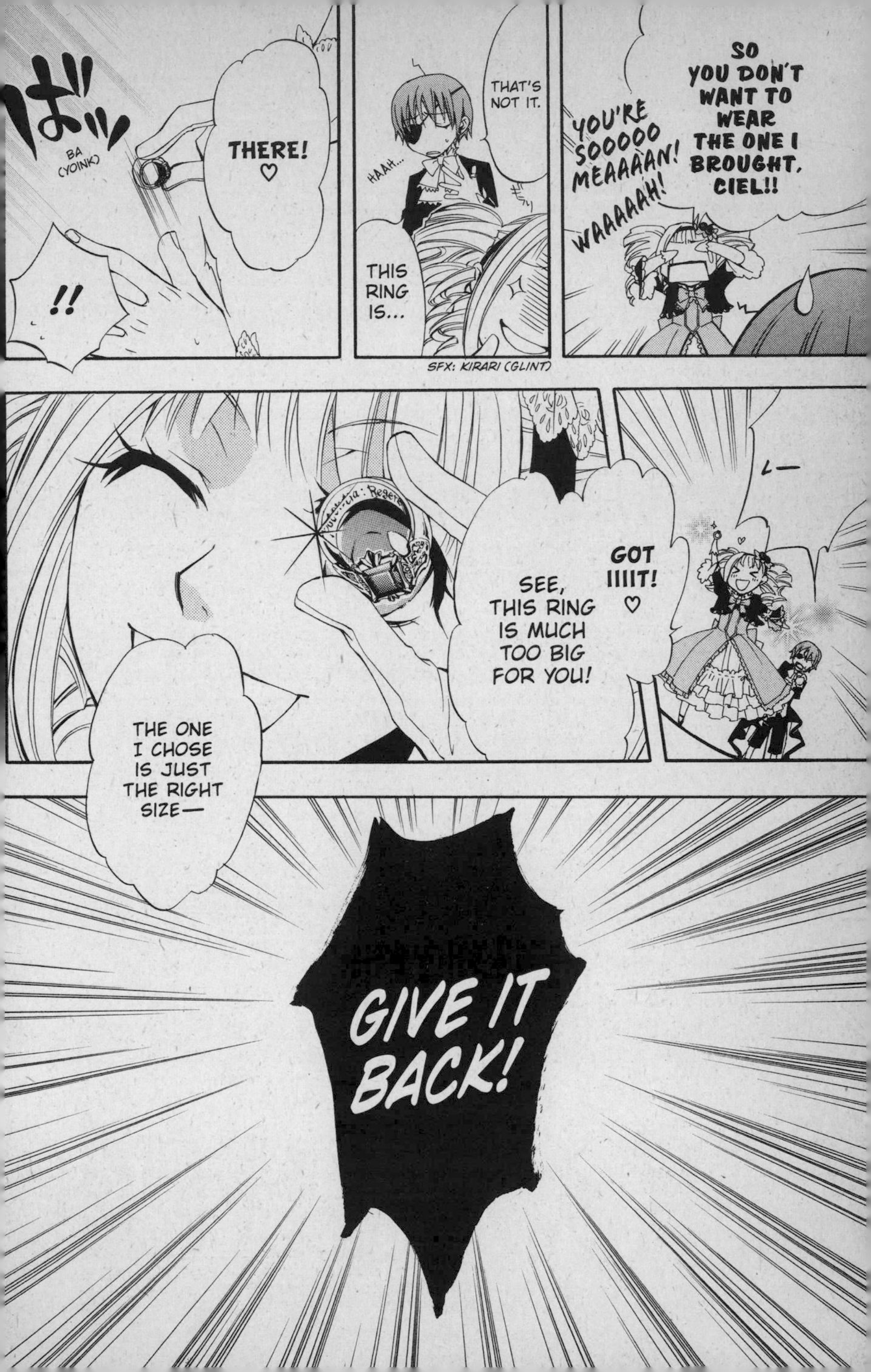
SO YOU DON'T WANT TO WEAR THE ONE I BROUGHT, CIEL!!
YOU'RE SOOOOO MEAAAAN! WAAAAAH!
THAT'S NOT IT.
HAAH...
THIS RING IS...
SFX: KIRARI (GLINT)
THERE! ♡
ばッ
BA (YOINK)
!!
GOT IIIIT! ♡
SEE, THIS RING IS MUCH TOO BIG FOR YOU!
THE ONE I CHOSE IS JUST THE RIGHT SIZE—
GIVE IT BACK!

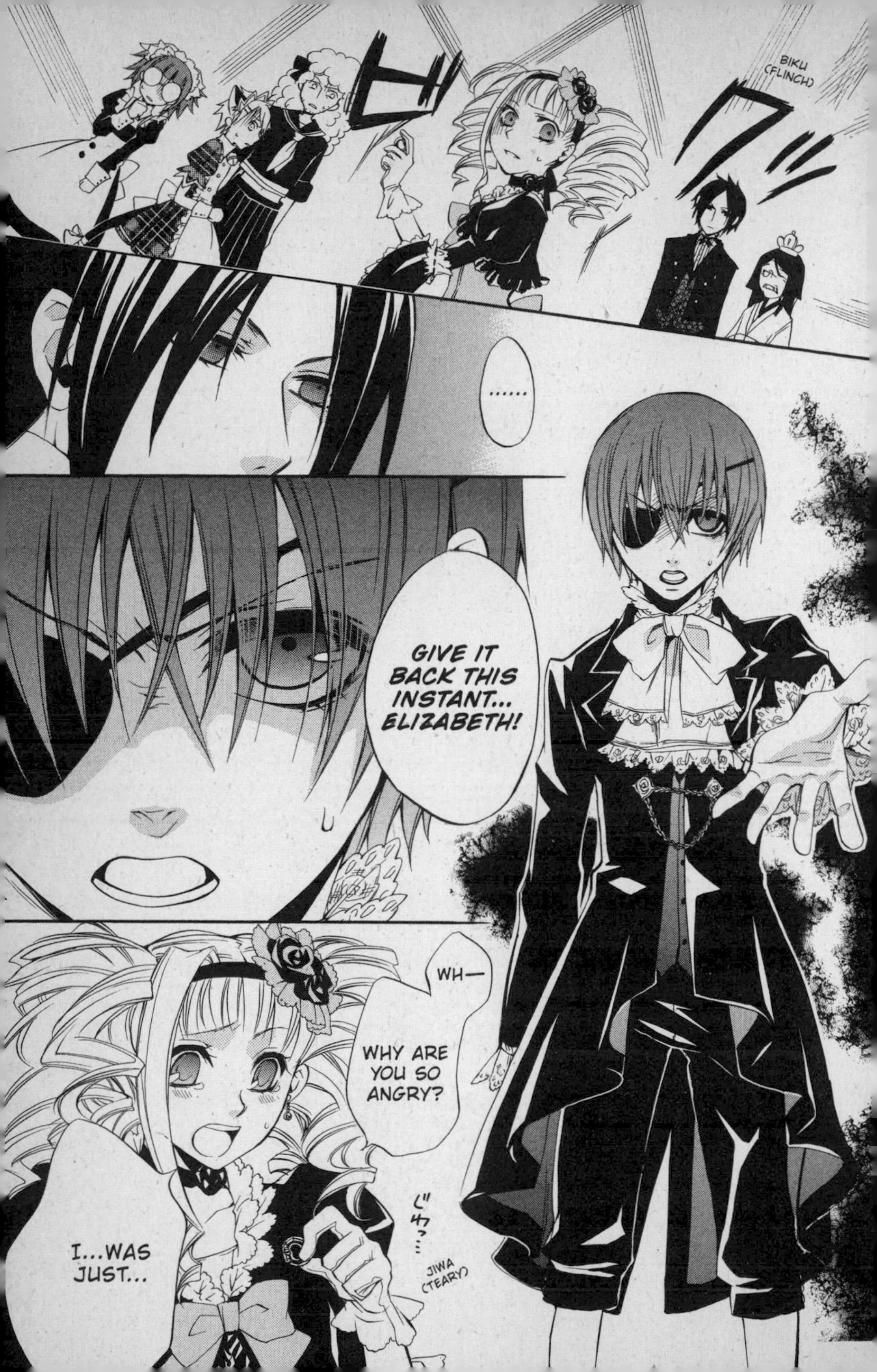
BIKU (FLINCH)
GIVE IT BACK THIS INSTANT... ELIZABETH!
......
WH—
WHY ARE YOU SO ANGRY?
じわっ…
JIWA (TEARY)
I...WAS JUST...

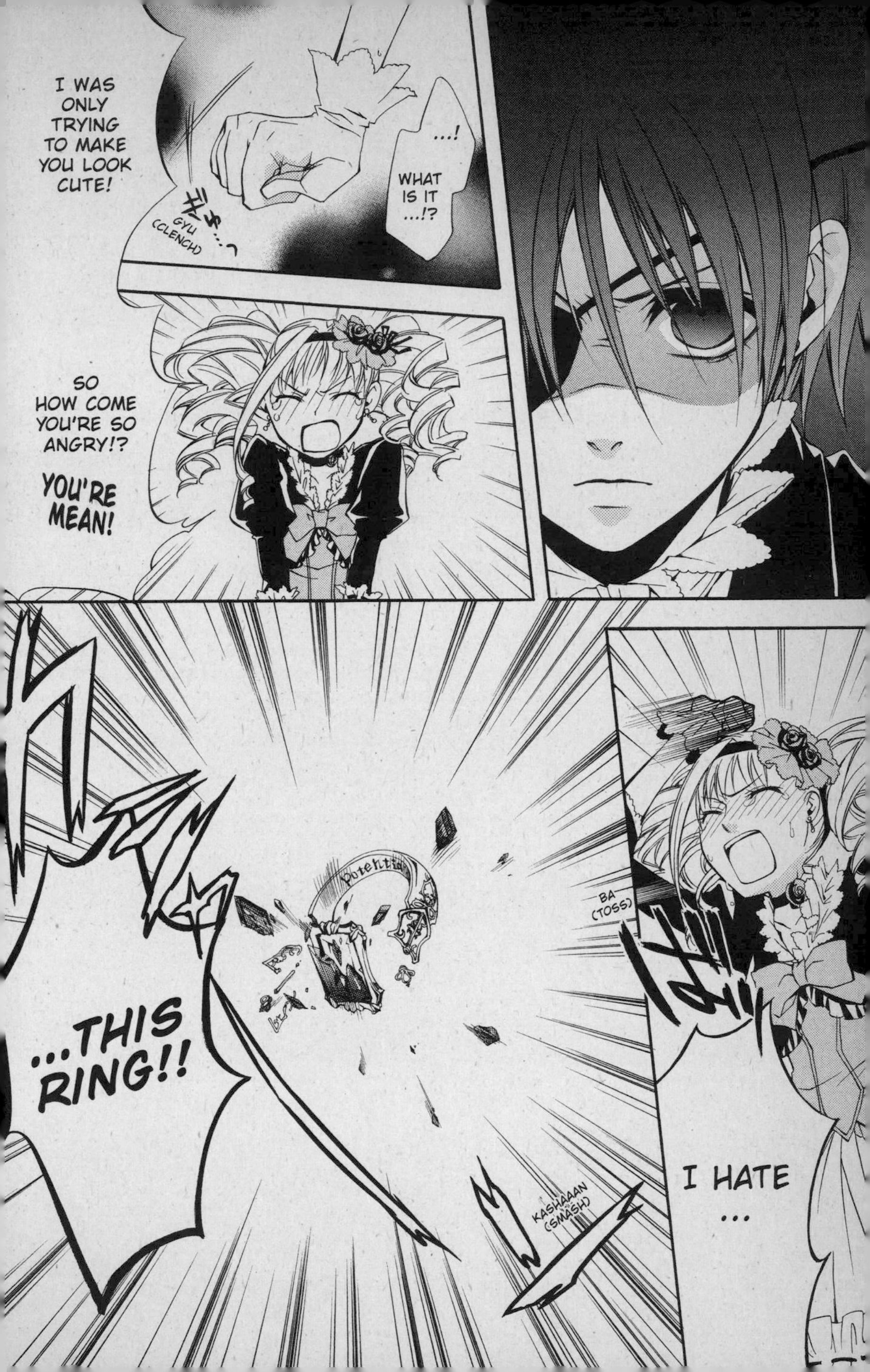
...!
WHAT IS IT ...!?
I WAS ONLY TRYING TO MAKE YOU LOOK CUTE!
GYU (CLENCH)
SO HOW COME YOU'RE SO ANGRY!?
YOU'RE MEAN!
BA (TOSS)
I HATE ...
...THIS RING!!
KASHAAAN (SMASH)

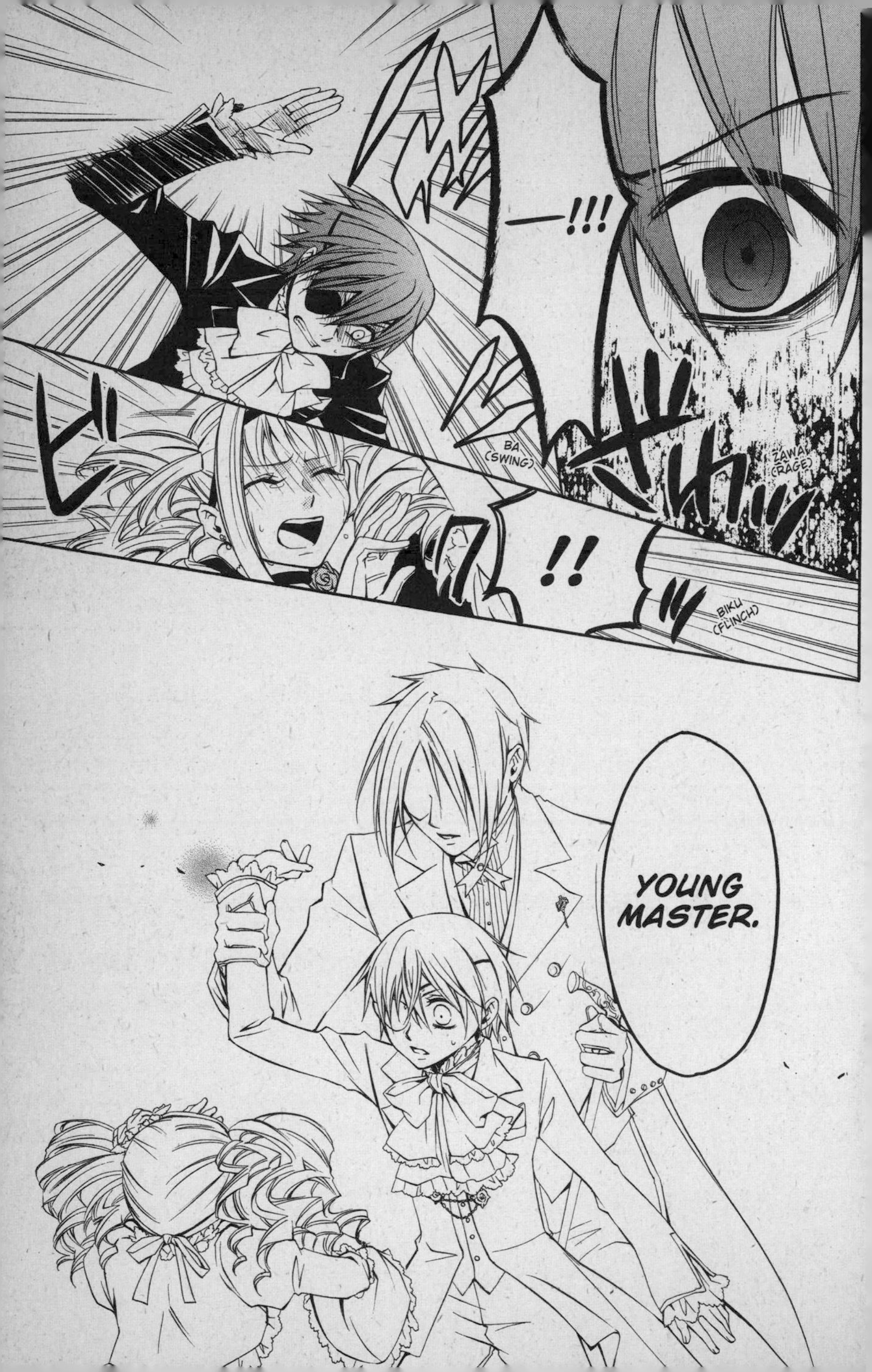

—!!!
ZAWA (RAGE)
BA (SWING)
BIKU (FLINCH)
!!
YOUNG MASTER.

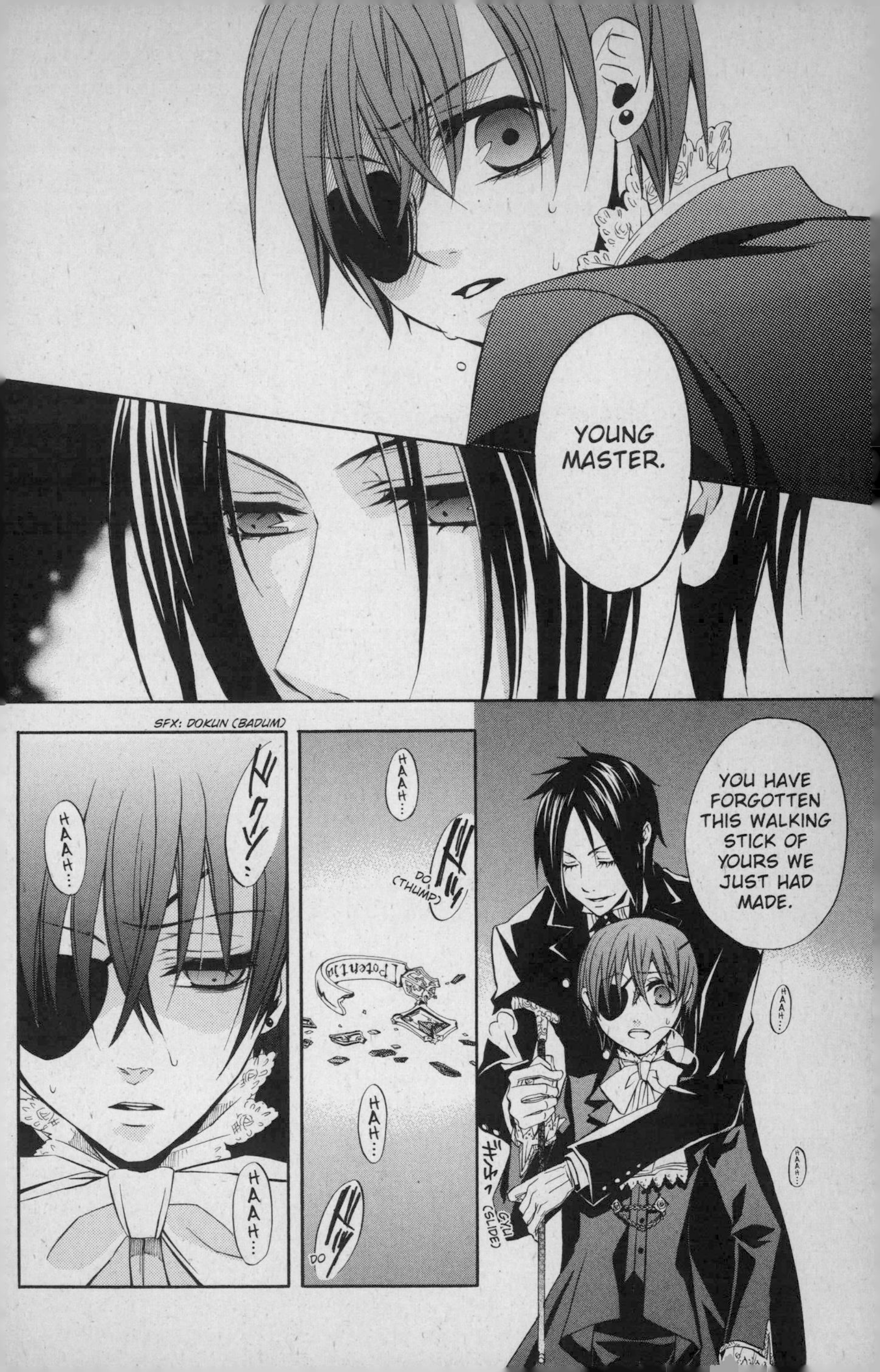
YOUNG MASTER.
YOU HAVE FORGOTTEN THIS WALKING STICK OF YOURS WE JUST HAD MADE.
HAAH...
GYU (SLIDE)
HAAH...
HAAH...
DO (THUMP)
HAH...
DO
SFX: DOKUN (BADUM)
HAAH...
HAAH...

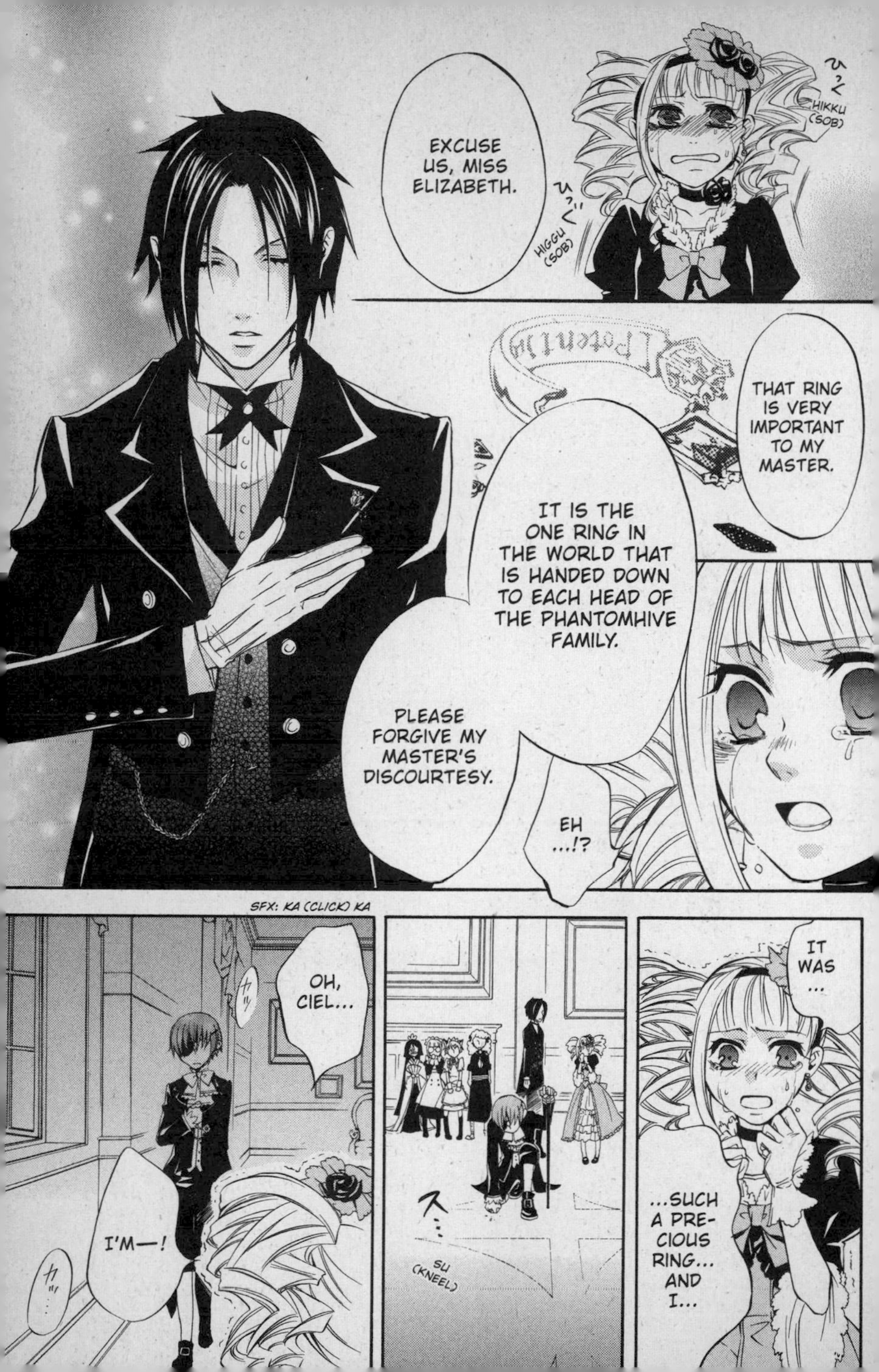
HIKKU (SOB)
EXCUSE US, MISS ELIZABETH.
HIGGU (SOB)
THAT RING IS VERY IMPORTANT TO MY MASTER.
IT IS THE ONE RING IN THE WORLD THAT IS HANDED DOWN TO EACH HEAD OF THE PHANTOMHIVE FAMILY.
PLEASE FORGIVE MY MASTER'S DISCOURTESY.
EH ...!?
SFX: KA (CLICK) KA
IT WAS ...
...SUCH A PRECIOUS RING... AND I...
SU (KNEEL)
OH, CIEL...
I'M—!

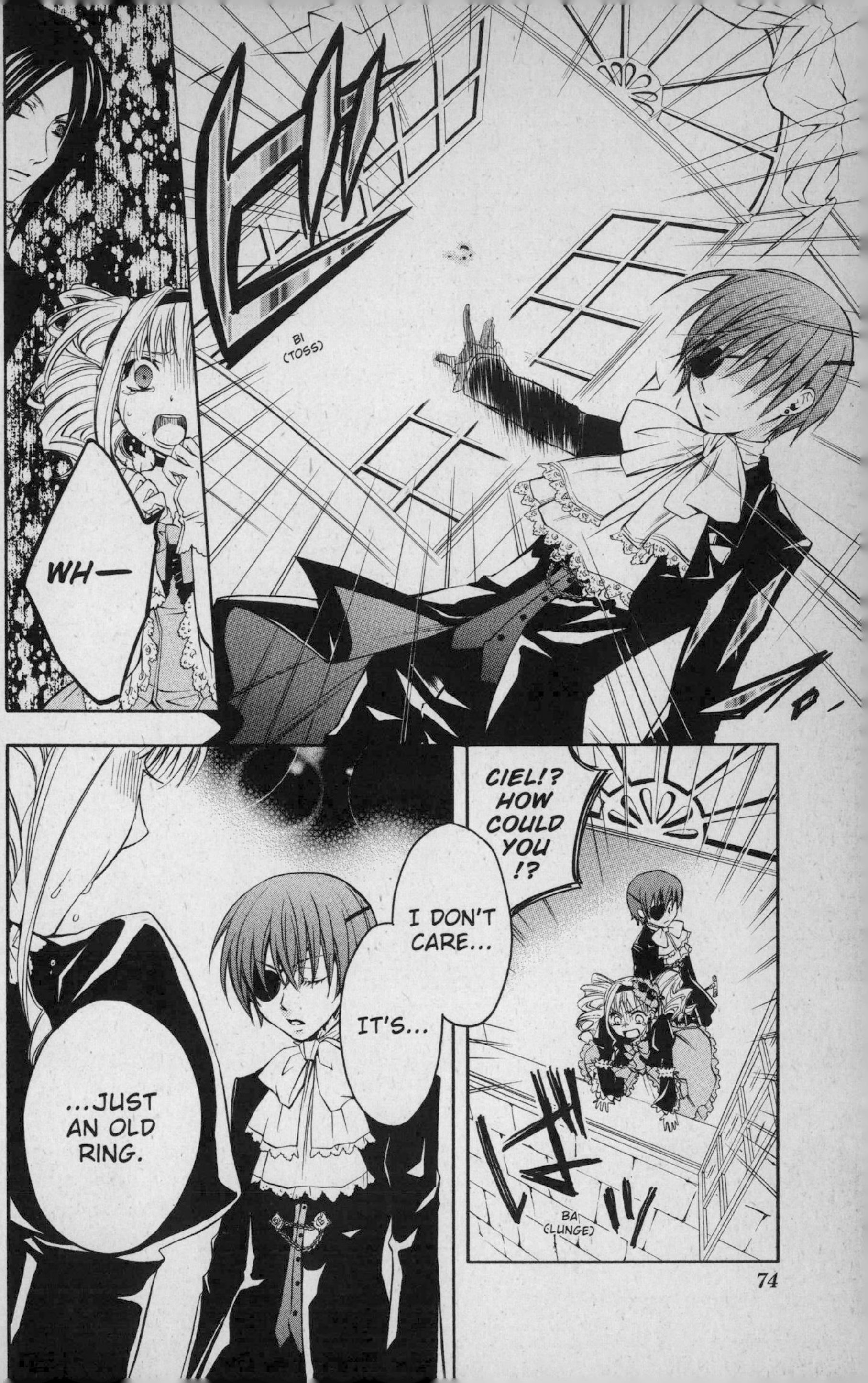
BI
(TOSS)
WH—
CIEL!? HOW COULD YOU !?
BA
(LUNGE)
I DON'T CARE...
IT'S...
...JUST AN OLD RING.

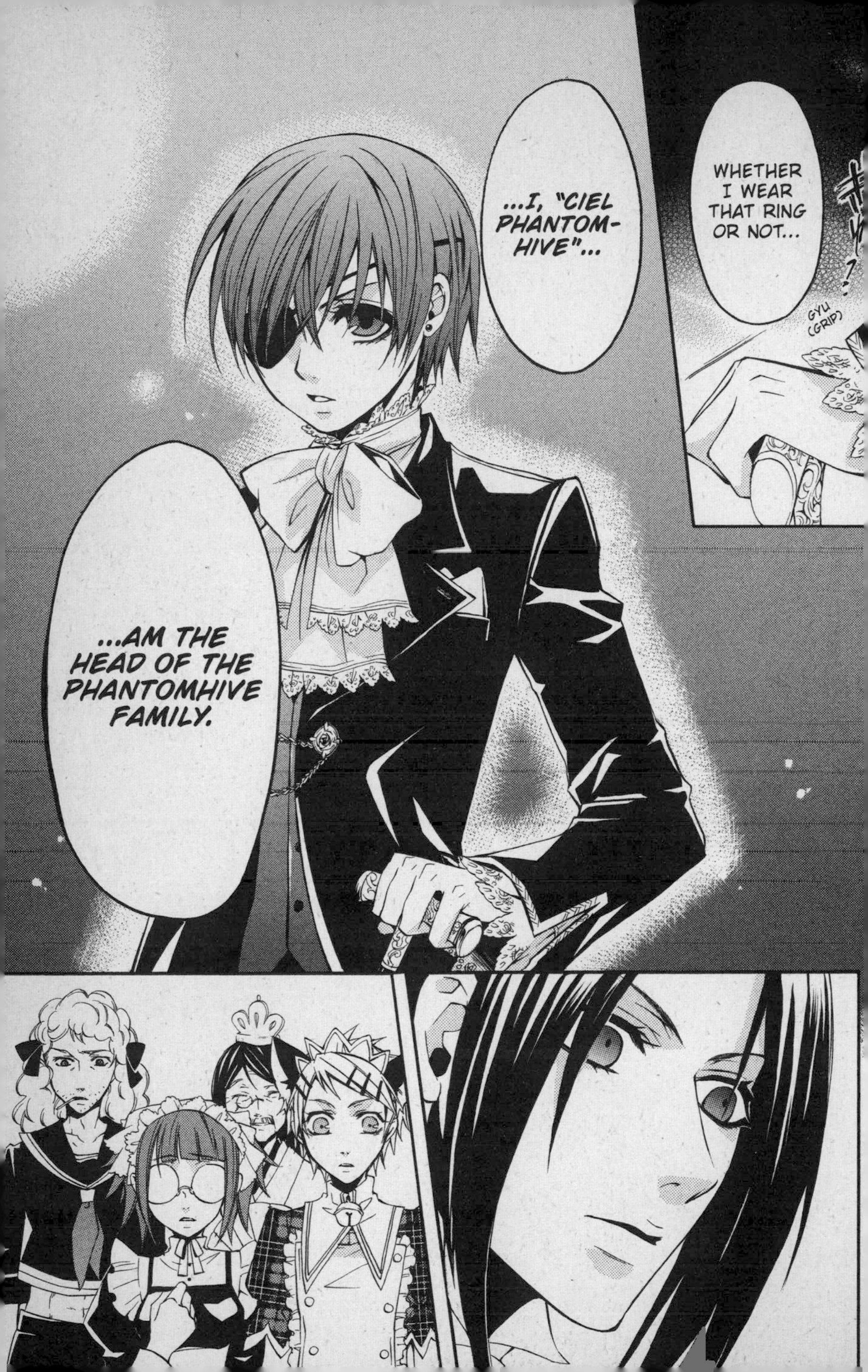
WHETHER I WEAR THAT RING OR NOT...
GYU (GRIP)
...I, "CIEL PHANTOM-HIVE"...
...AM THE HEAD OF THE PHANTOMHIVE FAMILY.

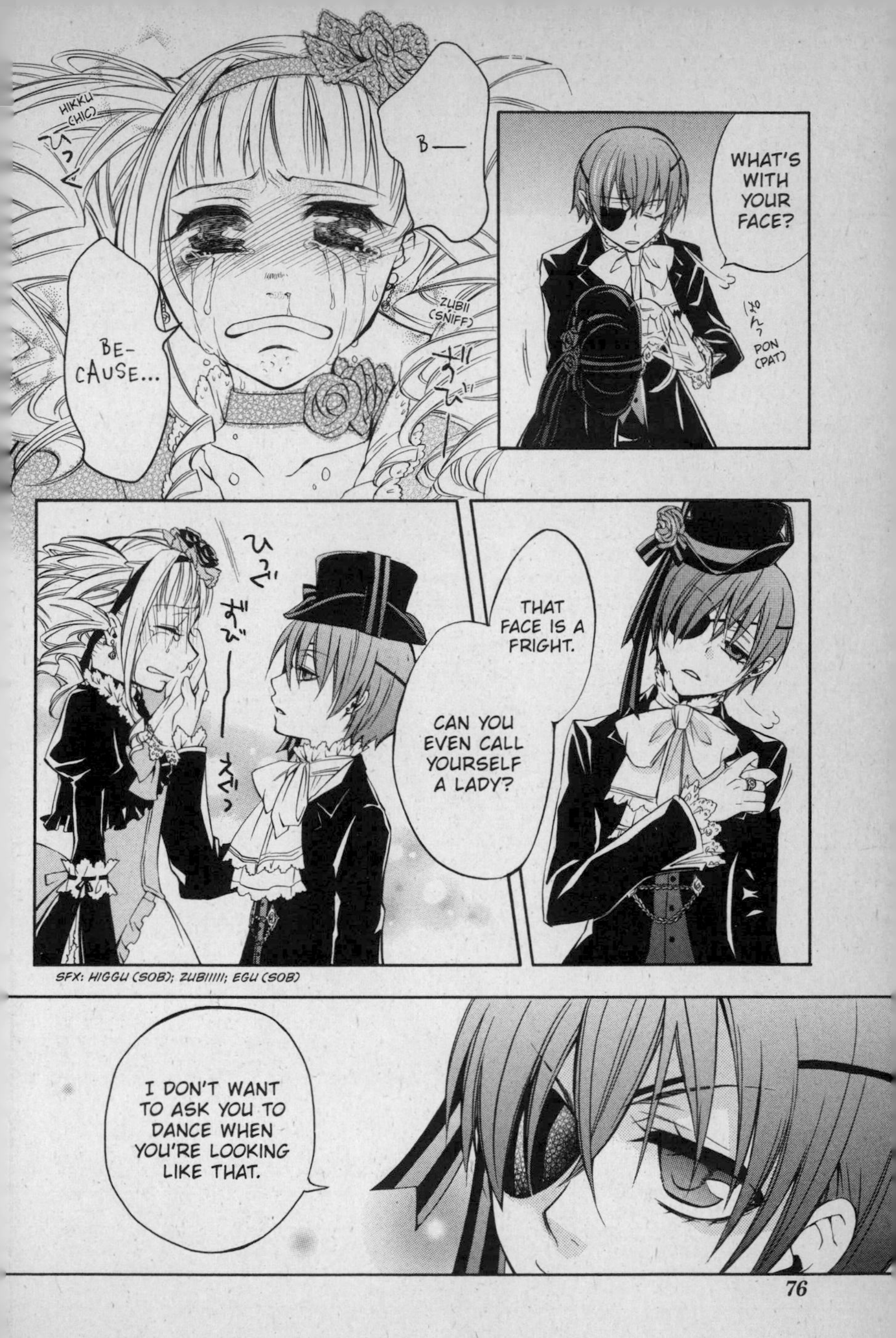
WHAT'S WITH YOUR FACE?
PON (PAT)
B—
HIKKU (HIC)
ZUBII (SNIFF)
BE-CAUSE...
THAT FACE IS A FRIGHT.
CAN YOU EVEN CALL YOURSELF A LADY?
SFX: HIGGU (SOB); ZUBIIIII; EGU (SOB)
I DON'T WANT TO ASK YOU TO DANCE WHEN YOU'RE LOOKING LIKE THAT.

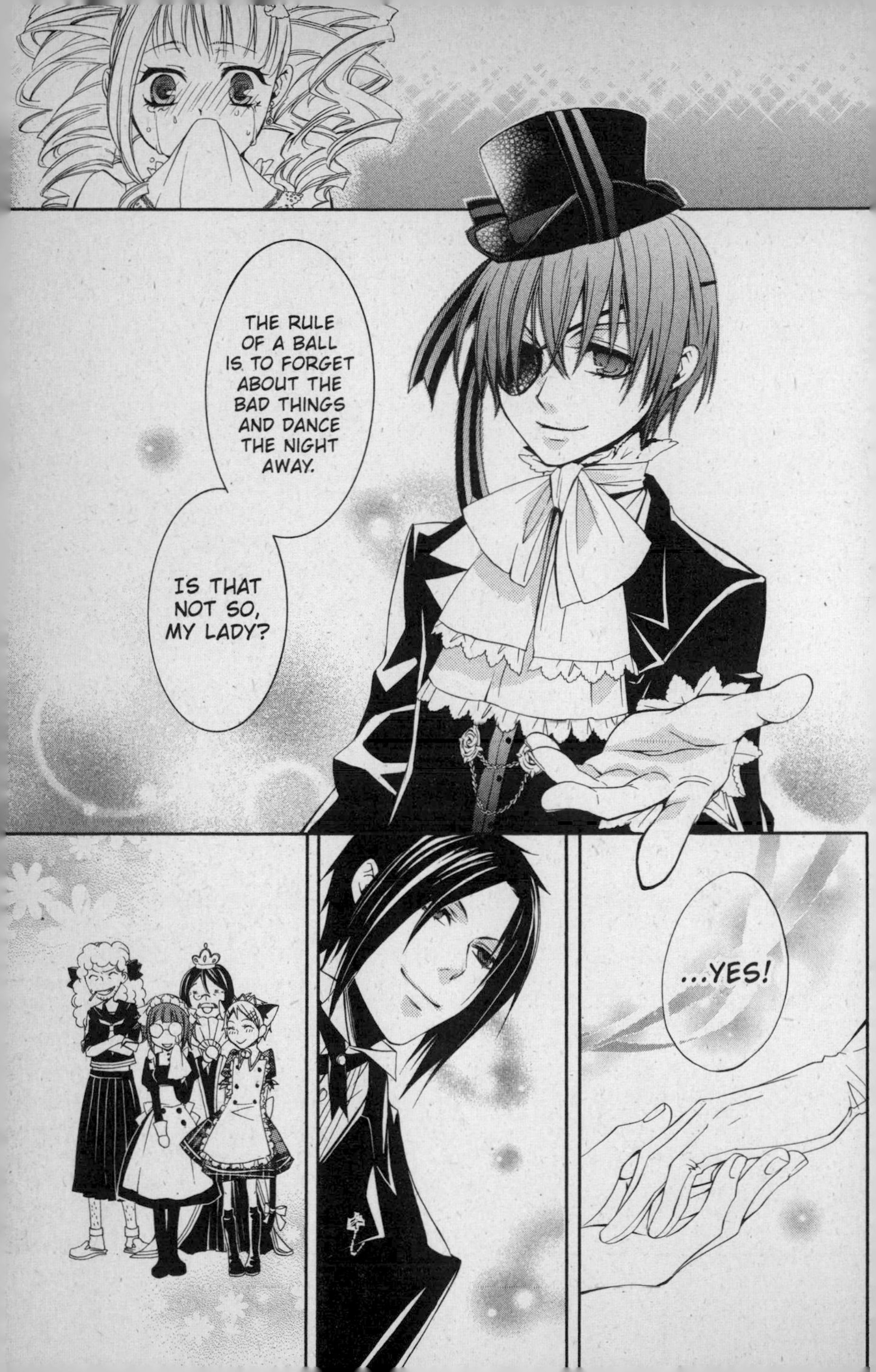
THE RULE OF A BALL IS TO FORGET ABOUT THE BAD THINGS AND DANCE THE NIGHT AWAY.
IS THAT NOT SO, MY LADY?
...YES!

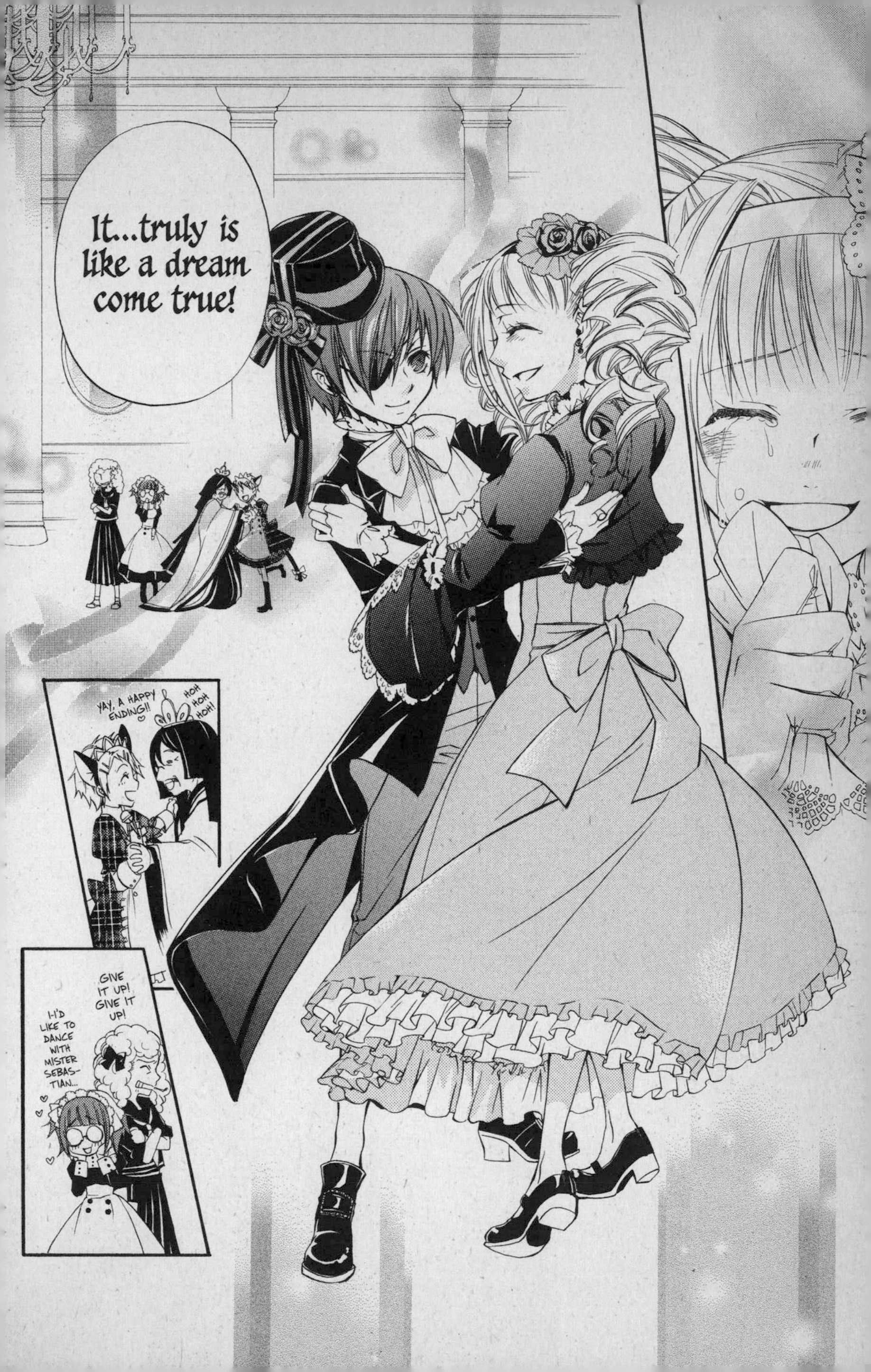
It...truly is like a dream come true!
HOH HOH HOH!
YAY, A HAPPY ENDING!!
GIVE IT UP! GIVE IT UP!
I-I'D LIKE TO DANCE WITH MISTER SEBASTIAN...

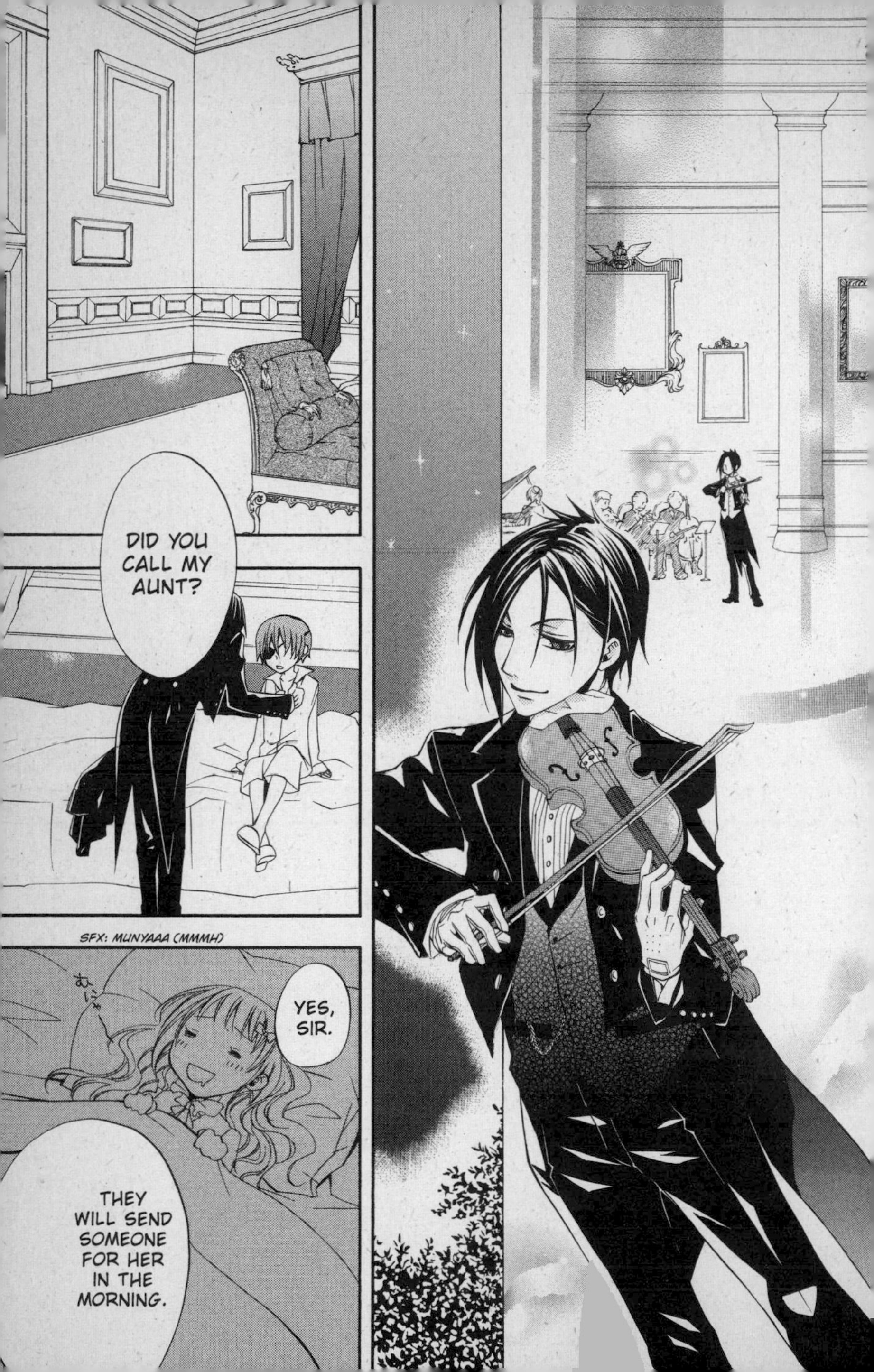
DID YOU CALL MY AUNT?
SFX: MUNYAAA (MMMH)
むにゃ
YES, SIR.
THEY WILL SEND SOMEONE FOR HER IN THE MORNING.

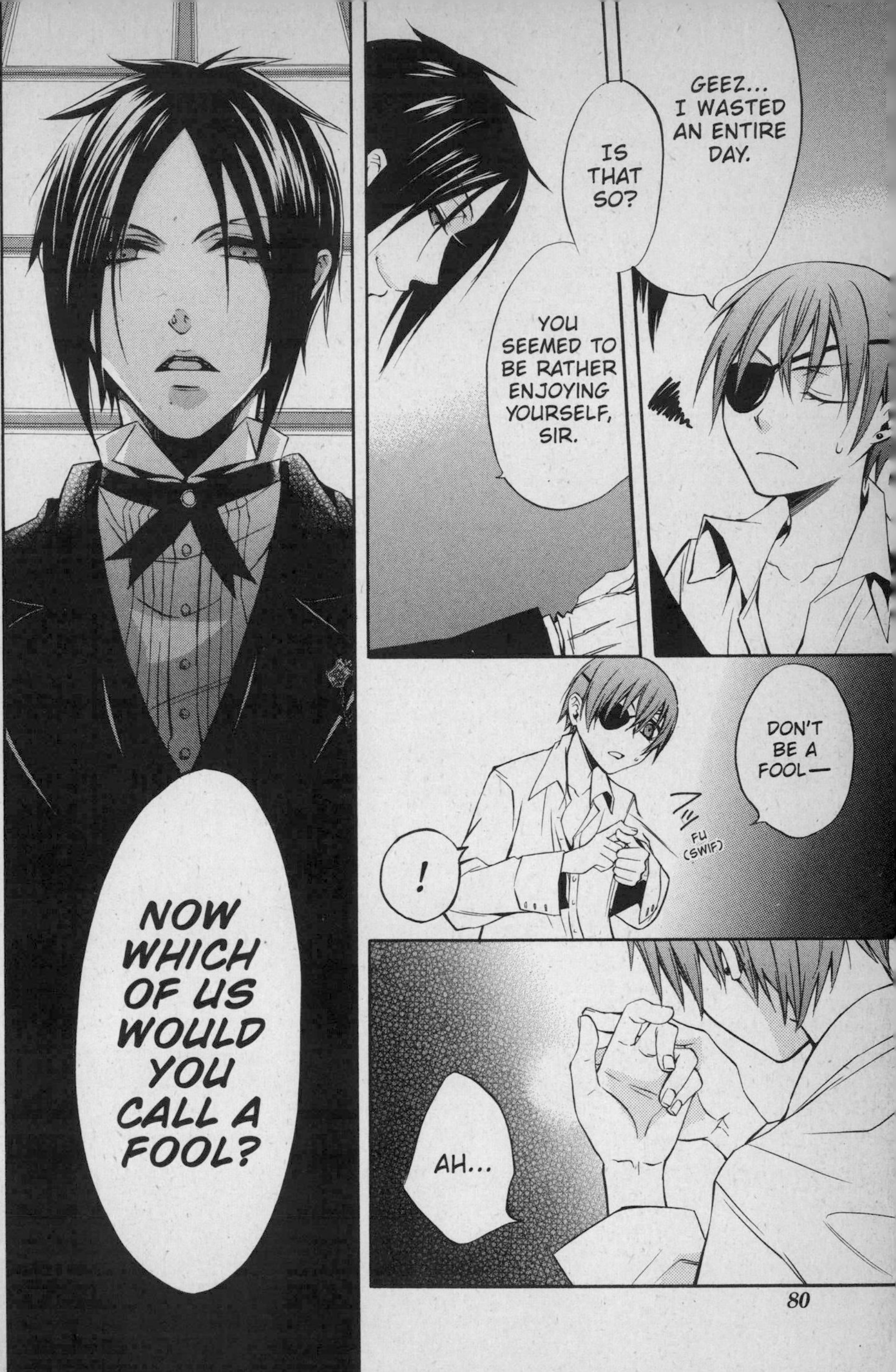
GEEZ... I WASTED AN ENTIRE DAY.
IS THAT SO?
YOU SEEMED TO BE RATHER ENJOYING YOURSELF, SIR.
DON'T BE A FOOL—
FU (SWIF)
!
AH...
NOW WHICH OF US WOULD YOU CALL A FOOL?

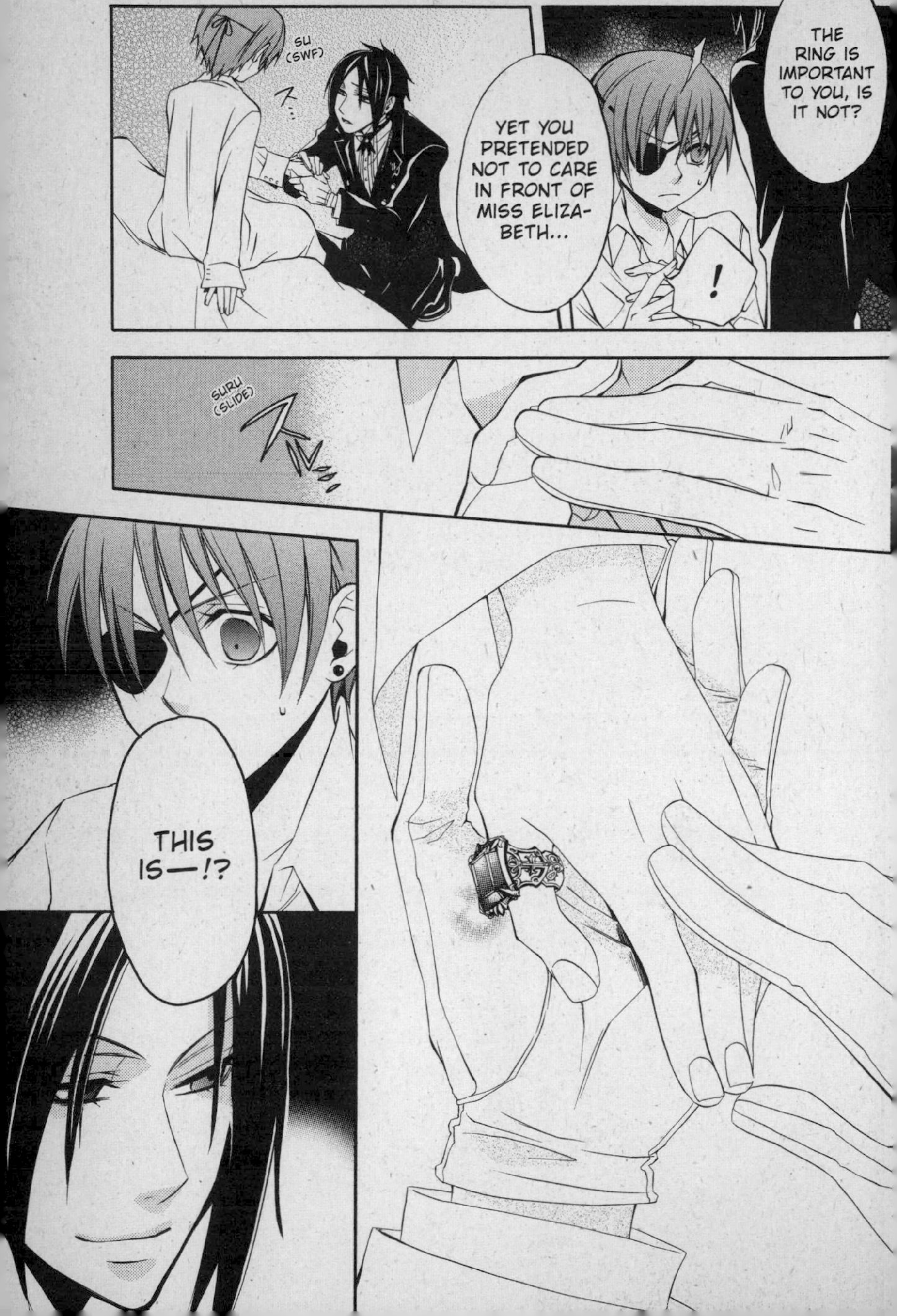
THE RING IS IMPORTANT TO YOU, IS IT NOT?
YET YOU PRETENDED NOT TO CARE IN FRONT OF MISS ELIZA-BETH...
!
SU (SWF)
SURU (SLIDE)
THIS IS—!?

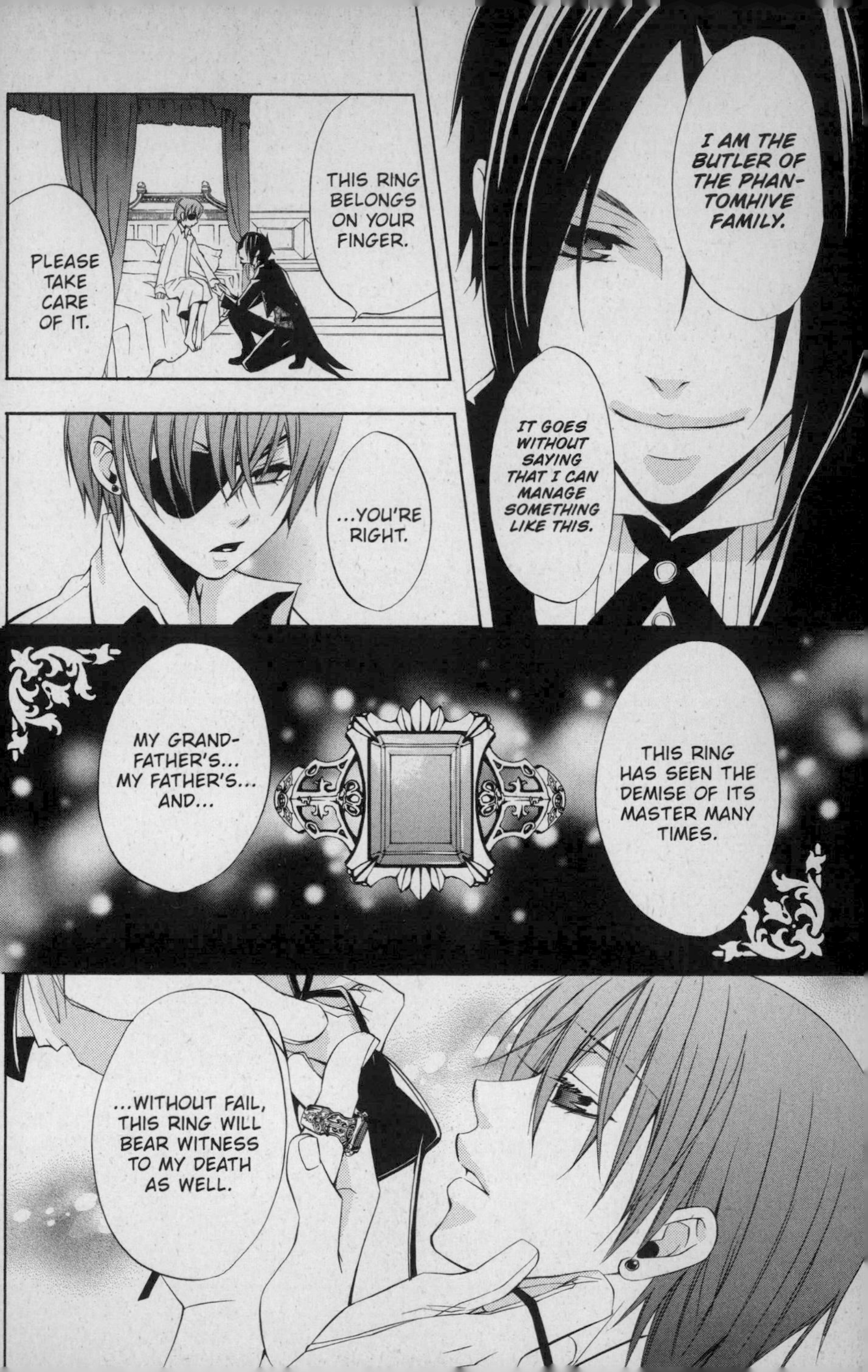
I AM THE BUTLER OF THE PHANTOMHIVE FAMILY.
IT GOES WITHOUT SAYING THAT I CAN MANAGE SOMETHING LIKE THIS.
THIS RING BELONGS ON YOUR FINGER.
PLEASE TAKE CARE OF IT.
...YOU'RE RIGHT.
THIS RING HAS SEEN THE DEMISE OF ITS MASTER MANY TIMES.
MY GRANDFATHER'S... MY FATHER'S... AND...
...WITHOUT FAIL, THIS RING WILL BEAR WITNESS TO MY DEATH AS WELL.

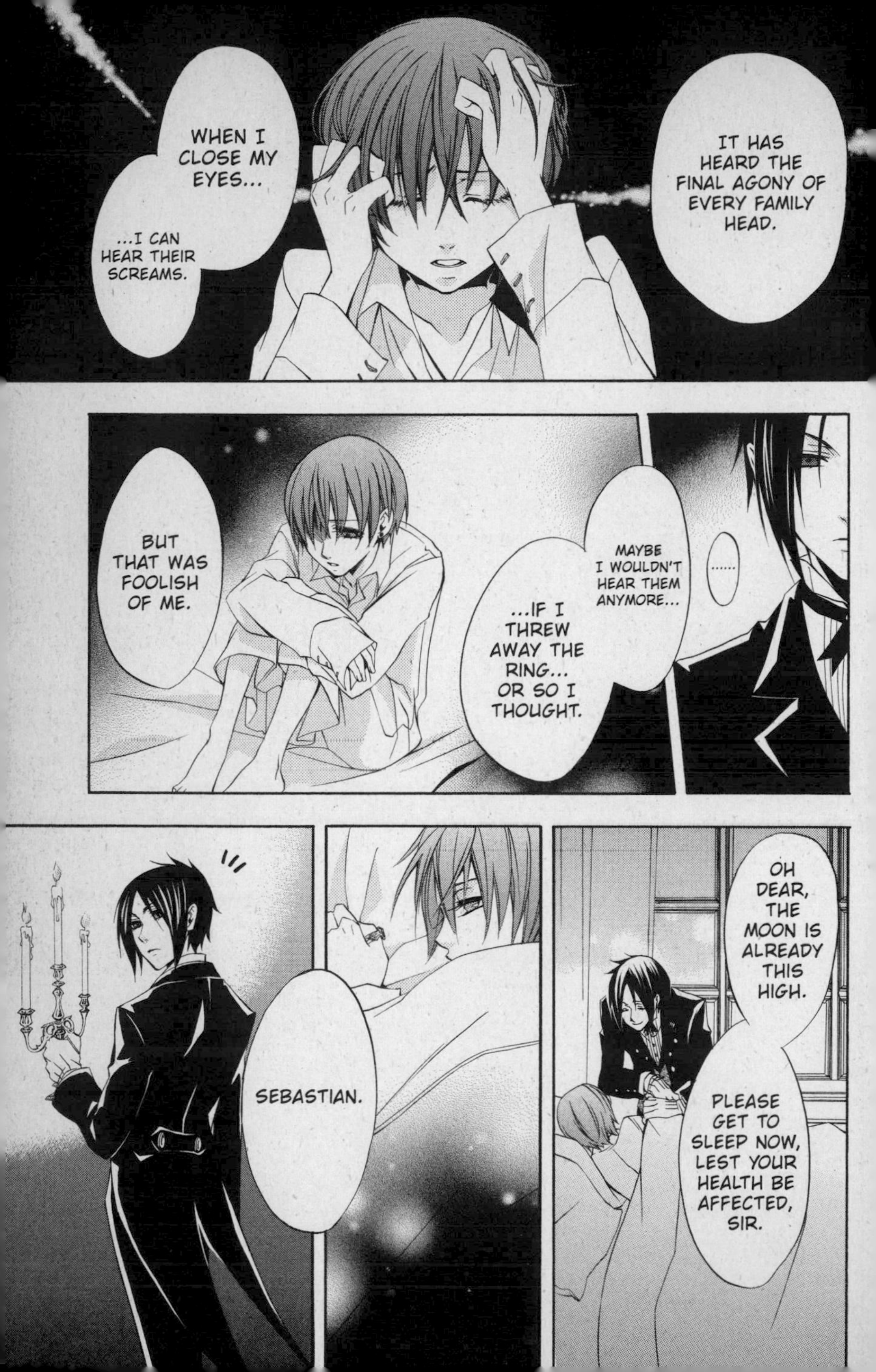
IT HAS HEARD THE FINAL AGONY OF EVERY FAMILY HEAD.
WHEN I CLOSE MY EYES...
...I CAN HEAR THEIR SCREAMS.
......
MAYBE I WOULDN'T HEAR THEM ANYMORE...
...IF I THREW AWAY THE RING... OR SO I THOUGHT.
BUT THAT WAS FOOLISH OF ME.
OH DEAR, THE MOON IS ALREADY THIS HIGH.
PLEASE GET TO SLEEP NOW, LEST YOUR HEALTH BE AFFECTED, SIR.
SEBASTIAN.

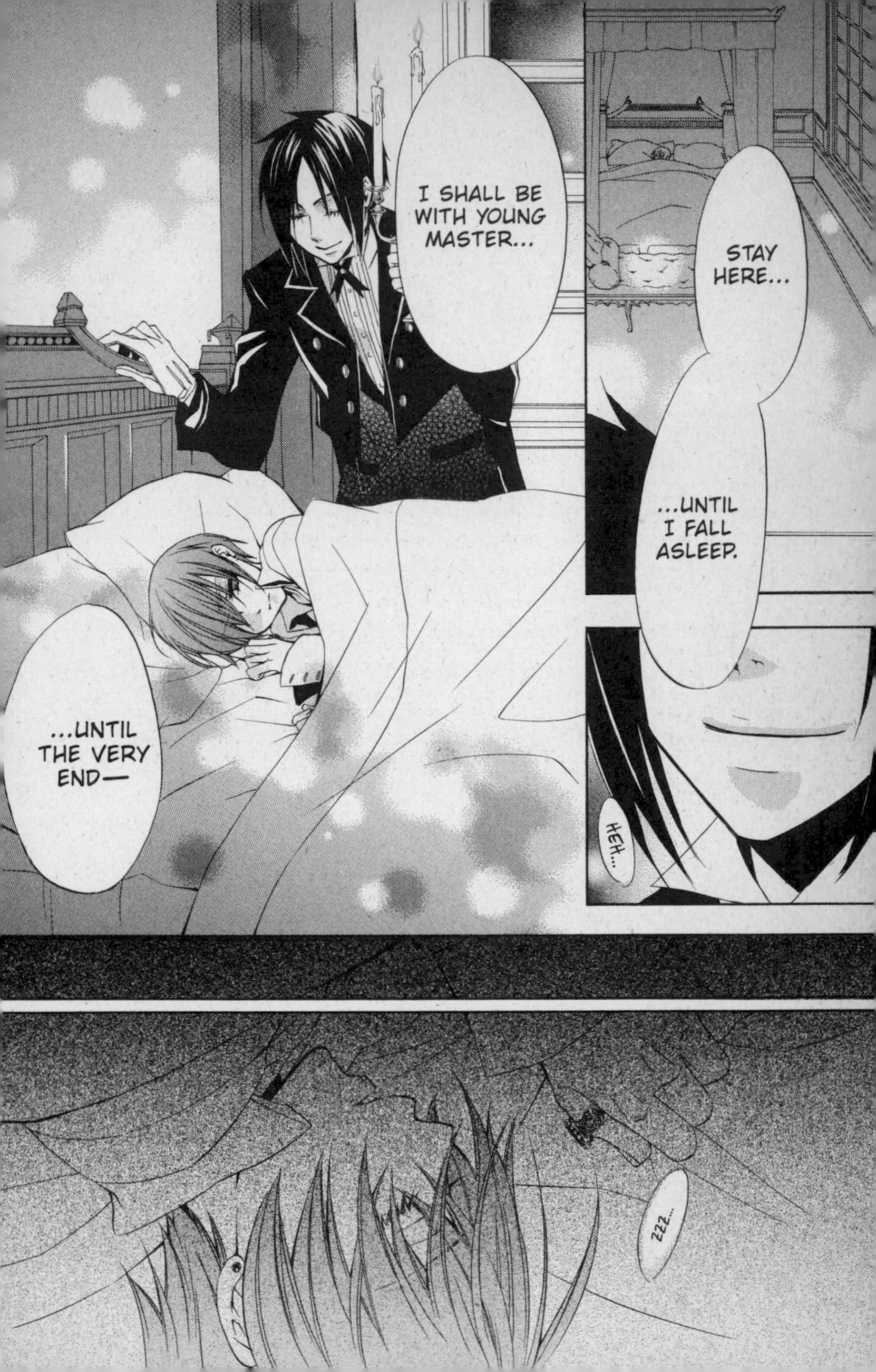
STAY HERE...
...UNTIL I FALL ASLEEP.
HEH...
I SHALL BE WITH YOUNG MASTER...
...UNTIL THE VERY END—
ZZZ...

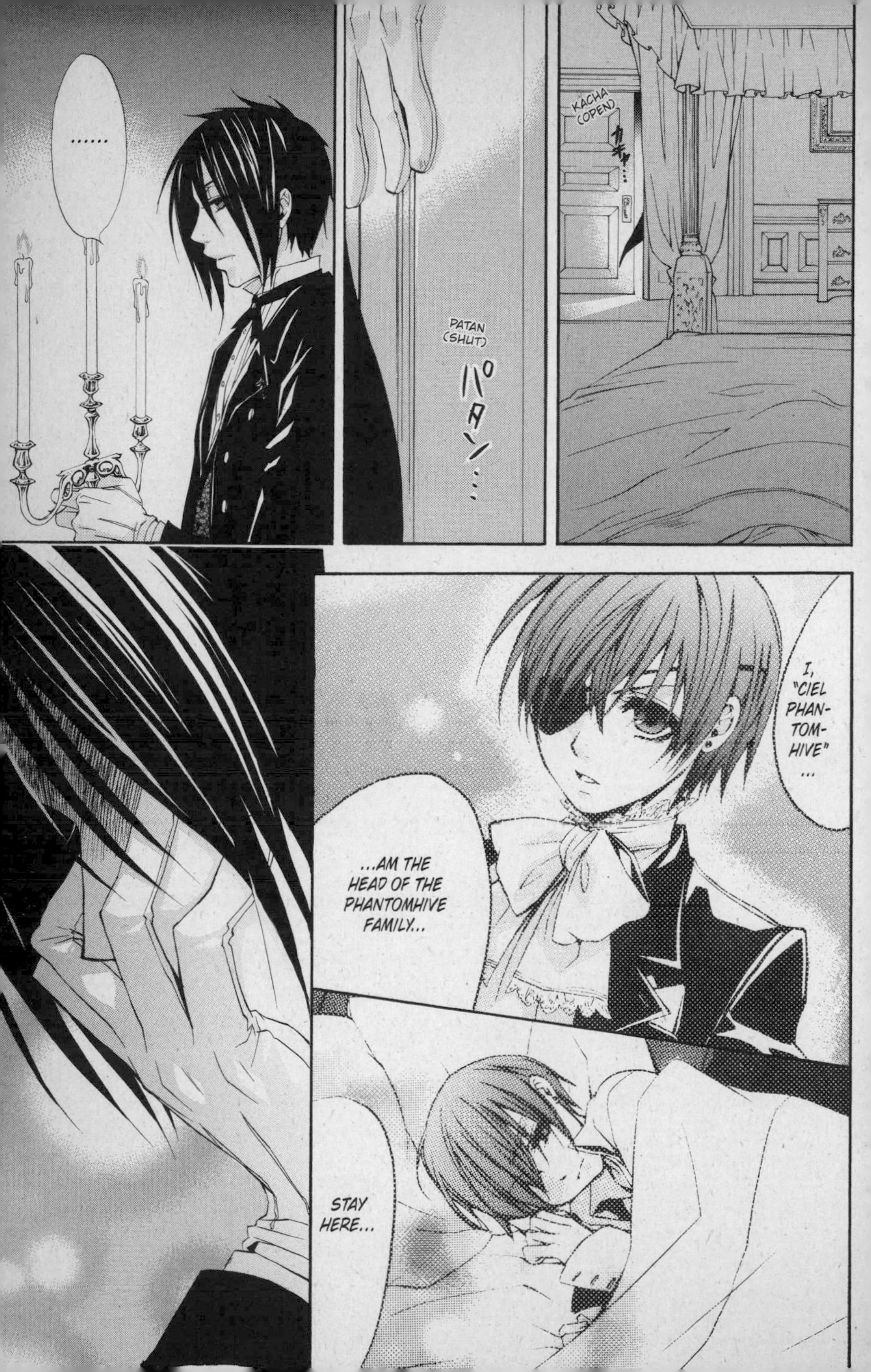
KACHA (OPEN)
カチャ…
PATAN (SHUT)
パタン…
......
I, "CIEL PHANTOMHIVE"...
...AM THE HEAD OF THE PHANTOMHIVE FAMILY...
STAY HERE...

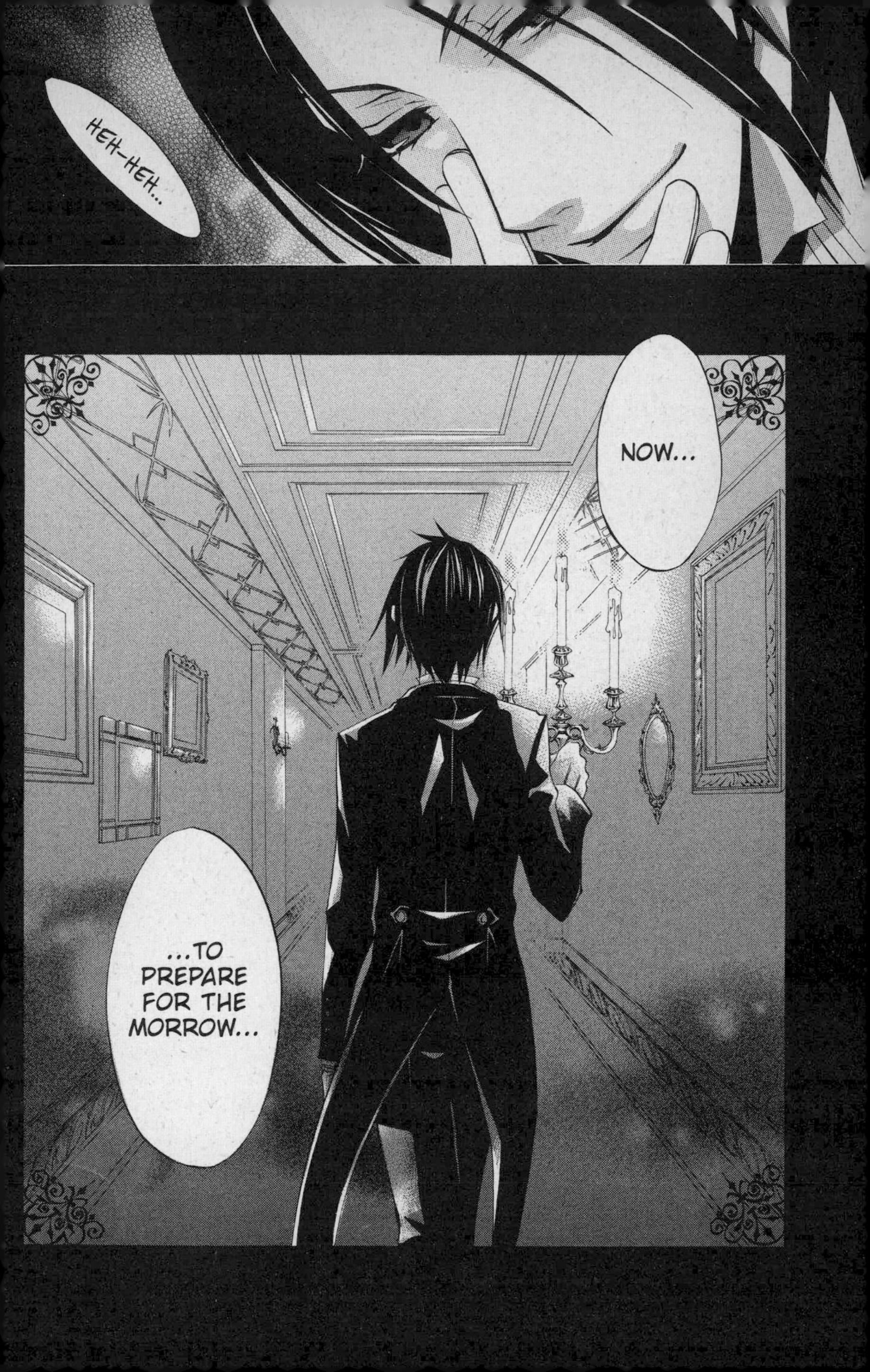
HEH-HEH...
NOW...
...TO PREPARE FOR THE MORROW...

**Black Butler**

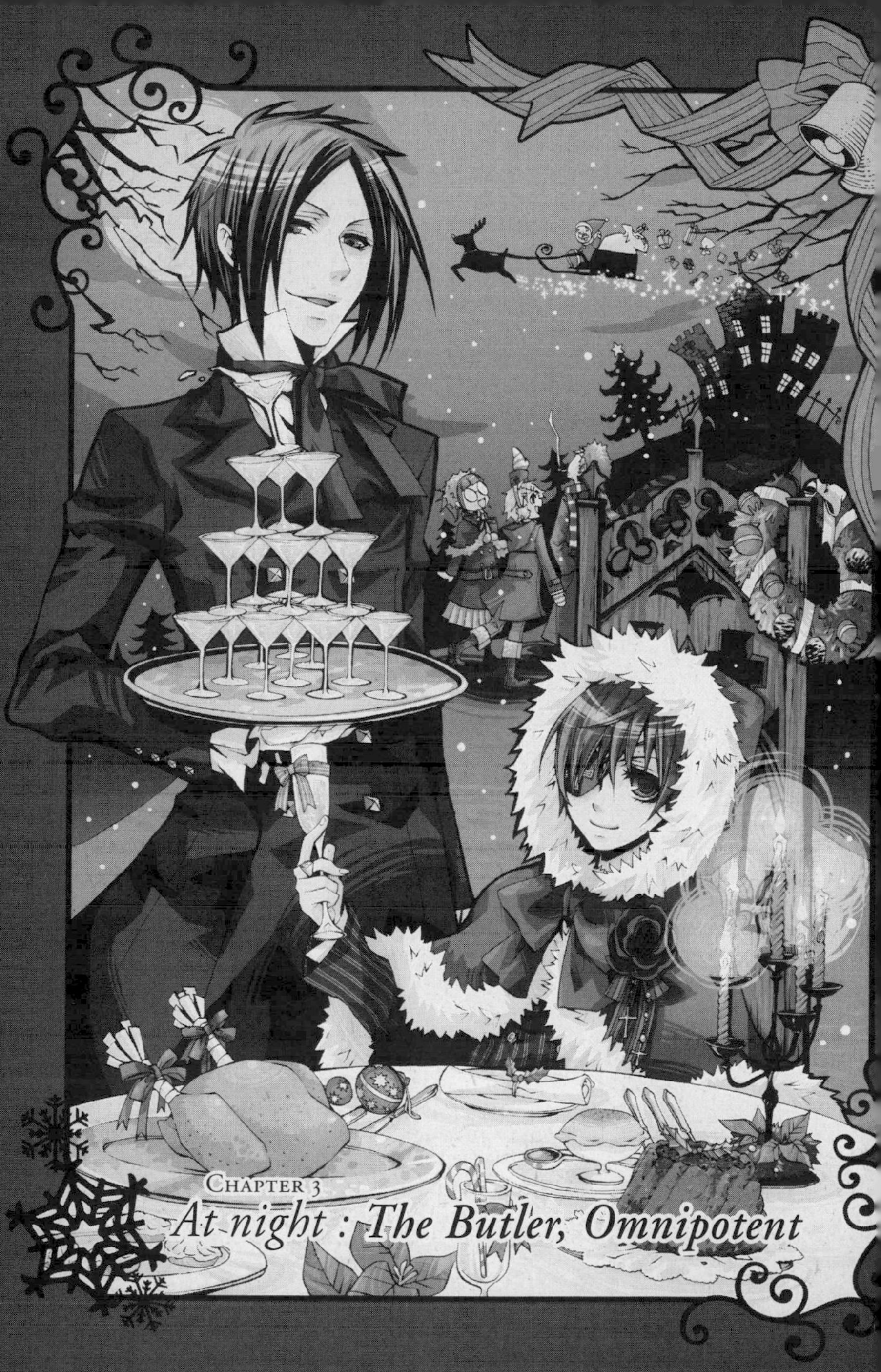

## Chapter 3
# At night : The Butler, Omnipotent

Black Butler

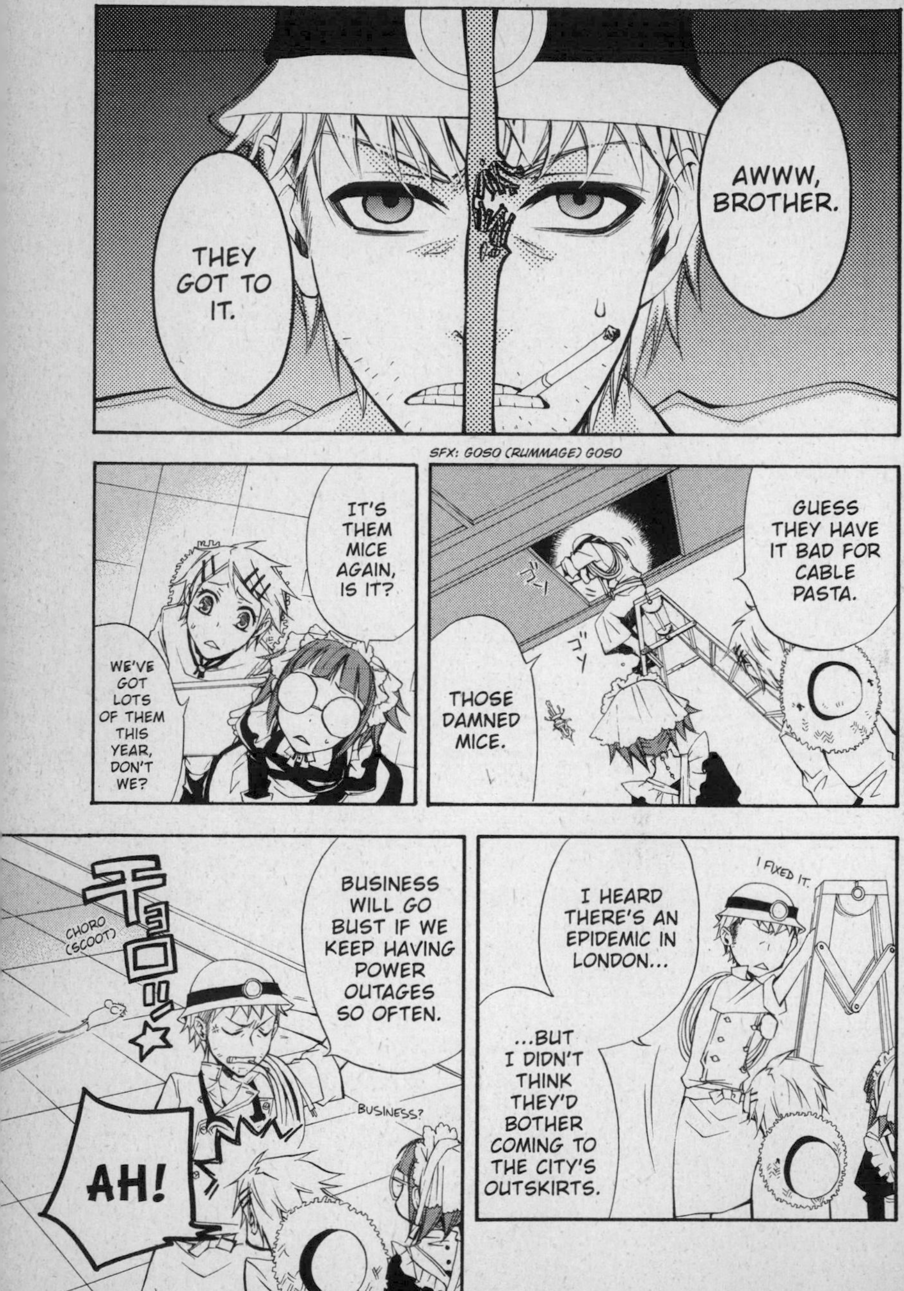
AWWW, BROTHER.
THEY GOT TO IT.
SFX: GOSO (RUMMAGE) GOSO
GUESS THEY HAVE IT BAD FOR CABLE PASTA.
THOSE DAMNED MICE.
IT'S THEM MICE AGAIN, IS IT?
WE'VE GOT LOTS OF THEM THIS YEAR, DON'T WE?
I FIXED IT.
I HEARD THERE'S AN EPIDEMIC IN LONDON...
...BUT I DIDN'T THINK THEY'D BOTHER COMING TO THE CITY'S OUTSKIRTS.
BUSINESS WILL GO BUST IF WE KEEP HAVING POWER OUTAGES SO OFTEN.
CHORO (SCOOT)
BUSINESS?
AH!

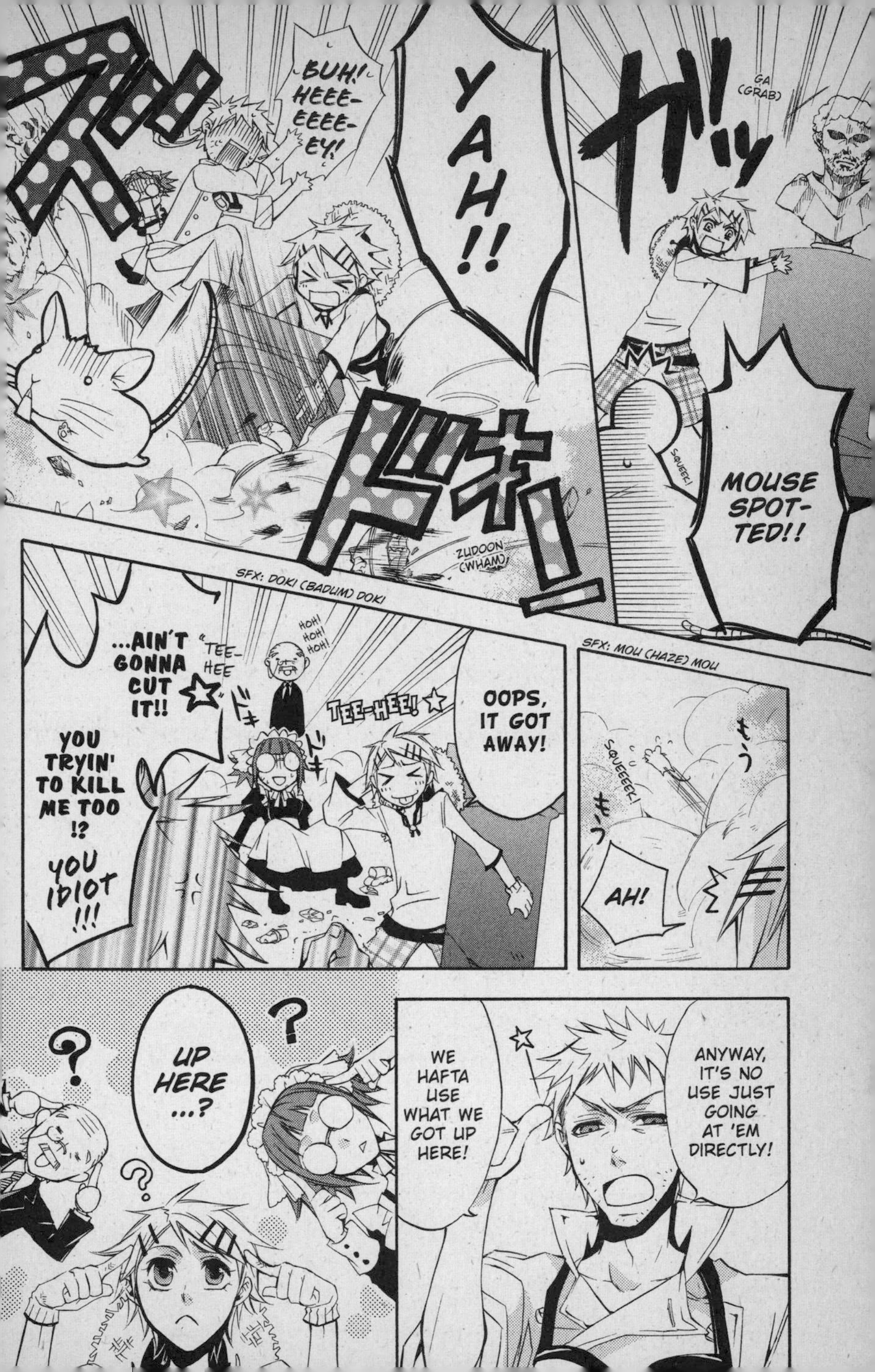
GA (GRAB)
MOUSE SPOT-TED!!
SQUEEK!
YAH!!
BUH! HEEEE-EEEEEY!
ZUDOON (WHAM)
SFX: MOU (HAZE) MOU
SQUEEEEK!
AH!
OOPS, IT GOT AWAY!
TEE-HEE! ☆
HOH! HOH! HOH!
"TEE-HEE ☆"
...AIN'T GONNA CUT IT!!
YOU TRYIN' TO KILL ME TOO!?
YOU IDIOT!!!
SFX: DOKI (BADUM) DOKI
ANYWAY, IT'S NO USE JUST GOING AT 'EM DIRECTLY!
WE HAFTA USE WHAT WE GOT UP HERE!
UP HERE ...?

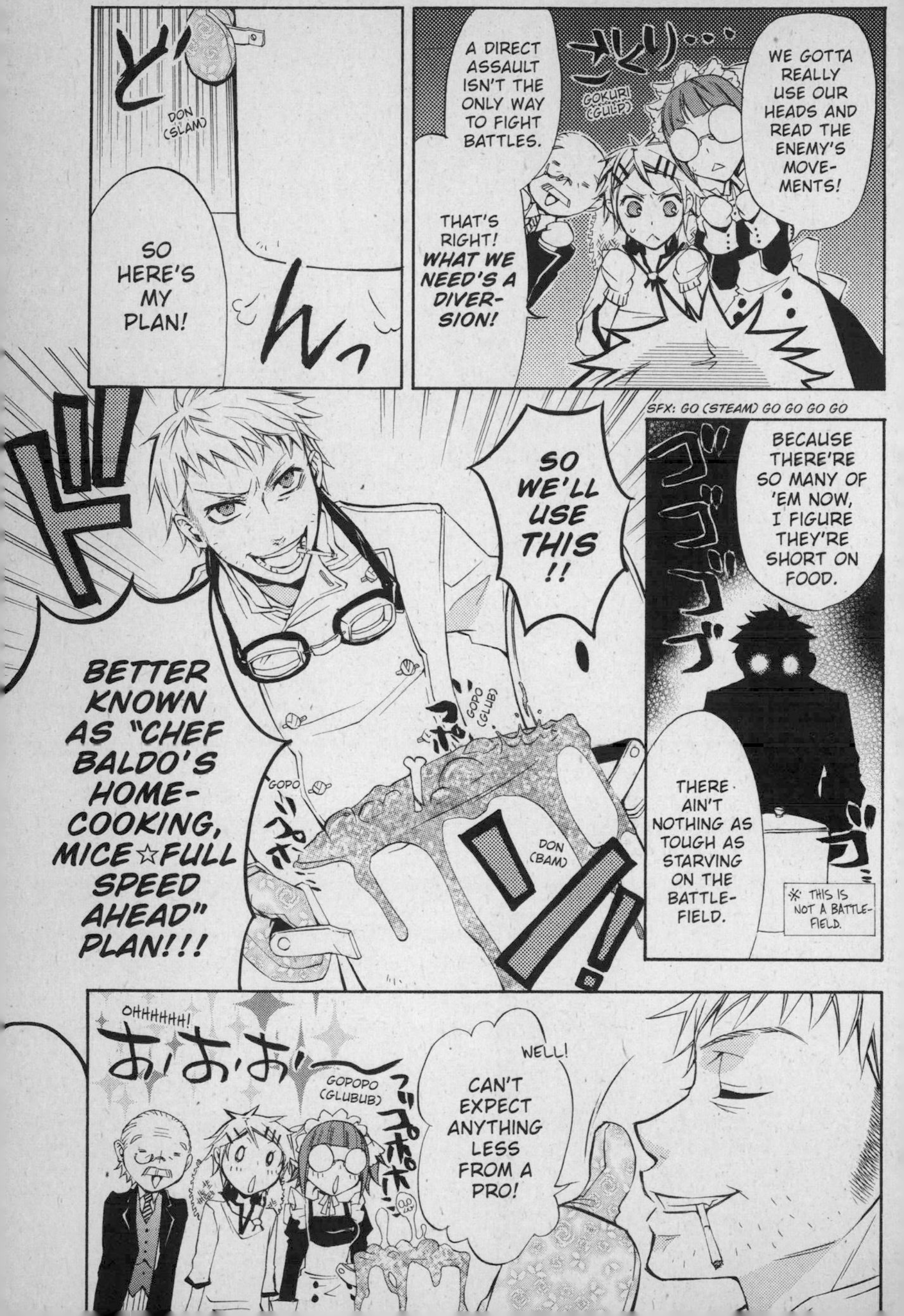
WE GOTTA REALLY USE OUR HEADS AND READ THE ENEMY'S MOVEMENTS!
GOKURI (GULP)
A DIRECT ASSAULT ISN'T THE ONLY WAY TO FIGHT BATTLES.
THAT'S RIGHT! WHAT WE NEED'S A DIVERSION!
DON (SLAM)
SO HERE'S MY PLAN!
SFX: GO (STEAM) GO GO GO GO
BECAUSE THERE'RE SO MANY OF 'EM NOW, I FIGURE THEY'RE SHORT ON FOOD.
THERE AIN'T NOTHING AS TOUGH AS STARVING ON THE BATTLEFIELD.
※ THIS IS NOT A BATTLEFIELD.
SO WE'LL USE THIS!!
GOPO (GLUB)
DON (BAM)
GOPO
BETTER KNOWN AS "CHEF BALDO'S HOME-COOKING, MICE☆FULL SPEED AHEAD" PLAN!!!
WELL!
CAN'T EXPECT ANYTHING LESS FROM A PRO!
GOPOPO (GLUBUB)
OHHHHHHH!

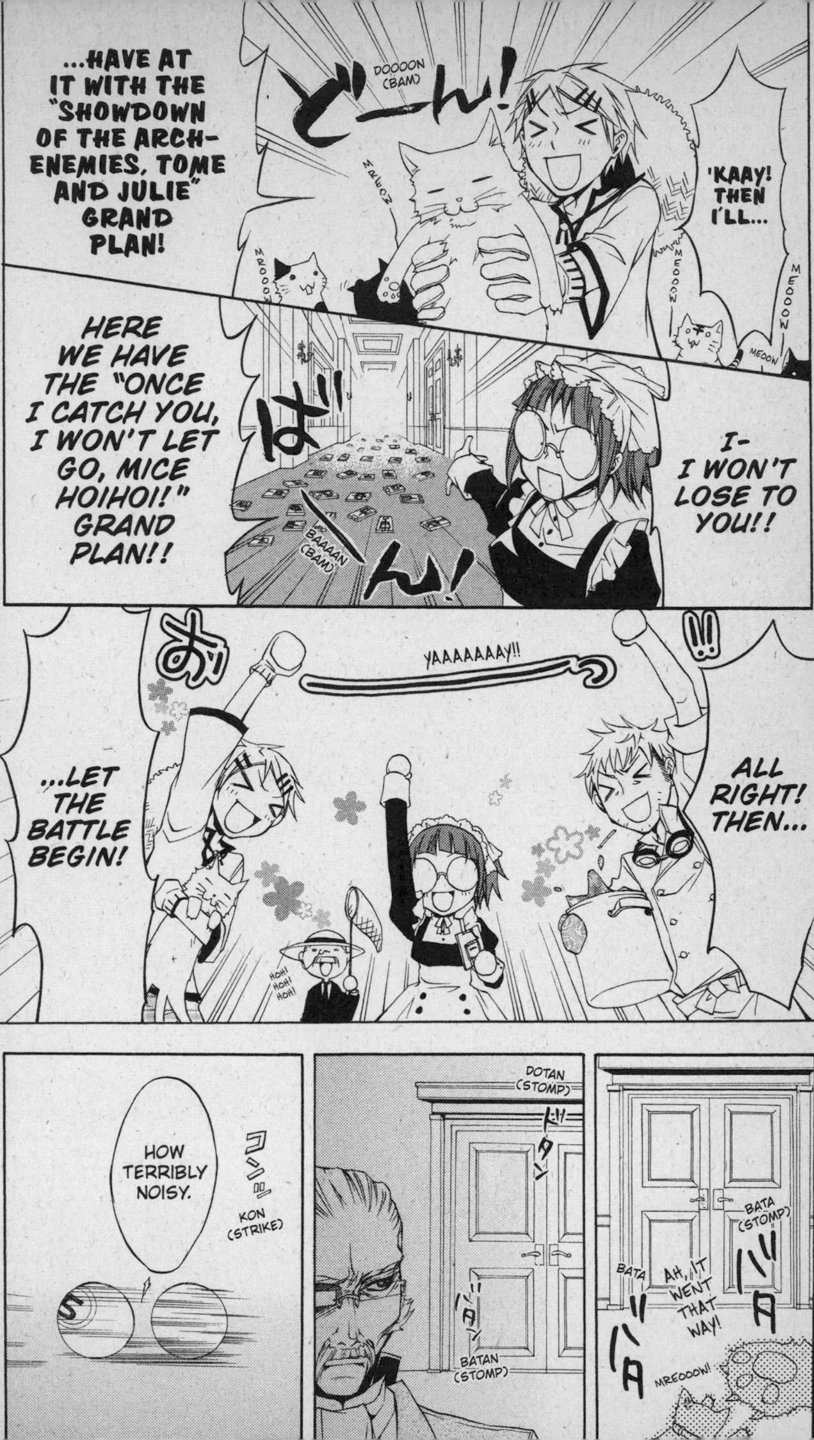
'KAAY! THEN I'LL...
DOOOON (BAM)
どーん!
MEOOOW
MEOOOW
MEOOW
MROOOOW
...HAVE AT IT WITH THE "SHOWDOWN OF THE ARCH-ENEMIES, TOME AND JULIE" GRAND PLAN!
I- I WON'T LOSE TO YOU!!
ばーん!
BAAAAN (BAM)
HERE WE HAVE THE "ONCE I CATCH YOU, I WON'T LET GO, MICE HOIHOI!" GRAND PLAN!!
ALL RIGHT! THEN...
!!
YAAAAAAAY!!
お
...LET THE BATTLE BEGIN!
HOH! HOH! HOH!
BATA (STOMP)
バタ
AH, IT WENT THAT WAY!
BATA
バタ
MREOOOW!
DOTAN (STOMP)
ドタン
バタン
BATAN (STOMP)
HOW TERRIBLY NOISY.
コン
KON (STRIKE)

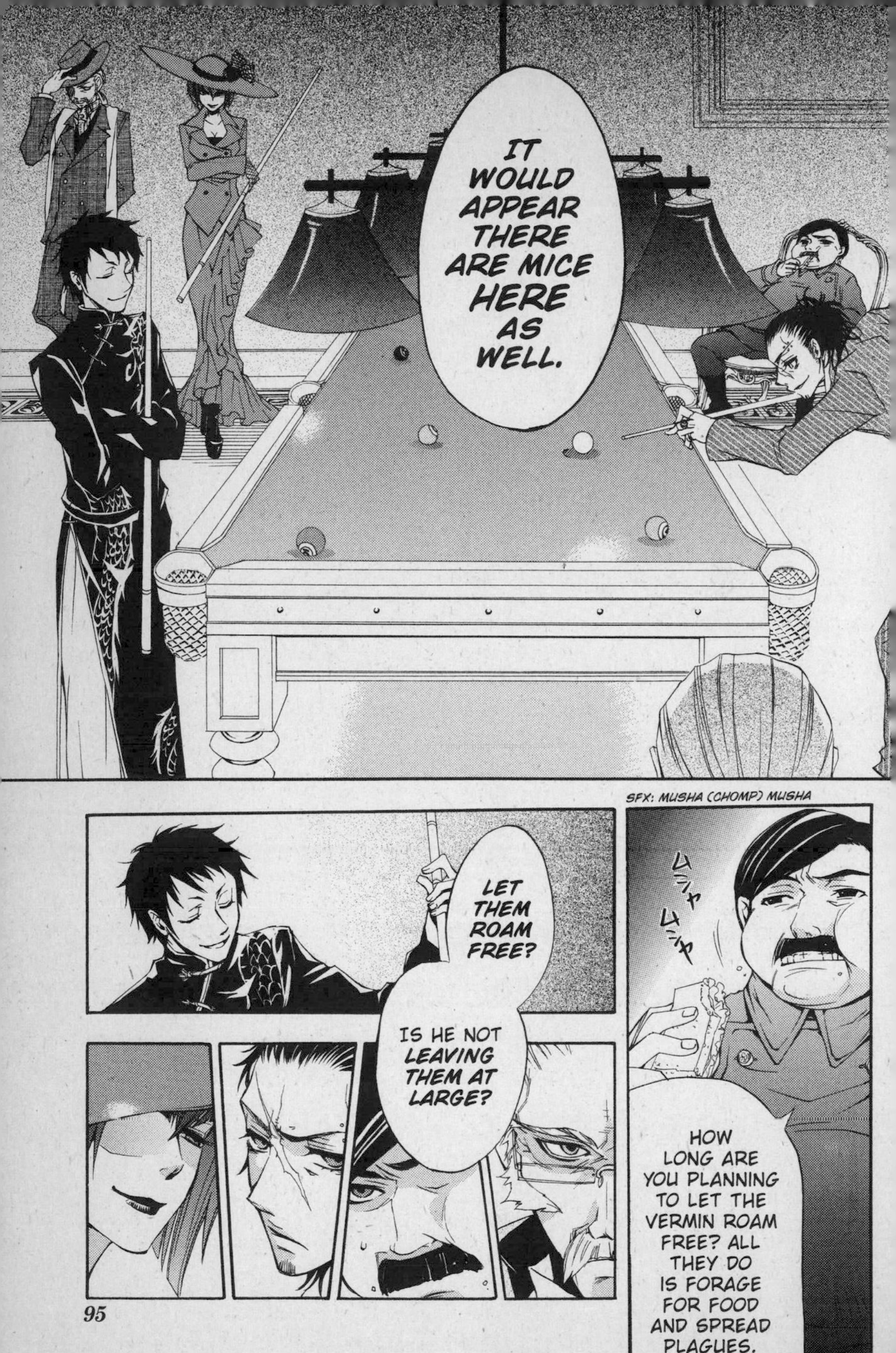
IT WOULD APPEAR THERE ARE MICE HERE AS WELL.
SFX: MUSHA (CHOMP) MUSHA
ムシャ ムシャ
HOW LONG ARE YOU PLANNING TO LET THE VERMIN ROAM FREE? ALL THEY DO IS FORAGE FOR FOOD AND SPREAD PLAGUES.
LET THEM ROAM FREE?
IS HE NOT *LEAVING* THEM AT LARGE?

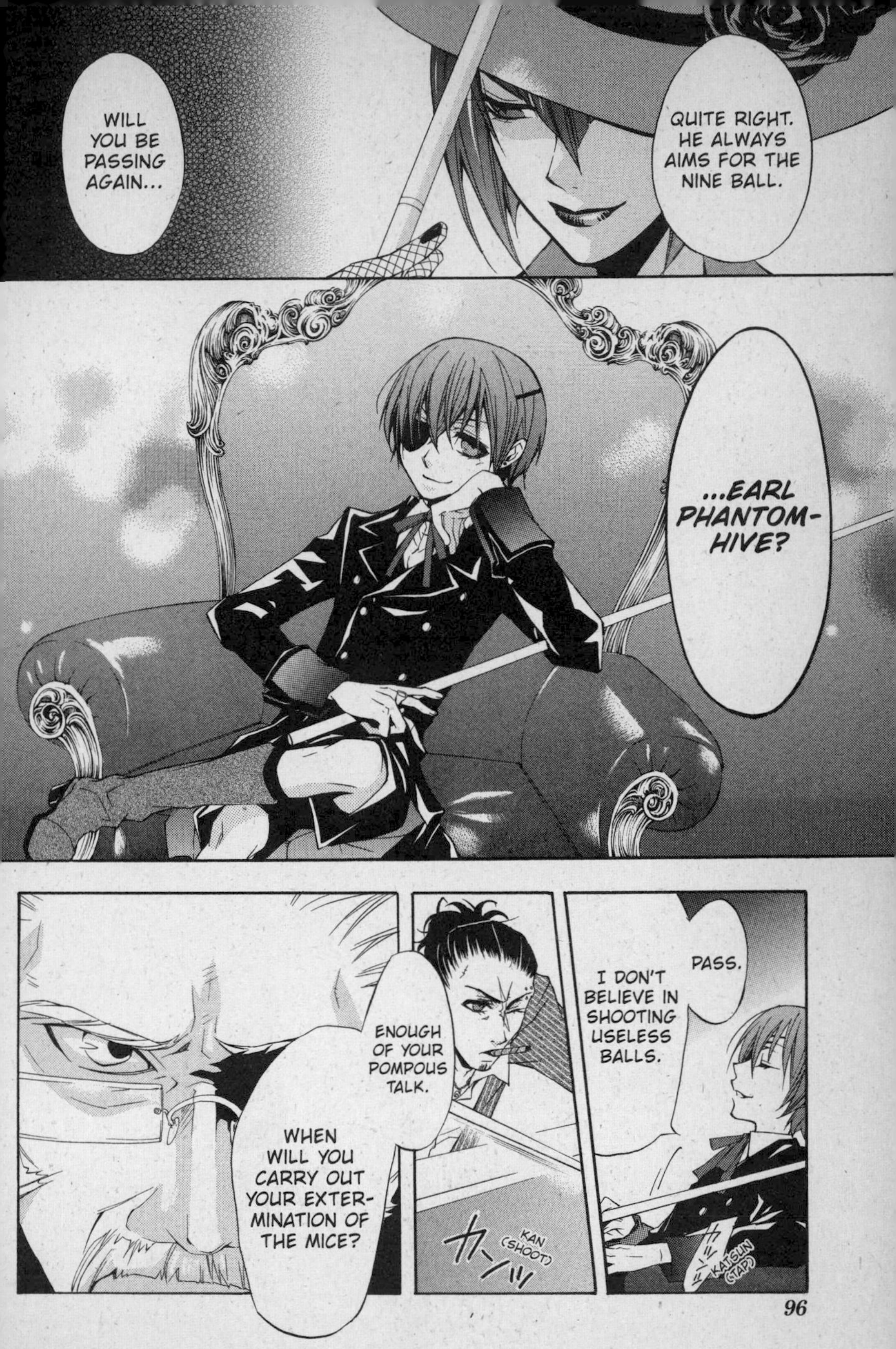
QUITE RIGHT. HE ALWAYS AIMS FOR THE NINE BALL.
WILL YOU BE PASSING AGAIN...
...EARL PHANTOM-HIVE?
PASS.
I DON'T BELIEVE IN SHOOTING USELESS BALLS.
KATSUN (TAP)
KAN (SHOOT)
ENOUGH OF YOUR POMPOUS TALK.
WHEN WILL YOU CARRY OUT YOUR EXTER-MINATION OF THE MICE?

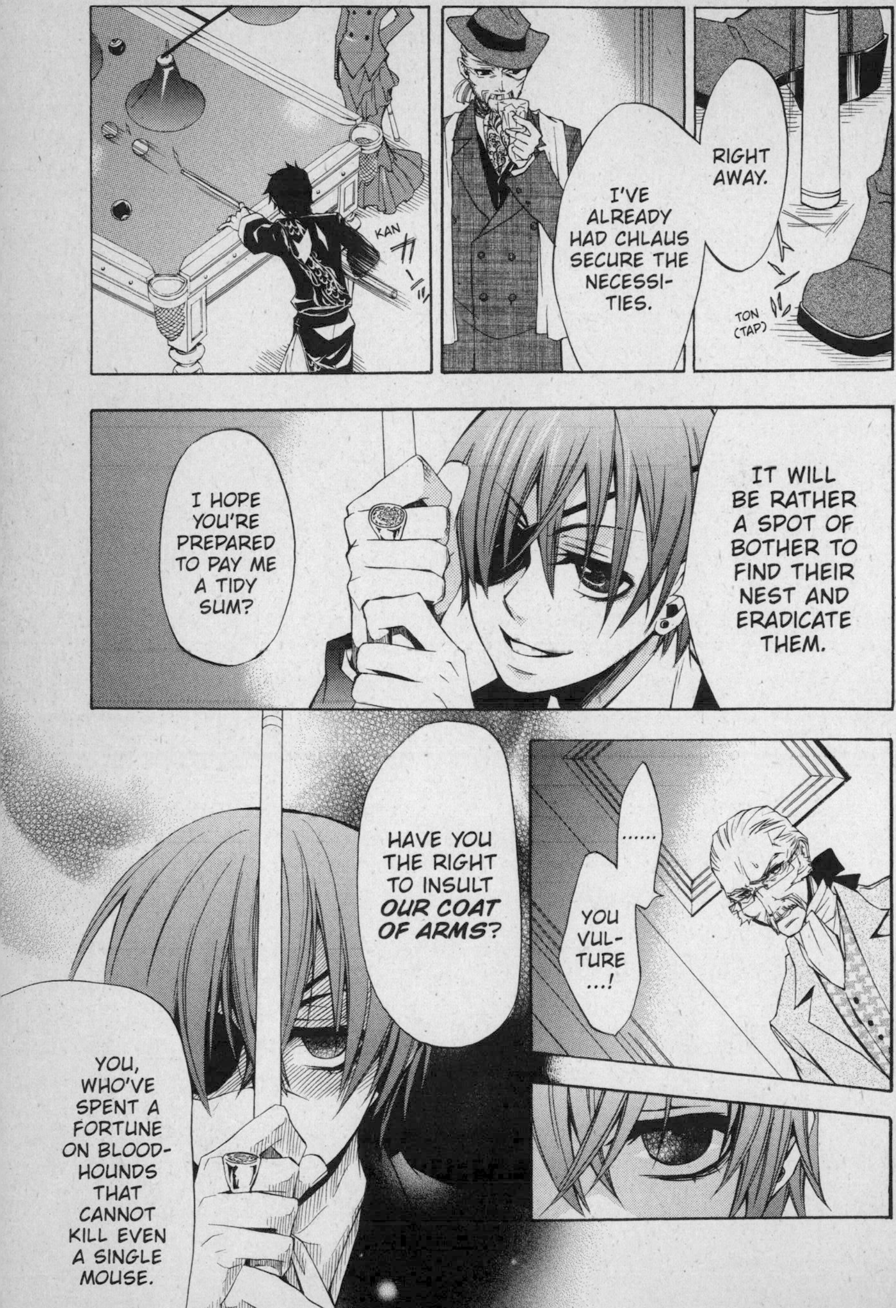
RIGHT AWAY.
TON (TAP)
I'VE ALREADY HAD CHLAUS SECURE THE NECESSITIES.
KAN
IT WILL BE RATHER A SPOT OF BOTHER TO FIND THEIR NEST AND ERADICATE THEM.
I HOPE YOU'RE PREPARED TO PAY ME A TIDY SUM?
......
YOU VULTURE...!
HAVE YOU THE RIGHT TO INSULT *OUR COAT OF ARMS*?
YOU, WHO'VE SPENT A FORTUNE ON BLOODHOUNDS THAT CANNOT KILL EVEN A SINGLE MOUSE.

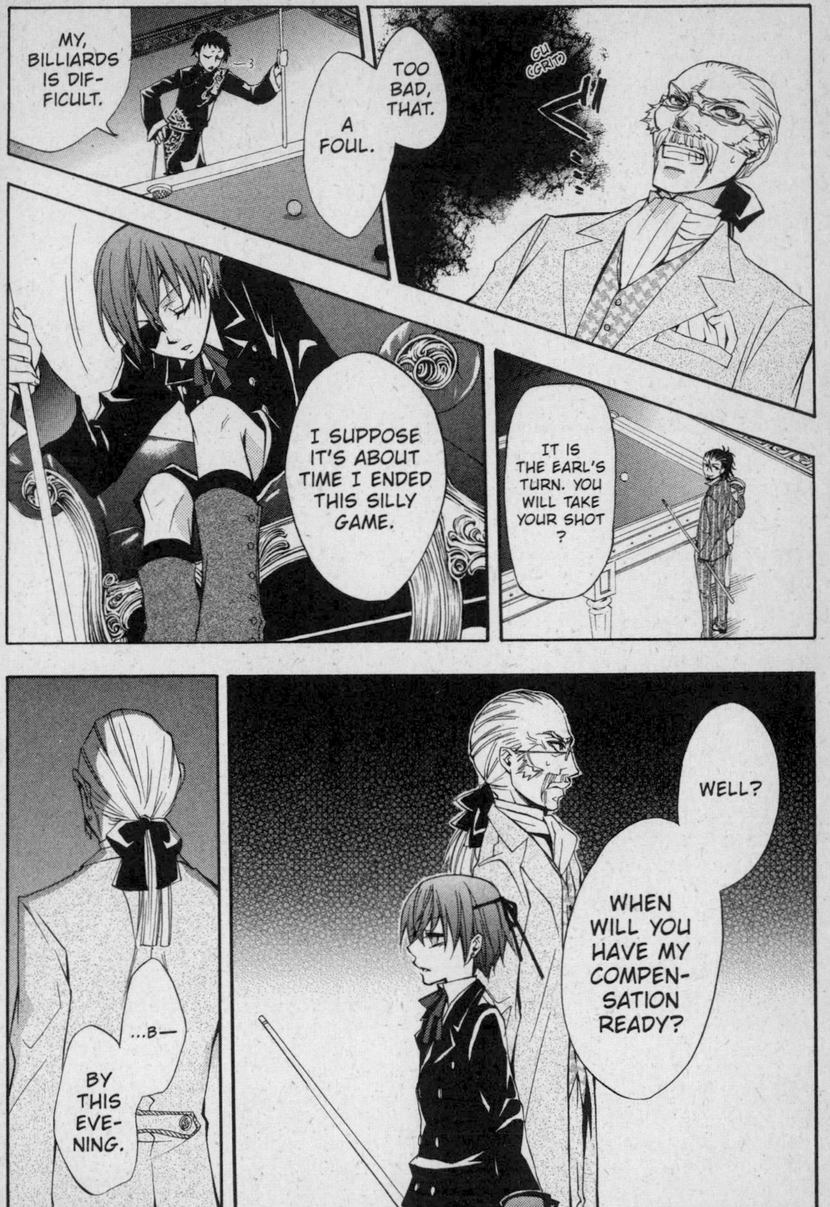
GU (GRIT)
TOO BAD, THAT.
A FOUL.
MY, BILLIARDS IS DIF-FICULT.
IT IS THE EARL'S TURN. YOU WILL TAKE YOUR SHOT?
I SUPPOSE IT'S ABOUT TIME I ENDED THIS SILLY GAME.
WELL?
WHEN WILL YOU HAVE MY COMPEN-SATION READY?
...B—
BY THIS EVE-NING.

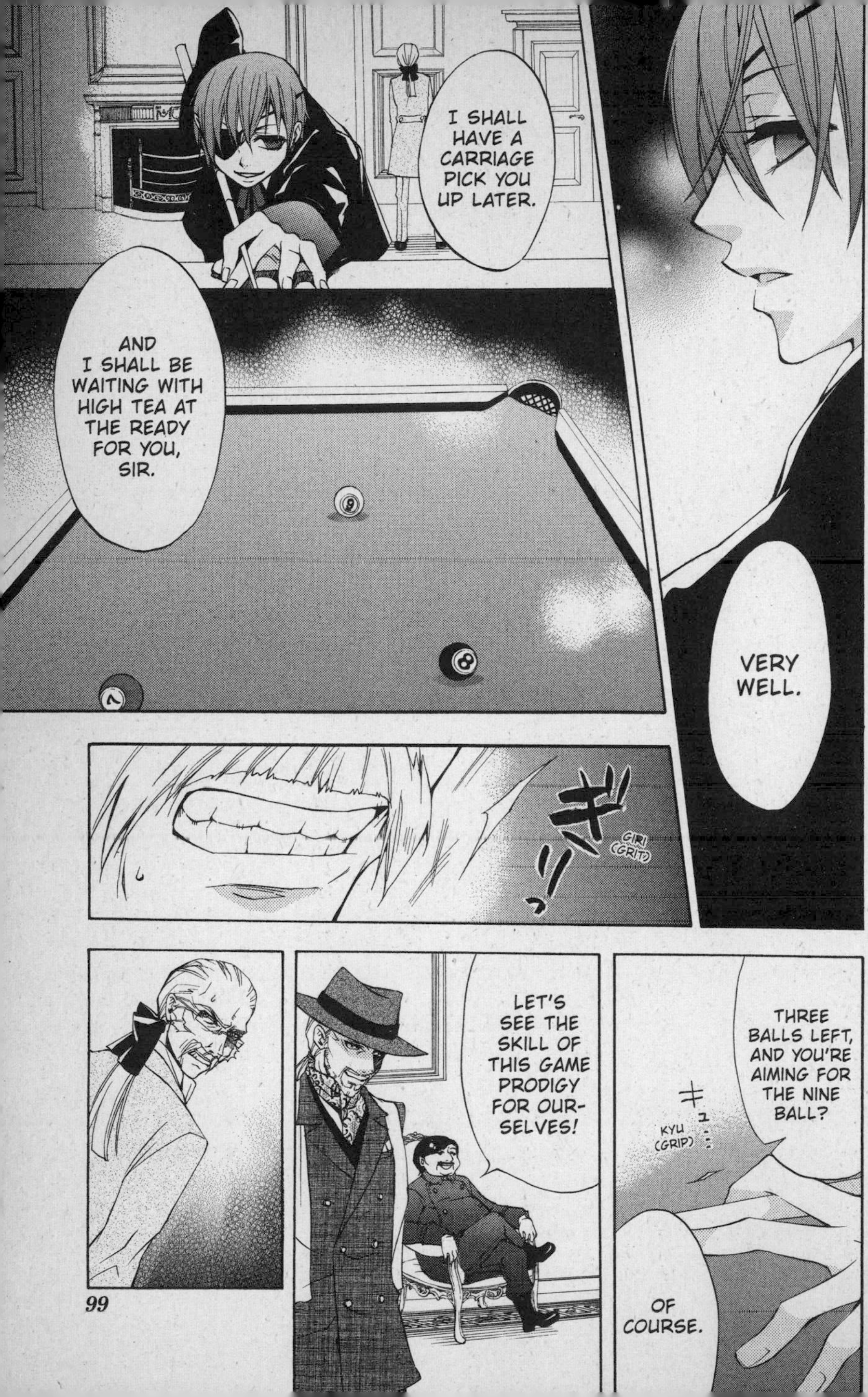
I SHALL HAVE A CARRIAGE PICK YOU UP LATER.
AND I SHALL BE WAITING WITH HIGH TEA AT THE READY FOR YOU, SIR.
VERY WELL.
GIRI (GRIT)
THREE BALLS LEFT, AND YOU'RE AIMING FOR THE NINE BALL?
KYU (GRIP)
OF COURSE.
LET'S SEE THE SKILL OF THIS GAME PRODIGY FOR OURSELVES!

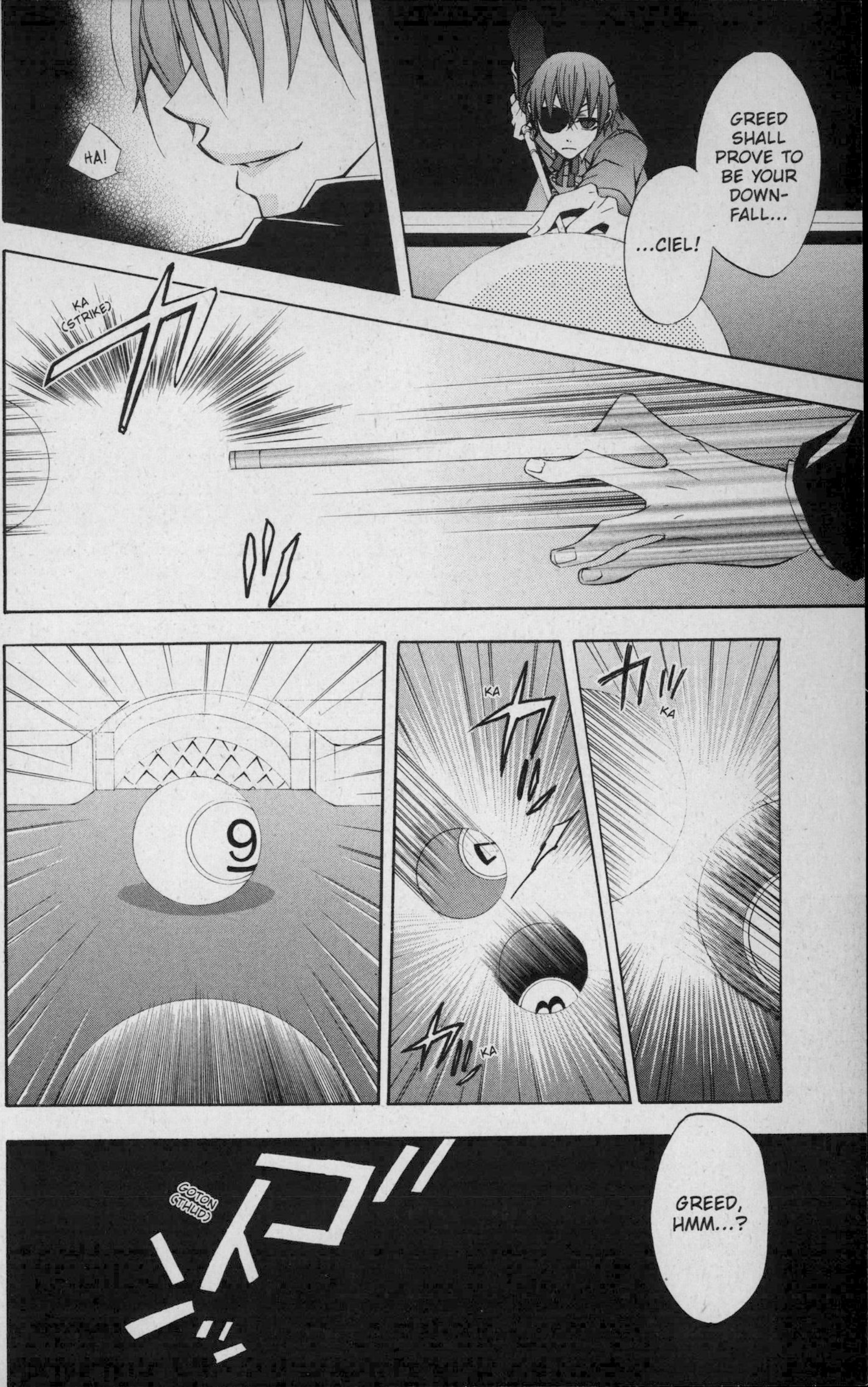
GREED SHALL PROVE TO BE YOUR DOWN-FALL...
...CIEL!
HA!
KA (STRIKE)
KA
KA
KA
GREED, HMM...?
GOTON (THUD)

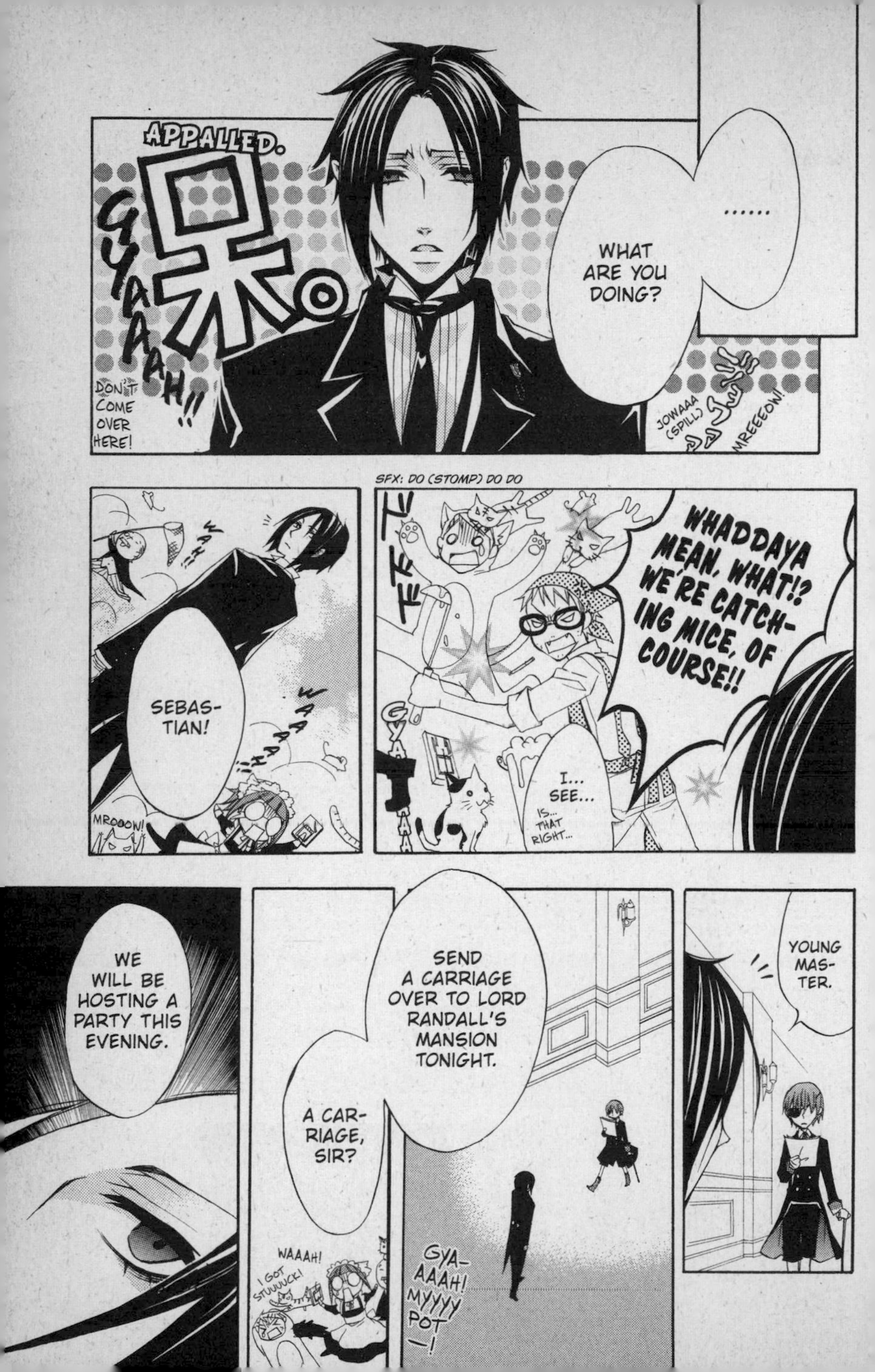
......
APPALLED.
GYAAAAAH!!
DON'T COME OVER HERE!
WHAT ARE YOU DOING?
JOWAAA (SPILL)
MREEEOW!
SFX: DO (STOMP) DO DO
WHADDAYA MEAN, WHAT!? WE'RE CATCHING MICE, OF COURSE!!
I... SEE...
IS... THAT RIGHT...
SEBASTIAN!
MROOON!
YOUNG MASTER.
SEND A CARRIAGE OVER TO LORD RANDALL'S MANSION TONIGHT.
A CARRIAGE, SIR?
GYAAAAH! MYYYY POT—!
WAAAH!
I GOT STUUUUCK!
WE WILL BE HOSTING A PARTY THIS EVENING.

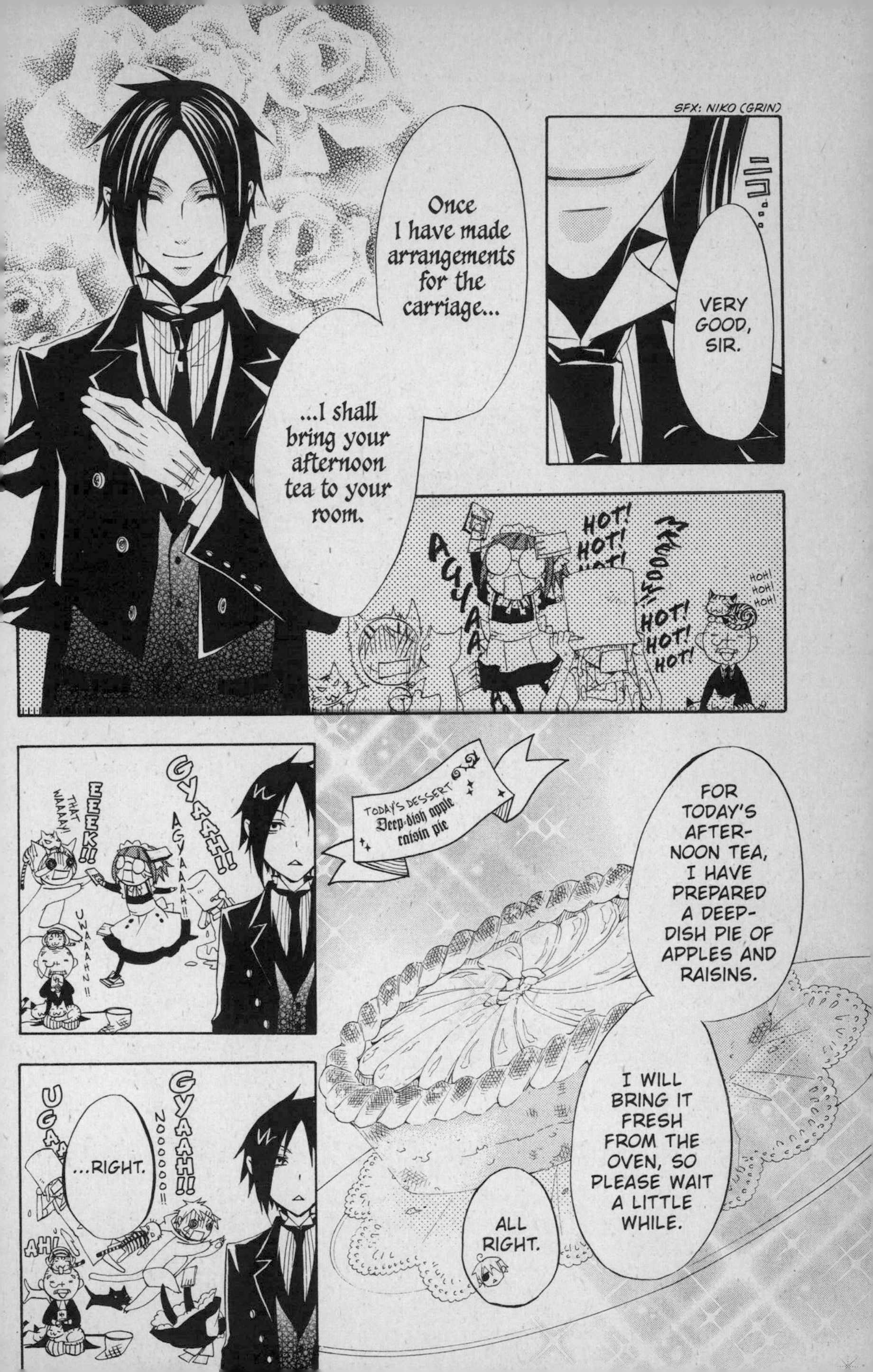
SFX: NIKO (GRIN)
VERY GOOD, SIR.
HOT! HOT!
HOH! HOH! HOH!
HOT! HOT! HOT!
Once I have made arrangements for the carriage...
...I shall bring your afternoon tea to your room.
TODAY'S DESSERT Deep-dish apple raisin pie
FOR TODAY'S AFTERNOON TEA, I HAVE PREPARED A DEEP-DISH PIE OF APPLES AND RAISINS.
I WILL BRING IT FRESH FROM THE OVEN, SO PLEASE WAIT A LITTLE WHILE.
ALL RIGHT.
GYAAAH!!
AGYAAAAH!!
EEEK!!
THAT WAAAAY!
UWAAAHN!!
...RIGHT.
GYAAAH!!
NOOOOOOO!!
AH!

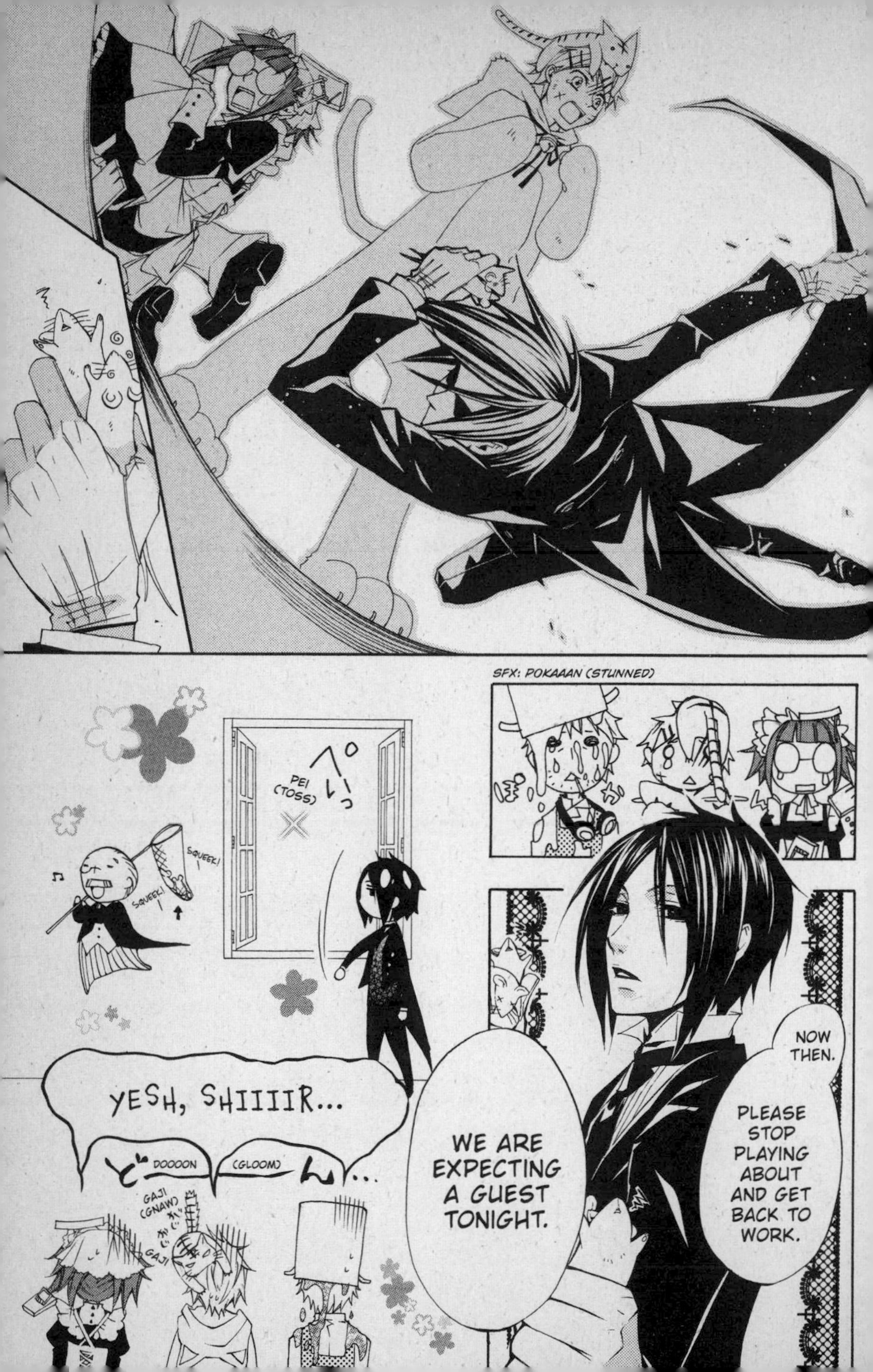
SFX: POKAAAN (STUNNED)
NOW THEN.
PLEASE STOP PLAYING ABOUT AND GET BACK TO WORK.
WE ARE EXPECTING A GUEST TONIGHT.
PEI (TOSS)
SQUEEK!
SQUEEK!
YESH, SHIIIIR...
DOOOON (GLOOM)
GAJI (GNAW)
GAJI

SFX: BUTSU (MUMBLE) BUTSU

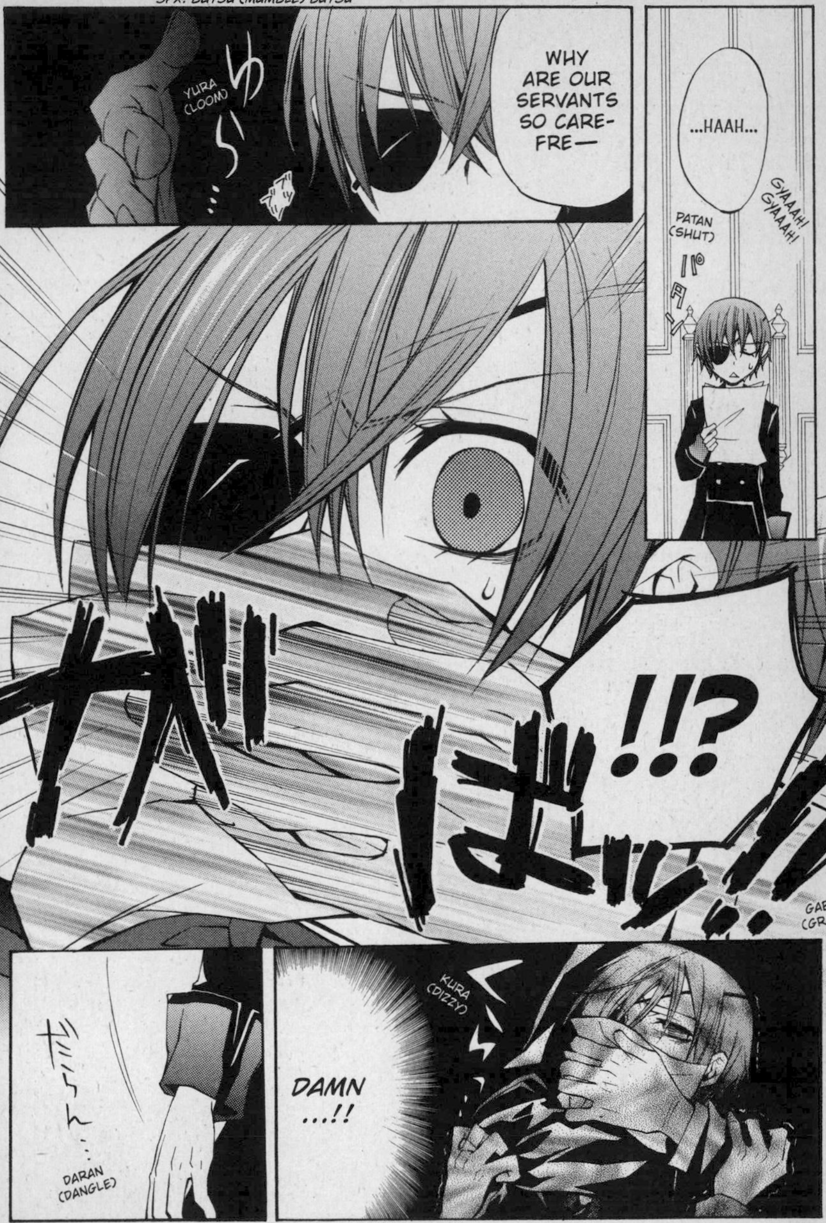
...HAAH...
GYAAAH! GYAAAH!
PATAN (SHUT)
WHY ARE OUR SERVANTS SO CARE-FRE—
YURA (LOOM)
!!?
GABA (GRAB)
KURA (DIZZY)
DAMN ...!!
DARAN (DANGLE)

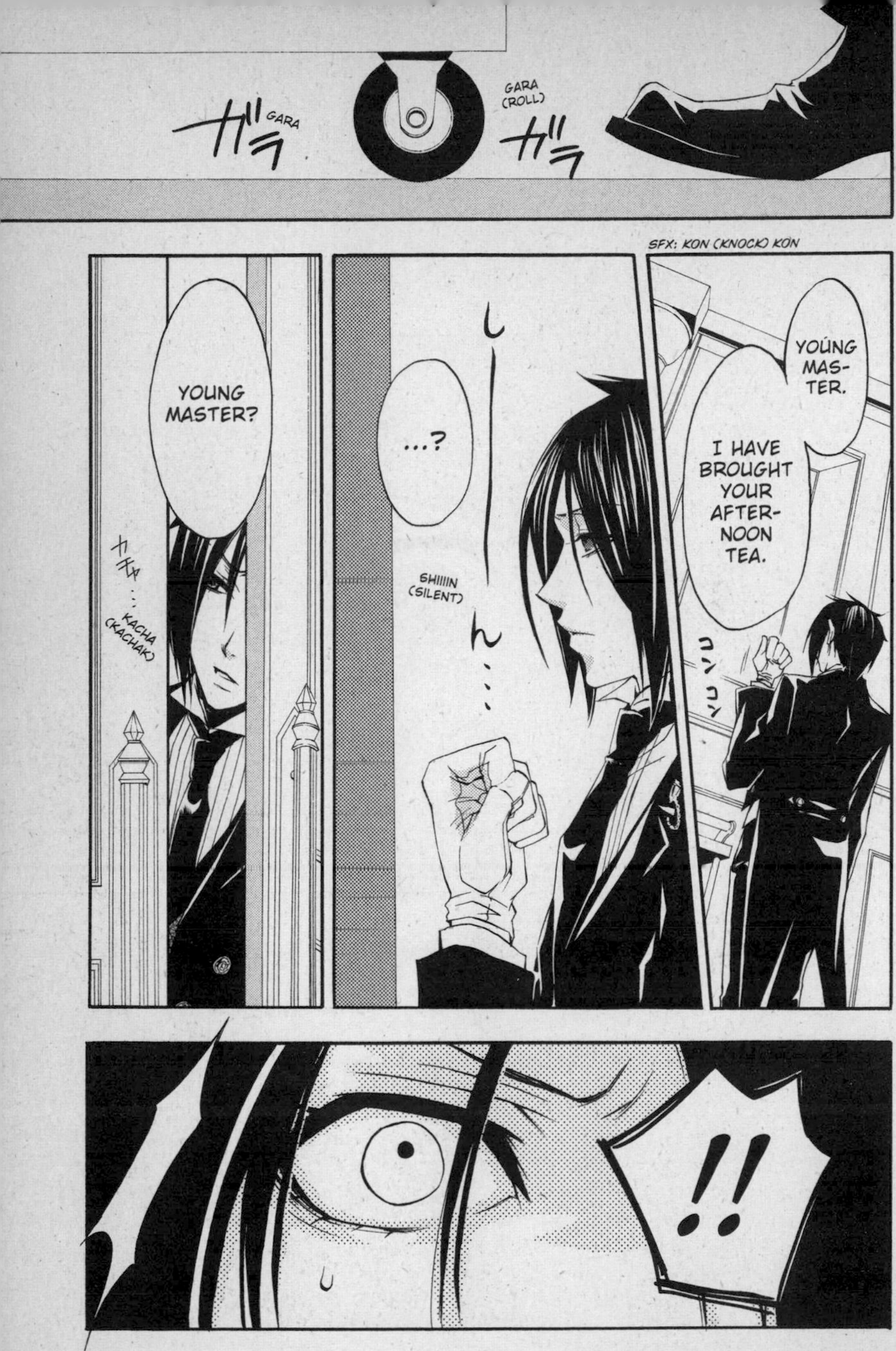
ガラ
GARA (ROLL)
ガラ
GARA
SFX: KON (KNOCK) KON
YOUNG MASTER.
I HAVE BROUGHT YOUR AFTERNOON TEA.
コンコン
...?
しーん...
SHIIIIN (SILENT)
YOUNG MASTER?
カチャ...
KACHA (KACHAK)
!!

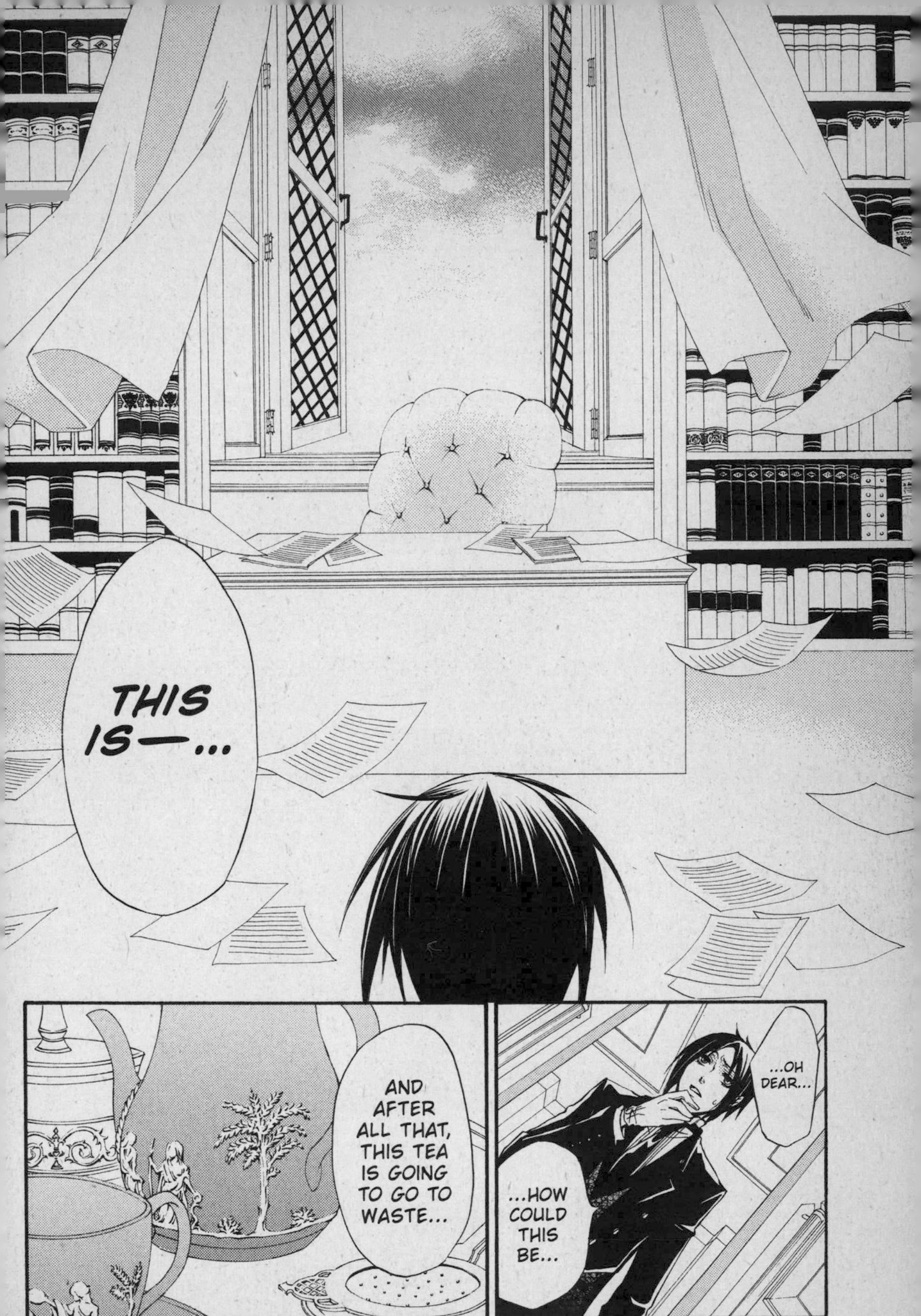
THIS IS—...
...OH DEAR...
...HOW COULD THIS BE...
AND AFTER ALL THAT, THIS TEA IS GOING TO GO TO WASTE...

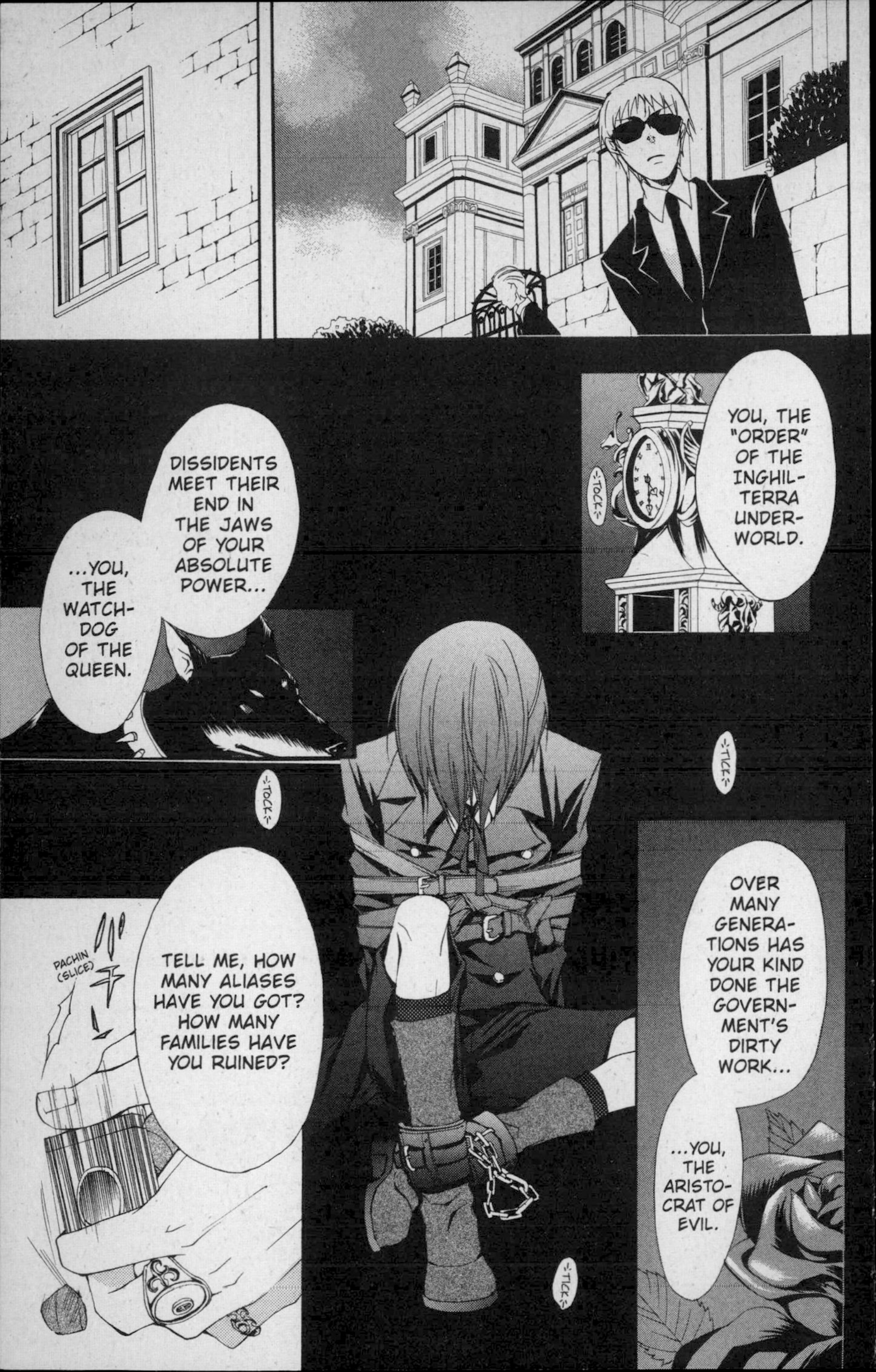
YOU, THE "ORDER" OF THE INGHIL-TERRA UNDER-WORLD.
-TOCK-
DISSIDENTS MEET THEIR END IN THE JAWS OF YOUR ABSOLUTE POWER...
...YOU, THE WATCH-DOG OF THE QUEEN.
-TICK-
-TOCK-
OVER MANY GENERA-TIONS HAS YOUR KIND DONE THE GOVERN-MENT'S DIRTY WORK...
...YOU, THE ARISTO-CRAT OF EVIL.
-TICK-
TELL ME, HOW MANY ALIASES HAVE YOU GOT? HOW MANY FAMILIES HAVE YOU RUINED?
PACHIN (SLICE)

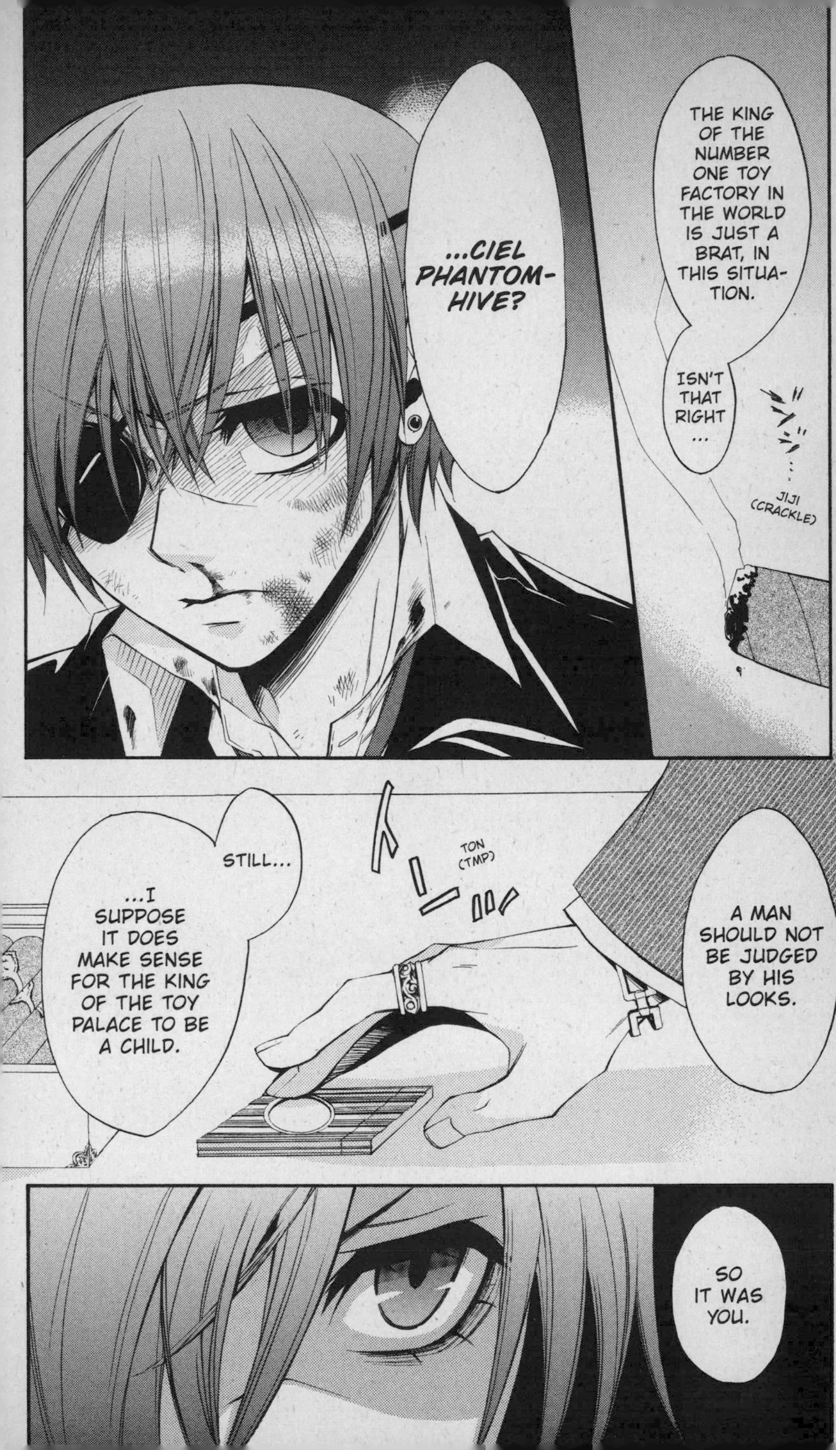
THE KING OF THE NUMBER ONE TOY FACTORY IN THE WORLD IS JUST A BRAT, IN THIS SITUATION.
ISN'T THAT RIGHT...
JIJI (CRACKLE)
...CIEL PHANTOMHIVE?
A MAN SHOULD NOT BE JUDGED BY HIS LOOKS.
TON (TMP)
STILL...
...I SUPPOSE IT DOES MAKE SENSE FOR THE KING OF THE TOY PALACE TO BE A CHILD.
SO IT WAS YOU.

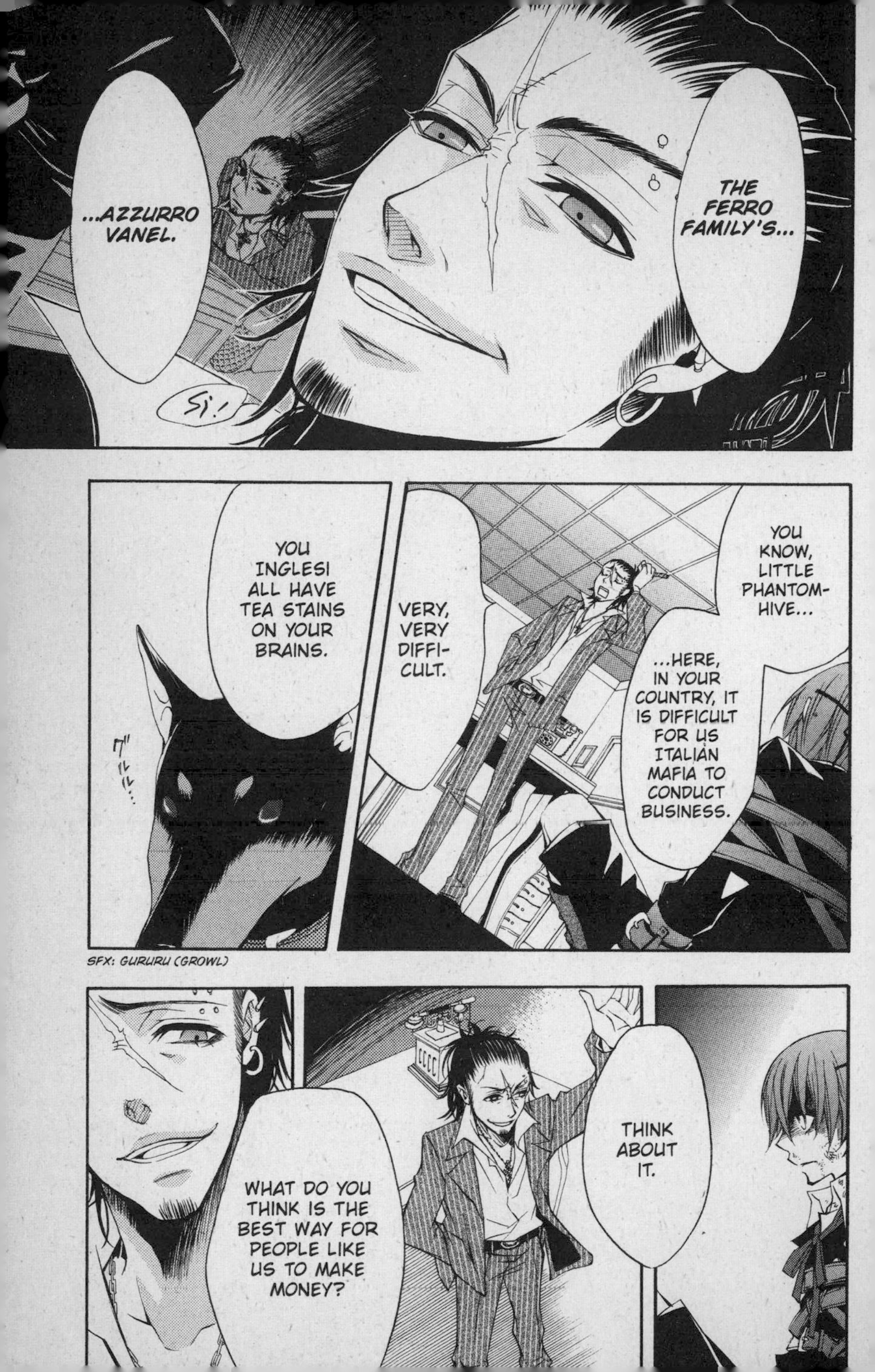
THE FERRO FAMILY'S...
...AZZURRO VANEL.
Sì!
YOU KNOW, LITTLE PHANTOM-HIVE...
...HERE, IN YOUR COUNTRY, IT IS DIFFICULT FOR US ITALIAN MAFIA TO CONDUCT BUSINESS.
VERY, VERY DIFFI-CULT.
YOU INGLESI ALL HAVE TEA STAINS ON YOUR BRAINS.
グルル…
THINK ABOUT IT.
WHAT DO YOU THINK IS THE BEST WAY FOR PEOPLE LIKE US TO MAKE MONEY?

SFX: GURURU (GROWL)

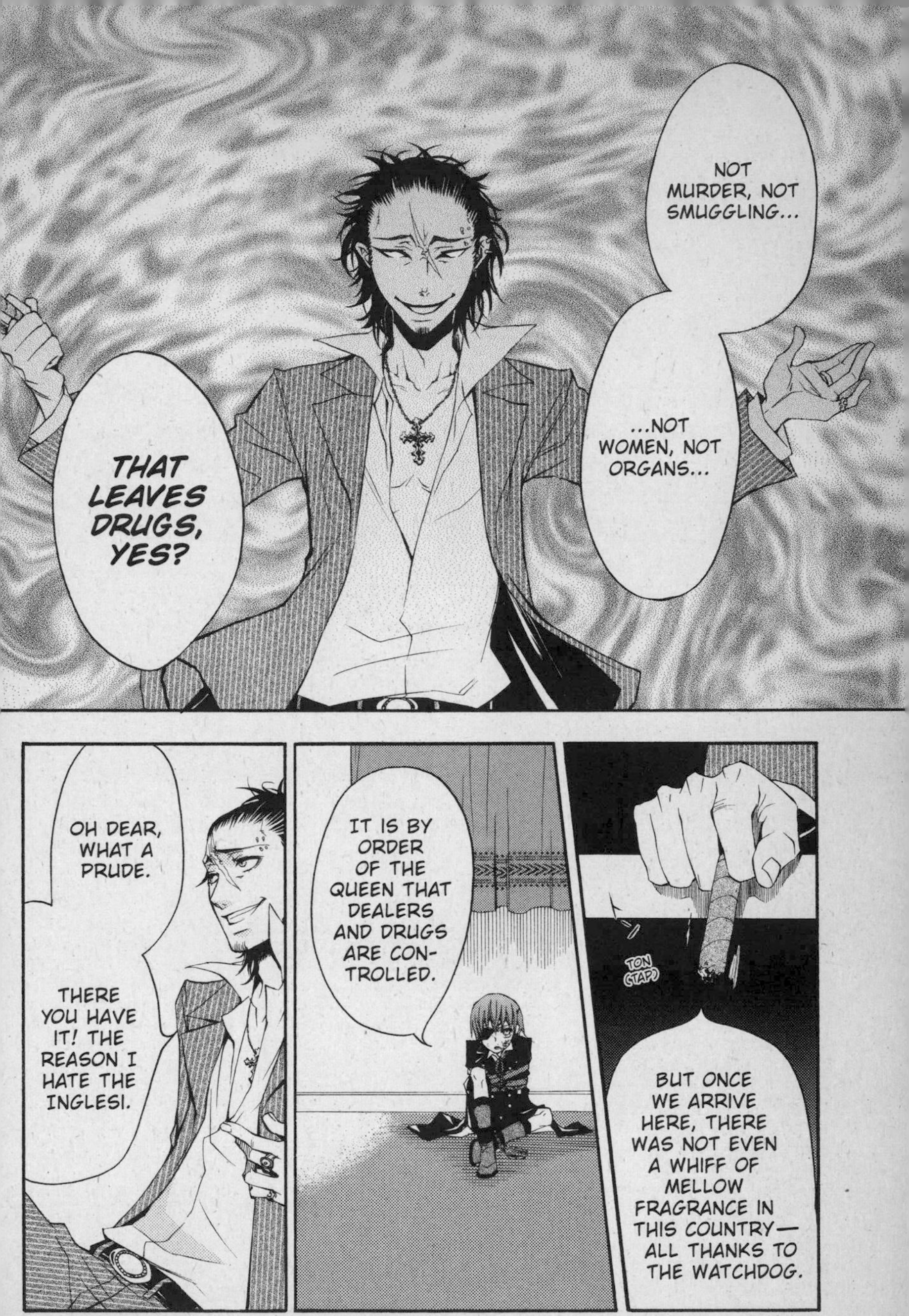

NOT MURDER, NOT SMUGGLING...
...NOT WOMEN, NOT ORGANS...
THAT LEAVES DRUGS, YES?
TON (TAP)
BUT ONCE WE ARRIVE HERE, THERE WAS NOT EVEN A WHIFF OF MELLOW FRAGRANCE IN THIS COUNTRY— ALL THANKS TO THE WATCHDOG.
IT IS BY ORDER OF THE QUEEN THAT DEALERS AND DRUGS ARE CON-TROLLED.
OH DEAR, WHAT A PRUDE.
THERE YOU HAVE IT! THE REASON I HATE THE INGLESI.

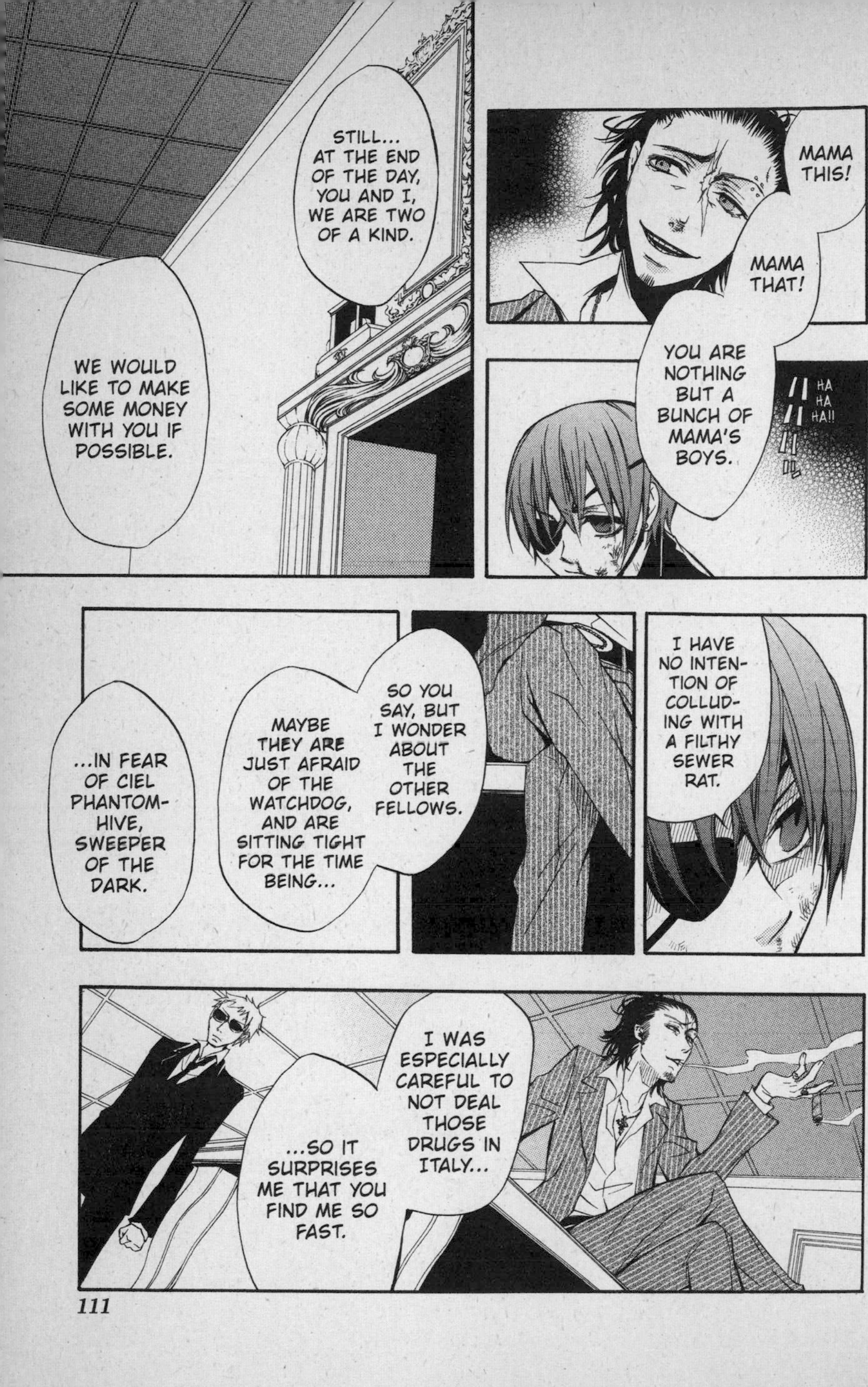
MAMA THIS!
MAMA THAT!
YOU ARE NOTHING BUT A BUNCH OF MAMA'S BOYS.
HA HA HA!!
STILL... AT THE END OF THE DAY, YOU AND I, WE ARE TWO OF A KIND.
WE WOULD LIKE TO MAKE SOME MONEY WITH YOU IF POSSIBLE.
I HAVE NO INTEN-TION OF COLLUD-ING WITH A FILTHY SEWER RAT.
SO YOU SAY, BUT I WONDER ABOUT THE OTHER FELLOWS.
MAYBE THEY ARE JUST AFRAID OF THE WATCHDOG, AND ARE SITTING TIGHT FOR THE TIME BEING...
...IN FEAR OF CIEL PHANTOM-HIVE, SWEEPER OF THE DARK.
I WAS ESPECIALLY CAREFUL TO NOT DEAL THOSE DRUGS IN ITALY...
...SO IT SURPRISES ME THAT YOU FIND ME SO FAST.

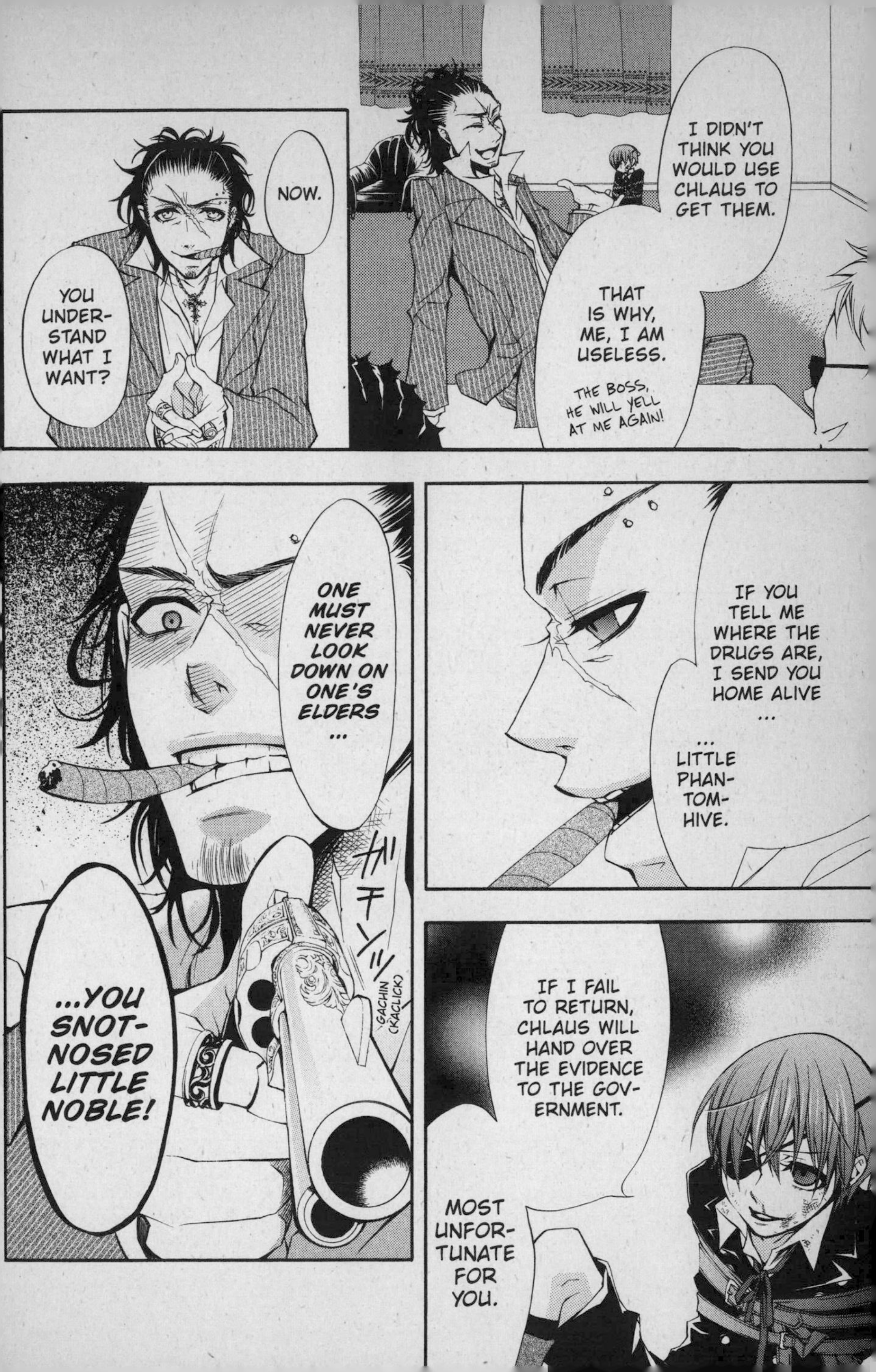
I DIDN'T THINK YOU WOULD USE CHLAUS TO GET THEM.
THAT IS WHY, ME, I AM USELESS.
THE BOSS, HE WILL YELL AT ME AGAIN!
NOW.
YOU UNDER-STAND WHAT I WANT?
IF YOU TELL ME WHERE THE DRUGS ARE, I SEND YOU HOME ALIVE ...
... LITTLE PHAN-TOM-HIVE.
IF I FAIL TO RETURN, CHLAUS WILL HAND OVER THE EVIDENCE TO THE GOV-ERNMENT.
MOST UNFOR-TUNATE FOR YOU.
ONE MUST NEVER LOOK DOWN ON ONE'S ELDERS ...
GACHIN (KACLICK)
...YOU SNOT-NOSED LITTLE NOBLE!

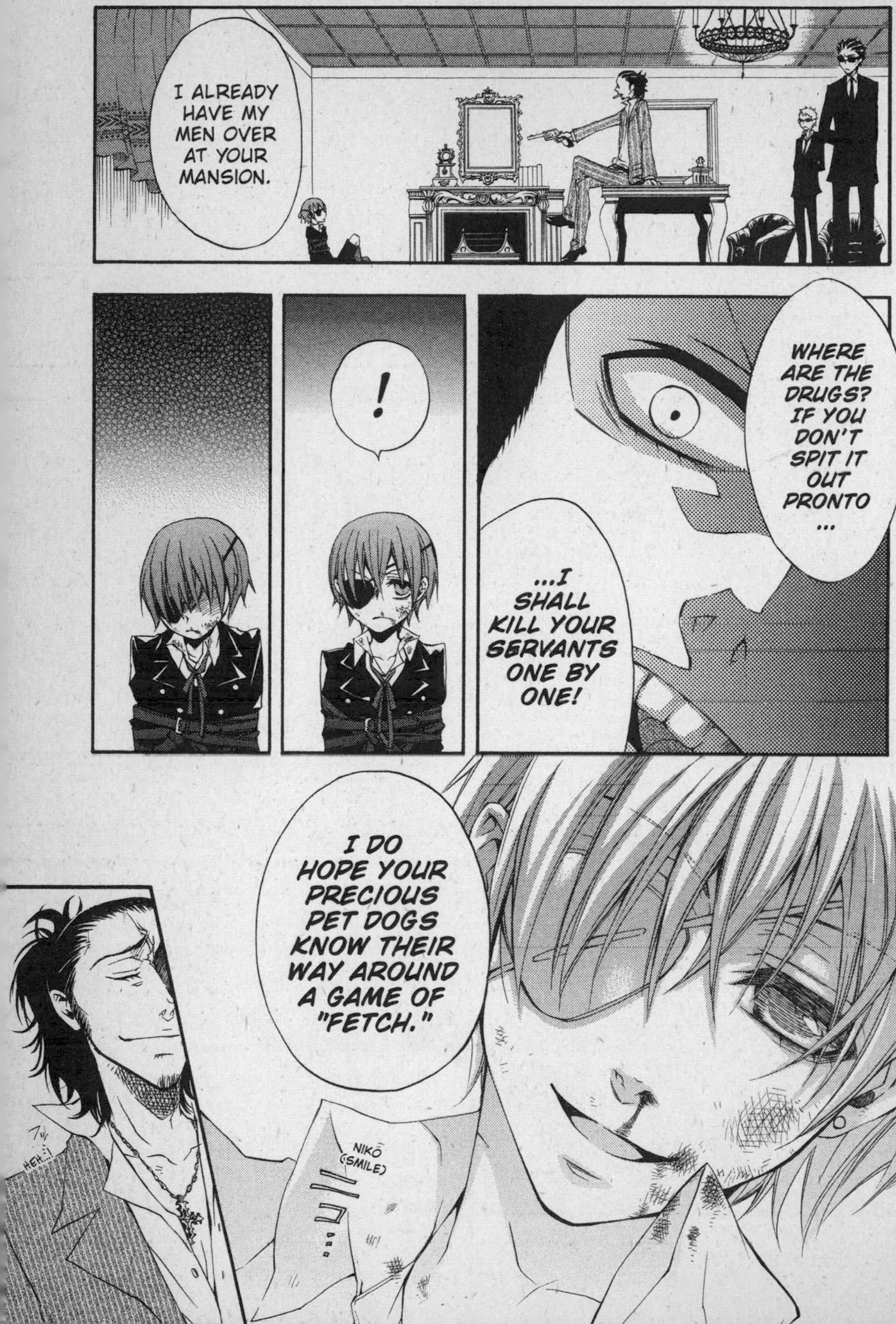
I ALREADY HAVE MY MEN OVER AT YOUR MANSION.
WHERE ARE THE DRUGS? IF YOU DON'T SPIT IT OUT PRONTO ...
...I SHALL KILL YOUR SERVANTS ONE BY ONE!
!
I DO HOPE YOUR PRECIOUS PET DOGS KNOW THEIR WAY AROUND A GAME OF "FETCH."
NIKO (SMILE)
HEH...!

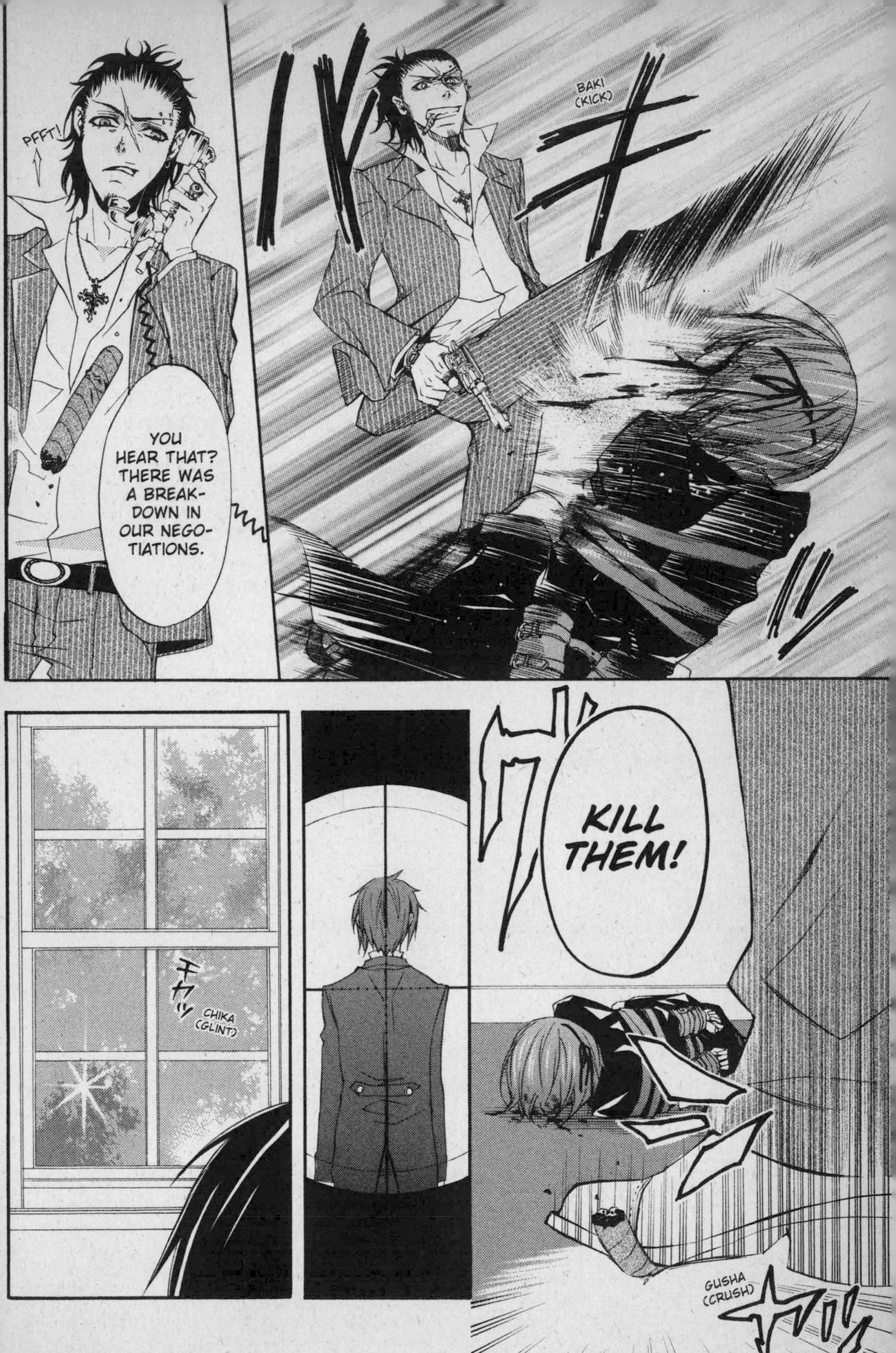
BAKI (KICK)
PFFT!
YOU HEAR THAT? THERE WAS A BREAK-DOWN IN OUR NEGO-TIATIONS.
KILL THEM!
GUSHA (CRUSH)
CHIKA (GLINT)

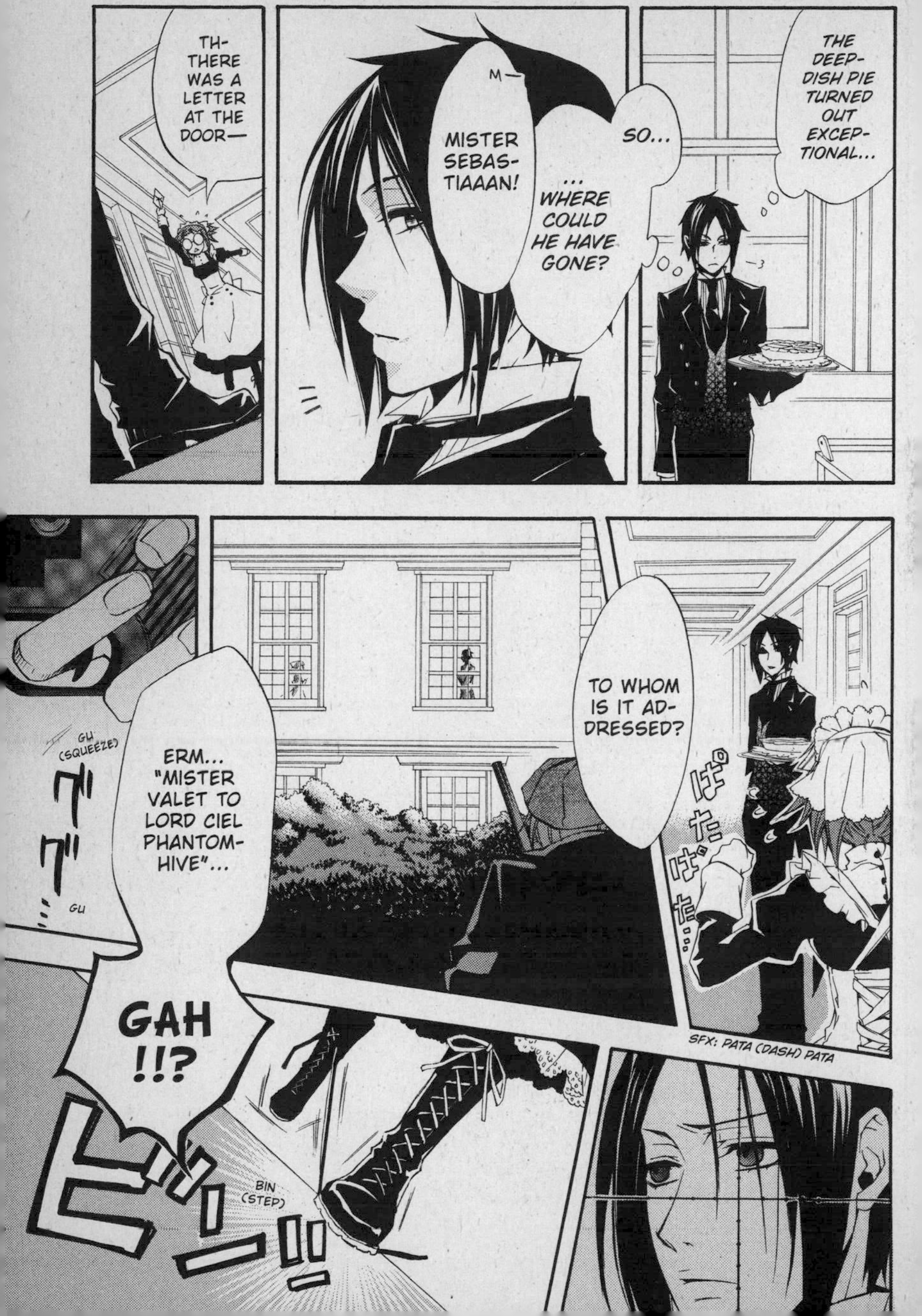
THE DEEP-DISH PIE TURNED OUT EXCEP-TIONAL...
SO...
...WHERE COULD HE HAVE GONE?
M—
MISTER SEBAS-TIAAAN!
TH-THERE WAS A LETTER AT THE DOOR—
TO WHOM IS IT AD-DRESSED?
SFX: PATA (DASH) PATA
ERM... "MISTER VALET TO LORD CIEL PHANTOM-HIVE"...
GU (SQUEEZE)
GU
GAH !!?
BIN (STEP)

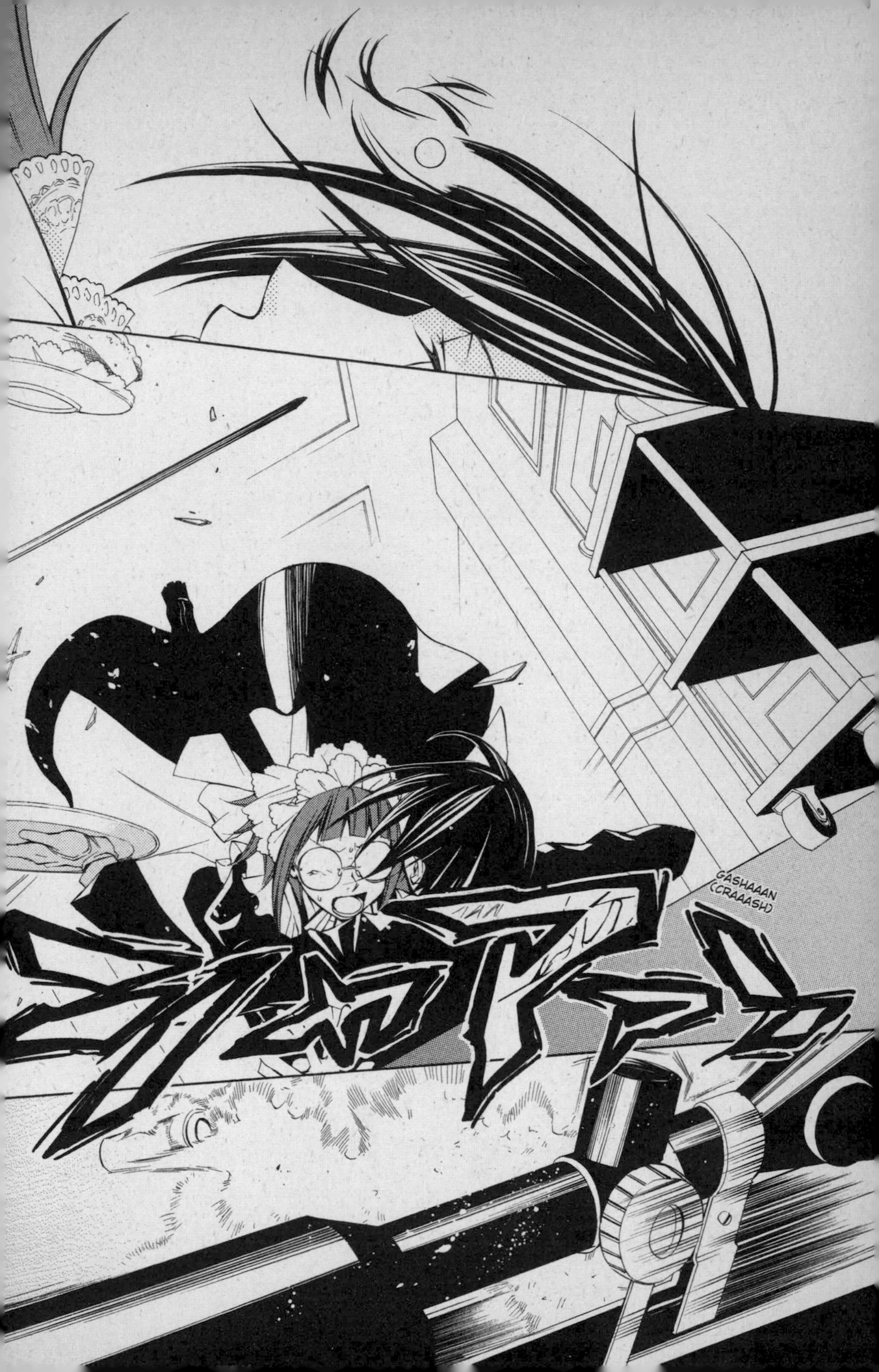
GASHAAAN
(CRAAASH)

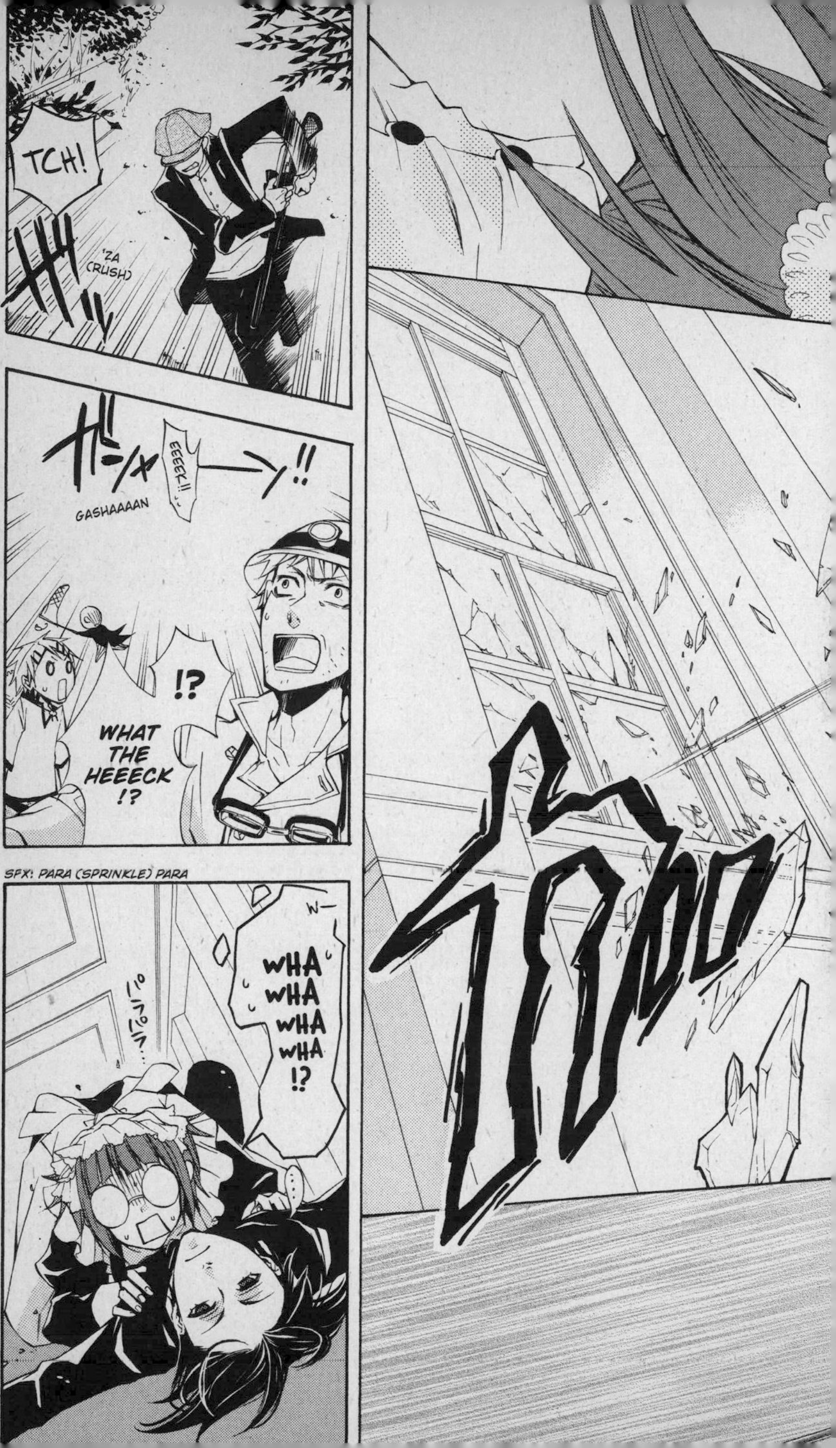
TCH!
'ZA (RUSH)
GASHAAAAN
EEEEK!!
!?
WHAT THE HEEECK!?
SFX: PARA (SPRINKLE) PARA
W--
WHA WHA WHA WHA!?

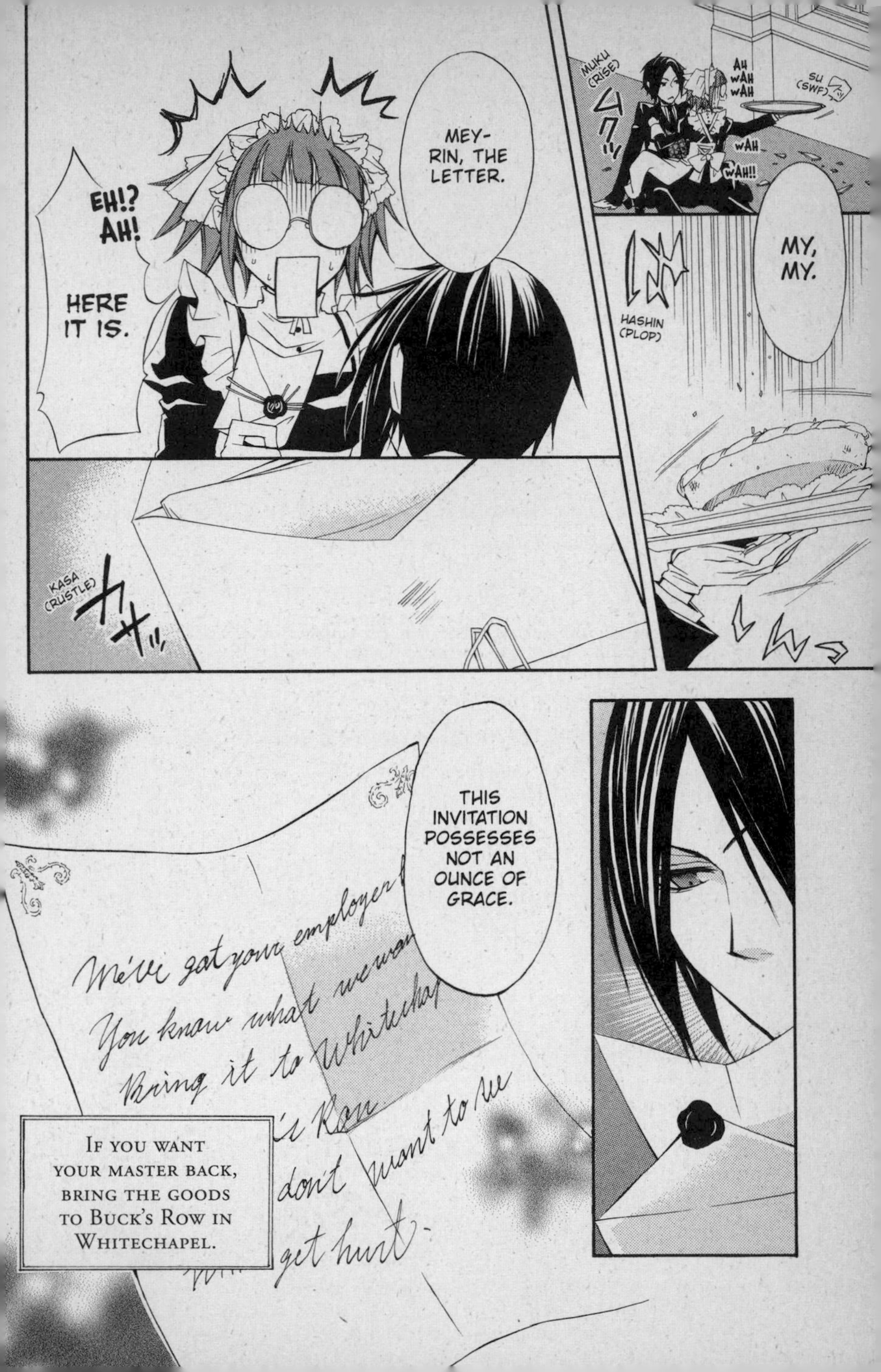
MUKU (RISE)
AH WAH WAH
SU (SWF)
WAH WAH!!
MY, MY.
HASHIN (PLOP)
MEY-RIN, THE LETTER.
EH!? AH!
HERE IT IS.
KASA (RUSTLE)
THIS INVITATION POSSESSES NOT AN OUNCE OF GRACE.
We've got your employer
You know what we wan
Bring it to Whitechap
's Row
don't want to see
get hurt
IF YOU WANT YOUR MASTER BACK, BRING THE GOODS TO BUCK'S ROW IN WHITECHAPEL.

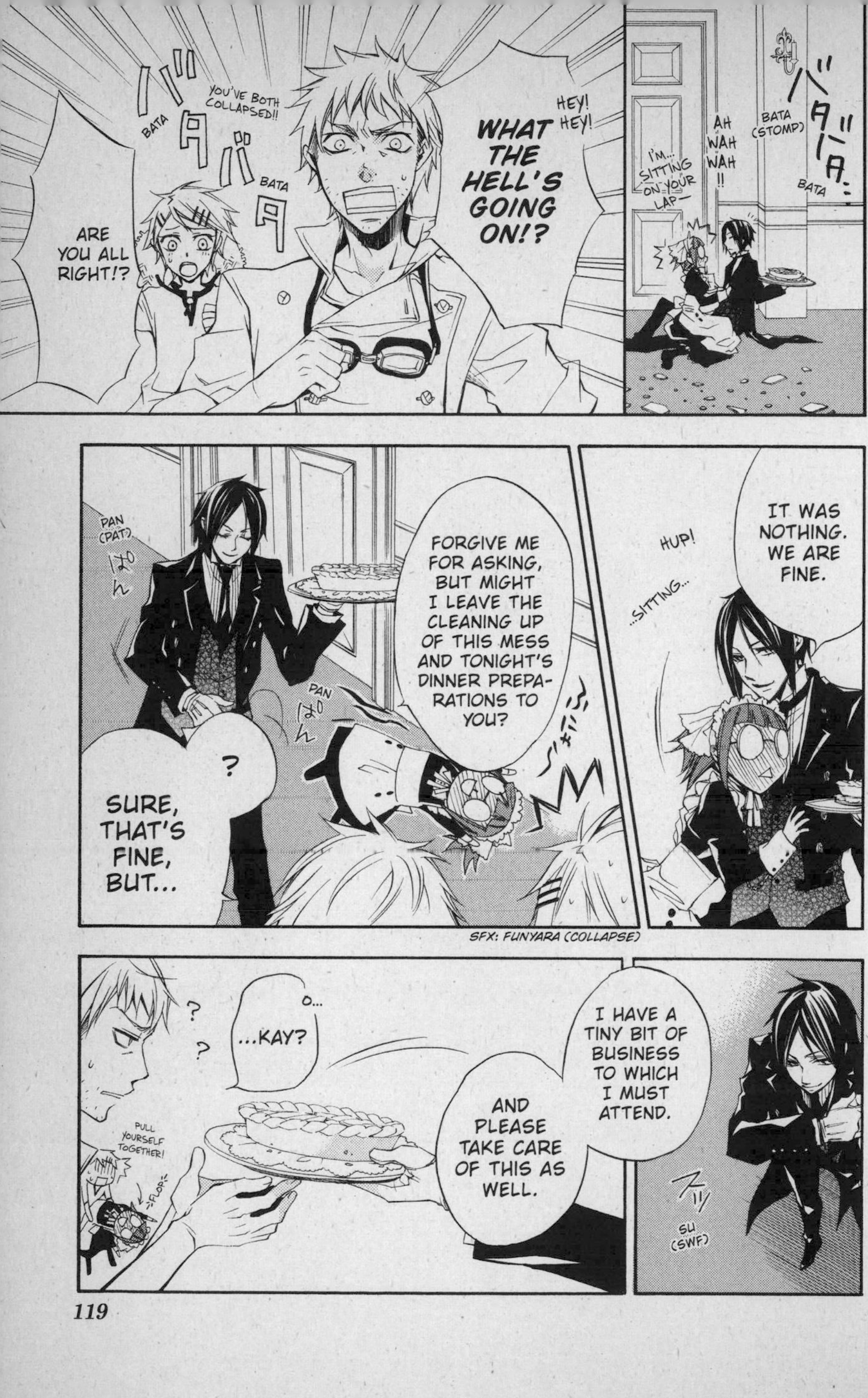
BATA (STOMP)
BATA
AH WAH WAH !!
I'M... SITTING ON YOUR LAP
WHAT THE HELL'S GOING ON!?
HEY! HEY!
YOU'VE BOTH COLLAPSED!!
BATA
BATA
ARE YOU ALL RIGHT!?
IT WAS NOTHING. WE ARE FINE.
HUP!
...SITTING...
FORGIVE ME FOR ASKING, BUT MIGHT I LEAVE THE CLEANING UP OF THIS MESS AND TONIGHT'S DINNER PREPARATIONS TO YOU?
PAN (PAT)
PAN
?
SURE, THAT'S FINE, BUT...
SFX: FUNYARA (COLLAPSE)
SU (SWF)
I HAVE A TINY BIT OF BUSINESS TO WHICH I MUST ATTEND.
AND PLEASE TAKE CARE OF THIS AS WELL.
O... ...KAY?
PULL YOURSELF TOGETHER!
FLOP

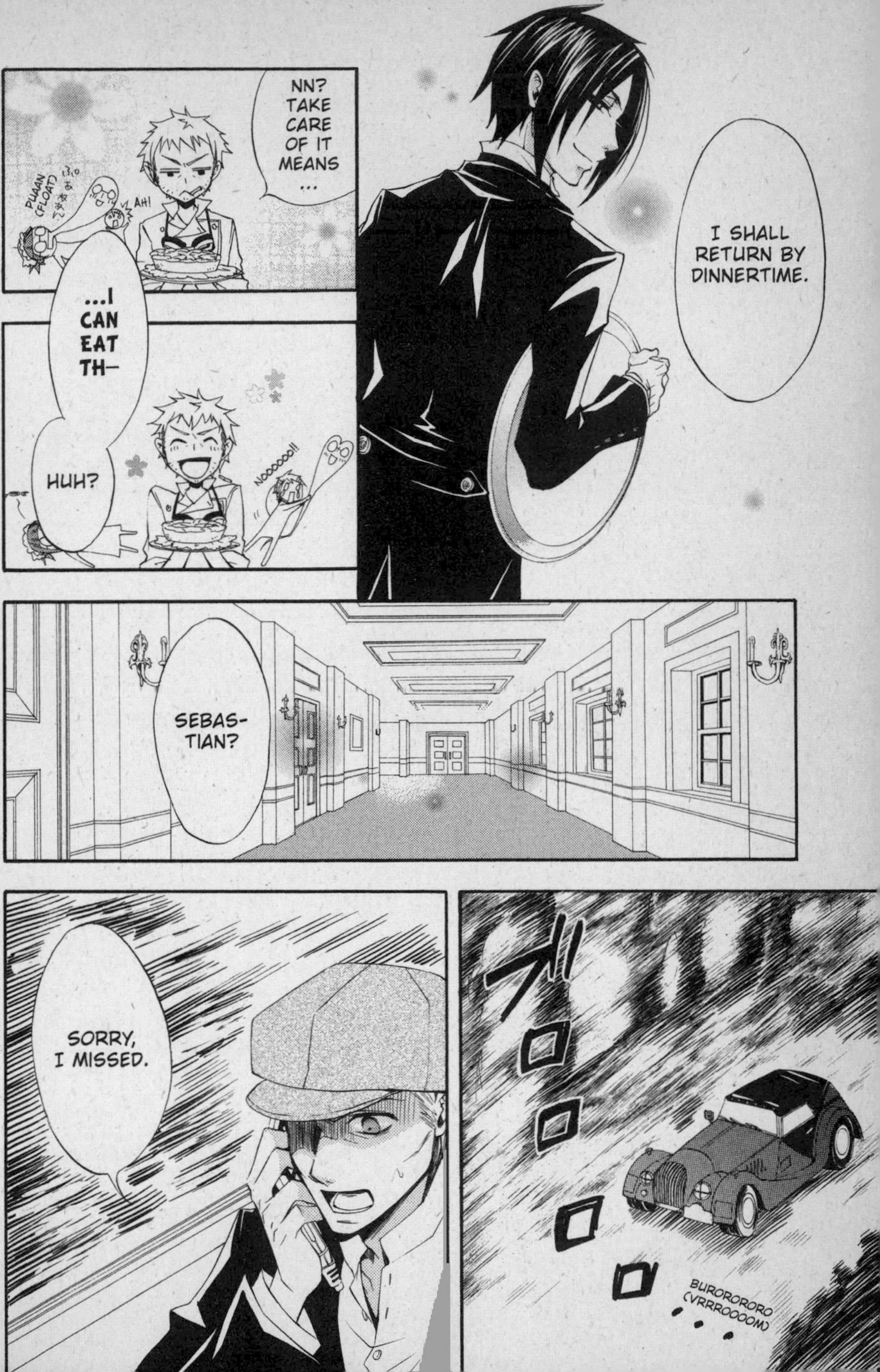
I SHALL RETURN BY DINNERTIME.
NN? TAKE CARE OF IT MEANS ...
PUAAN (FLOAT)
AH!
...I CAN EAT TH—
HUH?
NOOOOOO!!
SEBAS-TIAN?
BURORORORO (VRRROOOOM)
SORRY, I MISSED.

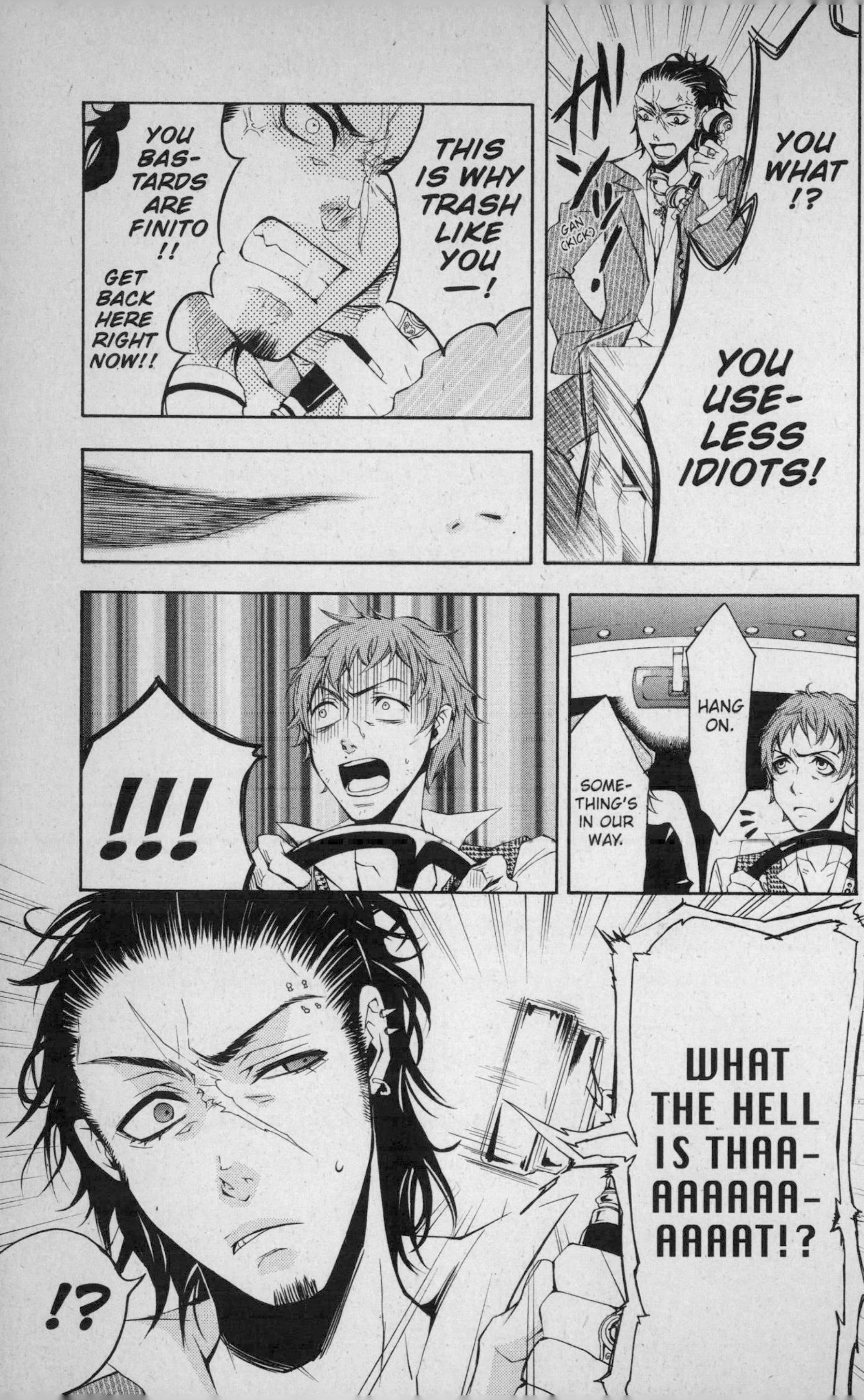
YOU WHAT!?
GAN (KICK)
YOU USELESS IDIOTS!
THIS IS WHY TRASH LIKE YOU—!
YOU BASTARDS ARE FINITO!!
GET BACK HERE RIGHT NOW!!
HANG ON.
SOMETHING'S IN OUR WAY.
!!!
WHAT THE HELL IS THAAAAAAAAAAAT!?
!?

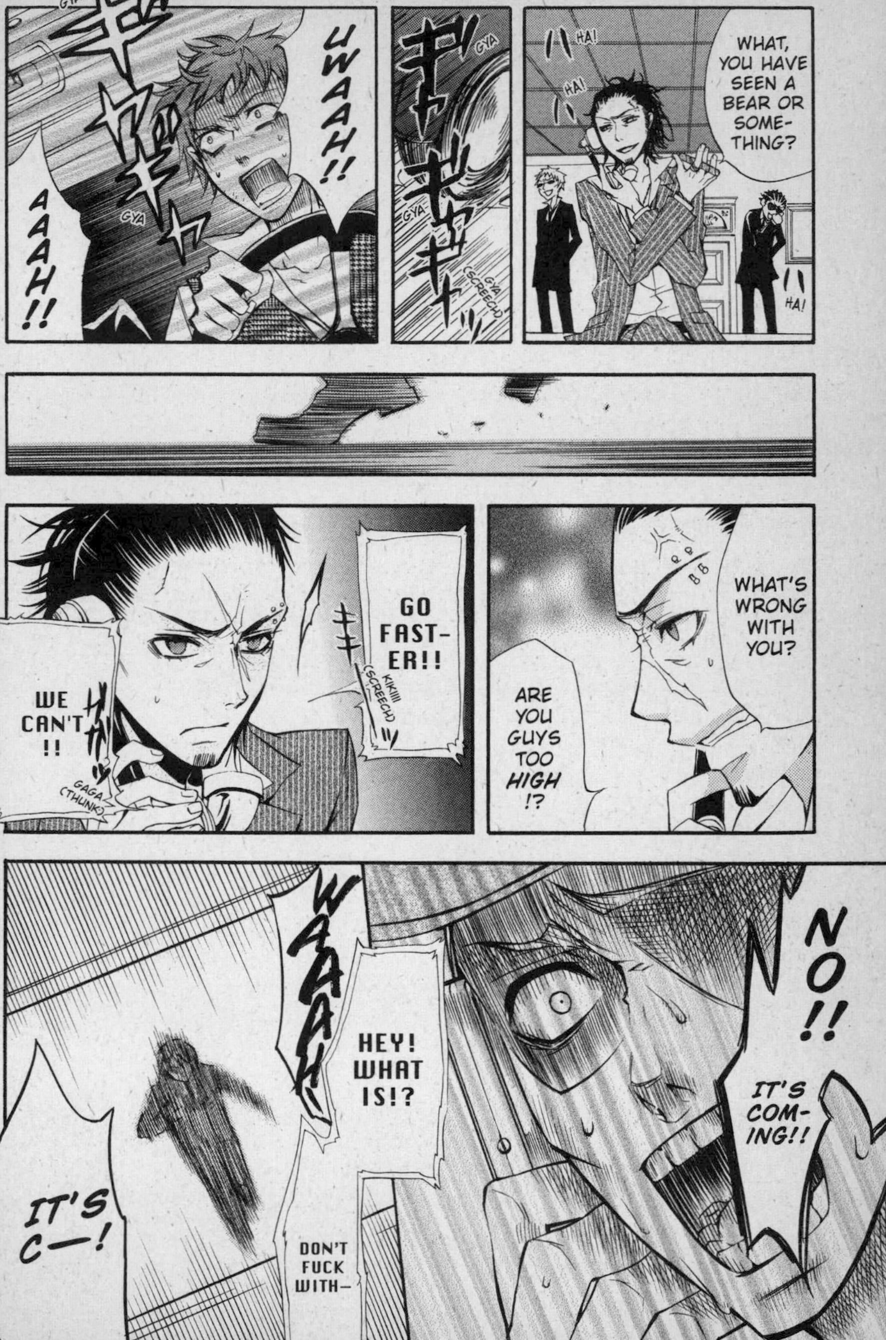
WHAT, YOU HAVE SEEN A BEAR OR SOMETHING?
HA!
HA!
HA!
GYA
GYA
GYA (SCREECH)
UWAAAH!!
AAAAH!!
GYA
GYA
WHAT'S WRONG WITH YOU?
ARE YOU GUYS TOO HIGH!?
GO FASTER!!
KIKIII (SCREECH)
WE CAN'T!!
GAGA (THUNK)
NO!!
IT'S COMING!!
WAAAAH
HEY! WHAT IS!?
DON'T FUCK WITH—
IT'S C—!

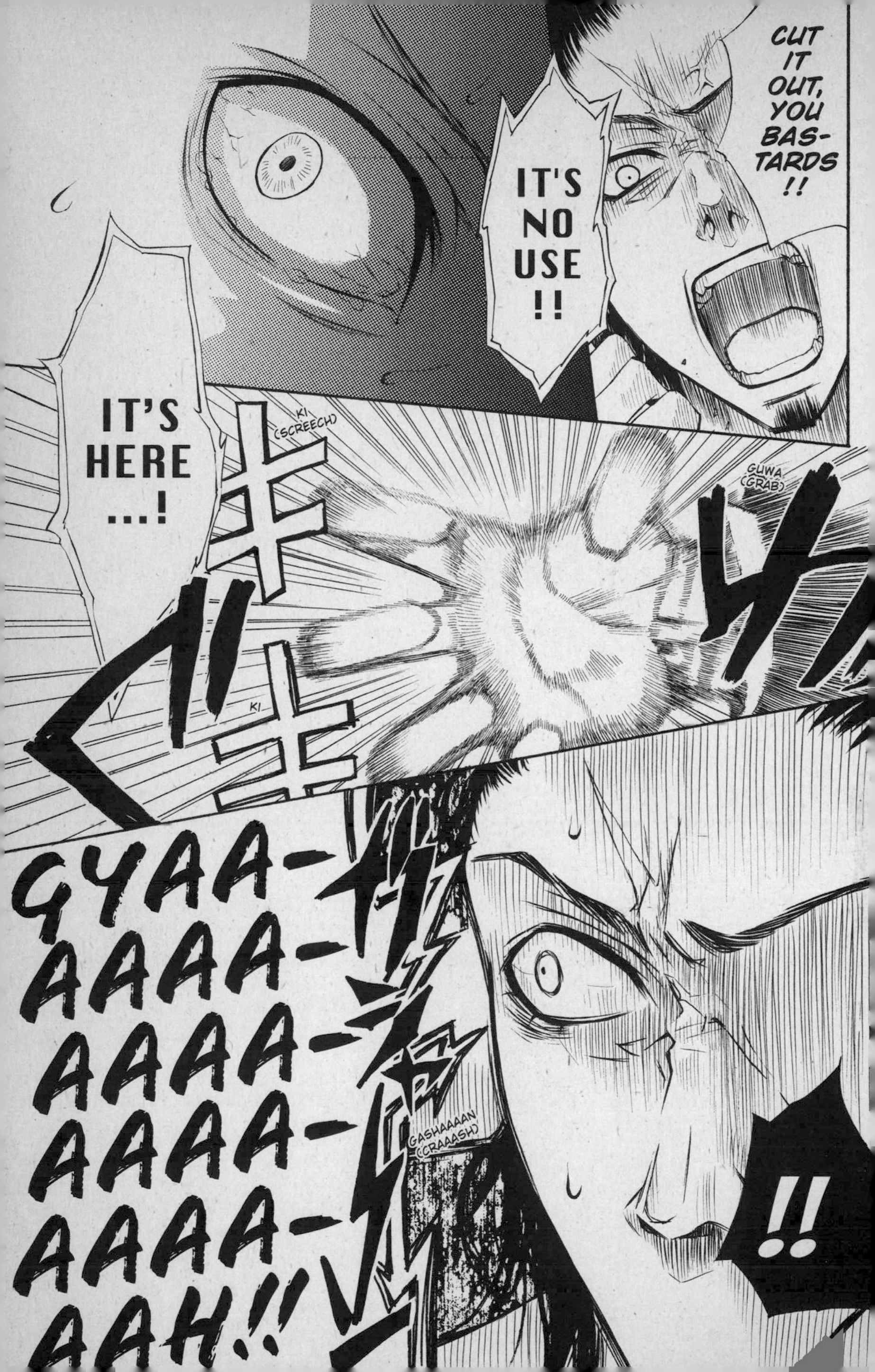
CUT IT OUT, YOU BASTARDS!!
IT'S NO USE!!
IT'S HERE...!
GUWA (GRAB)
KI (SCREECH)
KI
!!
GASHAAAAN (CRAAASH)
GYAA-AAAA-AAAA-AAAA-AAAA-AAH!!

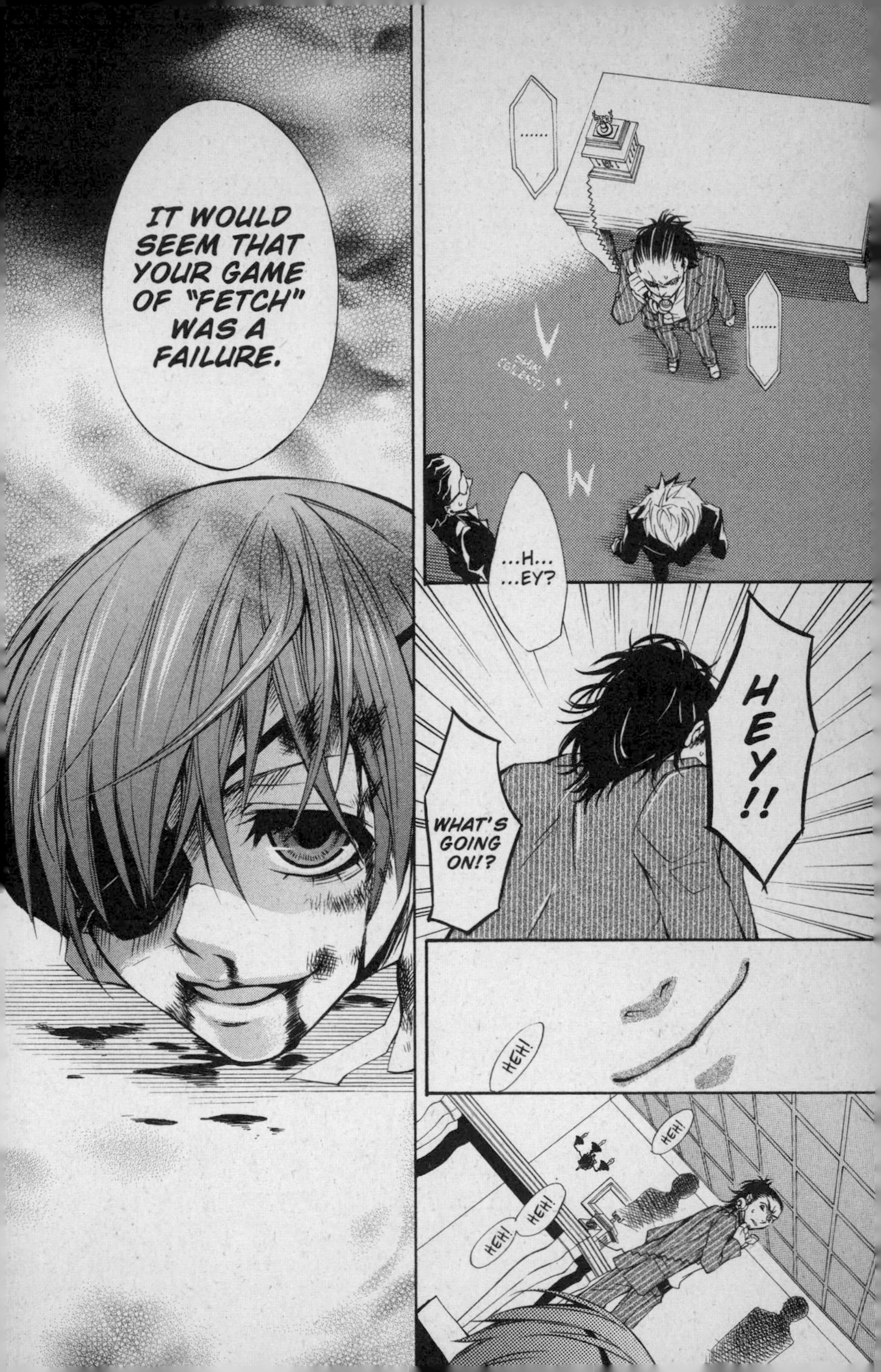
......
......
...H...
...EY?
HEY!!
WHAT'S GOING ON!?
HEH!
HEH!
HEH!
HEH!
IT WOULD SEEM THAT YOUR GAME OF "FETCH" WAS A FAILURE.

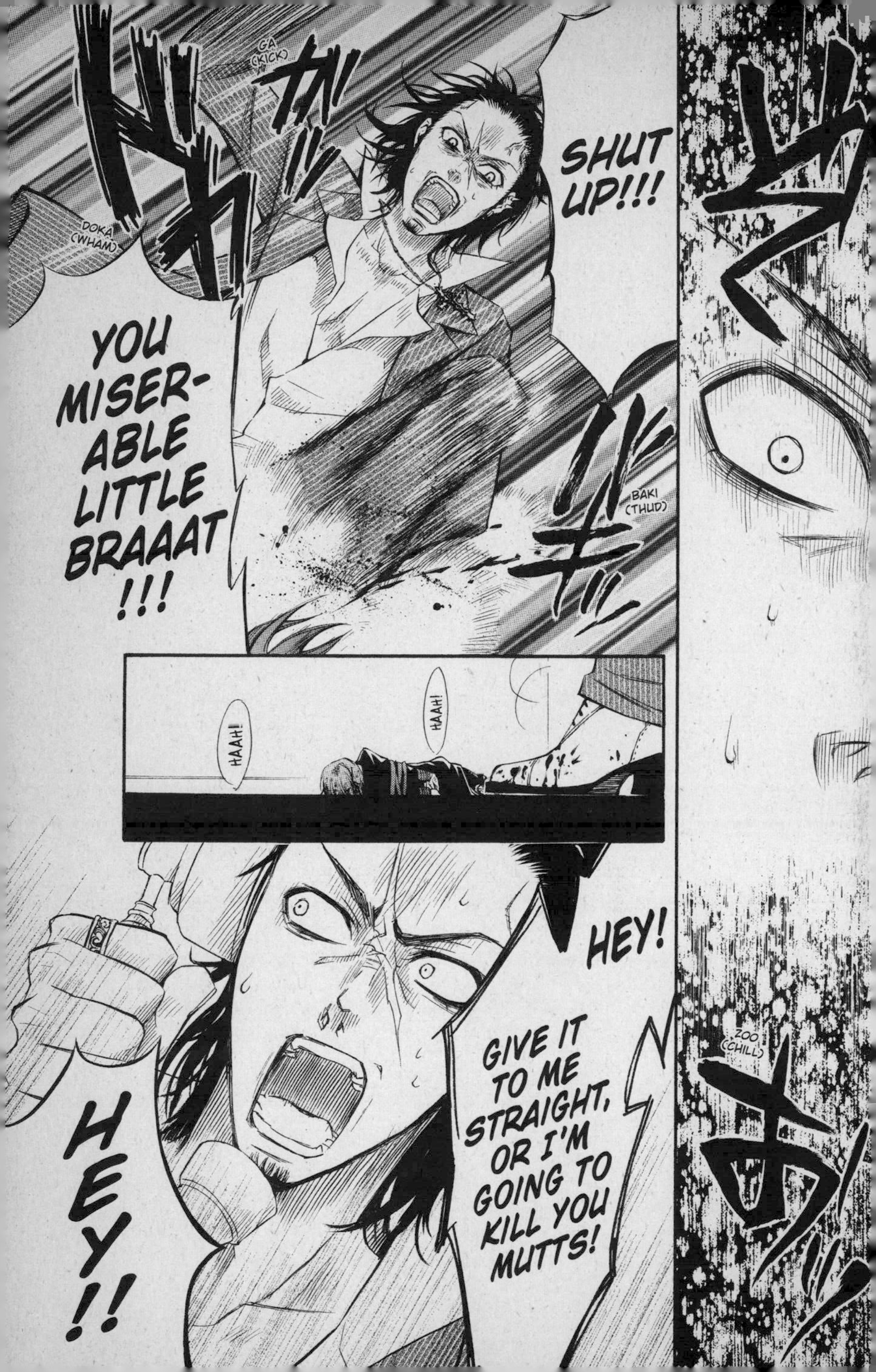
ZOO (CHILL)
GA (KICK)
SHUT UP!!!
DOKA (WHAM)
BAKI (THUD)
YOU MISER-ABLE LITTLE BRAAAT!!!
HAAH!
HAAH!
HEY!
GIVE IT TO ME STRAIGHT, OR I'M GOING TO KILL YOU MUTTS!
HEY HEY!!

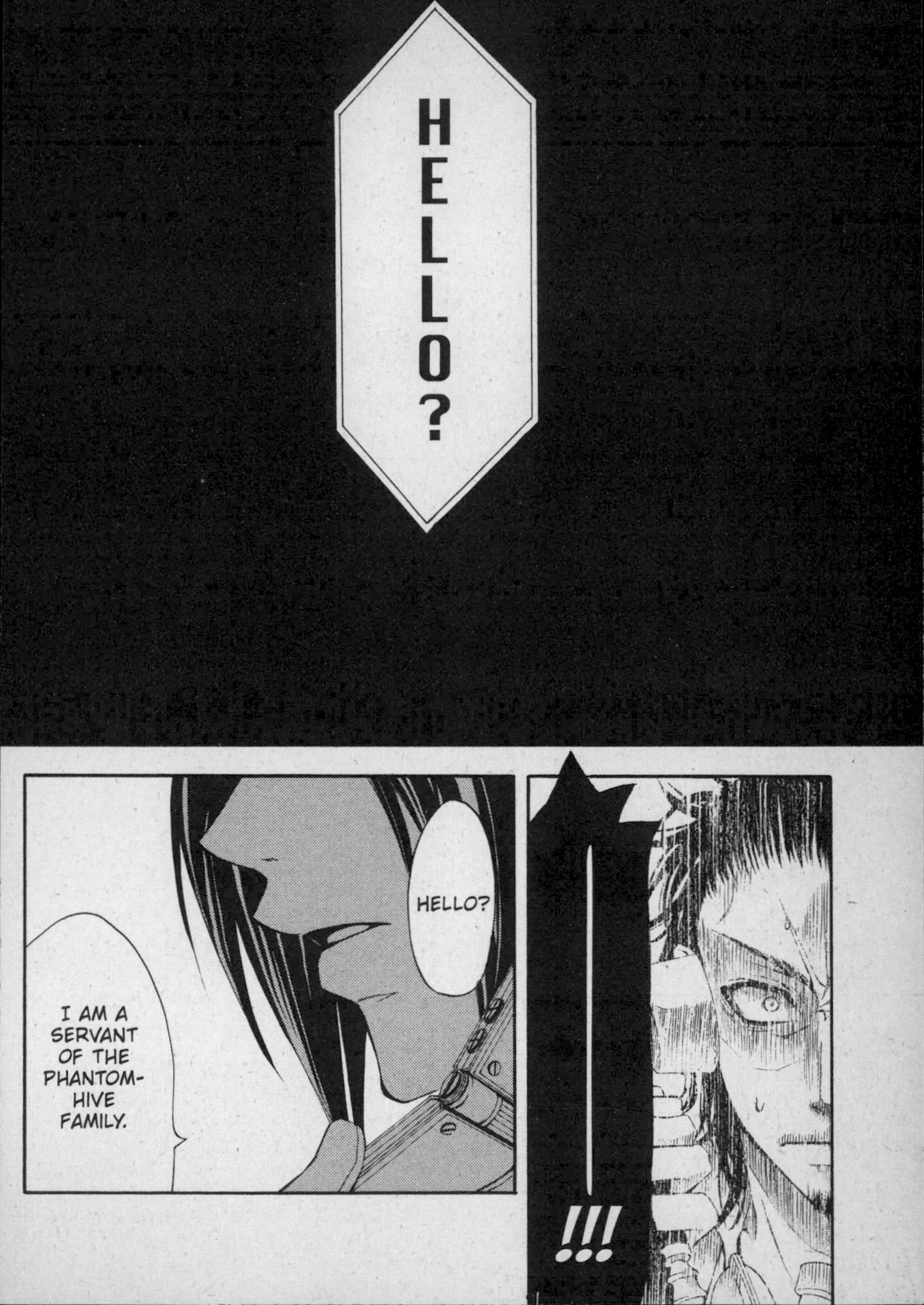
HELLO?
!!!
HELLO?
I AM A SERVANT OF THE PHANTOM-HIVE FAMILY.

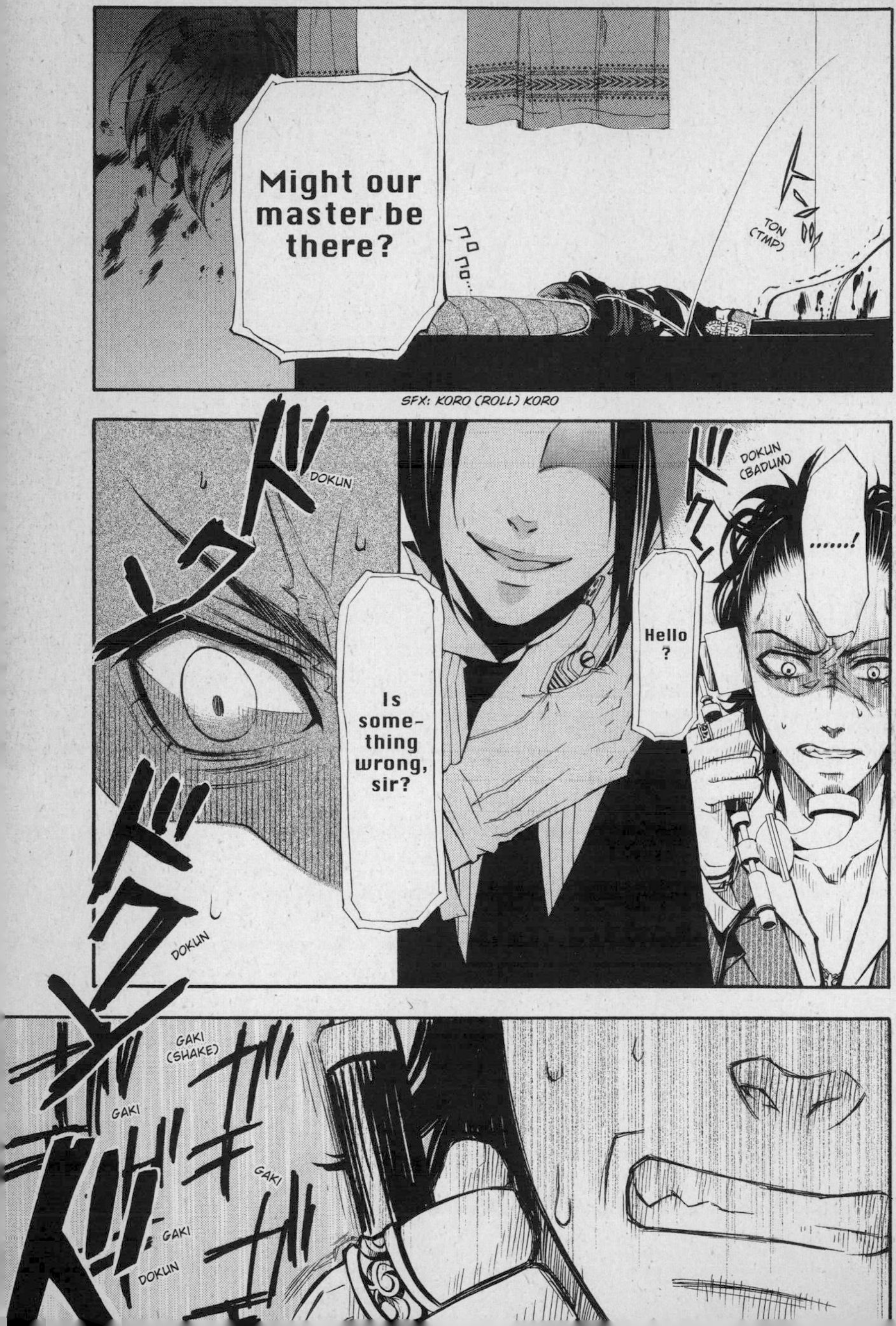

TON (TMP)
Might our master be there?
SFX: KORO (ROLL) KORO
DOKUN (BADUM)
......!
Hello?
Is something wrong, sir?
DOKUN
DOKUN
GAKI (SHAKE)
GAKI
GAKI
GAKI
DOKUN

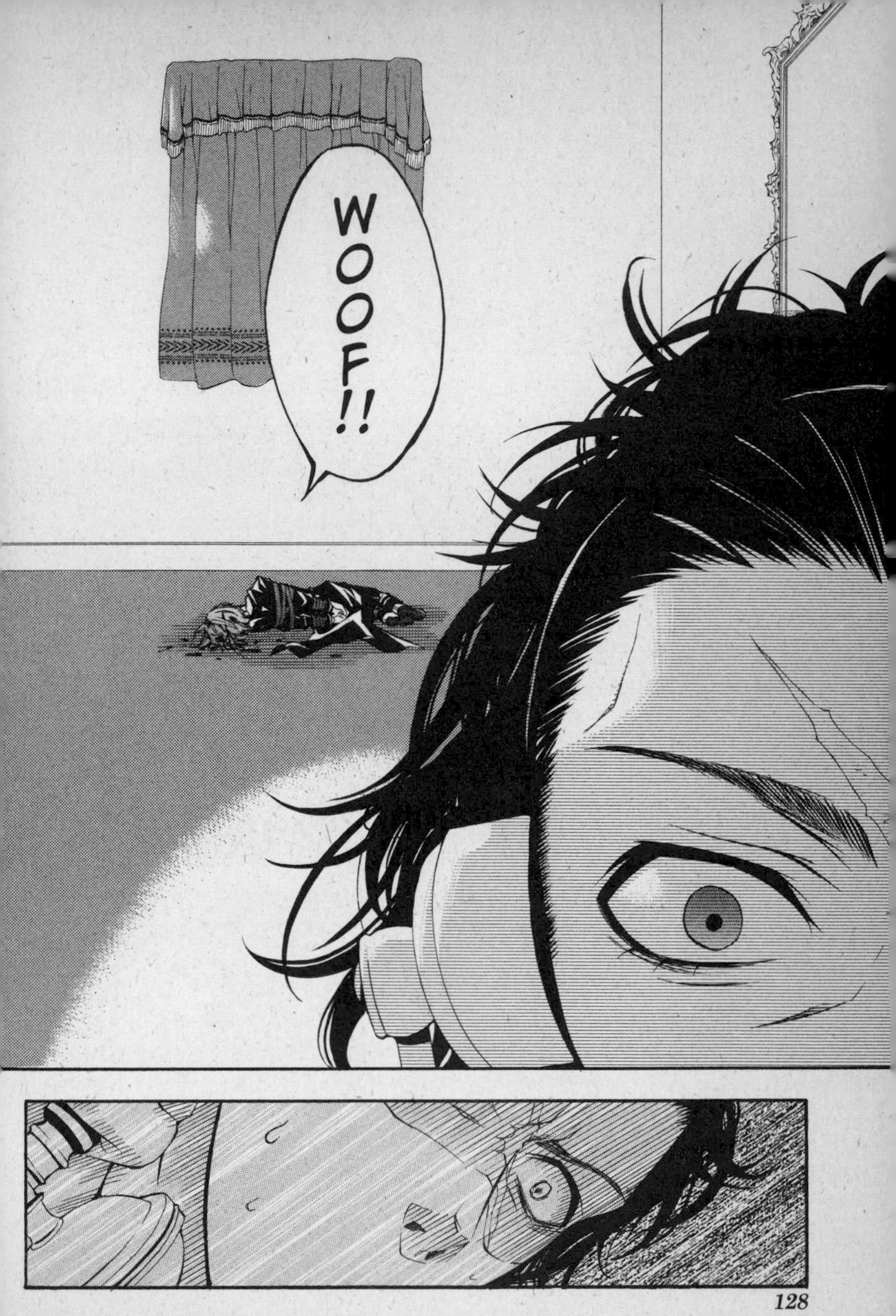
WOOF!!

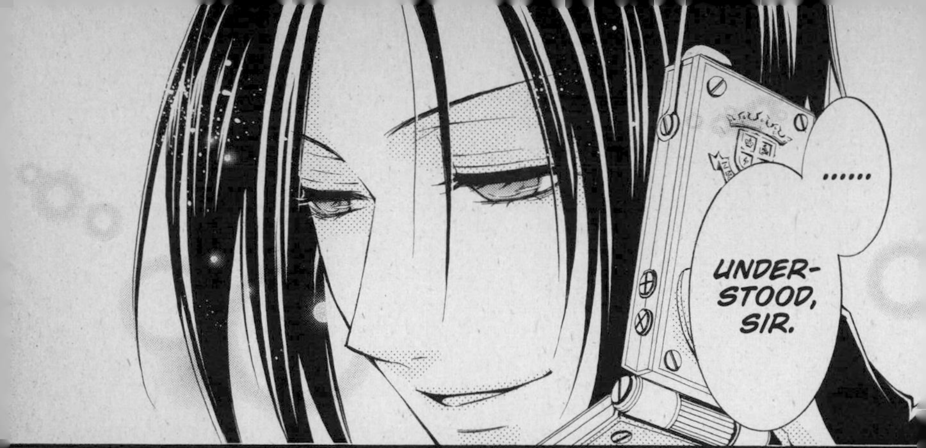
......
UNDER-STOOD, SIR.

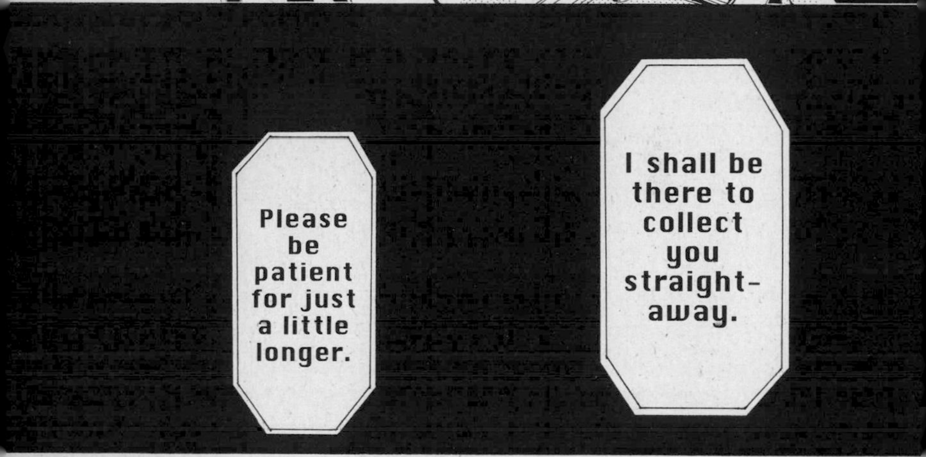
I shall be there to collect you straight-away.
Please be patient for just a little longer.

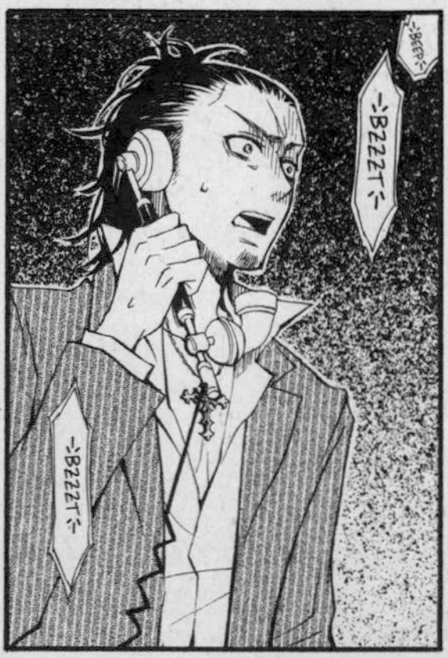
BEEP
BZZZT
BZZZT

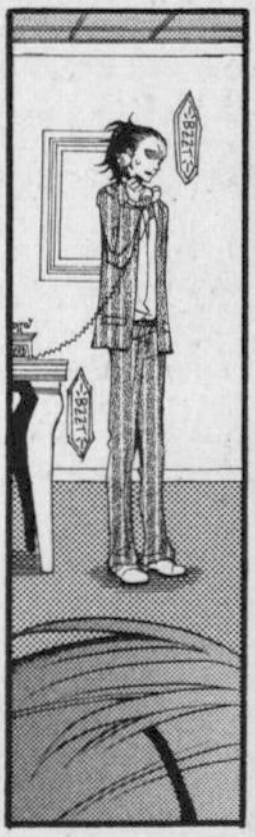
BZZT
BZZT

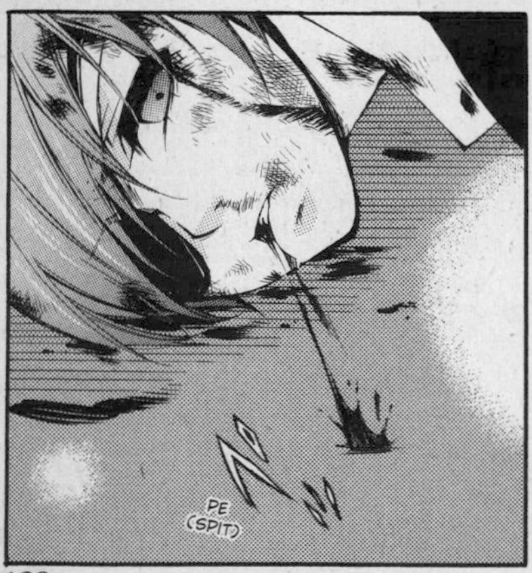
PE (SPIT)

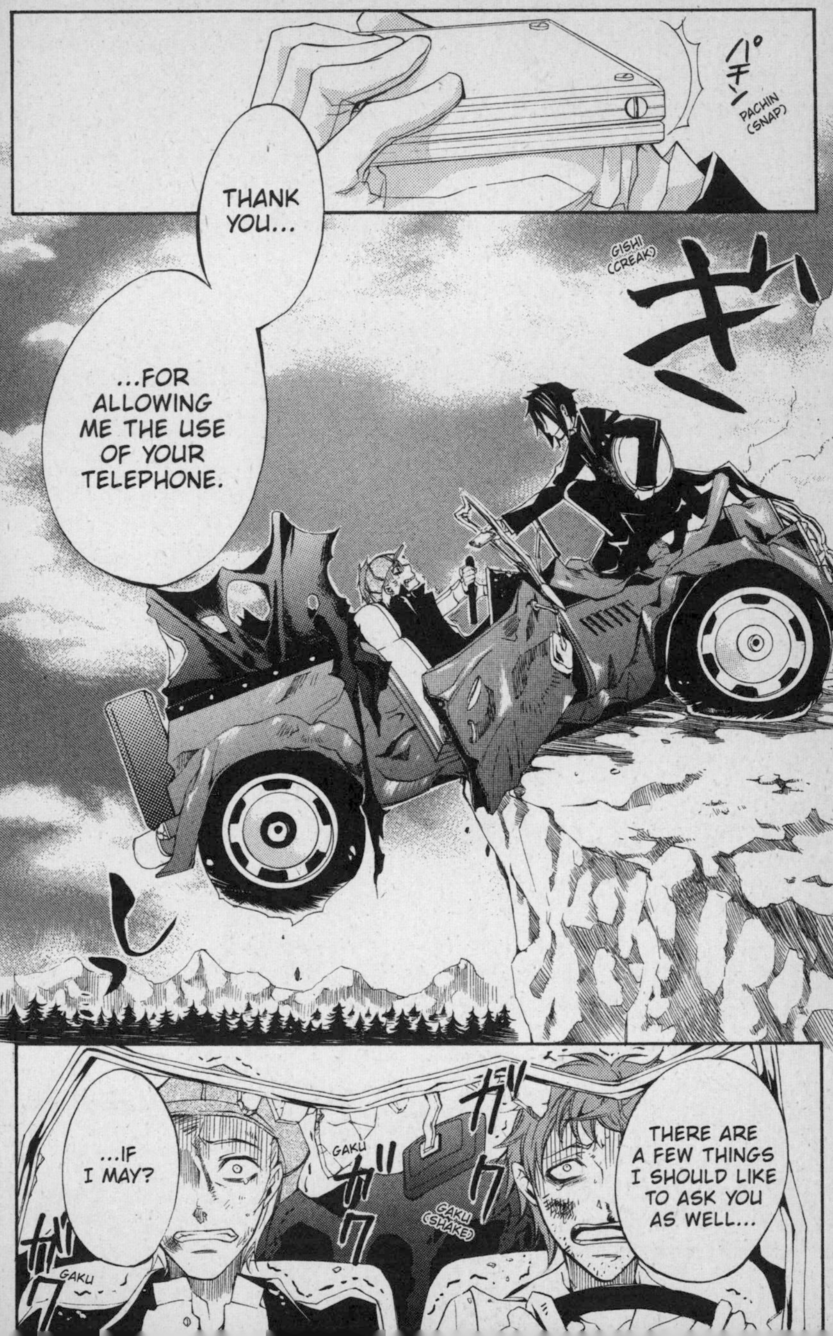
PACHIN (SNAP)
THANK YOU...
...FOR ALLOWING ME THE USE OF YOUR TELEPHONE.
GISHI (CREAK)
THERE ARE A FEW THINGS I SHOULD LIKE TO ASK YOU AS WELL...
GAKU (SHAKE)
GAKU
...IF I MAY?
GAKU

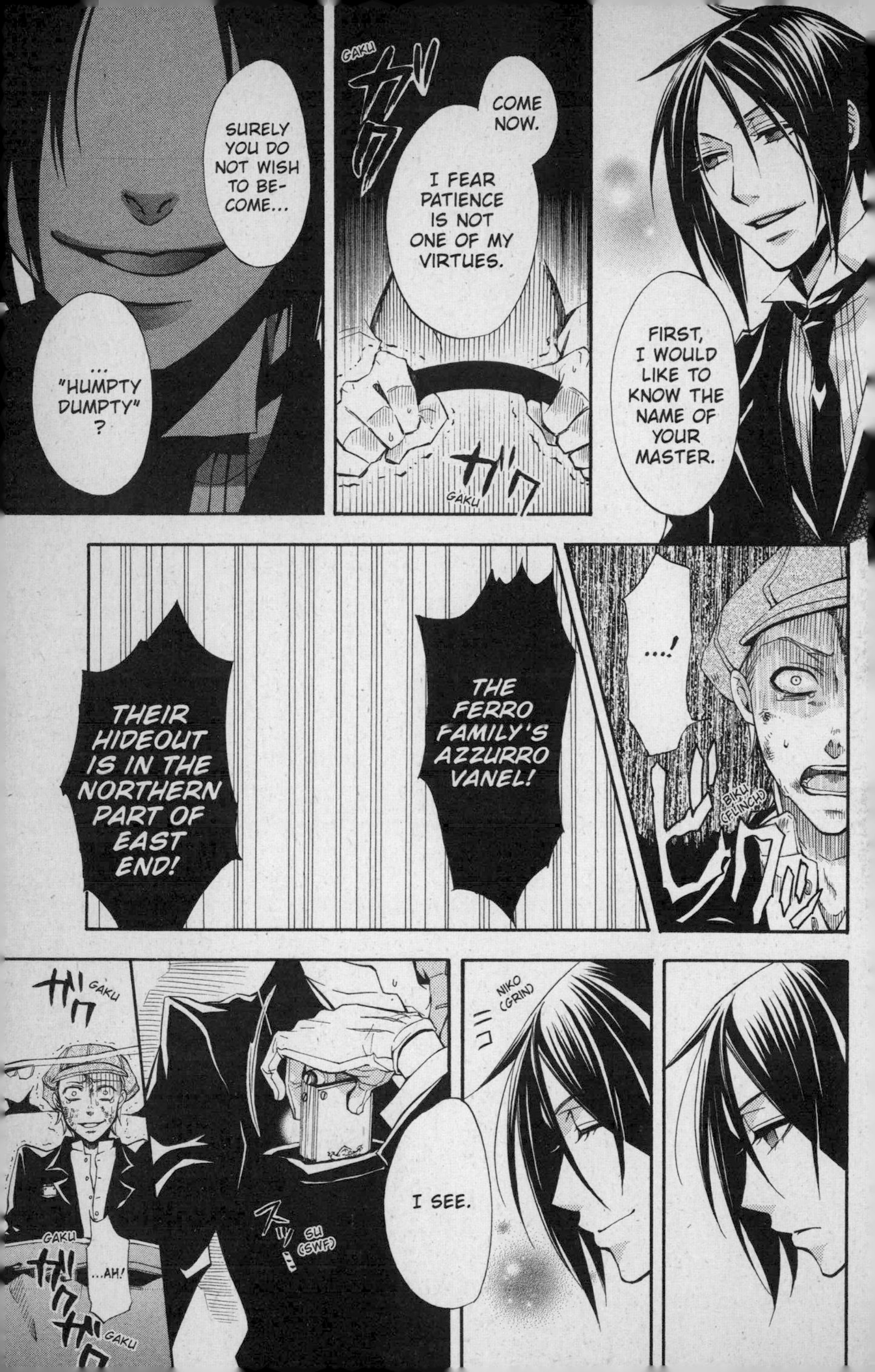
FIRST, I WOULD LIKE TO KNOW THE NAME OF YOUR MASTER.
GAKU
COME NOW.
I FEAR PATIENCE IS NOT ONE OF MY VIRTUES.
GAKU
SURELY YOU DO NOT WISH TO BE-COME...
..."HUMPTY DUMPTY"?
...!
BIKU (FLINCH)
THE FERRO FAMILY'S AZZURRO VANEL!
THEIR HIDEOUT IS IN THE NORTHERN PART OF EAST END!
NIKO (GRIN)
I SEE.
GAKU
SU (SWF)
GAKU
...AH!
GAKU

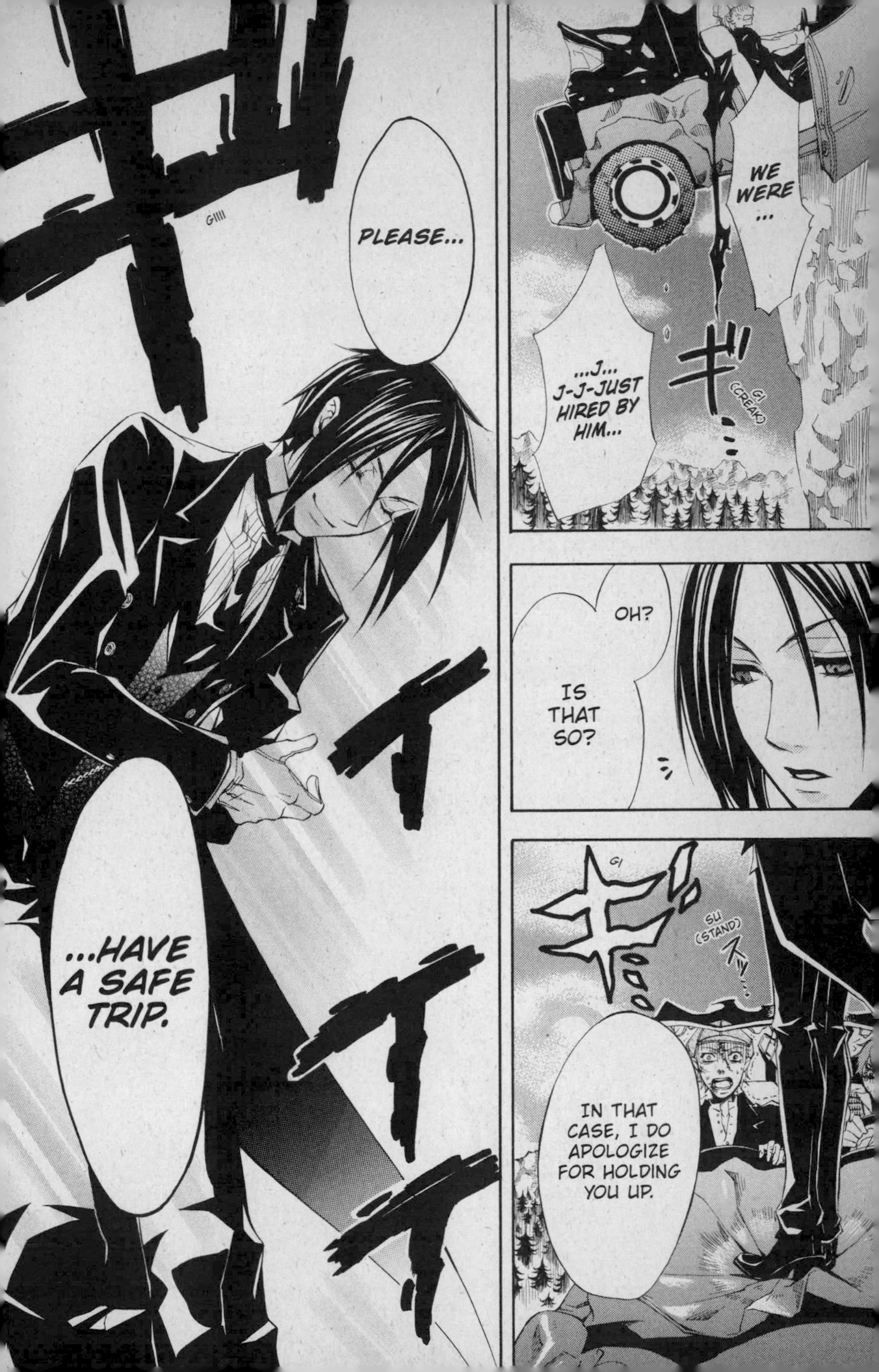
WE WERE ...
GI (CREAK)
...J... J-J-JUST HIRED BY HIM...
OH?
IS THAT SO?
GI
SU (STAND)
IN THAT CASE, I DO APOLOGIZE FOR HOLDING YOU UP.
GIIII
PLEASE...
...HAVE A SAFE TRIP.

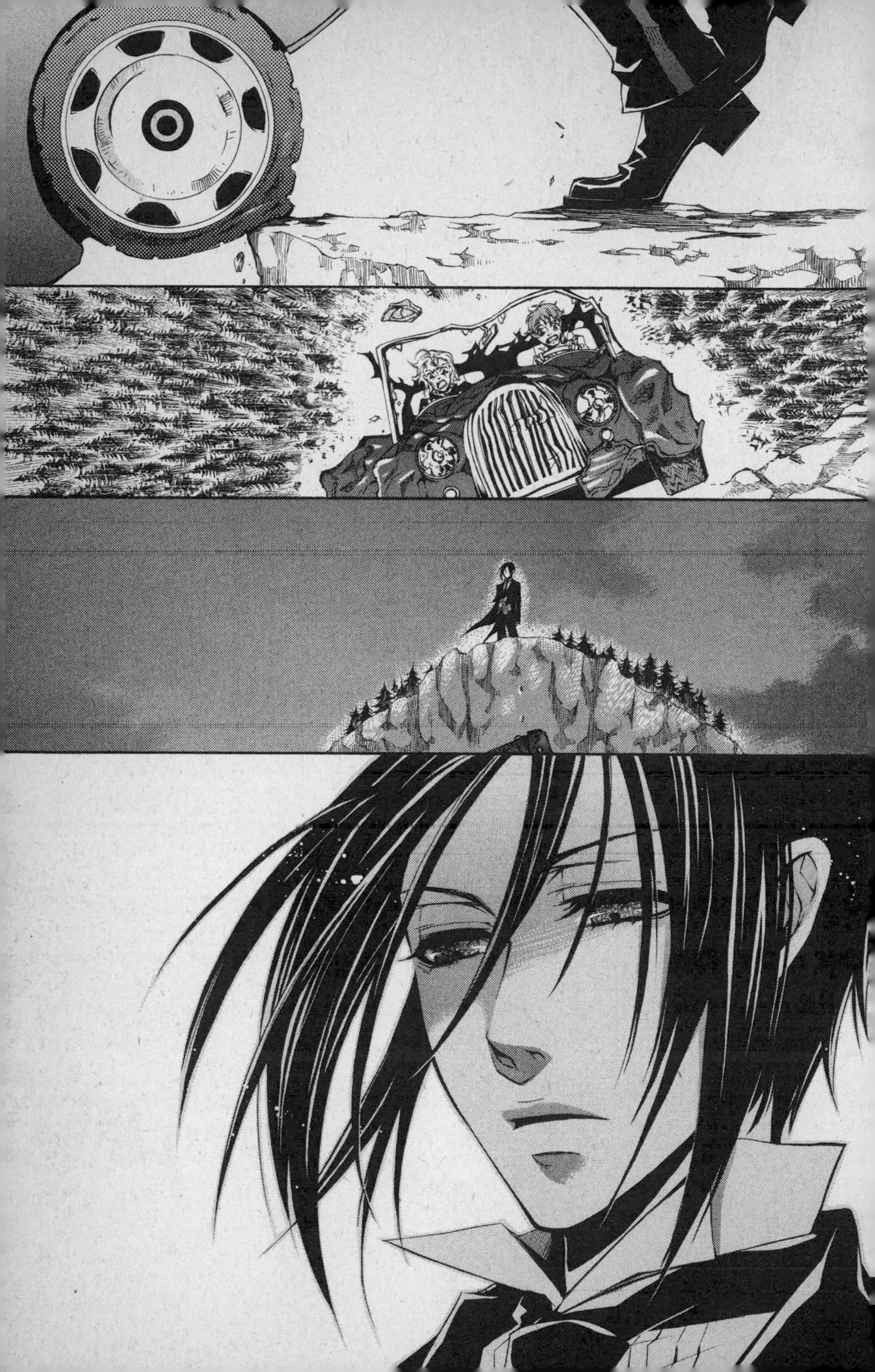

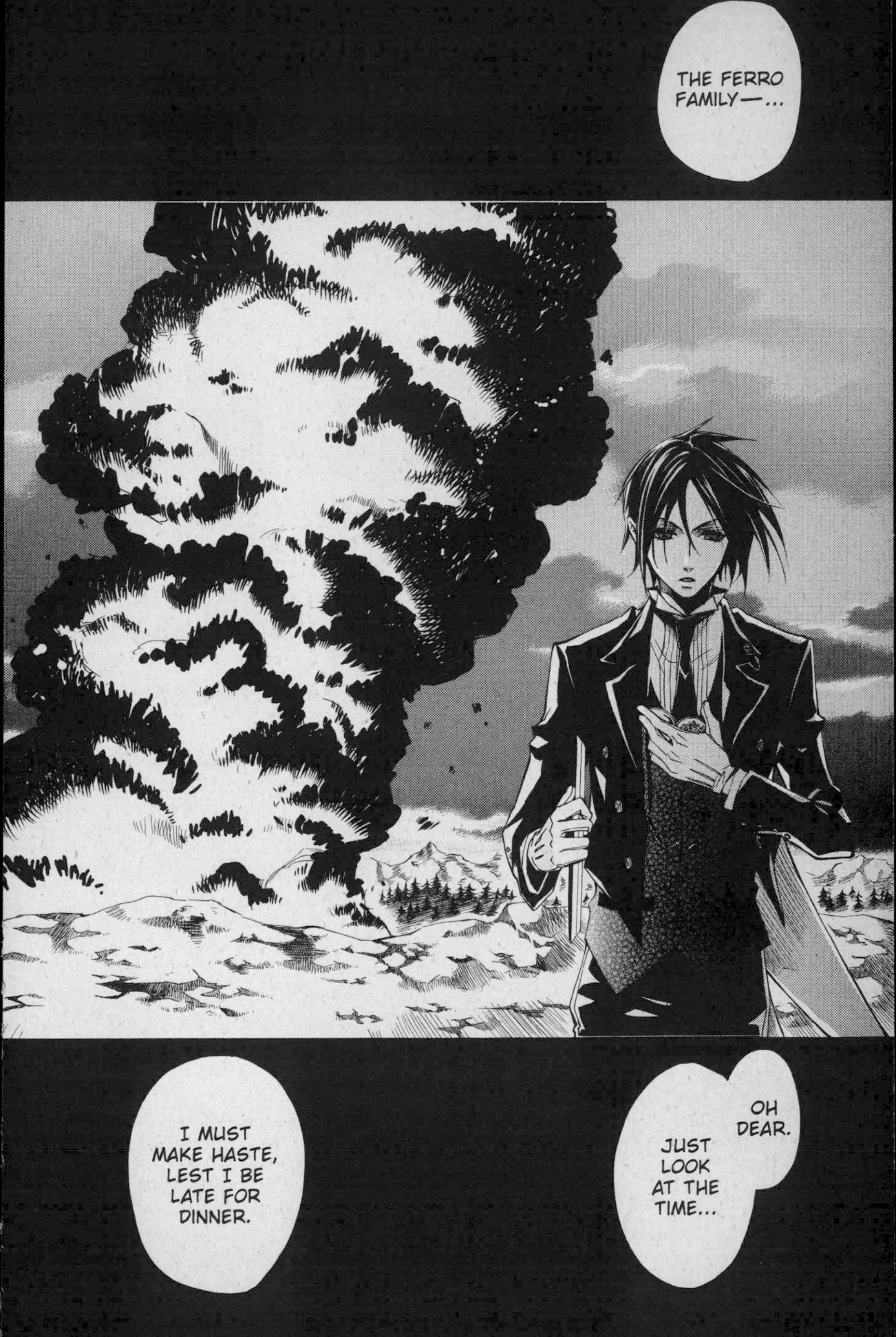
THE FERRO FAMILY—...
OH DEAR. JUST LOOK AT THE TIME...
I MUST MAKE HASTE, LEST I BE LATE FOR DINNER.

# Black Butler

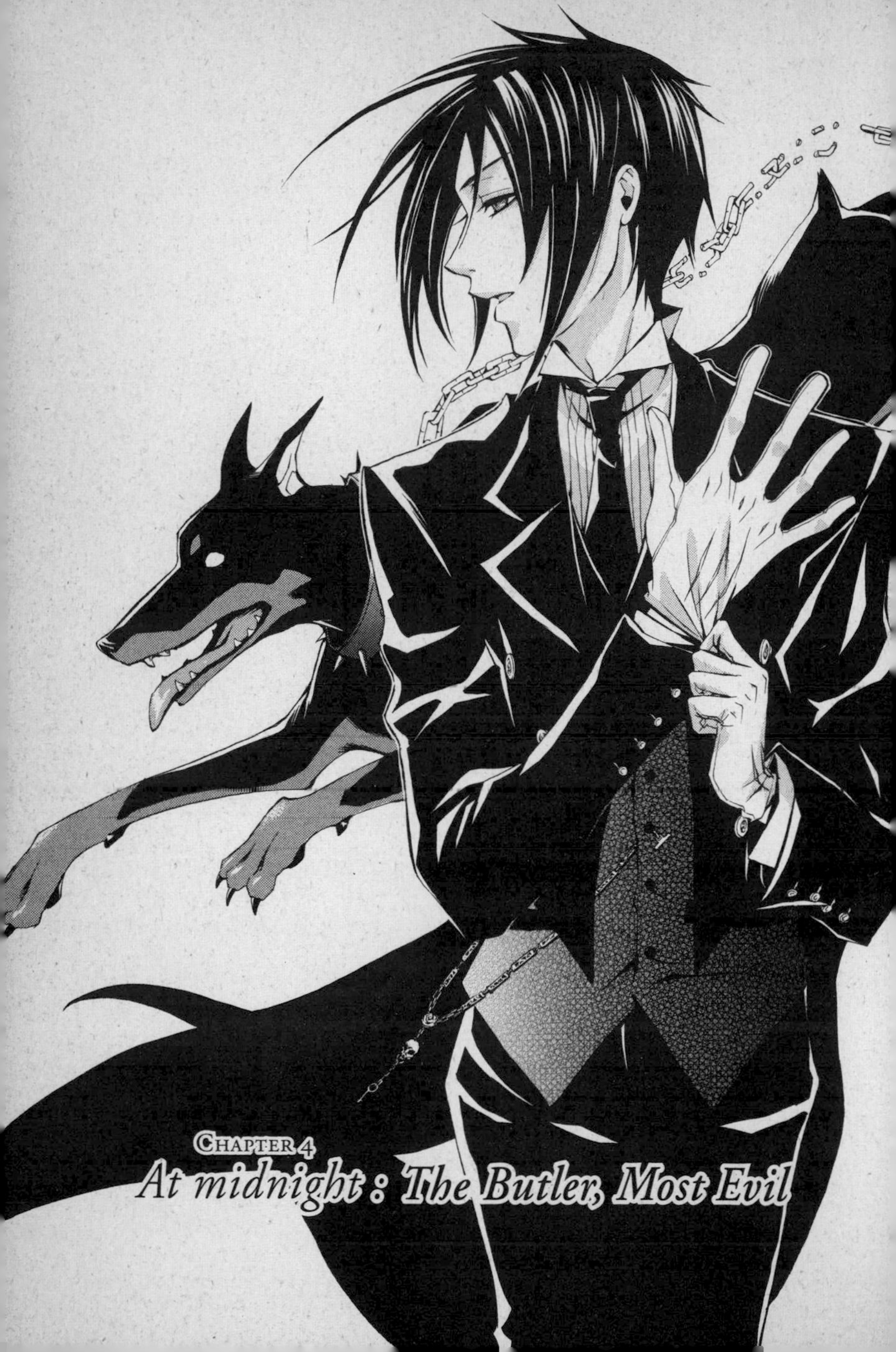
CHAPTER 4
At midnight : The Butler, Most Evil

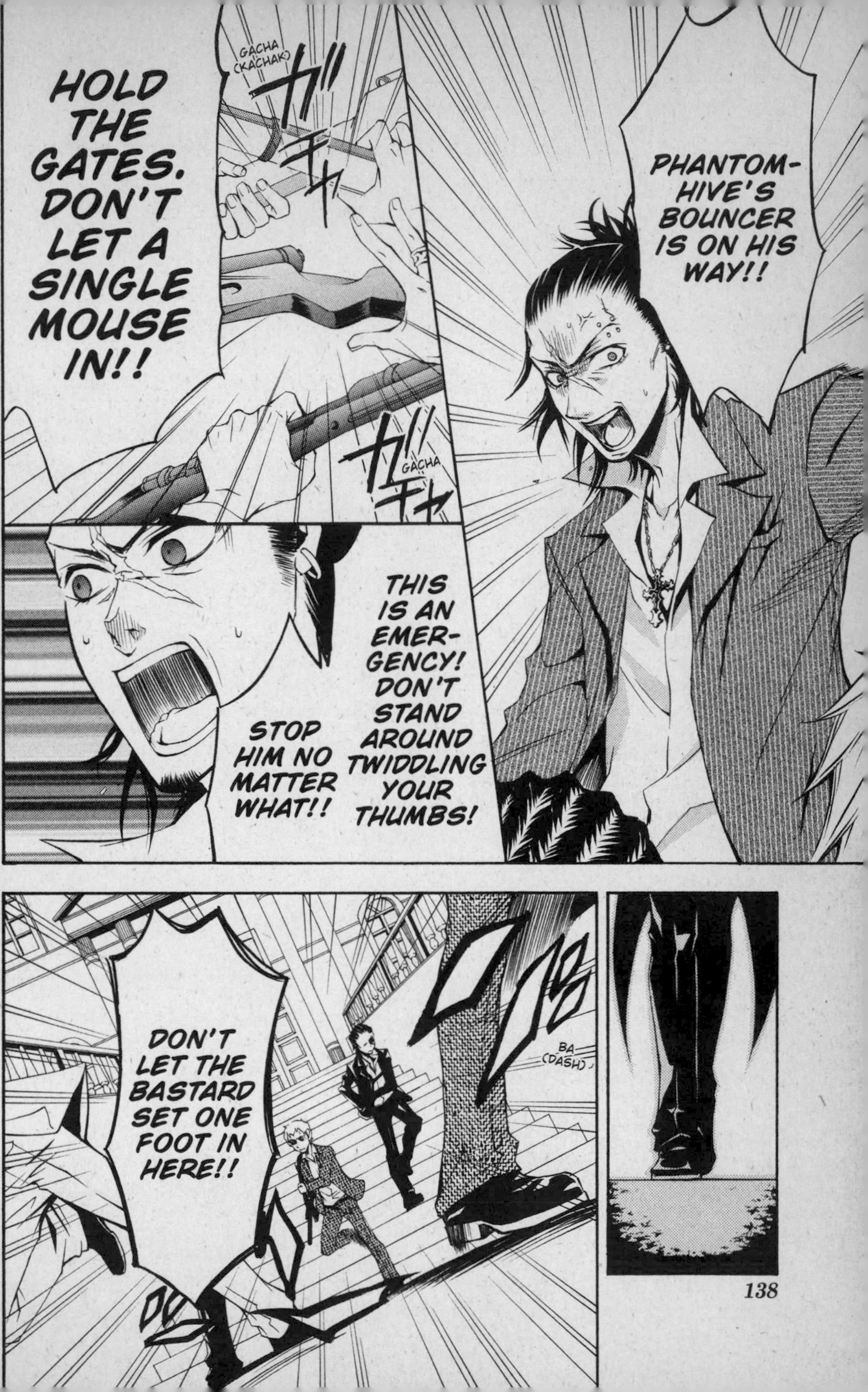
PHANTOM-HIVE'S BOUNCER IS ON HIS WAY!!
HOLD THE GATES. DON'T LET A SINGLE MOUSE IN!!
GACHA (KACHAK)
GACHA
THIS IS AN EMER-GENCY! DON'T STAND AROUND TWIDDLING YOUR THUMBS!
STOP HIM NO MATTER WHAT!!
BA (DASH)
DON'T LET THE BASTARD SET ONE FOOT IN HERE!!

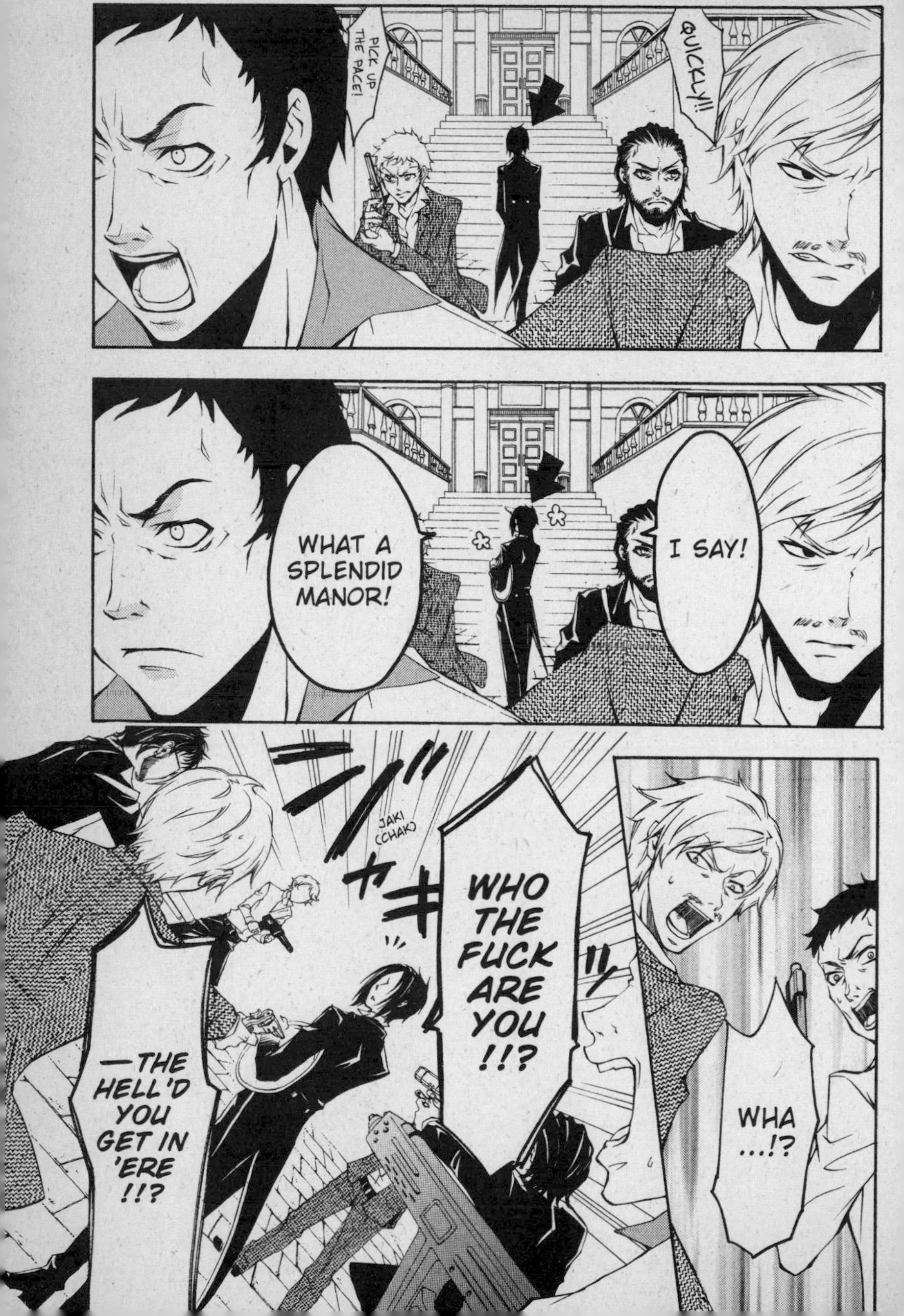
QUICKLY!!
PICK UP THE PACE!
I SAY!
WHAT A SPLENDID MANOR!
WHA ...!?
WHO THE FUCK ARE YOU!!?
JAKI (CHAK)
—THE HELL'D YOU GET IN 'ERE!!?

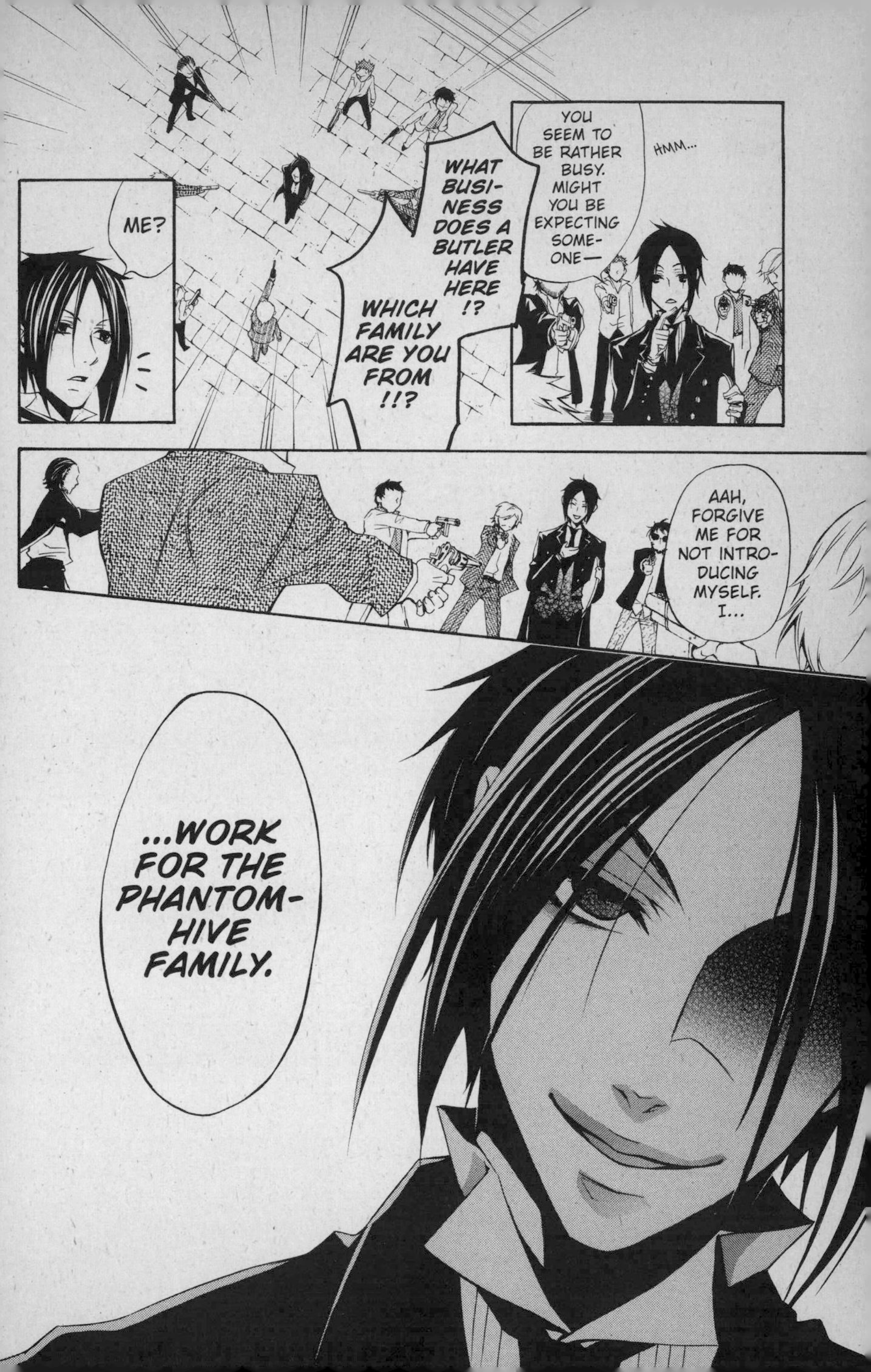
HMM...
YOU SEEM TO BE RATHER BUSY. MIGHT YOU BE EXPECTING SOME-ONE—
WHAT BUSI-NESS DOES A BUTLER HAVE HERE !?
WHICH FAMILY ARE YOU FROM !!?
ME?
AAH, FORGIVE ME FOR NOT INTRO-DUCING MYSELF. I...
...WORK FOR THE PHANTOM-HIVE FAMILY.

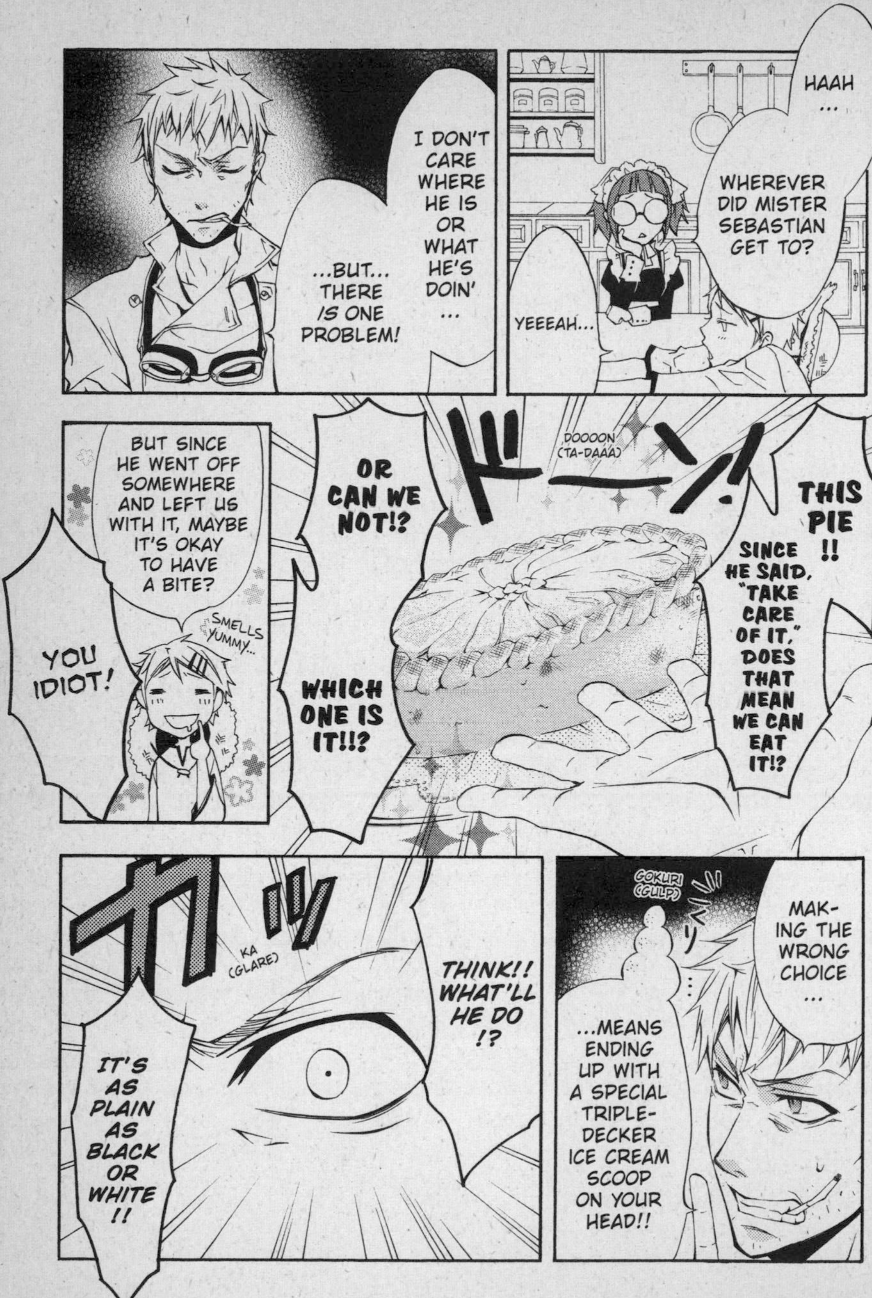
HAAH ...
WHEREVER DID MISTER SEBASTIAN GET TO?
YEEEAH...
I DON'T CARE WHERE HE IS OR WHAT HE'S DOIN' ...
...BUT... THERE IS ONE PROBLEM!
THIS PIE !!
DOOOON (TA-DAAA)
SINCE HE SAID, "TAKE CARE OF IT," DOES THAT MEAN WE CAN EAT IT!?
OR CAN WE NOT!?
WHICH ONE IS IT!!?
BUT SINCE HE WENT OFF SOMEWHERE AND LEFT US WITH IT, MAYBE IT'S OKAY TO HAVE A BITE?
SMELLS YUMMY...
YOU IDIOT!
GOKURI (GULP)
MAK-ING THE WRONG CHOICE ...
...MEANS ENDING UP WITH A SPECIAL TRIPLE-DECKER ICE CREAM SCOOP ON YOUR HEAD!!
KA (GLARE)
THINK!! WHAT'LL HE DO !?
IT'S AS PLAIN AS BLACK OR WHITE !!

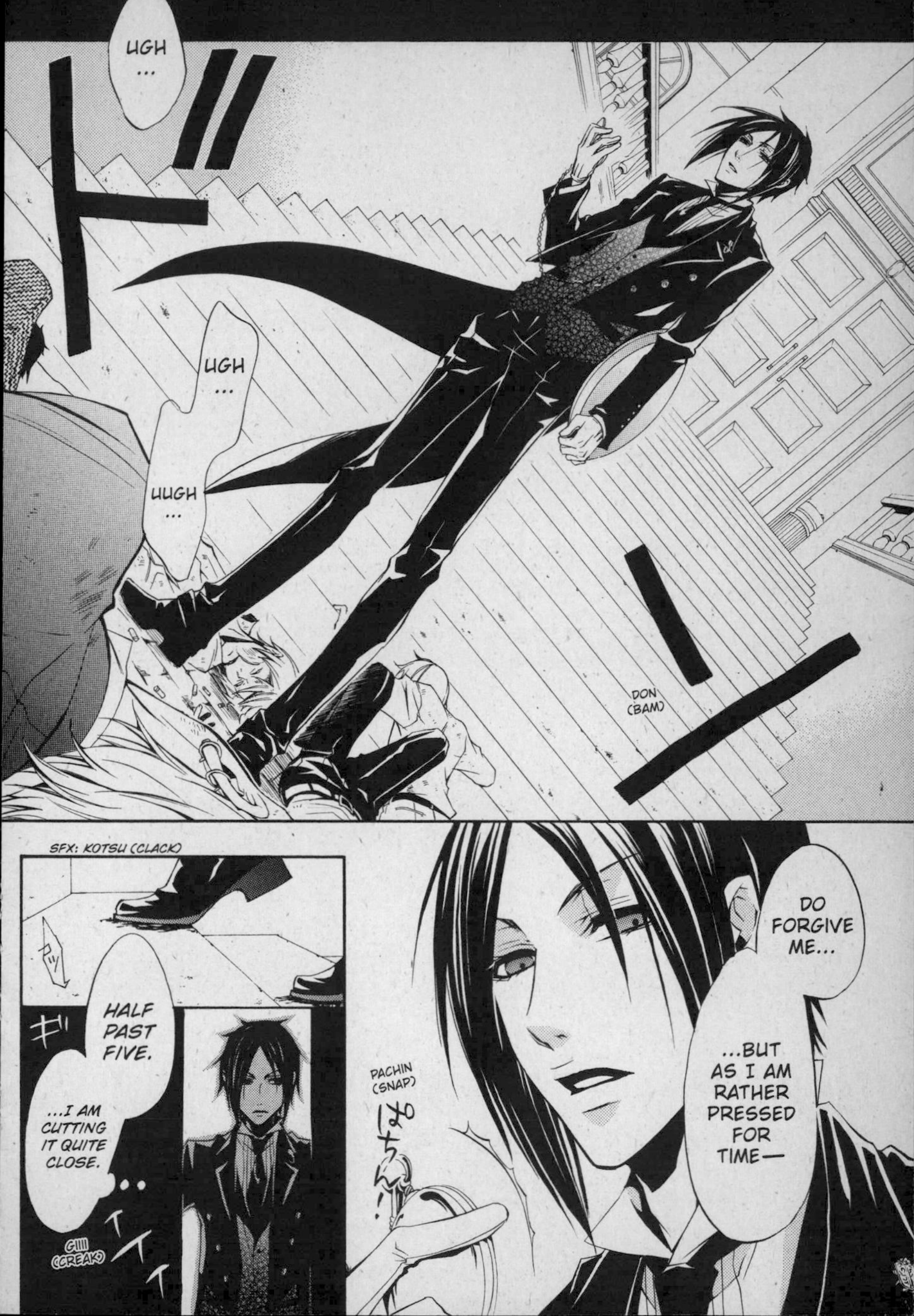
UGH...
UGH...
UUGH...
DON (BAM)
DO FORGIVE ME...
...BUT AS I AM RATHER PRESSED FOR TIME—
PACHIN (SNAP)
SFX: KOTSU (CLACK)
HALF PAST FIVE.
...I AM CUTTING IT QUITE CLOSE.
GIIII (CREAK)

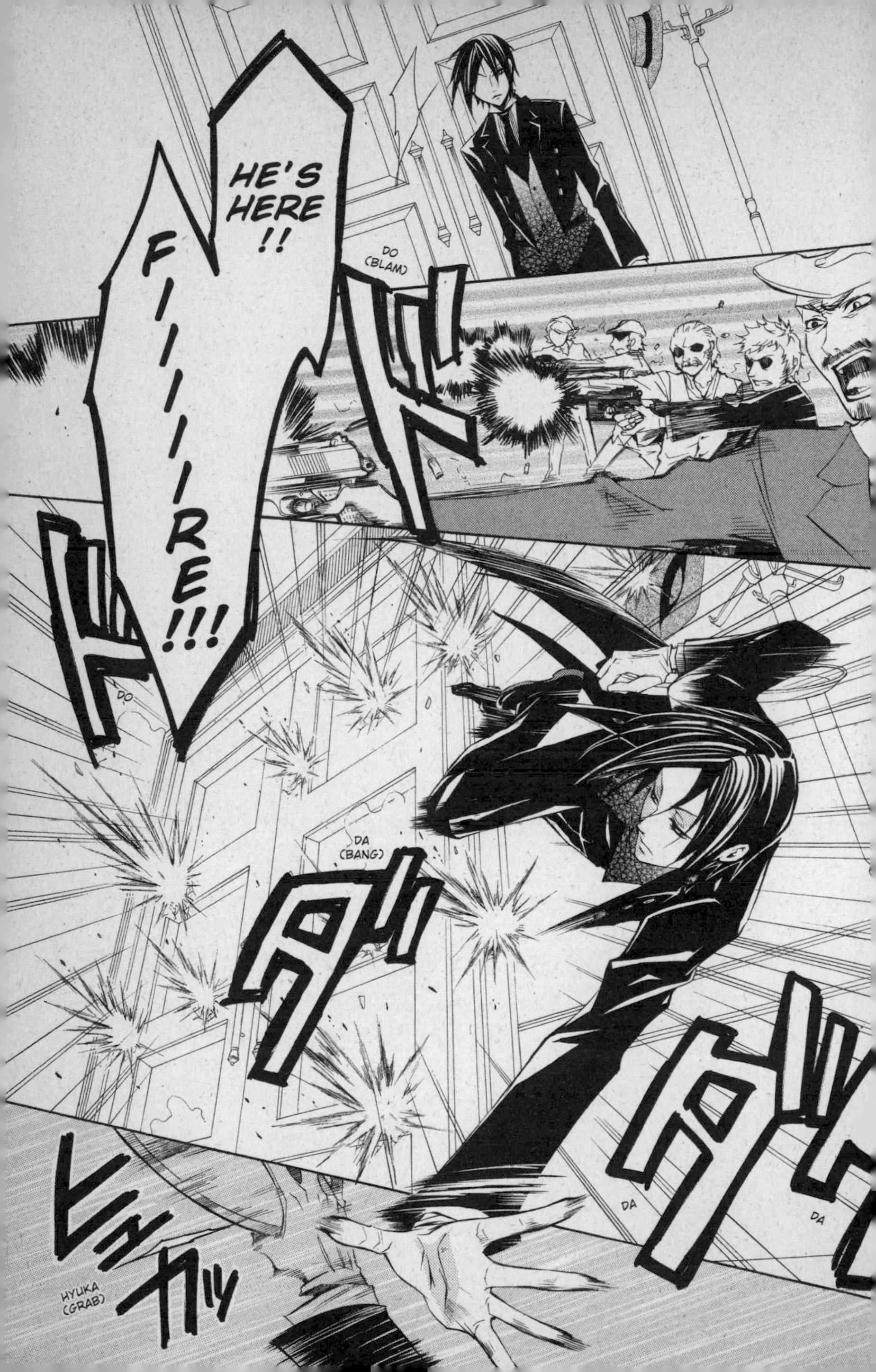

DO
(BLAM)
HE'S HERE!!
FI-I-I-IRE!!!
DO
DA
(BANG)
DA
DA
HYUKA
(GRAB)

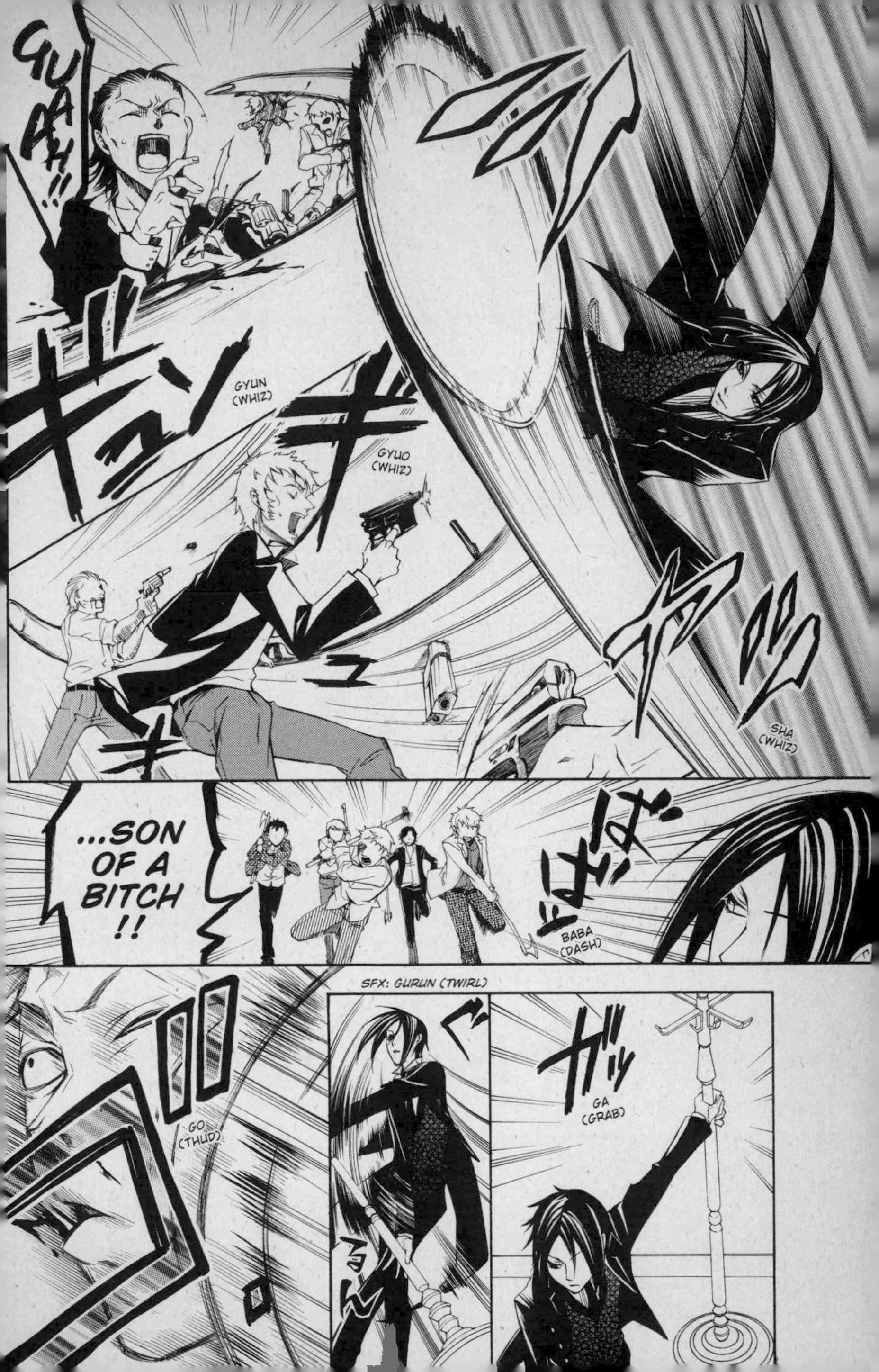
GUAAH!!
GYUN (WHIZ)
GYUO (WHIZ)
SHA (WHIZ)
BABA (DASH)
...SON OF A BITCH!!
GA (GRAB)
SFX: GURUN (TWIRL)
GO (THUD)

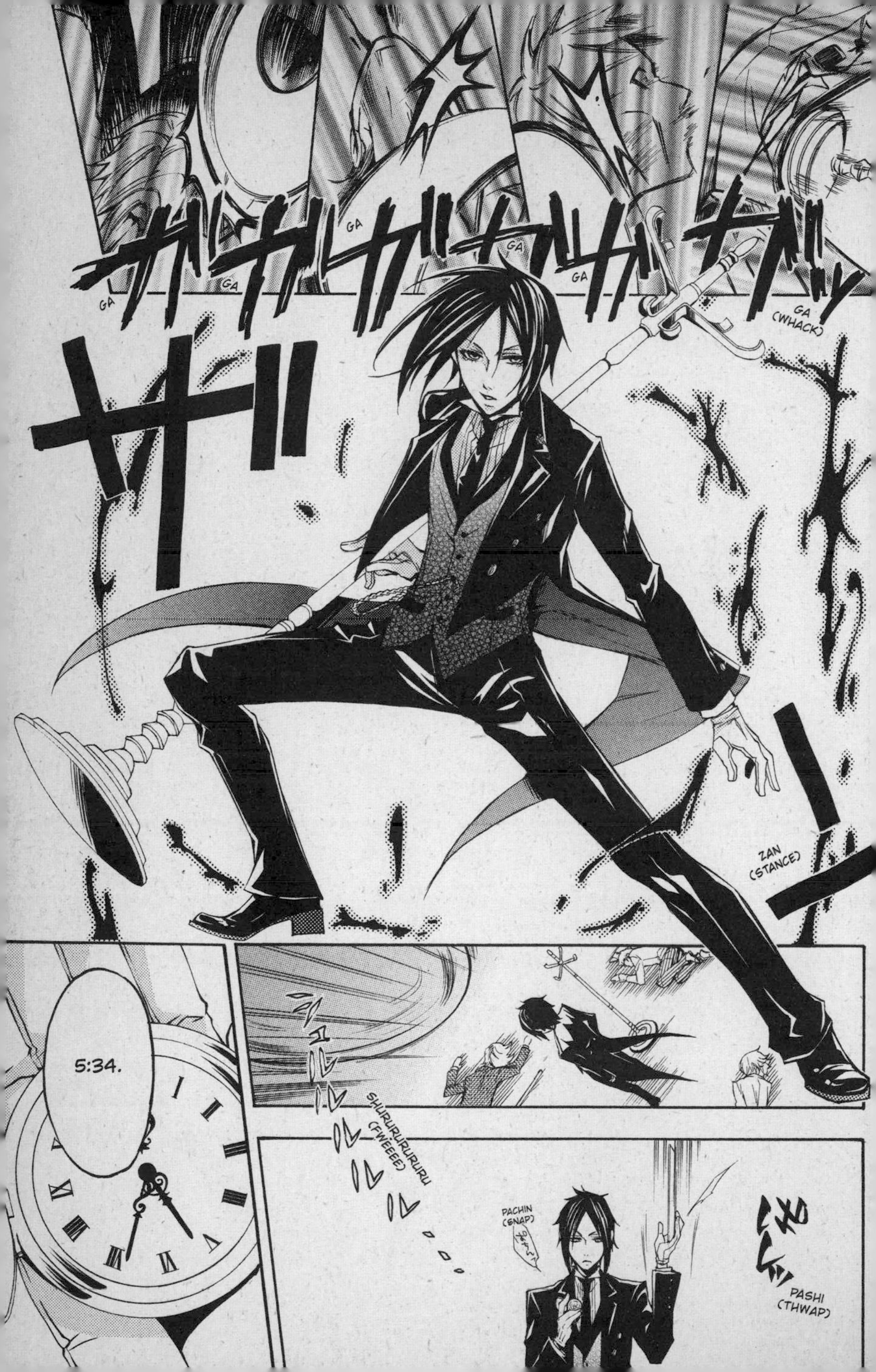
GA (WHACK)
GA
GA
GA
GA
GA
ZAN (STANCE)
SHURURURURU (FWEEEE)
PACHIN (SNAP)
PASHI (THWAP)
5:34.

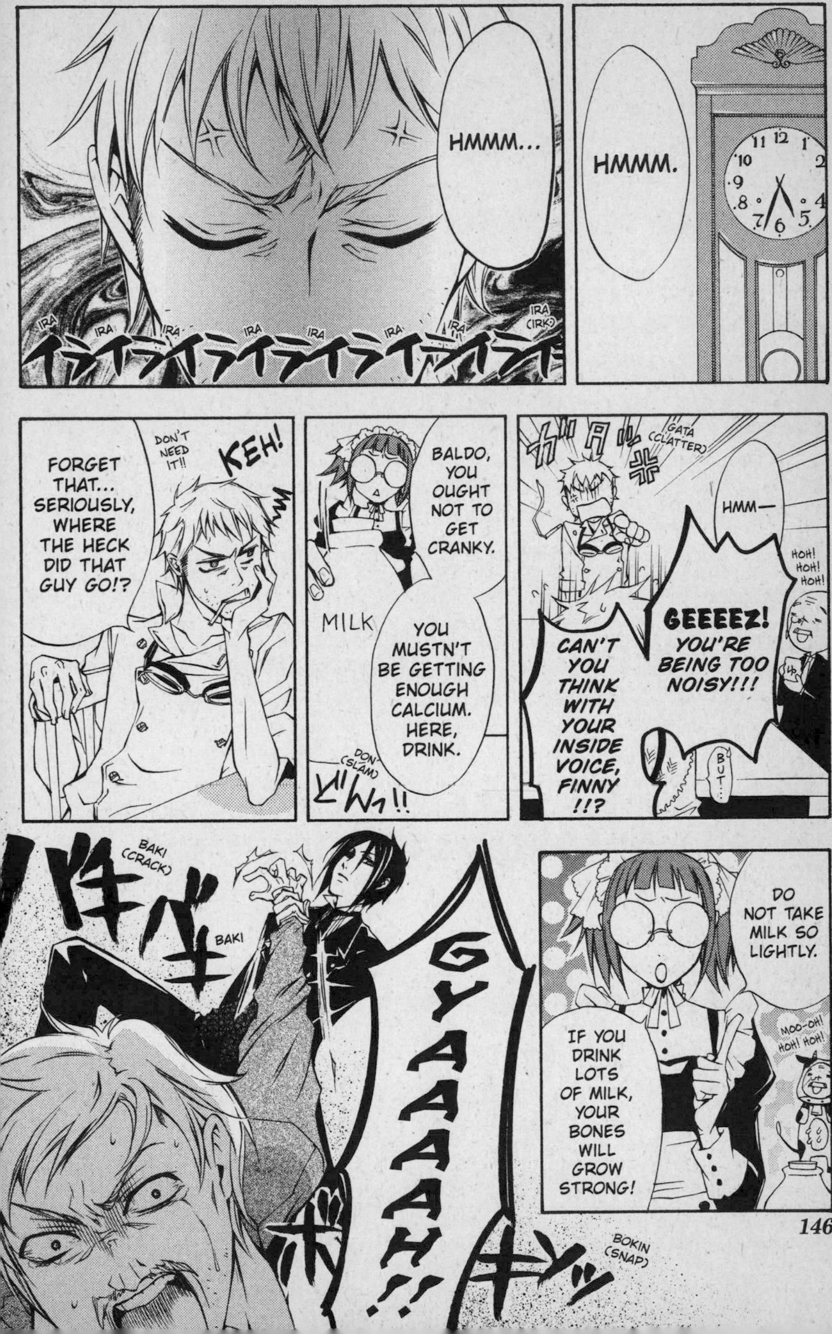
HMMM.
HMMM...
IRA IRA IRA IRA IRA IRA IRA IRA (IRK)
GATA (CLATTER)
HMM—
GEEEEZ! YOU'RE BEING TOO NOISY!!!
CAN'T YOU THINK WITH YOUR INSIDE VOICE, FINNY!!?
BUT...
HOH! HOH! HOH!
UP
BALDO, YOU OUGHT NOT TO GET CRANKY.
MILK
YOU MUSTN'T BE GETTING ENOUGH CALCIUM. HERE, DRINK.
DON' (SLAM)
FORGET THAT... SERIOUSLY, WHERE THE HECK DID THAT GUY GO!?
DON'T NEED IT!!
KEH!
DO NOT TAKE MILK SO LIGHTLY.
IF YOU DRINK LOTS OF MILK, YOUR BONES WILL GROW STRONG!
MOO-OH! HOH! HOH!
BAKI (CRACK)
BAKI
GYAAAAAH!!!
BOKIN (SNAP)

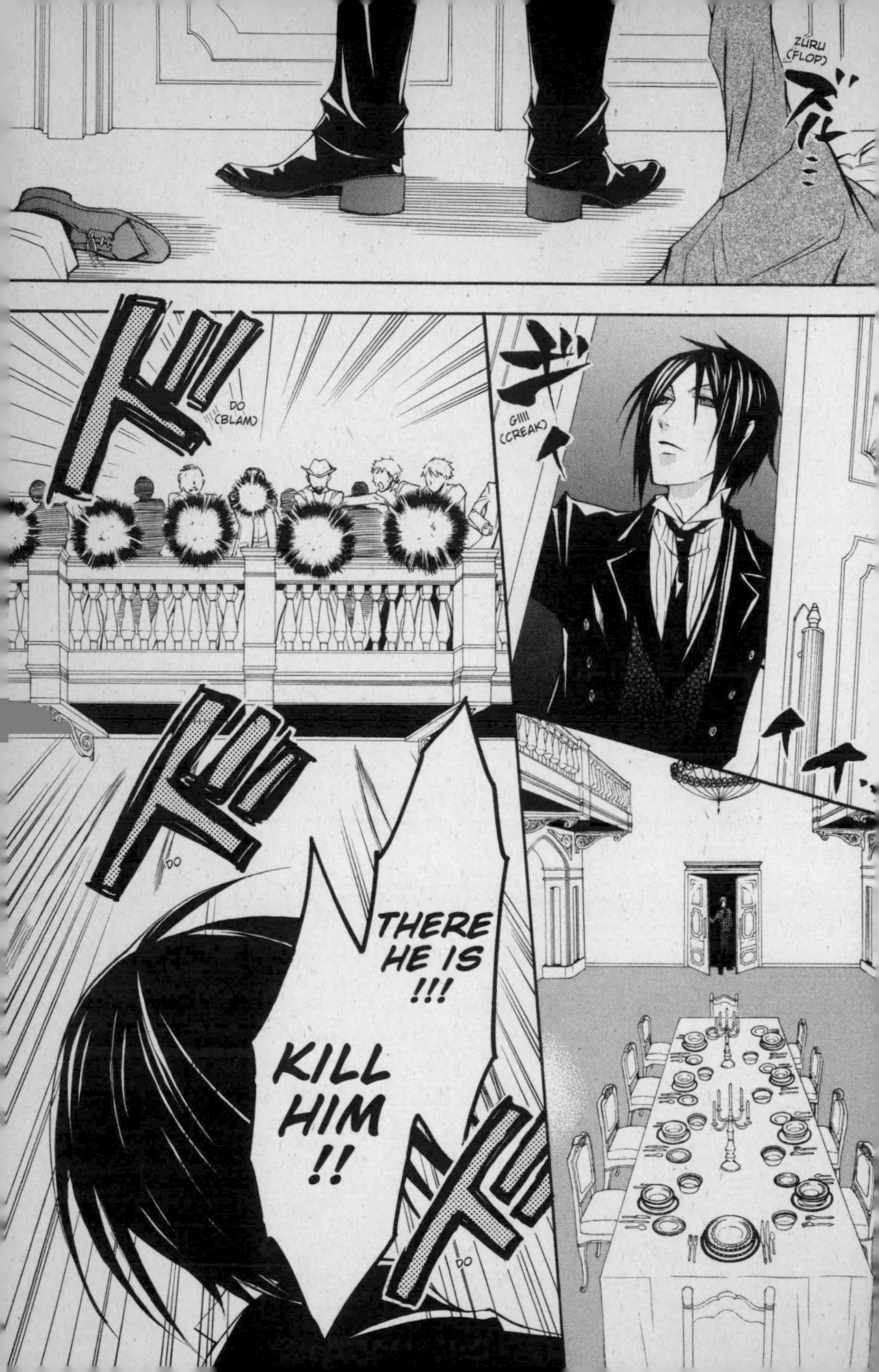
ZURU (FLOP)
GIIII (CREAK)
DO (BLAM)
DO
THERE HE IS !!!
KILL HIM !!
DO

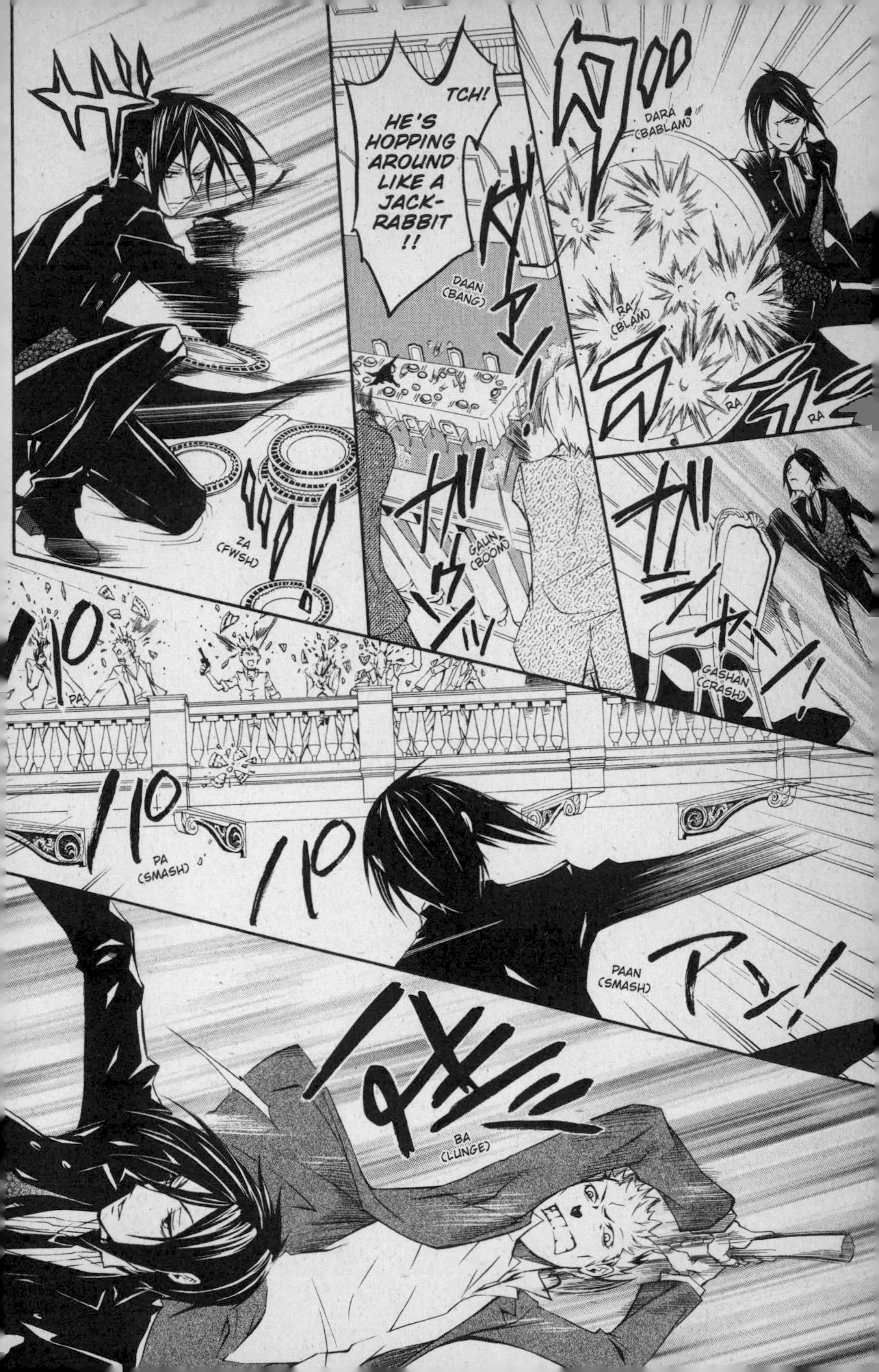
DARA (BABLAM)
RA (BLAM)
RA
RA
GASHAN (CRASH)
TCH!
HE'S HOPPING AROUND LIKE A JACK-RABBIT !!
DAAN (BANG)
GAUN (BOOM)
ZA (FWSH)
PA
PA (SMASH)
PAAN (SMASH)
BA (LUNGE)

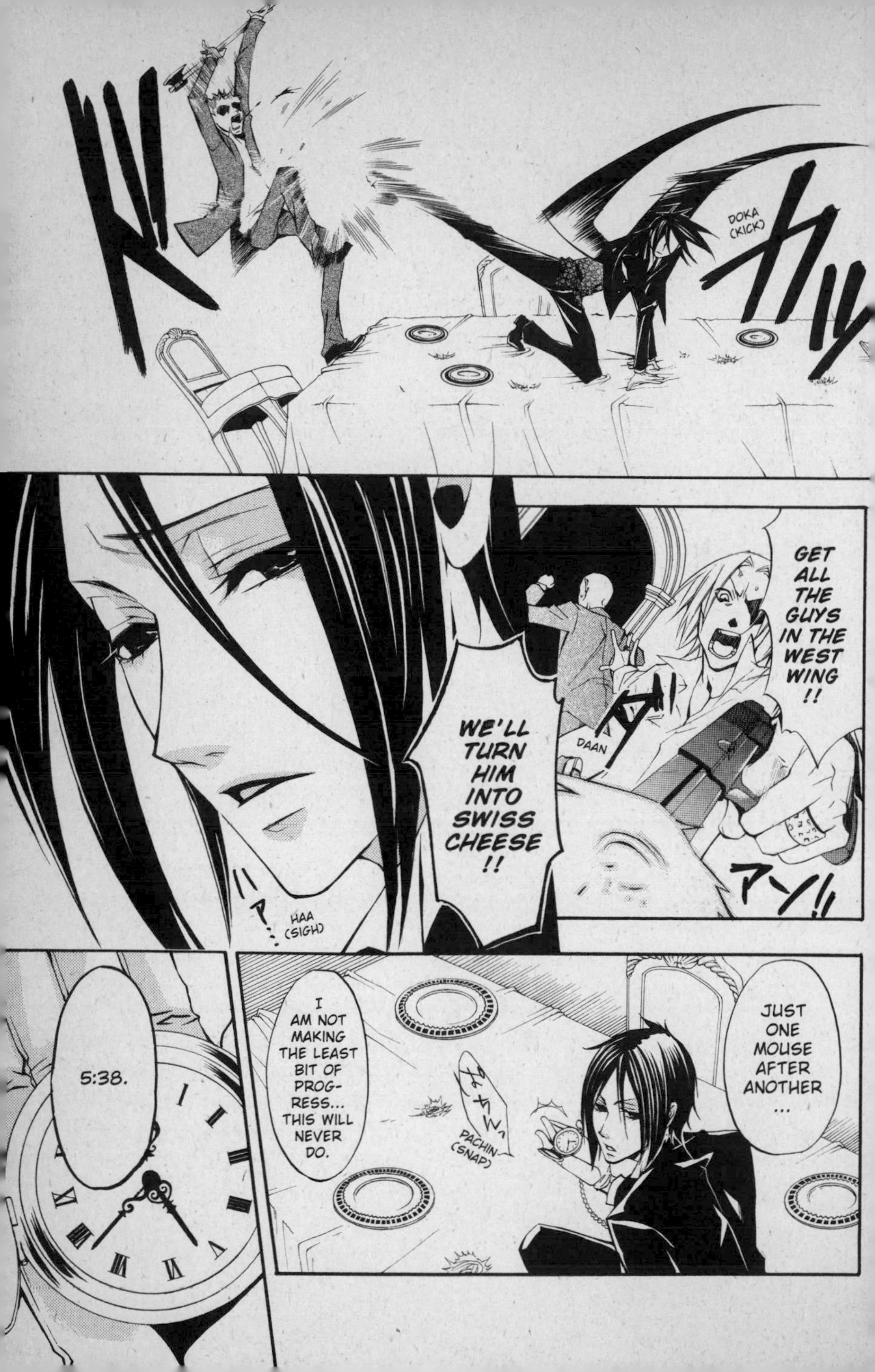
DOKA (KICK)
GET ALL THE GUYS IN THE WEST WING!!
DAAN
WE'LL TURN HIM INTO SWISS CHEESE!!
HAA (SIGH)
JUST ONE MOUSE AFTER ANOTHER...
I AM NOT MAKING THE LEAST BIT OF PROG-RESS... THIS WILL NEVER DO.
PACHIN (SNAP)
5:38.

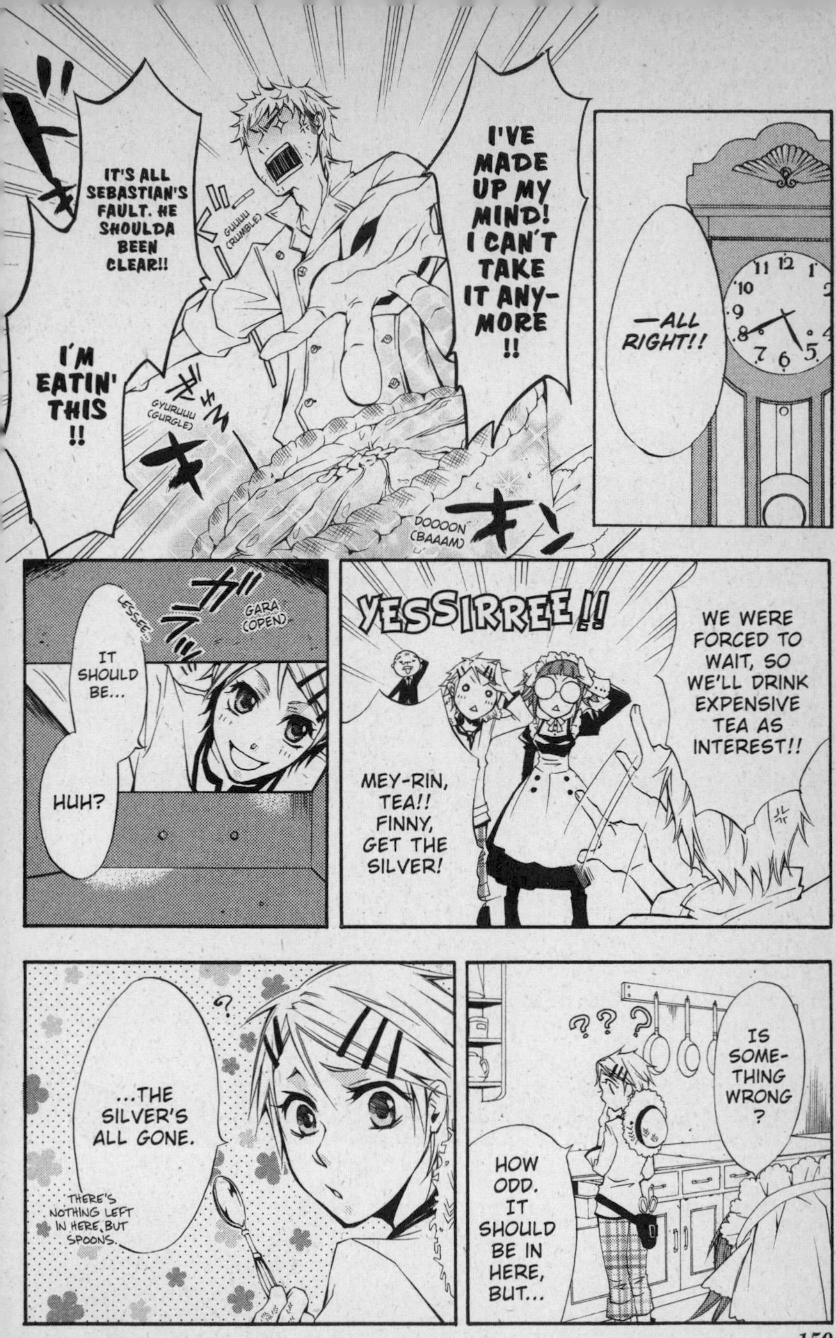
—ALL RIGHT!!
I'VE MADE UP MY MIND! I CAN'T TAKE IT ANYMORE!!
IT'S ALL SEBASTIAN'S FAULT. HE SHOULDA BEEN CLEAR!!
GUUUU (RUMBLE)
I'M EATIN' THIS!!
GYURUUU (GURGLE)
DOOOON (BAAAM)
YESSIRREE!!
WE WERE FORCED TO WAIT, SO WE'LL DRINK EXPENSIVE TEA AS INTEREST!!
MEY-RIN, TEA!! FINNY, GET THE SILVER!
GARA (OPEN)
LESSEE...
IT SHOULD BE...
HUH?
IS SOMETHING WRONG?
HOW ODD. IT SHOULD BE IN HERE, BUT...
...THE SILVER'S ALL GONE.
THERE'S NOTHING LEFT IN HERE, BUT SPOONS.

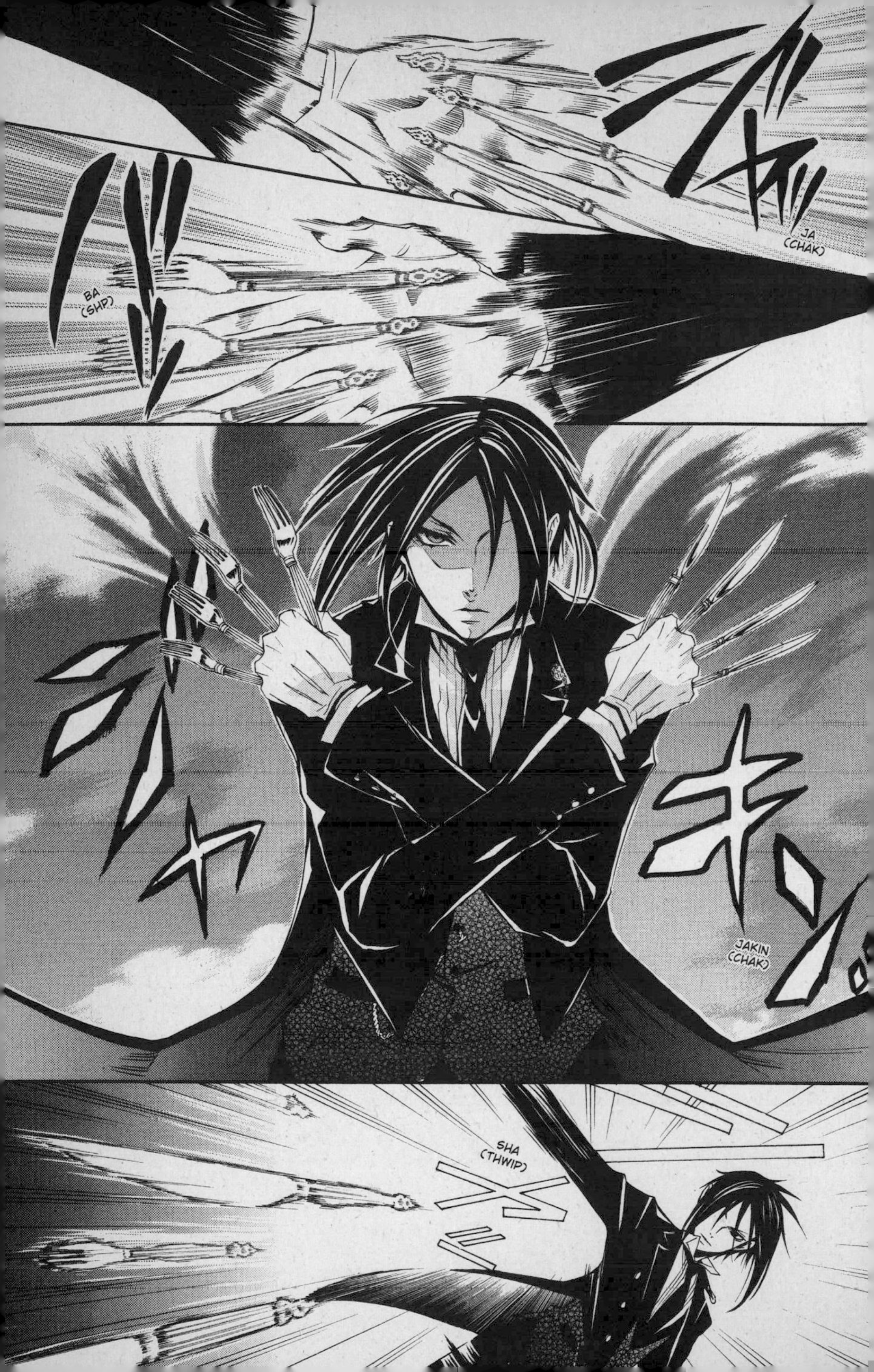
JA
(CHAK)
BA
(SHP)
JAKIN
(CHAK)
SHA
(THWIP)

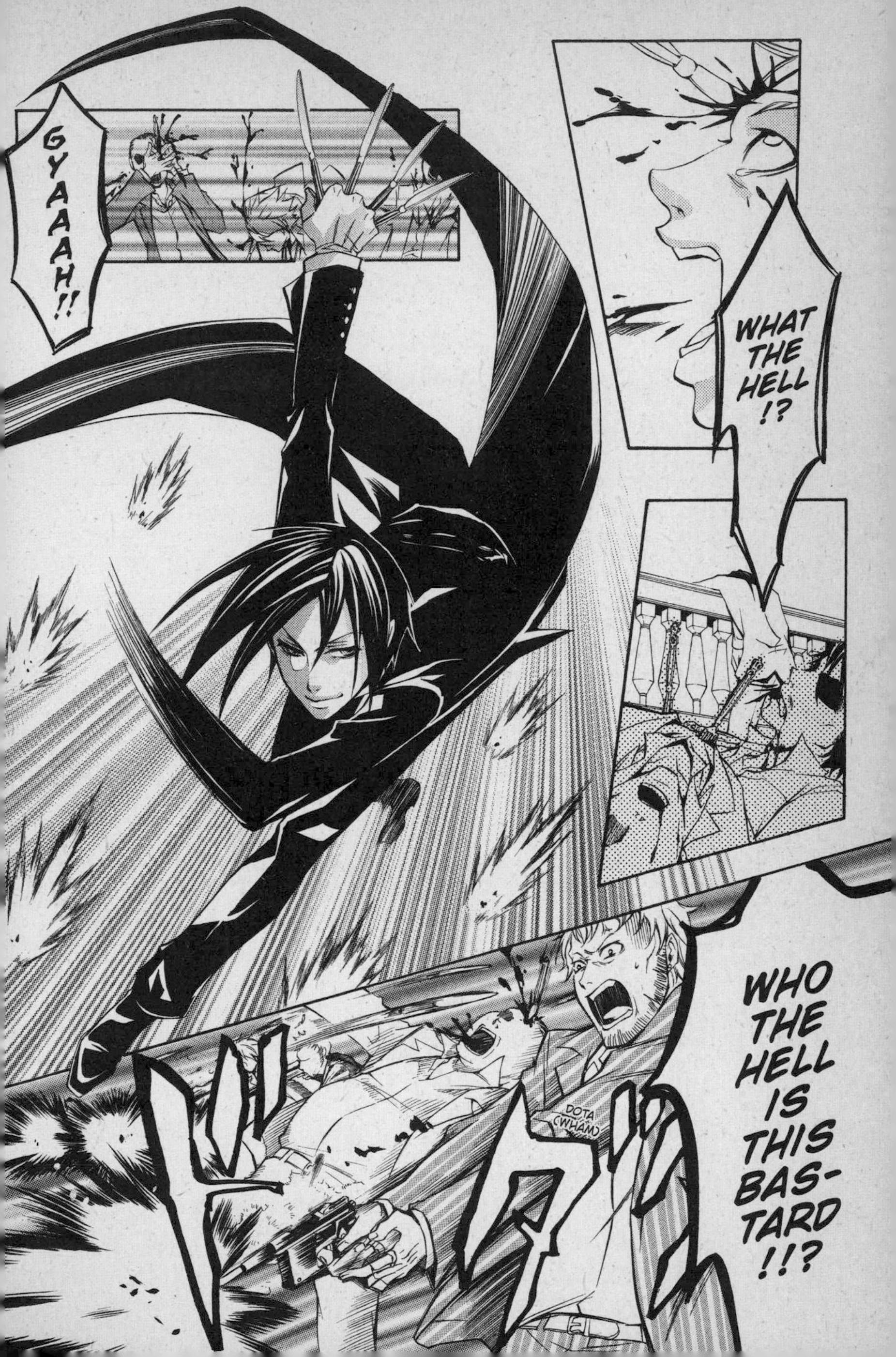
WHAT THE HELL!?
GYAAAH!!
WHO THE HELL IS THIS BAS-TARD!!?
DOTA (WHAM)

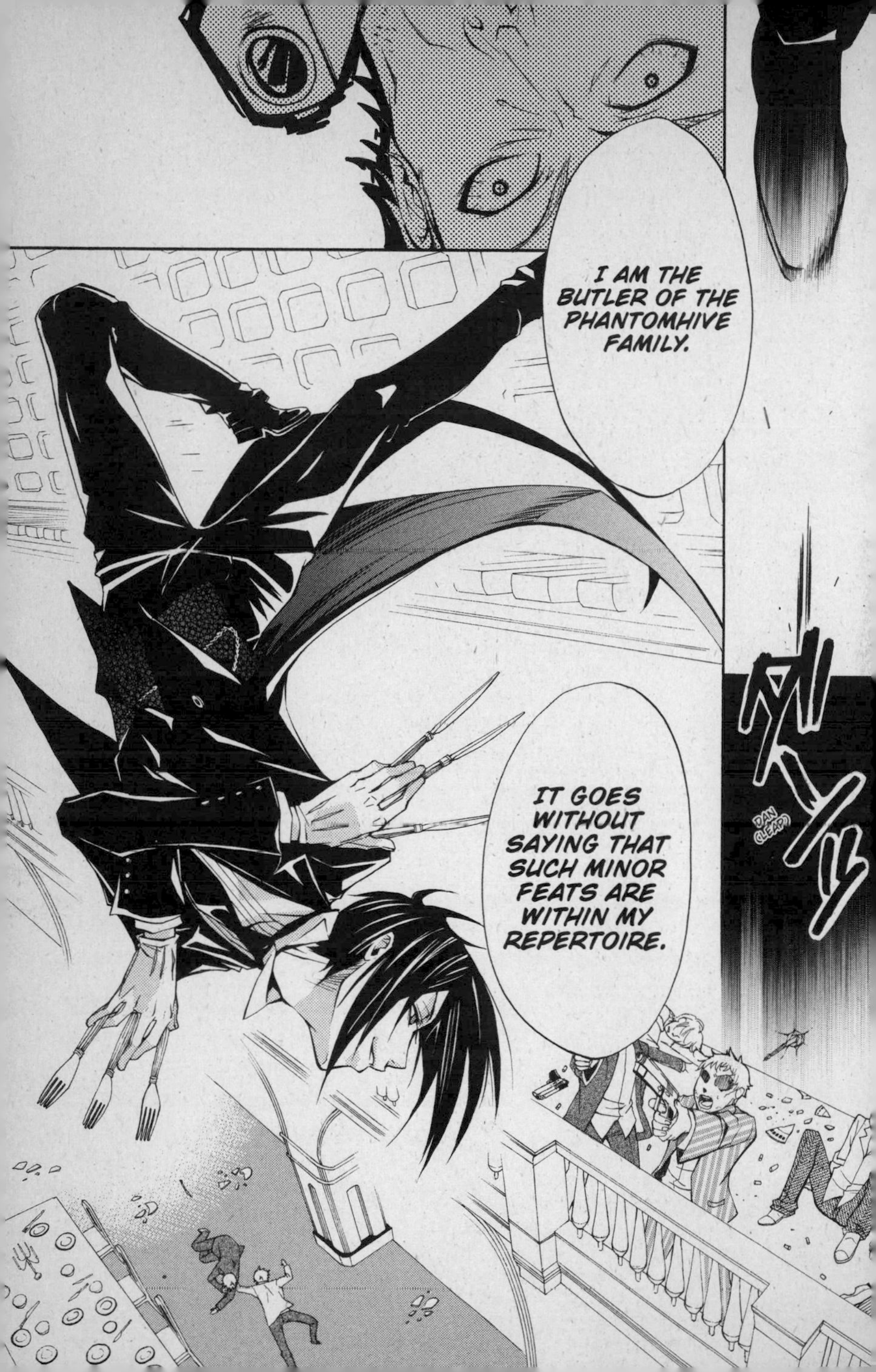
I AM THE BUTLER OF THE PHANTOMHIVE FAMILY.
DAN (LEAP)
IT GOES WITHOUT SAYING THAT SUCH MINOR FEATS ARE WITHIN MY REPERTOIRE.

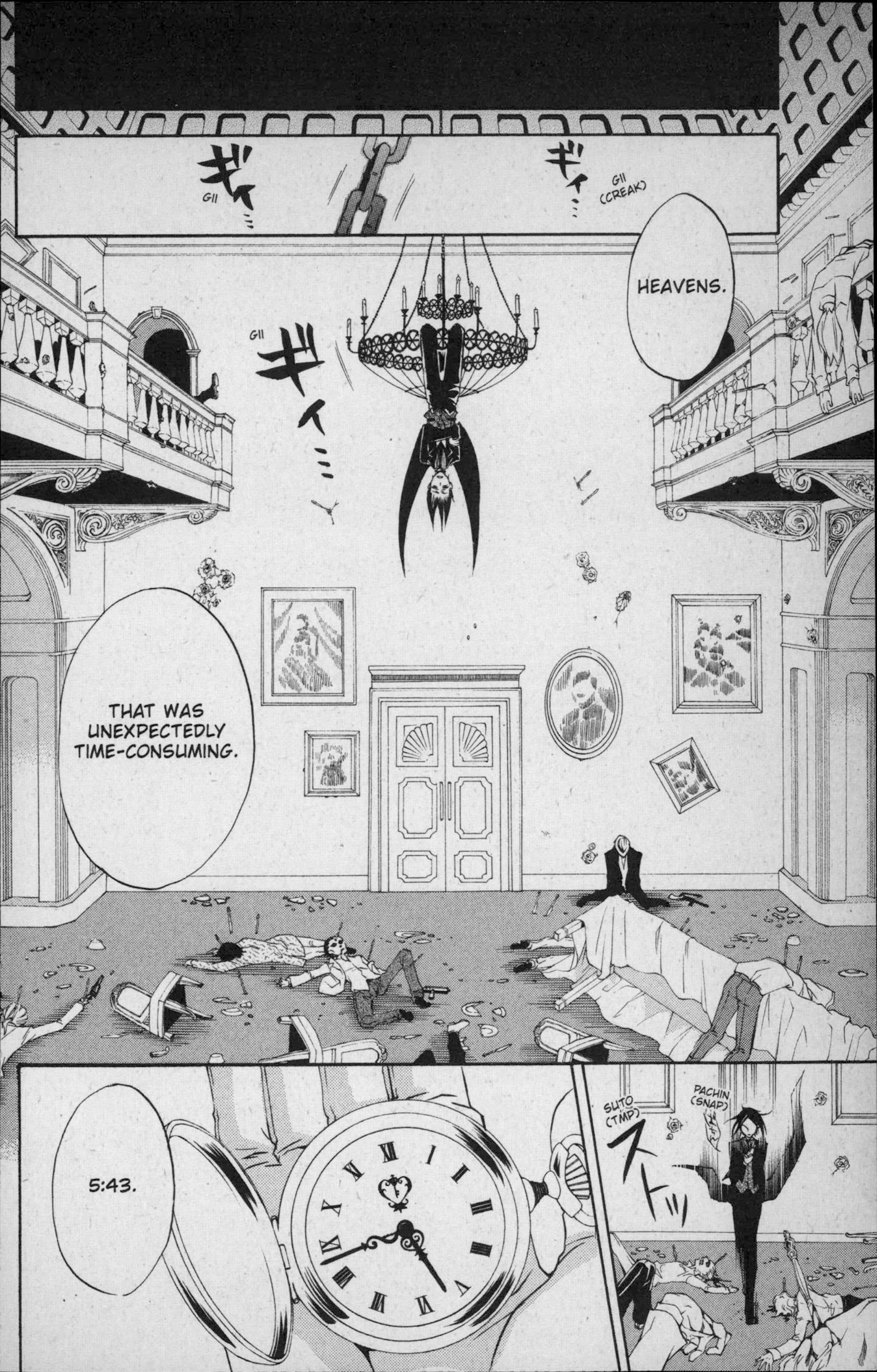
GII (CREAK)
GII
GII
HEAVENS.
THAT WAS UNEXPECTEDLY TIME-CONSUMING.
PACHIN (SNAP)
SUTO (TMP)
5:43.

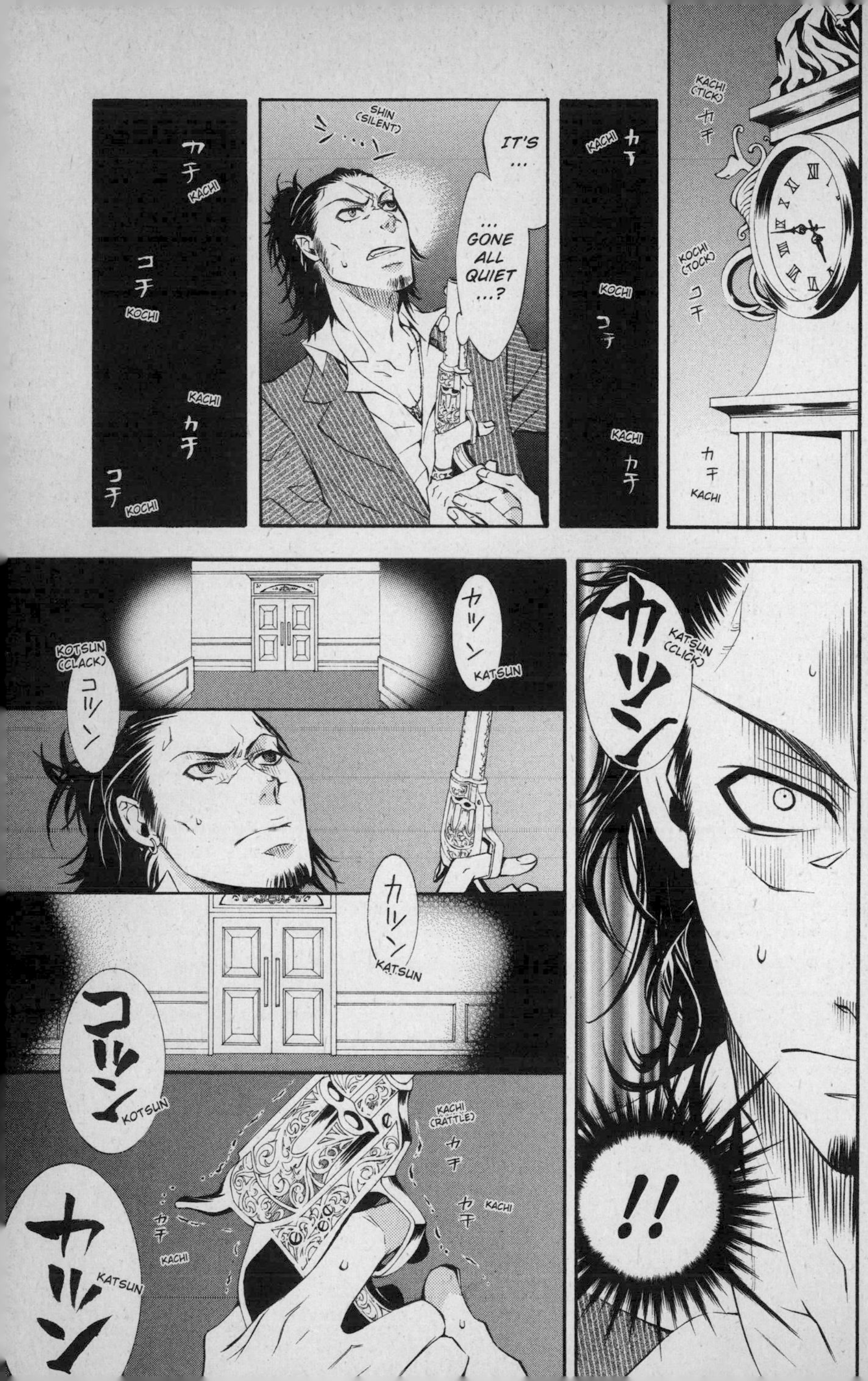

KACHI (TICK)
カチ
KOCHI (TOCK)
コチ
カチ
KACHI
KACHI
カチ
KOCHI
コチ
KACHI
カチ
SHIN (SILENT)
IT'S ...
... GONE ALL QUIET ...?
カチ
KACHI
コチ
KOCHI
KACHI
カチ
コチ
KOCHI
カツン
KATSUN (CLICK)
!!
カツン
KATSUN
KOTSUN (CLACK)
コツン
カツン
KATSUN
コツン
KOTSUN
KACHI (RATTLE)
カチ
カチ
KACHI
カチ
KACHI
カツン
KATSUN

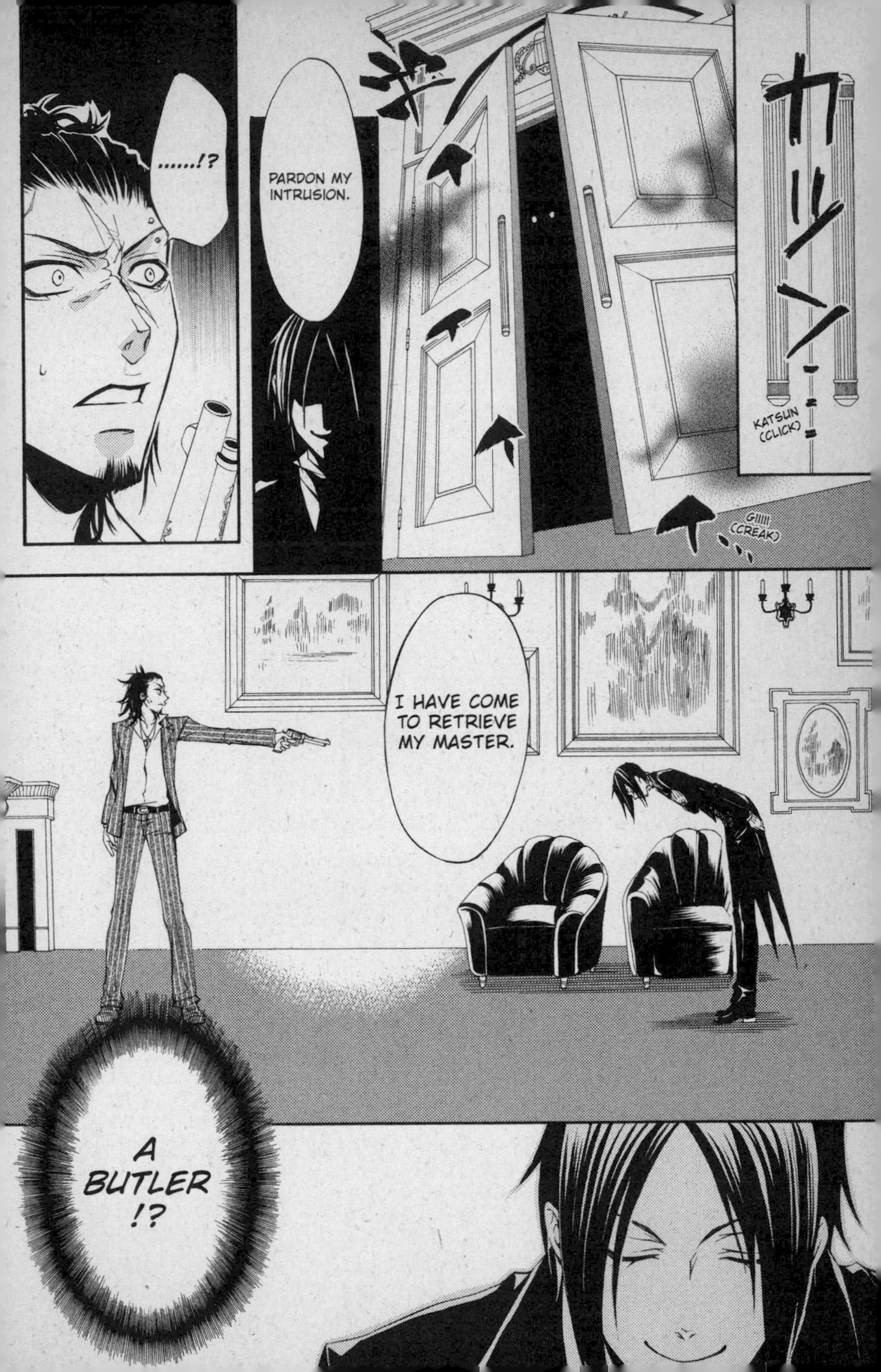
KATSUN (CLICK)
GIIII (CREAK)
PARDON MY INTRUSION.
......!?
I HAVE COME TO RETRIEVE MY MASTER.
A BUTLER !?

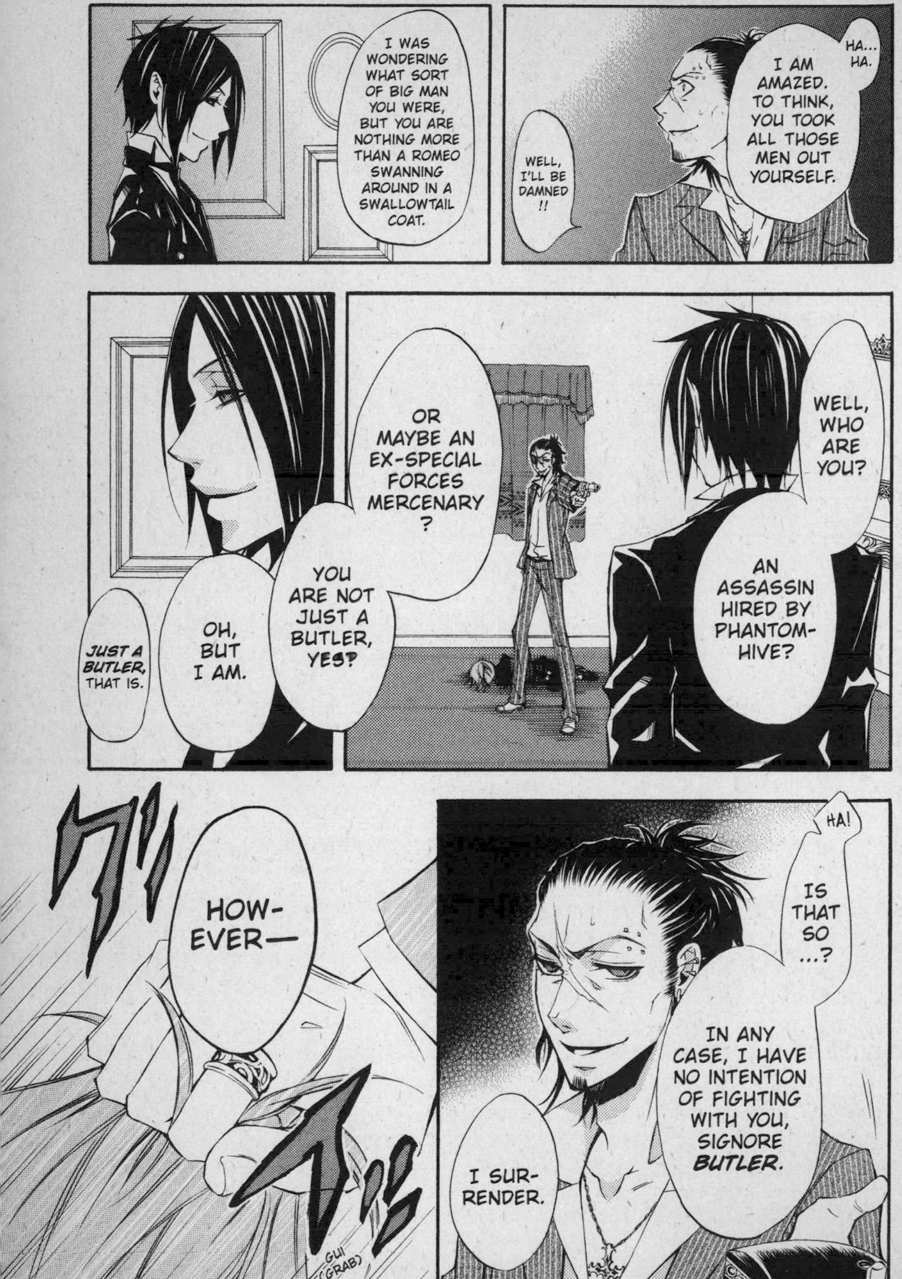
HA... HA.
I AM AMAZED. TO THINK, YOU TOOK ALL THOSE MEN OUT YOURSELF.
WELL, I'LL BE DAMNED!!
I WAS WONDERING WHAT SORT OF BIG MAN YOU WERE, BUT YOU ARE NOTHING MORE THAN A ROMEO SWANNING AROUND IN A SWALLOWTAIL COAT.
WELL, WHO ARE YOU?
AN ASSASSIN HIRED BY PHANTOM-HIVE?
OR MAYBE AN EX-SPECIAL FORCES MERCENARY?
YOU ARE NOT JUST A BUTLER, YES?
OH, BUT I AM.
*JUST A BUTLER*, THAT IS.
HA!
IS THAT SO...?
IN ANY CASE, I HAVE NO INTENTION OF FIGHTING WITH YOU, SIGNORE *BUTLER*.
I SUR-RENDER.
HOW-EVER—
GUI (GRAB)

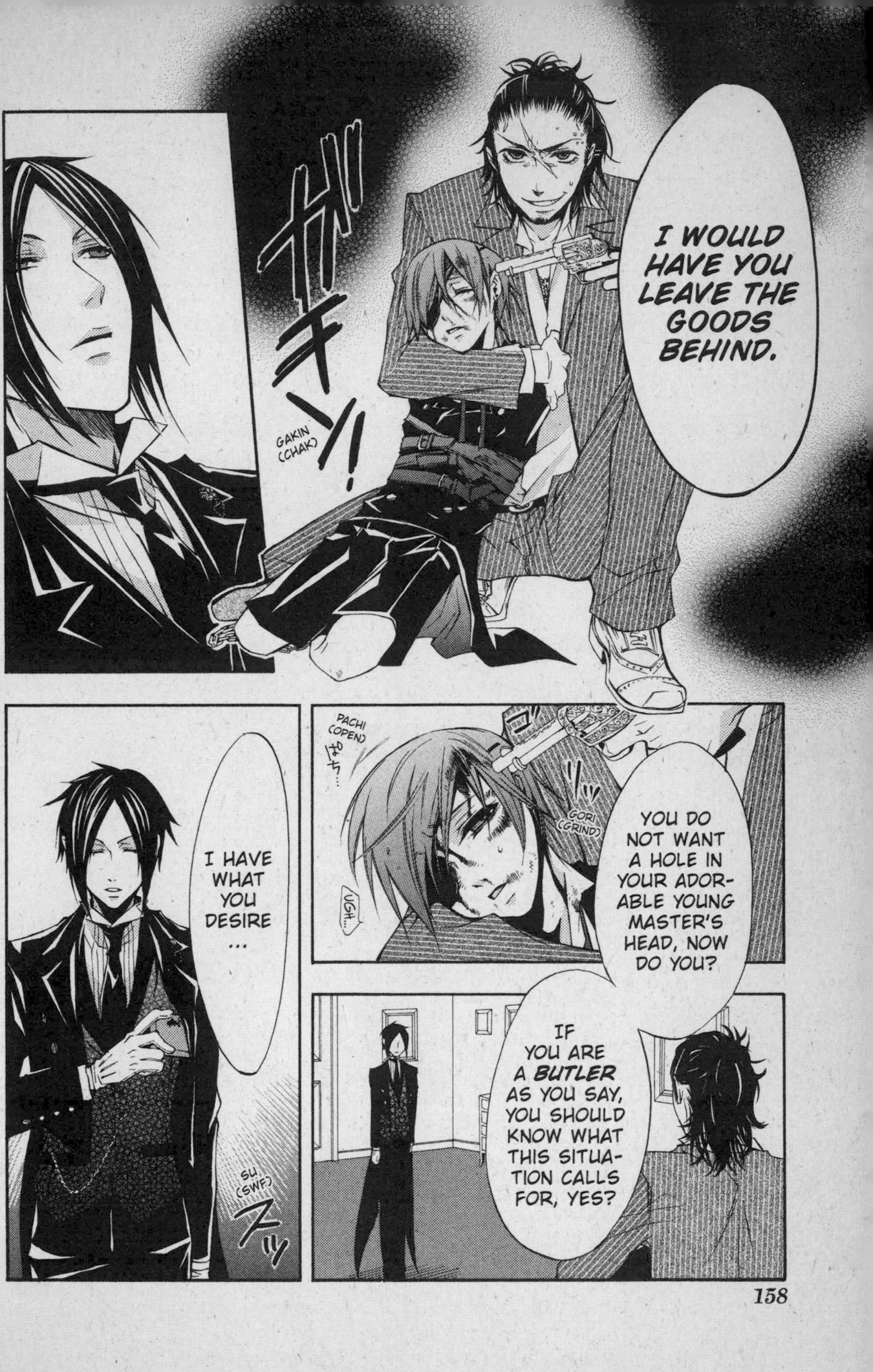
GAKIN (CHAK)
I WOULD HAVE YOU LEAVE THE GOODS BEHIND.
PACHI (OPEN)
GORI (GRIND)
UGH...
YOU DO NOT WANT A HOLE IN YOUR ADOR-ABLE YOUNG MASTER'S HEAD, NOW DO YOU?
IF YOU ARE A ***BUTLER*** AS YOU SAY, YOU SHOULD KNOW WHAT THIS SITUA-TION CALLS FOR, YES?
I HAVE WHAT YOU DESIRE ...
SU (SWF)

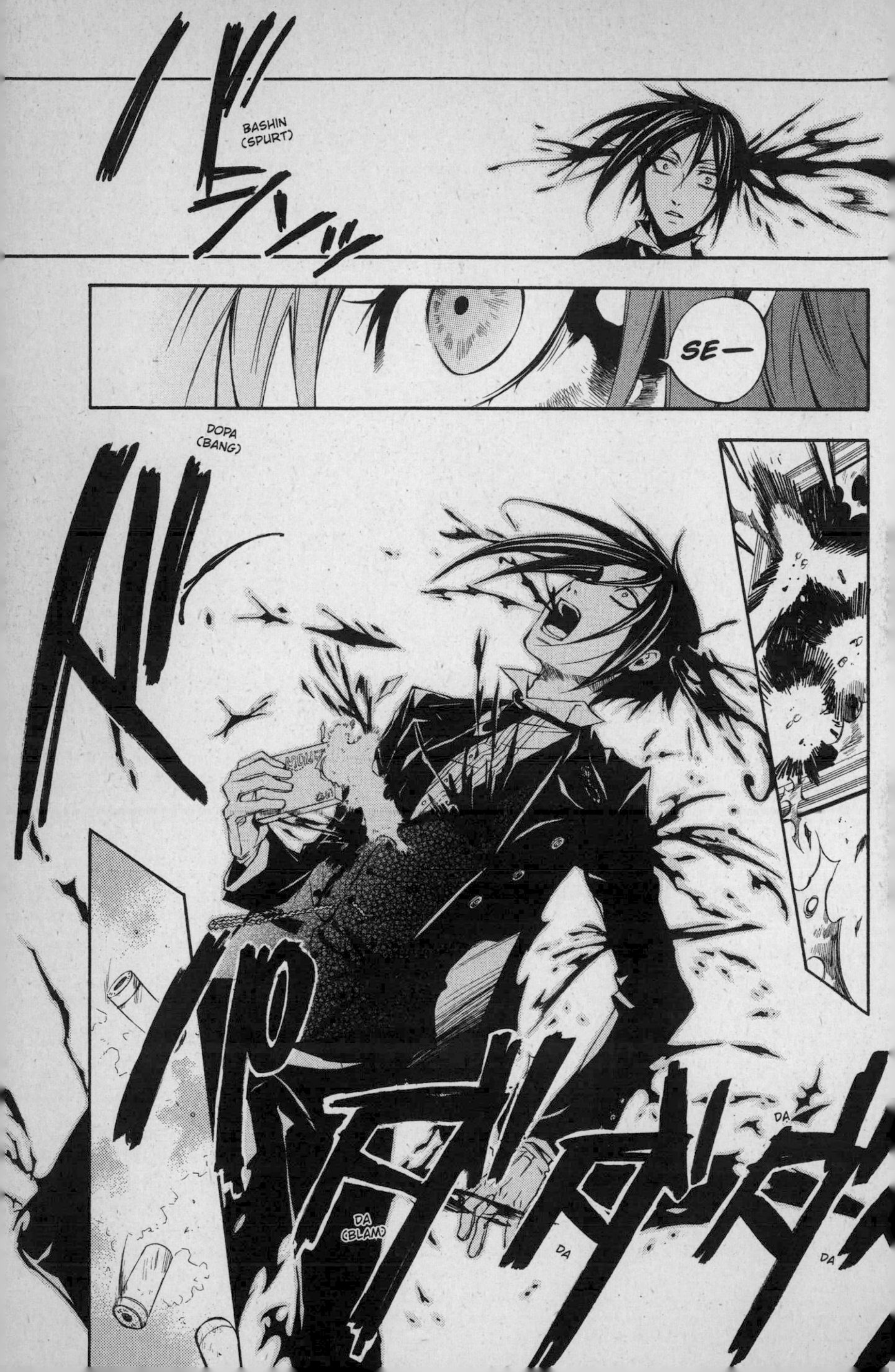
BASHIN (SPURT)
SE—
DOPA (BANG)
DA
DA
DA
DA (BLAM)

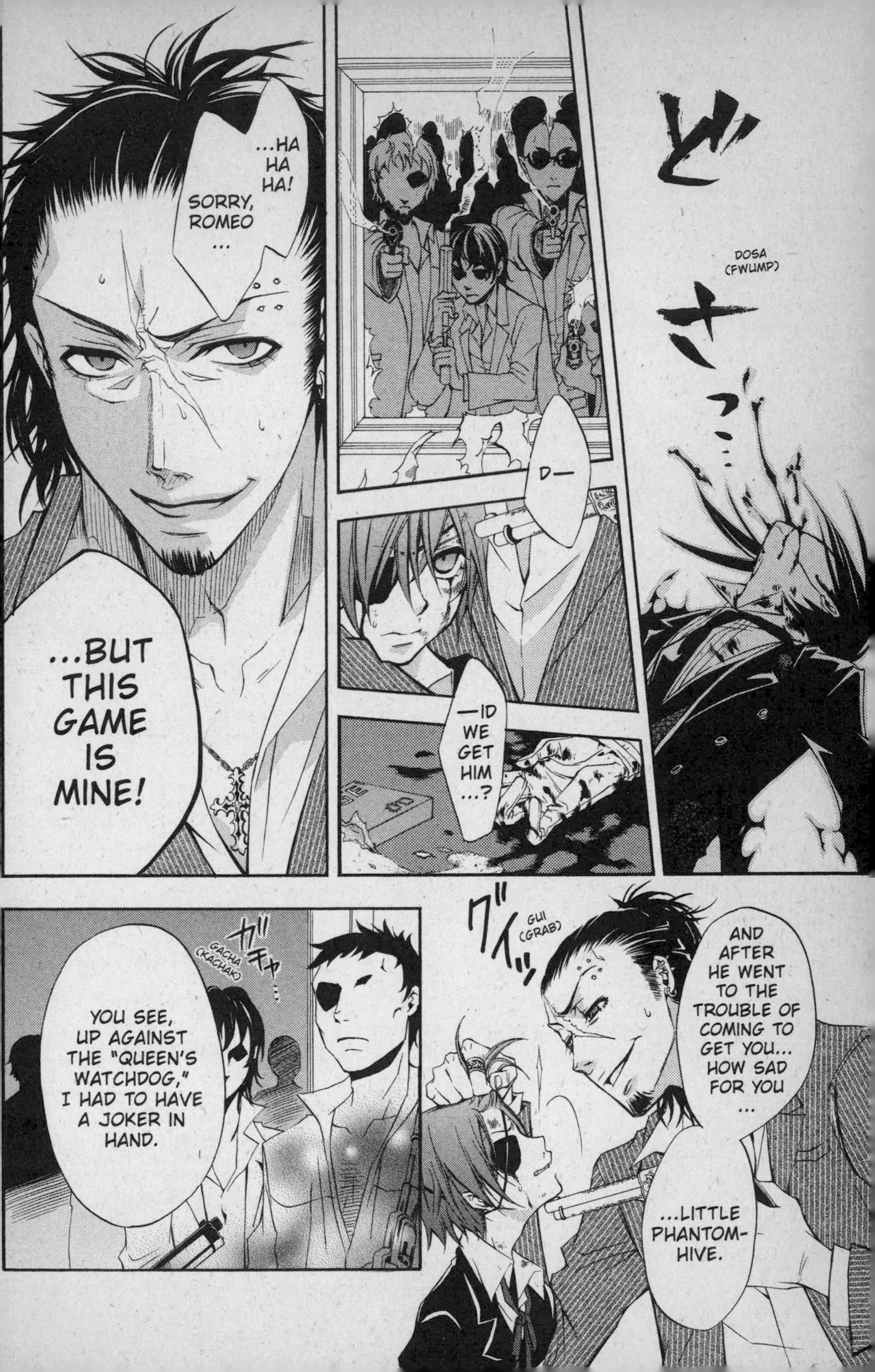
DOSA (FWUMP)
D—
—ID WE GET HIM ...?
...HA HA HA!
SORRY, ROMEO ...
...BUT THIS GAME IS MINE!
GUI (GRAB)
AND AFTER HE WENT TO THE TROUBLE OF COMING TO GET YOU... HOW SAD FOR YOU ...
...LITTLE PHANTOM-HIVE.
GACHA (KACHAK)
YOU SEE, UP AGAINST THE "QUEEN'S WATCHDOG," I HAD TO HAVE A JOKER IN HAND.

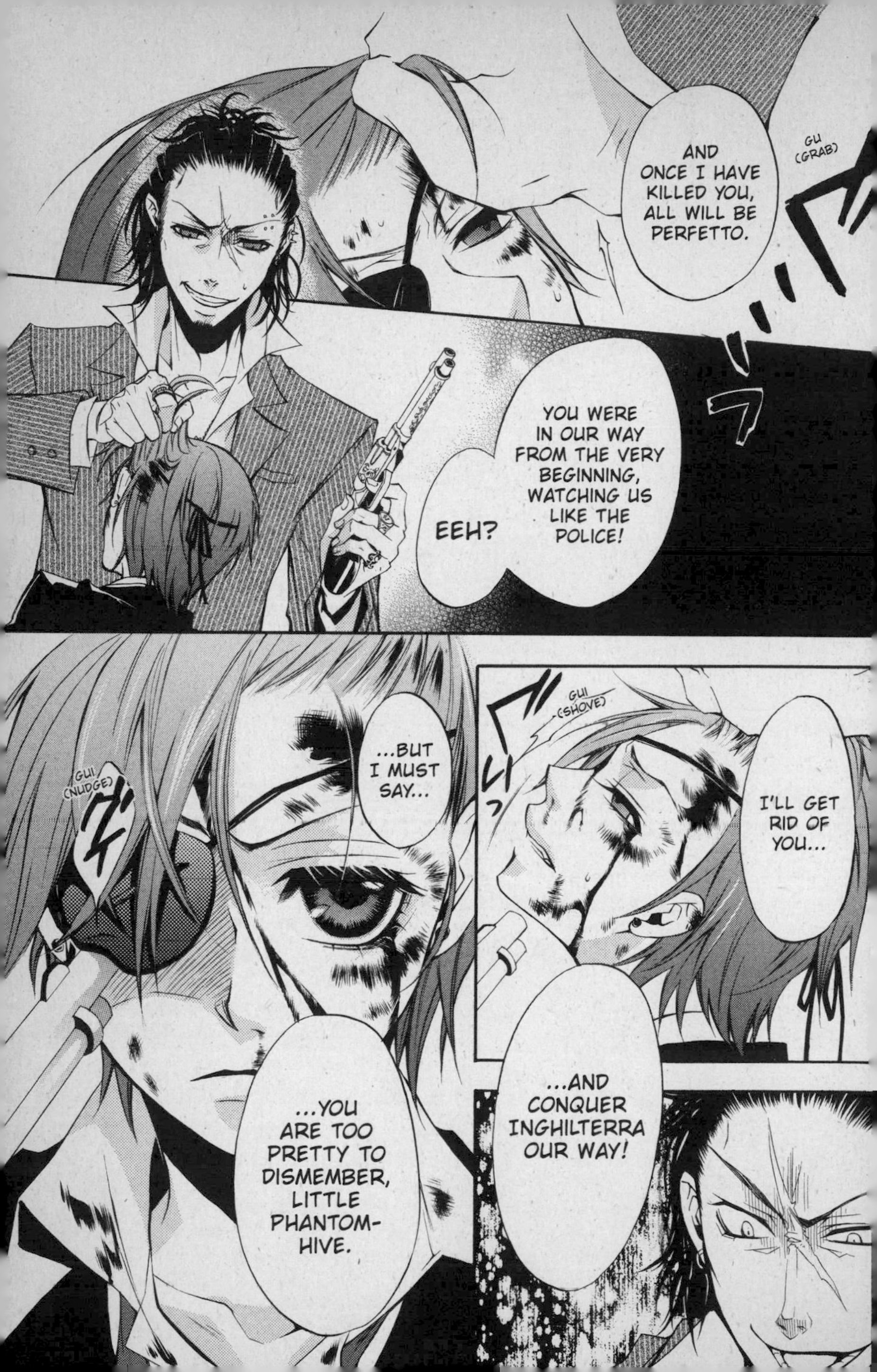
GU (GRAB)
AND ONCE I HAVE KILLED YOU, ALL WILL BE PERFETTO.
YOU WERE IN OUR WAY FROM THE VERY BEGINNING, WATCHING US LIKE THE POLICE!
EEH?
GUI (SHOVE)
I'LL GET RID OF YOU...
...AND CONQUER INGHILTERRA OUR WAY!
...BUT I MUST SAY...
GUI (NUDGE)
...YOU ARE TOO PRETTY TO DISMEMBER, LITTLE PHANTOM-HIVE.

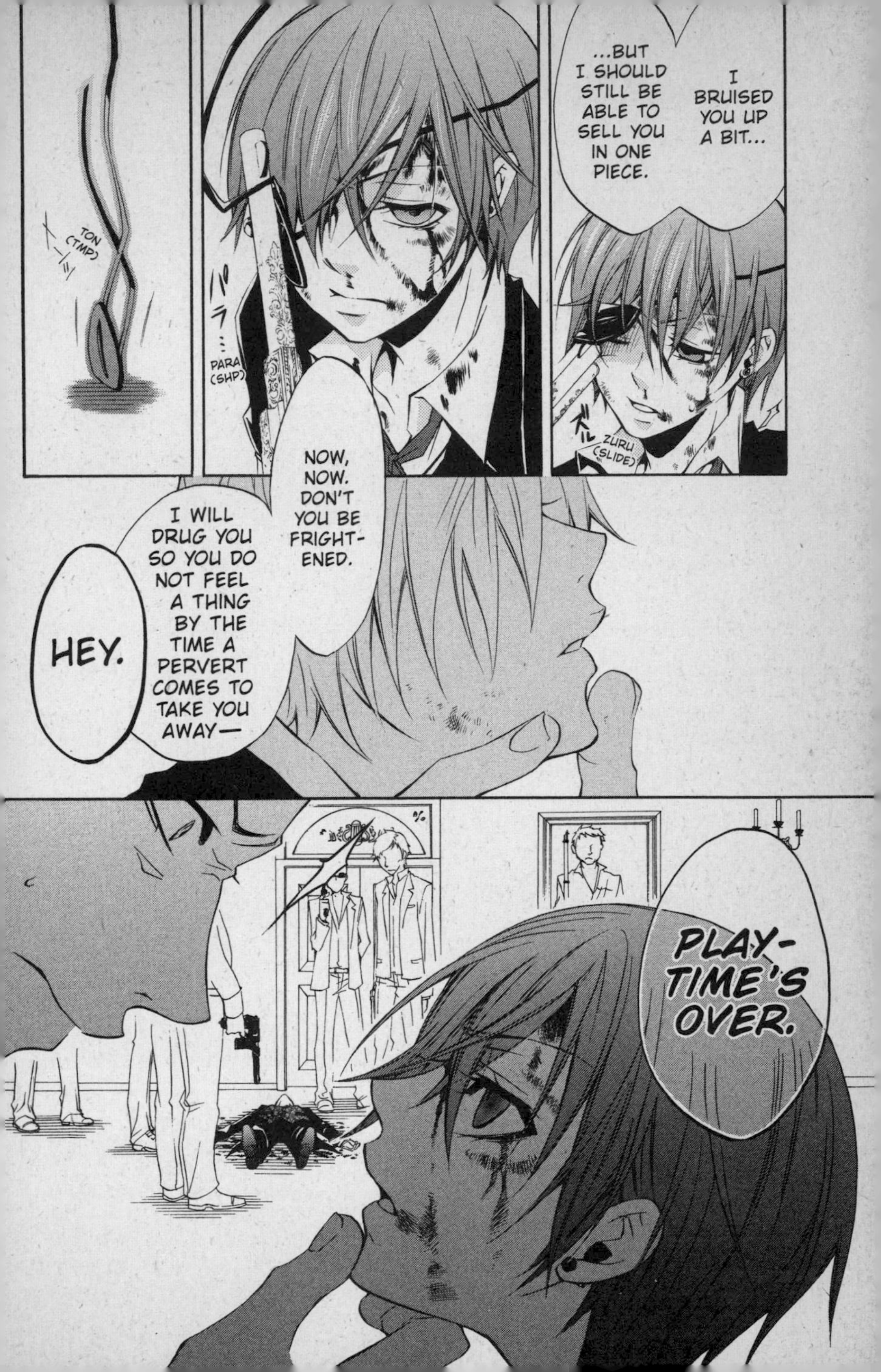
I BRUISED YOU UP A BIT...
...BUT I SHOULD STILL BE ABLE TO SELL YOU IN ONE PIECE.
ZURU (SLIDE)
PARA (SHP)
TON (TMP)
NOW, NOW. DON'T YOU BE FRIGHT-ENED.
I WILL DRUG YOU SO YOU DO NOT FEEL A THING BY THE TIME A PERVERT COMES TO TAKE YOU AWAY—
HEY.
PLAY-TIME'S OVER.

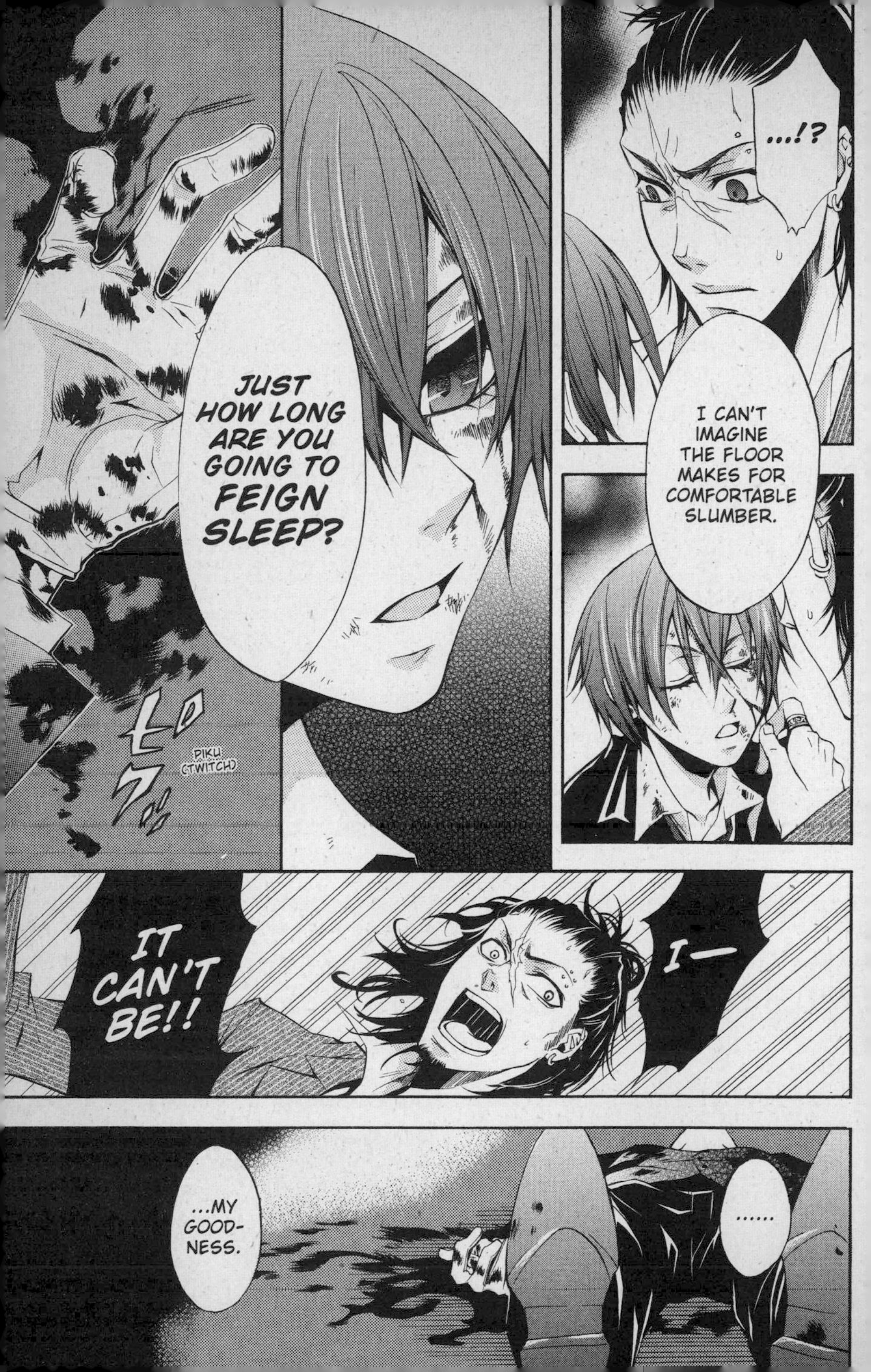
...!?
I CAN'T IMAGINE THE FLOOR MAKES FOR COMFORTABLE SLUMBER.
JUST HOW LONG ARE YOU GOING TO FEIGN SLEEP?
PIKU (TWITCH)
I—
IT CAN'T BE!!
......
...MY GOODNESS.

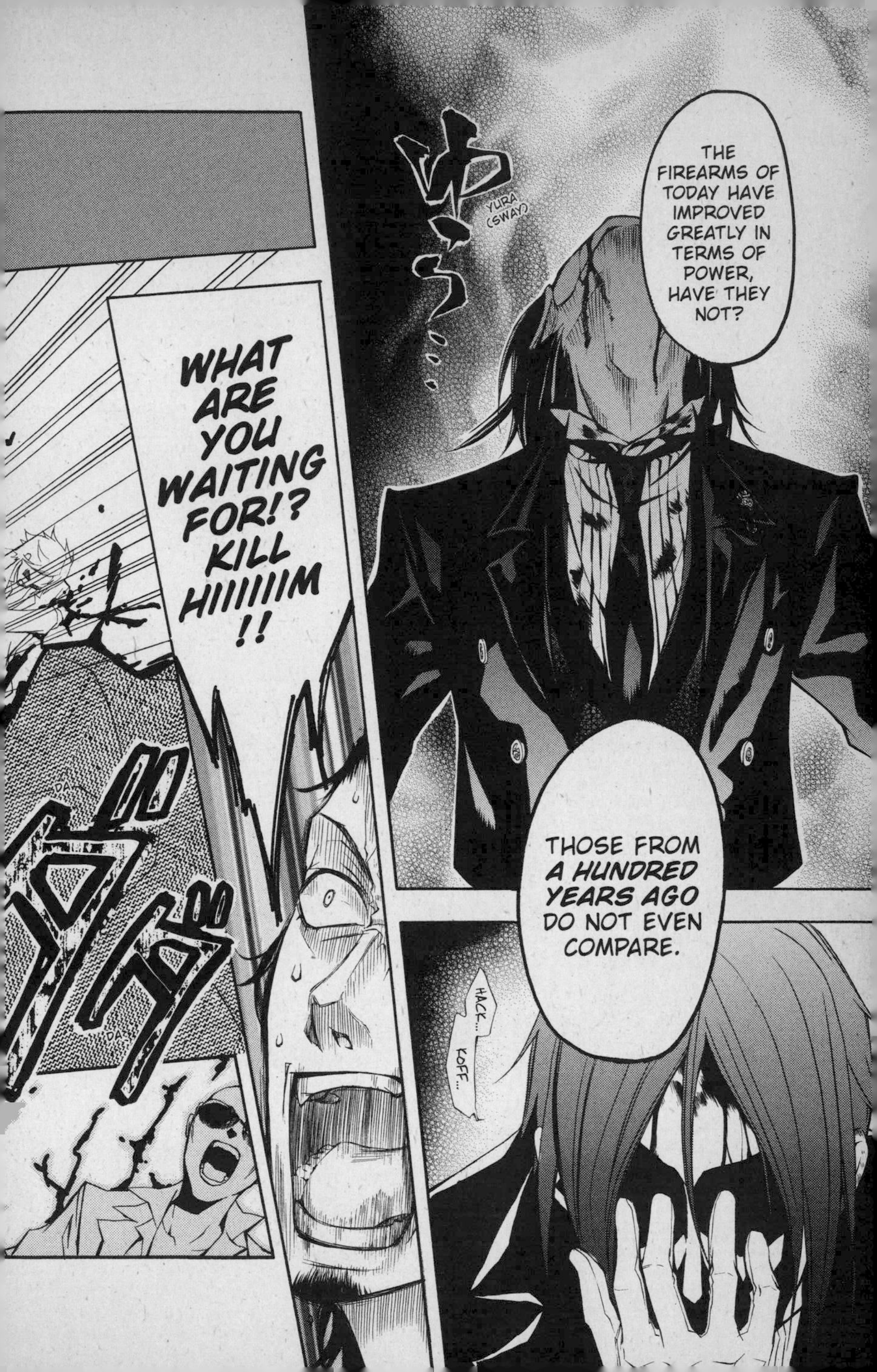
YURA (SWAY)
THE FIREARMS OF TODAY HAVE IMPROVED GREATLY IN TERMS OF POWER, HAVE THEY NOT?
THOSE FROM A HUNDRED YEARS AGO DO NOT EVEN COMPARE.
HACK... KOFF...
WHAT ARE YOU WAITING FOR!? KILL HIIIIIIM!!
DA
DA

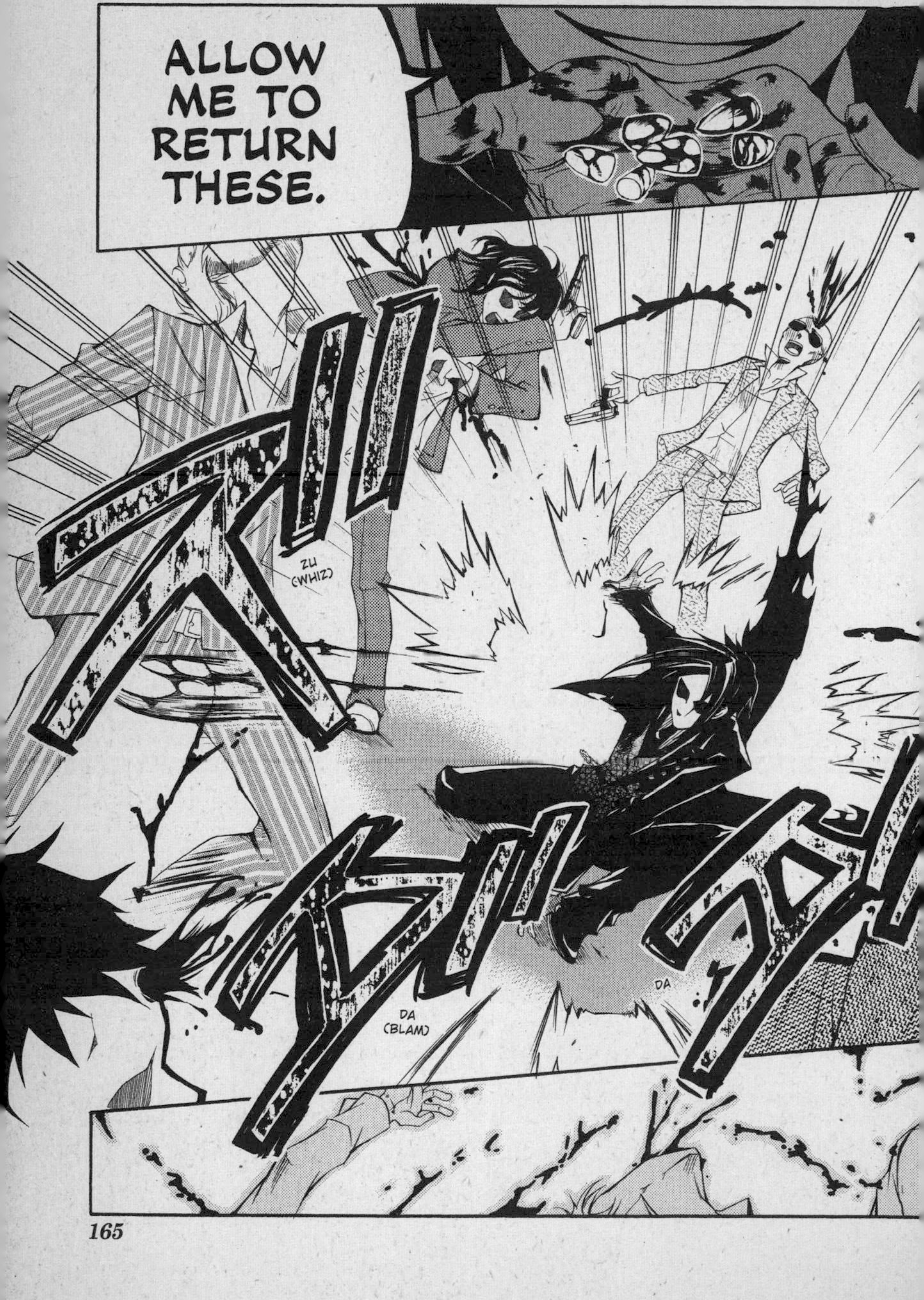
ALLOW ME TO RETURN THESE.
ZU (WHIZ)
DA
DA (BLAM)

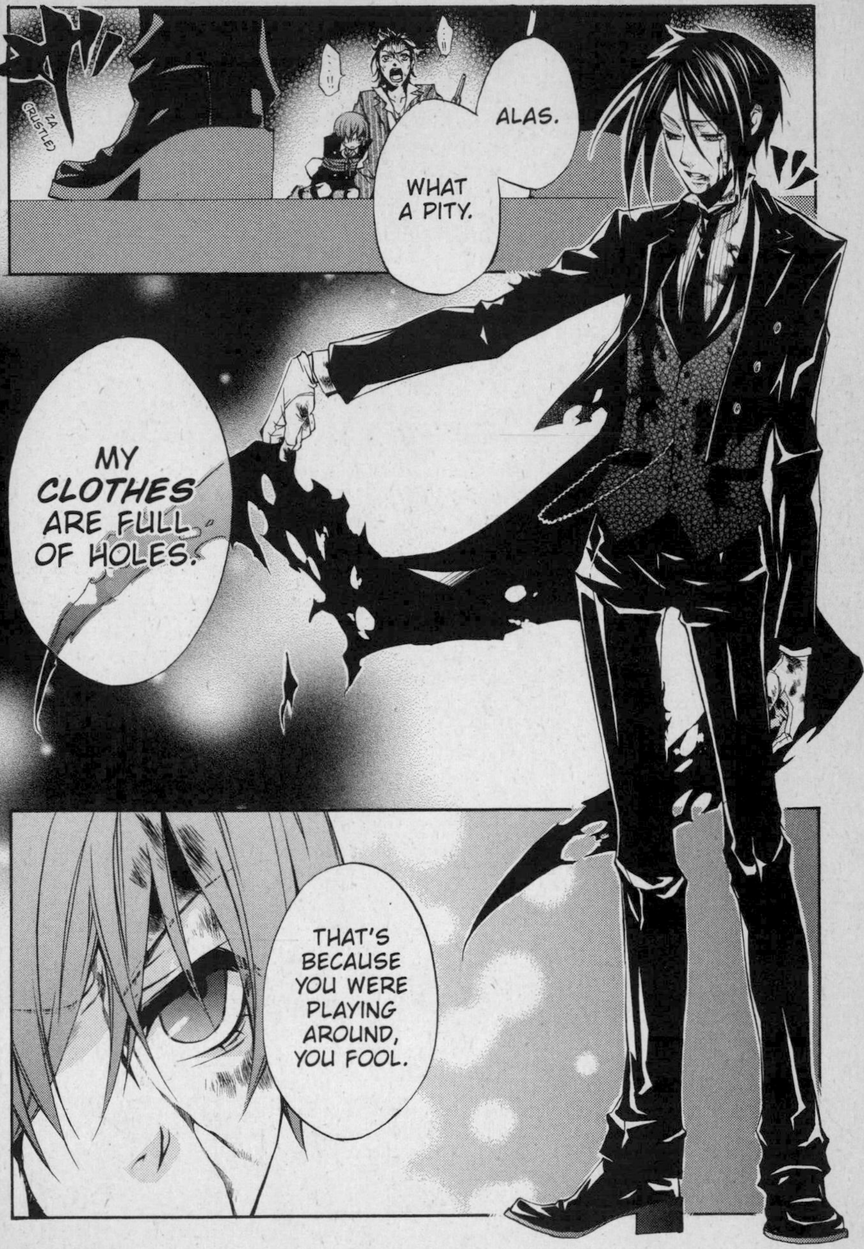
ALAS.
WHAT A PITY.
...!!
...!!
ZA (RUSTLE)
MY CLOTHES ARE FULL OF HOLES.
THAT'S BECAUSE YOU WERE PLAYING AROUND, YOU FOOL.

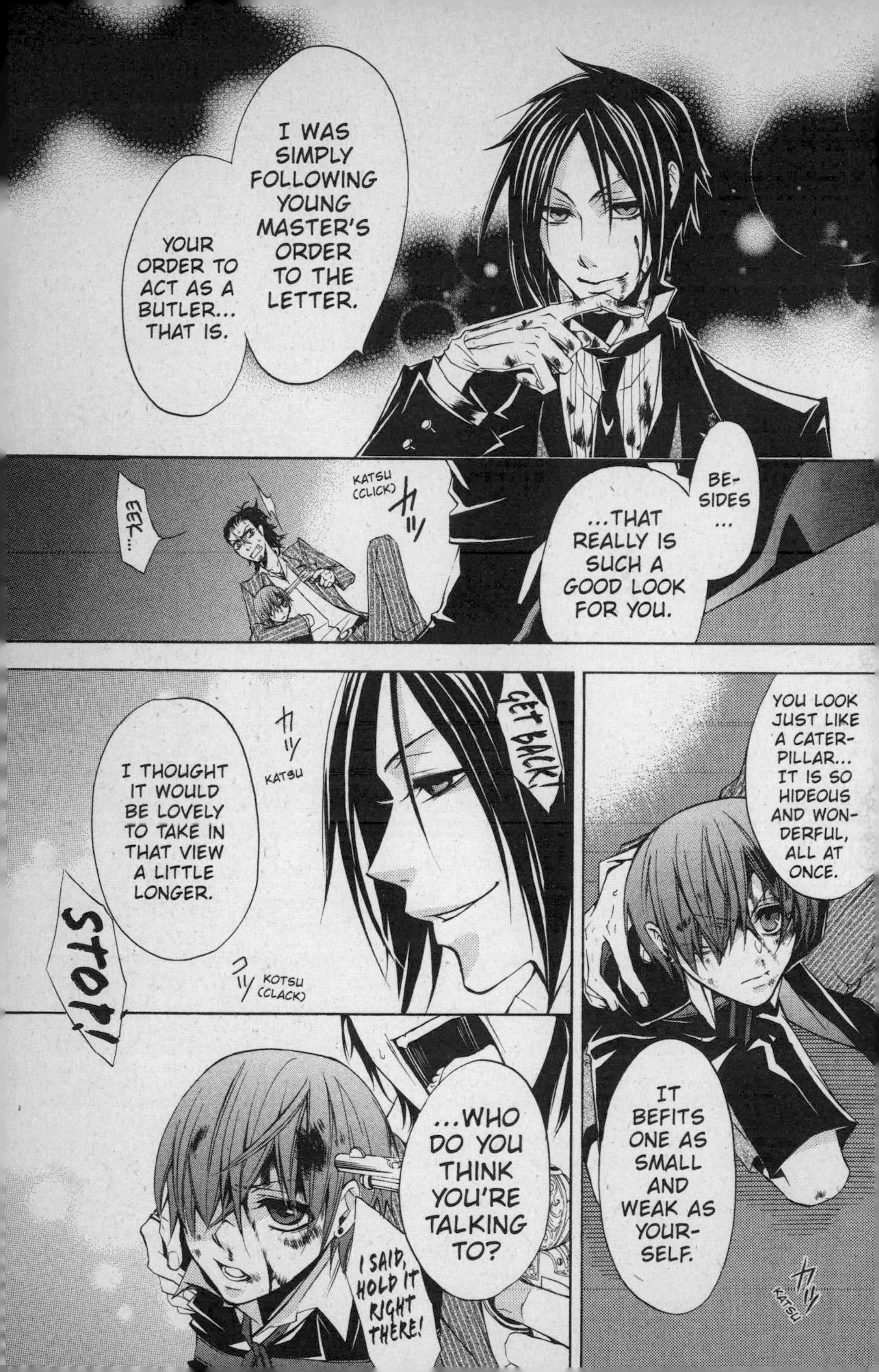
I WAS SIMPLY FOLLOWING YOUNG MASTER'S ORDER TO THE LETTER.
YOUR ORDER TO ACT AS A BUTLER... THAT IS.
BE-SIDES...
...THAT REALLY IS SUCH A GOOD LOOK FOR YOU.
KATSU (CLICK)
EEK...
YOU LOOK JUST LIKE A CATER-PILLAR... IT IS SO HIDEOUS AND WON-DERFUL, ALL AT ONCE.
IT BEFITS ONE AS SMALL AND WEAK AS YOUR-SELF.
KATSU
GET BACK!
KATSU
I THOUGHT IT WOULD BE LOVELY TO TAKE IN THAT VIEW A LITTLE LONGER.
KOTSU (CLACK)
STOP!
...WHO DO YOU THINK YOU'RE TALKING TO?
I SAID, HOLD IT RIGHT THERE!

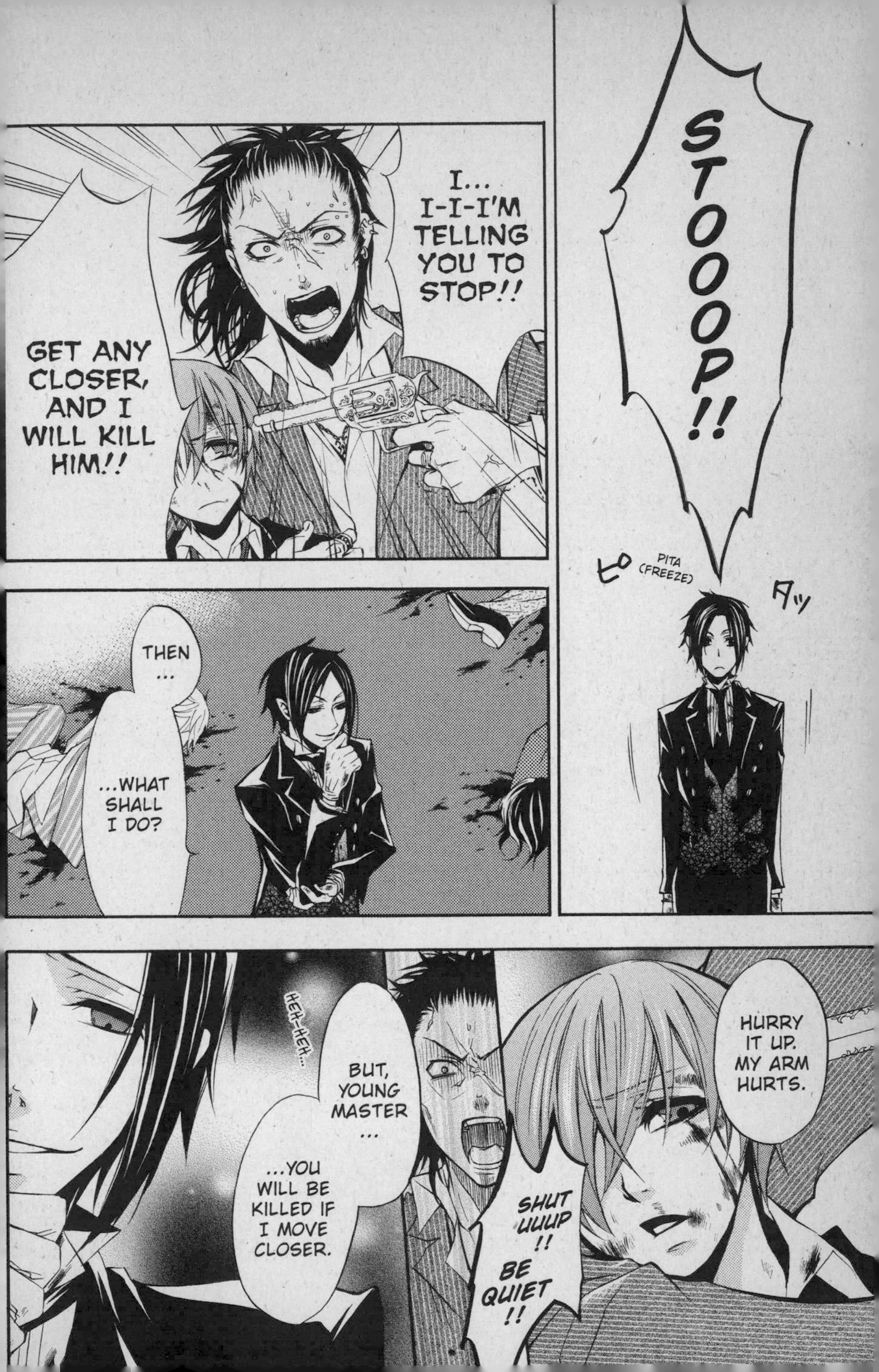
STOOOP!!
ピ PITA (FREEZE)
タッ
I... I-I-I'M TELLING YOU TO STOP!!
GET ANY CLOSER, AND I WILL KILL HIM!!
THEN...
...WHAT SHALL I DO?
HURRY IT UP. MY ARM HURTS.
SHUT UUUP!! BE QUIET!!
HEH-HEH...
BUT, YOUNG MASTER...
...YOU WILL BE KILLED IF I MOVE CLOSER.

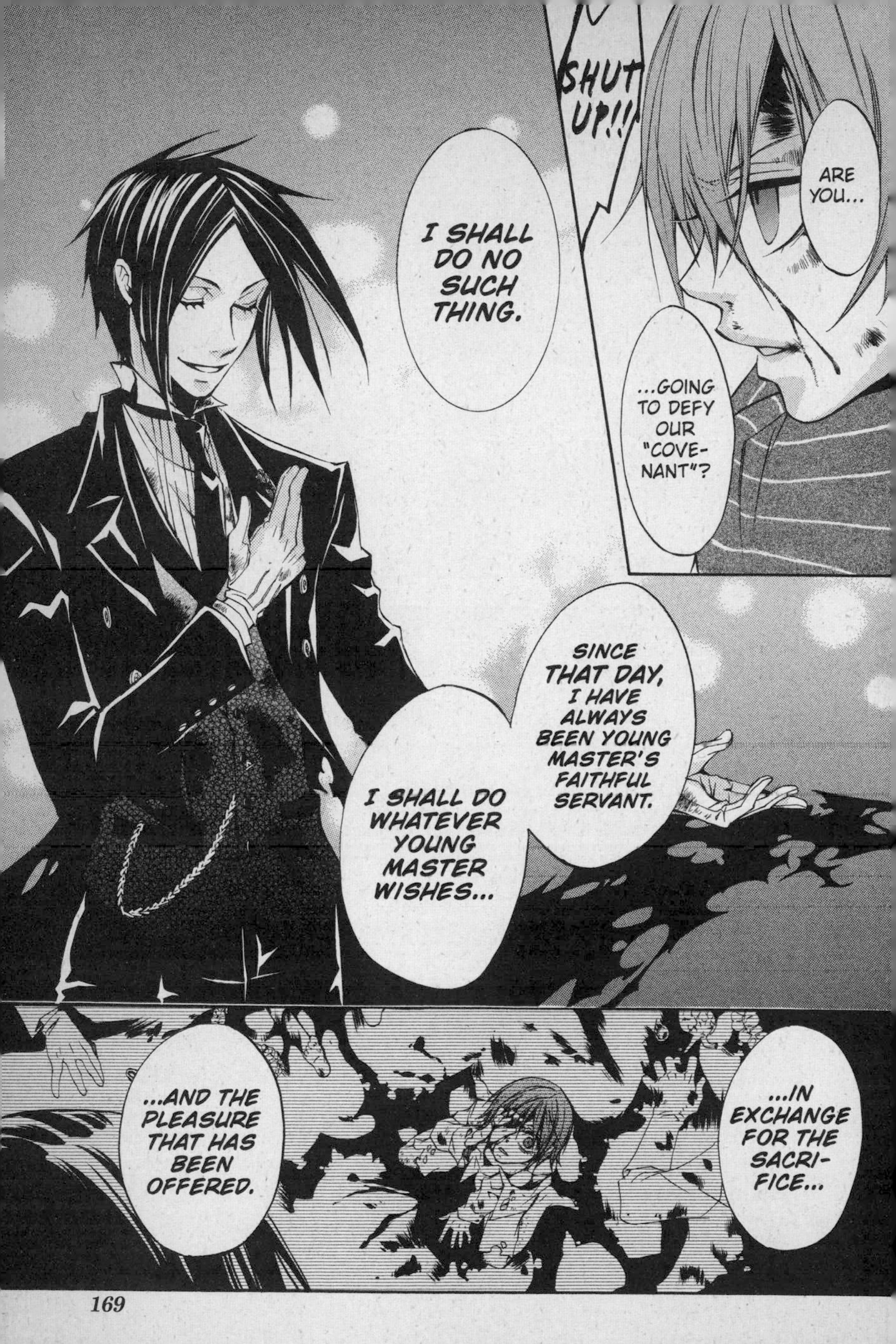
ARE YOU...
...GOING TO DEFY OUR "COVENANT"?
SHUT UP!!
I SHALL DO NO SUCH THING.
SINCE THAT DAY, I HAVE ALWAYS BEEN YOUNG MASTER'S FAITHFUL SERVANT.
I SHALL DO WHATEVER YOUNG MASTER WISHES...
...IN EXCHANGE FOR THE SACRIFICE...
...AND THE PLEASURE THAT HAS BEEN OFFERED.

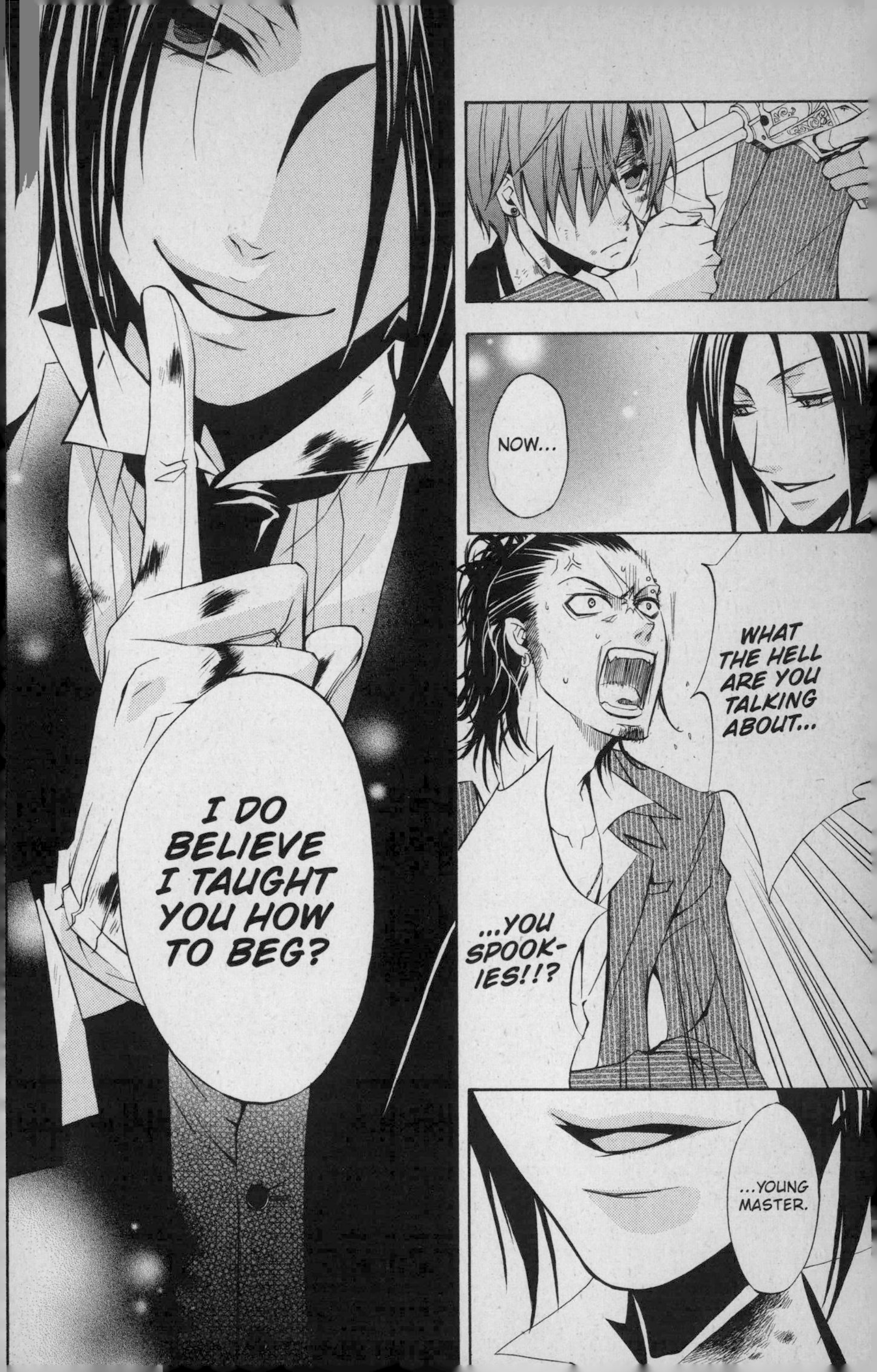
NOW...
WHAT THE HELL ARE YOU TALKING ABOUT...
...YOU SPOOK-IES!!?
...YOUNG MASTER.
I DO BELIEVE I TAUGHT YOU HOW TO BEG?

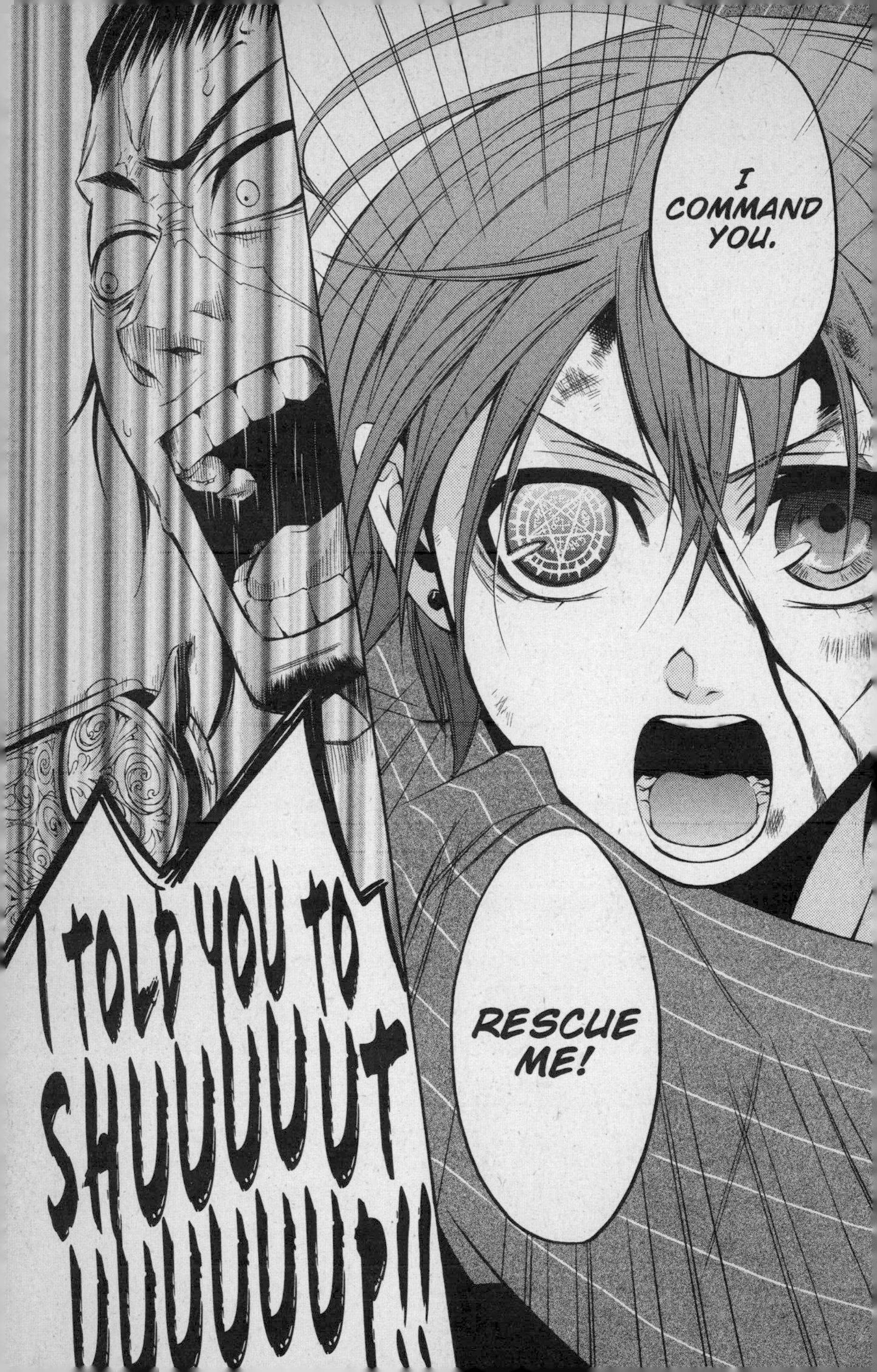
I COMMAND YOU.
RESCUE ME!
I TOLD YOU TO SHUUUUUT UUUUUUP!!

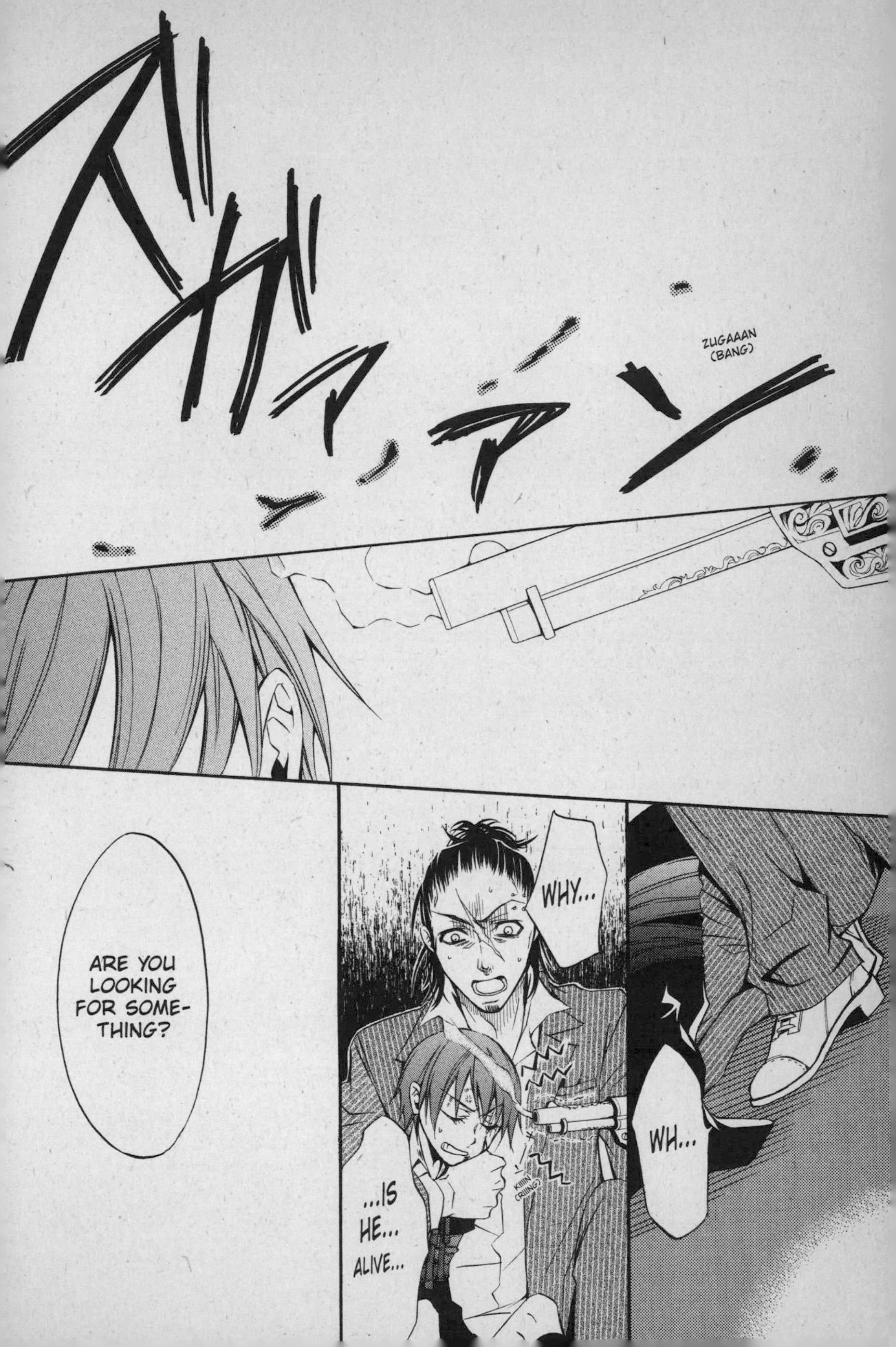
ZUGAAAN (BANG)
WH...
WHY...
KIIIN (RIING)
...IS HE... ALIVE...
ARE YOU LOOKING FOR SOME-THING?

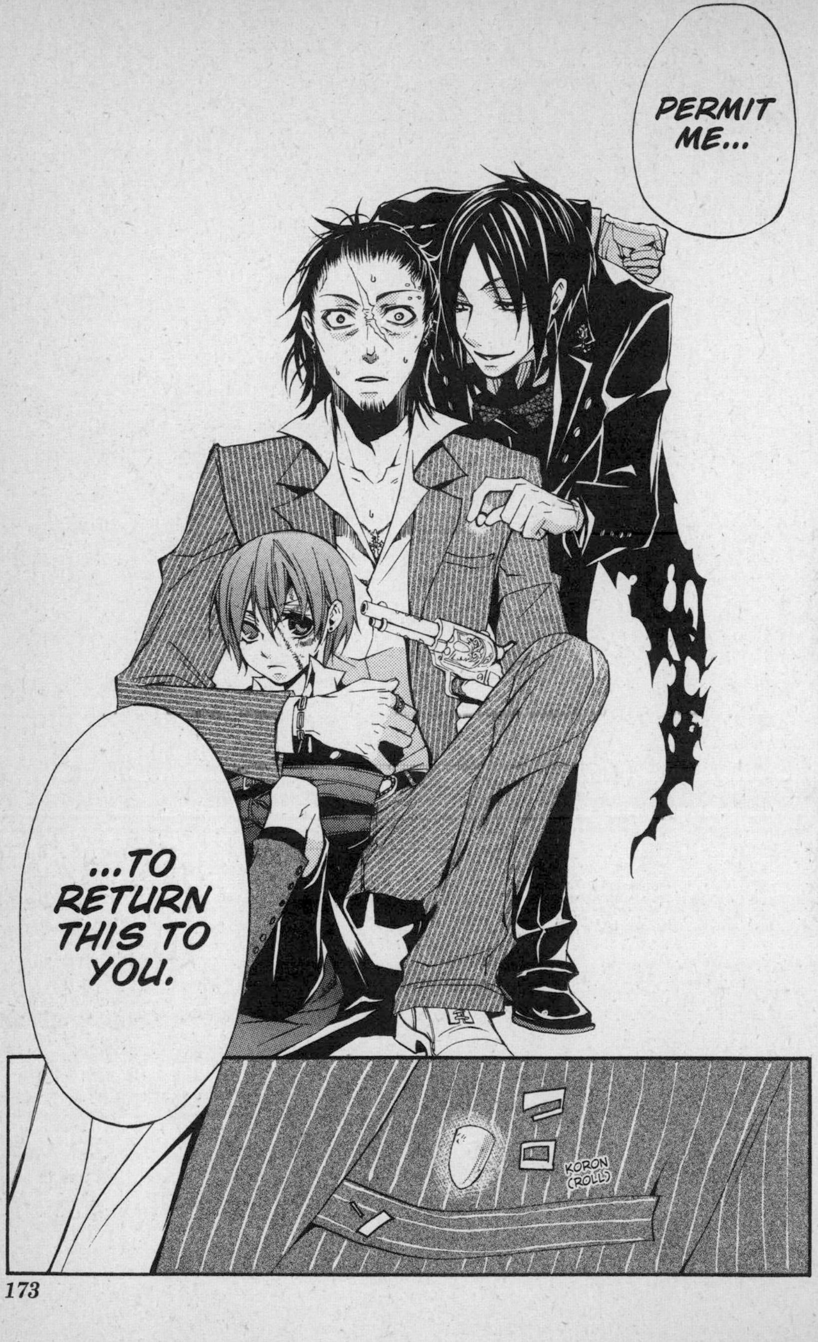

PERMIT ME...
...TO RETURN THIS TO YOU.
KORON (ROLL)

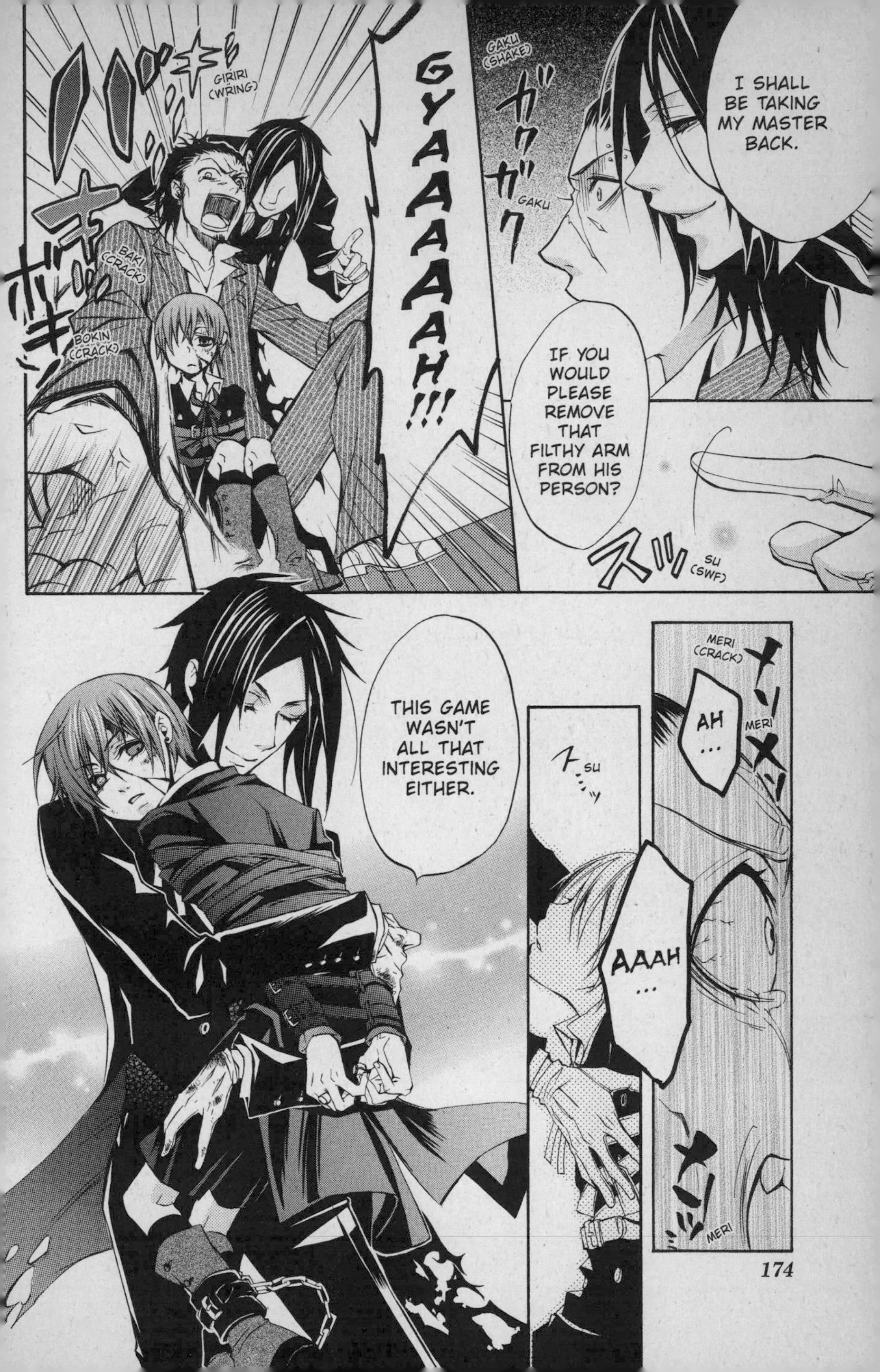

I SHALL BE TAKING MY MASTER BACK.
GAKU (SHAKE)
GAKU
IF YOU WOULD PLEASE REMOVE THAT FILTHY ARM FROM HIS PERSON?
SU (SWF)
GYAAAAAH!!!
GIRIRI (WRING)
BAKI (CRACK)
BOKIN (CRACK)
MERI (CRACK)
AH ...
MERI
MERI
SU
AAAH ...
THIS GAME WASN'T ALL THAT INTERESTING EITHER.

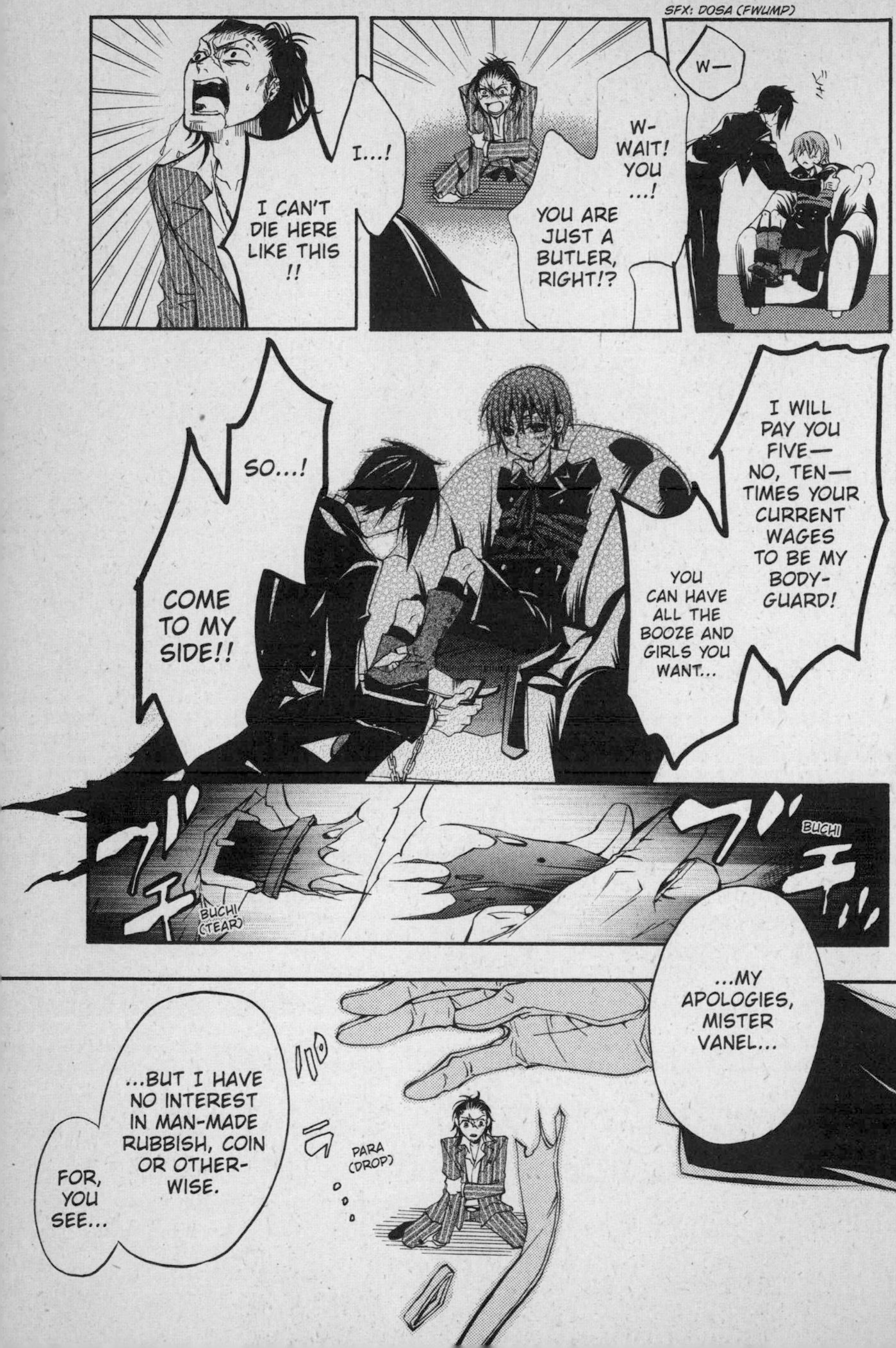
SFX: DOSA (FWUMP)
W—
W- WAIT! YOU ...!
YOU ARE JUST A BUTLER, RIGHT!?
I...!
I CAN'T DIE HERE LIKE THIS !!
I WILL PAY YOU FIVE— NO, TEN— TIMES YOUR CURRENT WAGES TO BE MY BODY-GUARD!
YOU CAN HAVE ALL THE BOOZE AND GIRLS YOU WANT...
SO...!
COME TO MY SIDE!!
BUCHI
BUCHI (TEAR)
...MY APOLOGIES, MISTER VANEL...
PARA (DROP)
...BUT I HAVE NO INTEREST IN MAN-MADE RUBBISH, COIN OR OTHER-WISE.
FOR, YOU SEE...

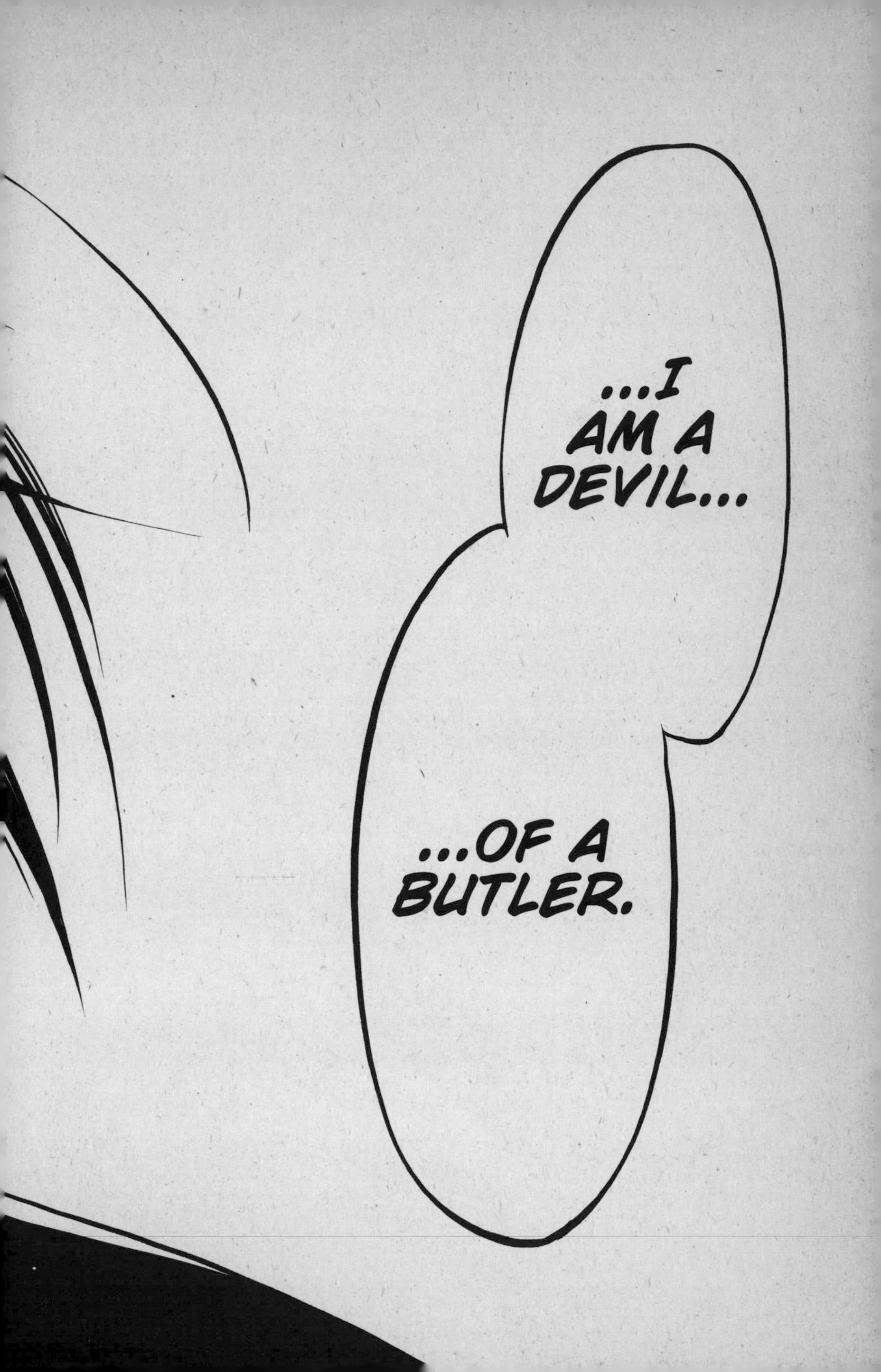
...I AM A DEVIL...
...OF A BUTLER.

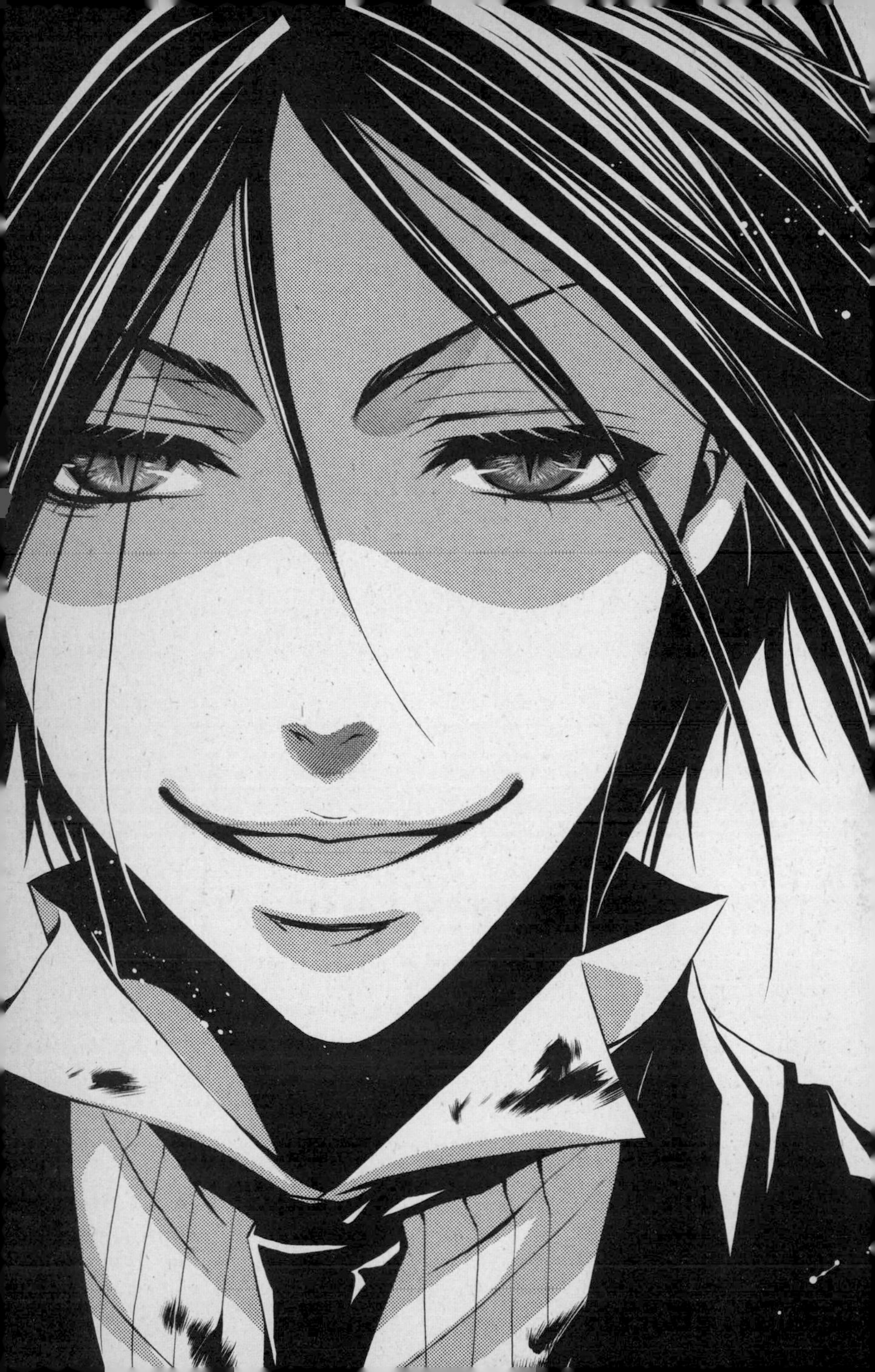

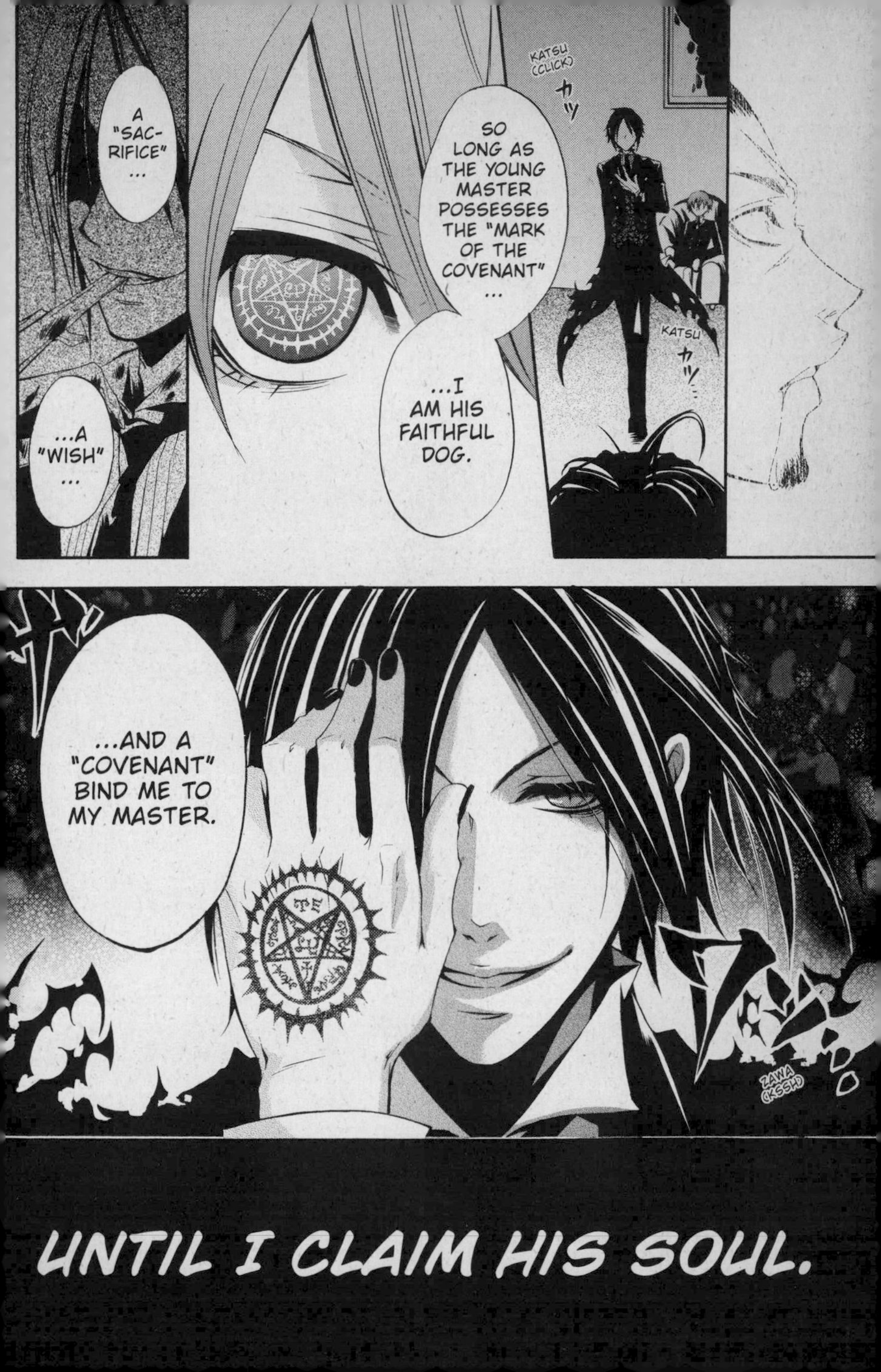
KATSU (CLICK)
カッ
KATSU
カッ
SO LONG AS THE YOUNG MASTER POSSESSES THE "MARK OF THE COVENANT" ...
...I AM HIS FAITHFUL DOG.
A "SAC-RIFICE" ...
...A "WISH" ...
...AND A "COVENANT" BIND ME TO MY MASTER.
ZAWA (KSSH)
UNTIL I CLAIM HIS SOUL.

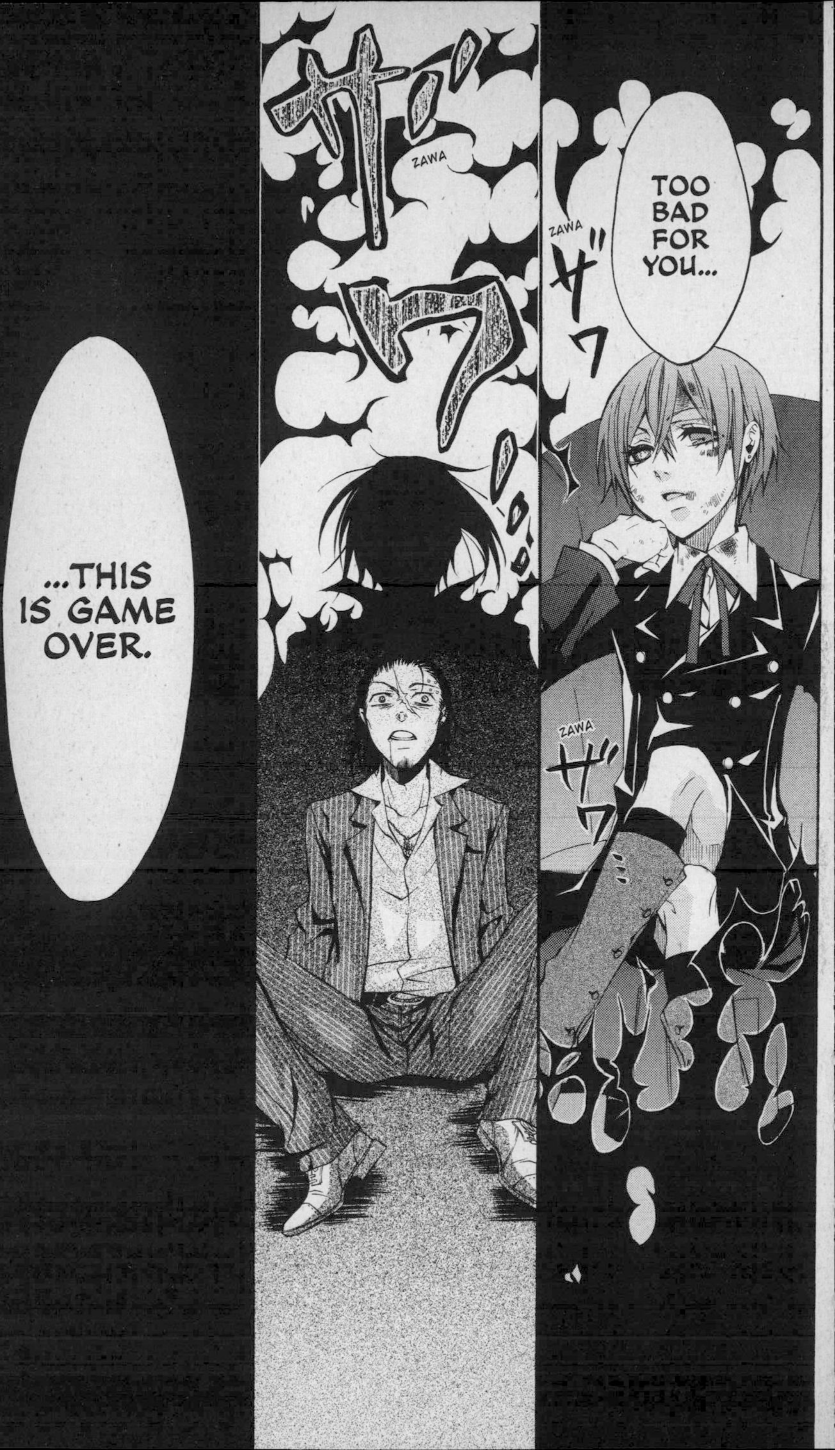
TOO BAD FOR YOU...
ザワ
ZAWA
ザワ
ZAWA
ザワ
ZAWA
...THIS IS GAME OVER.

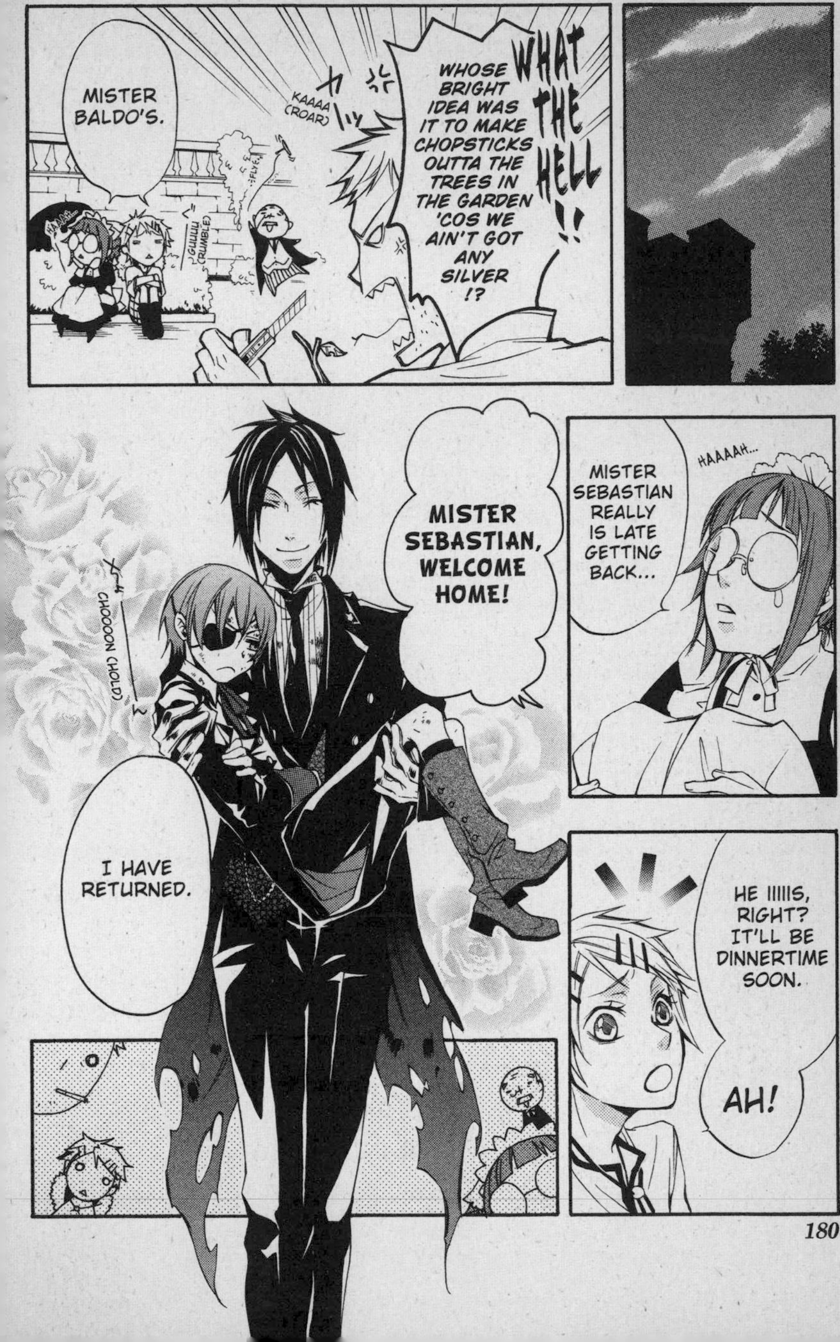
WHAT THE HELL!!
WHOSE BRIGHT IDEA WAS IT TO MAKE CHOPSTICKS OUTTA THE TREES IN THE GARDEN 'COS WE AIN'T GOT ANY SILVER!?
KAAAA (ROAR)
MISTER BALDO'S.
HAAAAH...
MISTER SEBASTIAN REALLY IS LATE GETTING BACK...
HE IIIIIS, RIGHT? IT'LL BE DINNERTIME SOON.
AH!
MISTER SEBASTIAN, WELCOME HOME!
CHOOOON (HOLD)
I HAVE RETURNED.

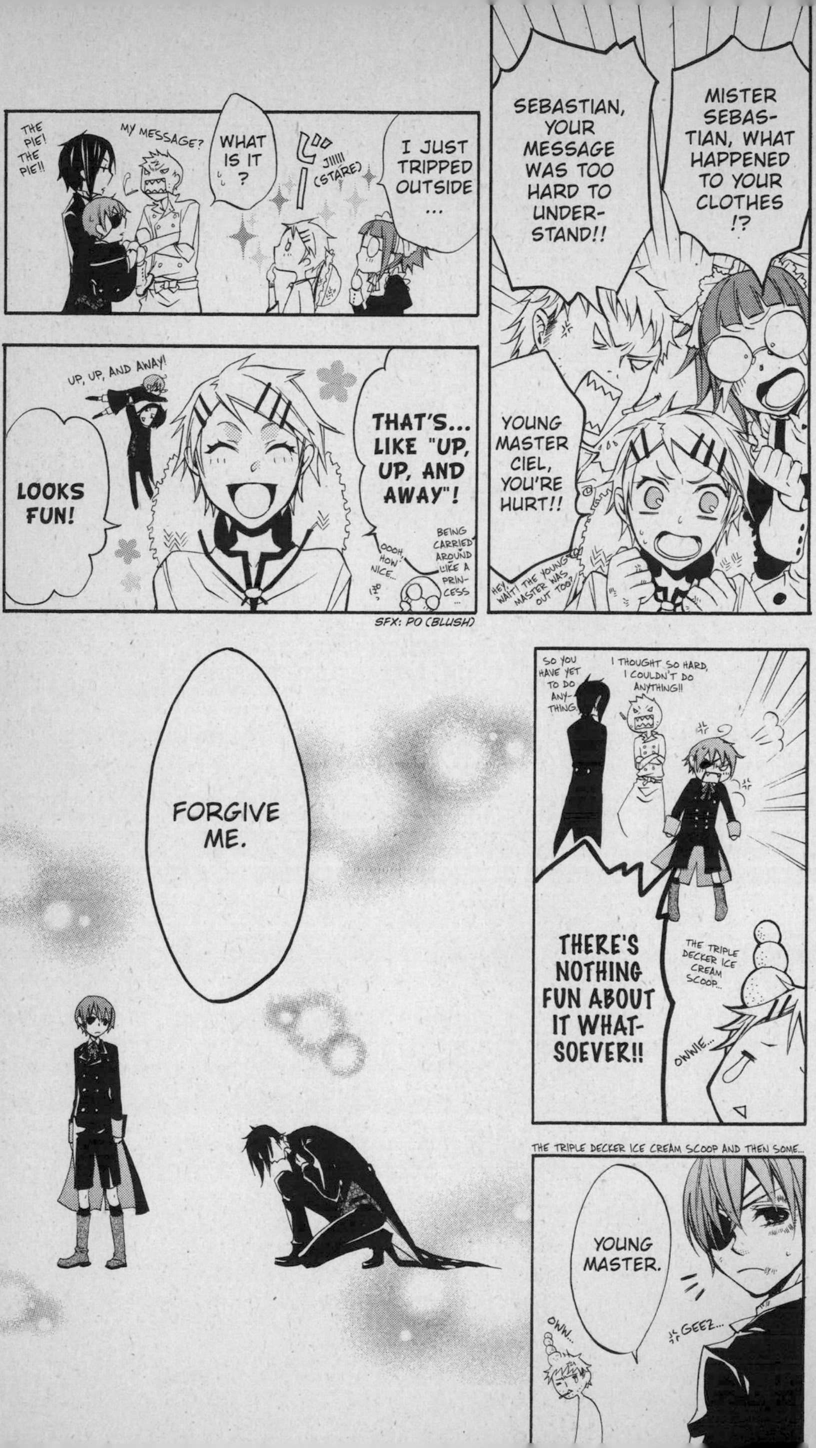
MISTER SEBAS-TIAN, WHAT HAPPENED TO YOUR CLOTHES !?
SEBASTIAN, YOUR MESSAGE WAS TOO HARD TO UNDER-STAND!!
YOUNG MASTER CIEL, YOU'RE HURT!!
HEY, WAIT! THE YOUNG MASTER WAS OUT TOO?
I JUST TRIPPED OUTSIDE ...
JI!!!!! (STARE)
WHAT IS IT ?
MY MESSAGE?
THE PIE! THE PIE!!
THAT'S... LIKE "UP, UP, AND AWAY"!
BEING CARRIED AROUND LIKE A PRIN-CESS ...
OOOH, HOW NICE...
LOOKS FUN!
UP, UP, AND AWAY!
SFX: PO (BLUSH)
I THOUGHT SO HARD, I COULDN'T DO ANYTHING!!
SO YOU HAVE YET TO DO ANY-THING.
THERE'S NOTHING FUN ABOUT IT WHAT-SOEVER!!
THE TRIPLE DECKER ICE CREAM SCOOP...
OWWIE...
THE TRIPLE DECKER ICE CREAM SCOOP AND THEN SOME...
YOUNG MASTER.
GEEZ...
OWW...
FORGIVE ME.

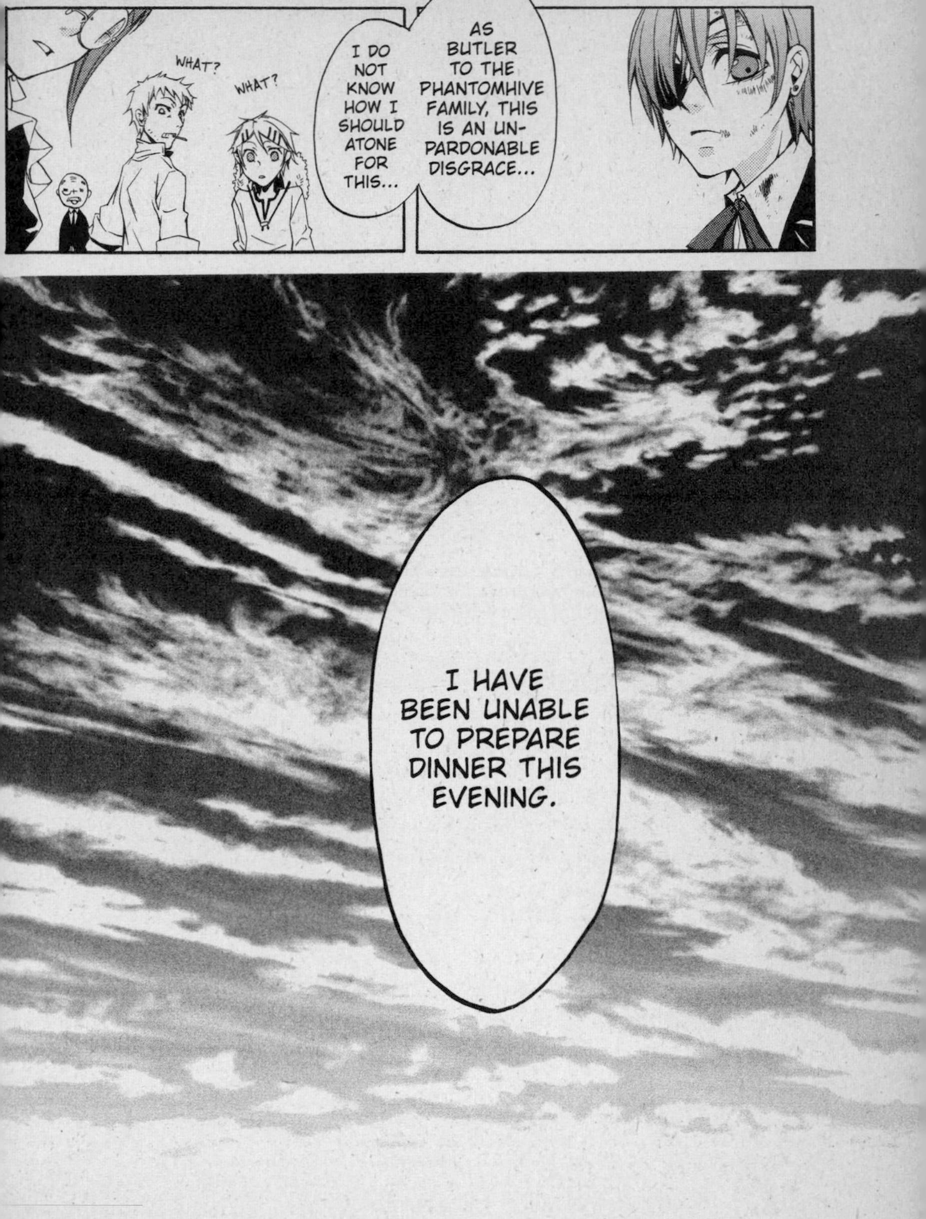
AS BUTLER TO THE PHANTOMHIVE FAMILY, THIS IS AN UN-PARDONABLE DISGRACE...
I DO NOT KNOW HOW I SHOULD ATONE FOR THIS...
WHAT?
WHAT?
I HAVE BEEN UNABLE TO PREPARE DINNER THIS EVENING.

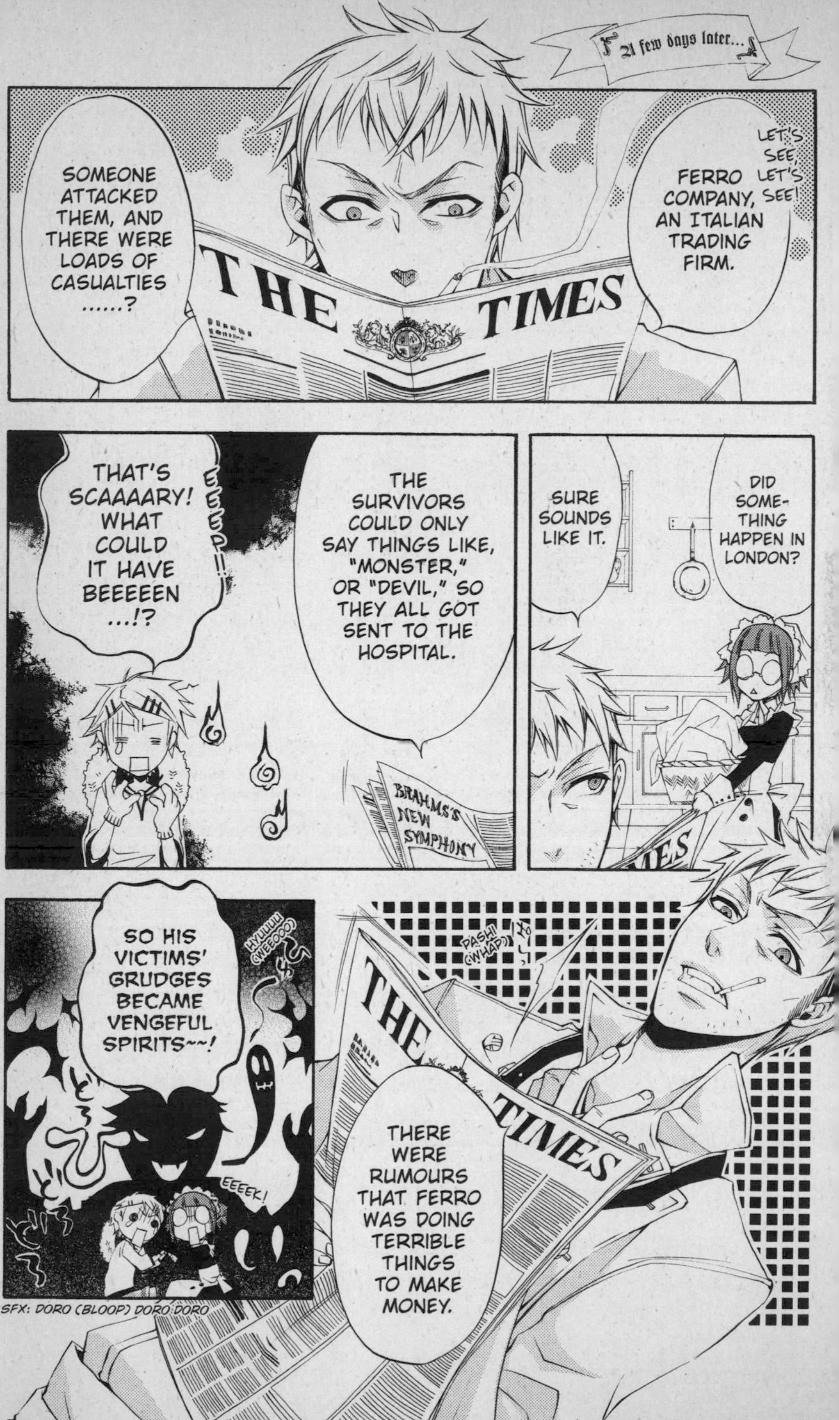
A few days later...
LET'S SEE, LET'S SEE!
FERRO COMPANY, AN ITALIAN TRADING FIRM.
THE TIMES
SOMEONE ATTACKED THEM, AND THERE WERE LOADS OF CASUALTIES ......?
DID SOMETHING HAPPEN IN LONDON?
SURE SOUNDS LIKE IT.
THE SURVIVORS COULD ONLY SAY THINGS LIKE, "MONSTER," OR "DEVIL," SO THEY ALL GOT SENT TO THE HOSPITAL.
BRAHMS'S NEW SYMPHONY
EEEP!!
THAT'S SCAAAARY! WHAT COULD IT HAVE BEEEEEN ...!?
PASH! (WHAP)
THE TIMES
THERE WERE RUMOURS THAT FERRO WAS DOING TERRIBLE THINGS TO MAKE MONEY.
HYUUUU (WEEOOO)
SO HIS VICTIMS' GRUDGES BECAME VENGEFUL SPIRITS~~!
EEEEK!
SFX: DORO (BLOOP) DORO DORO

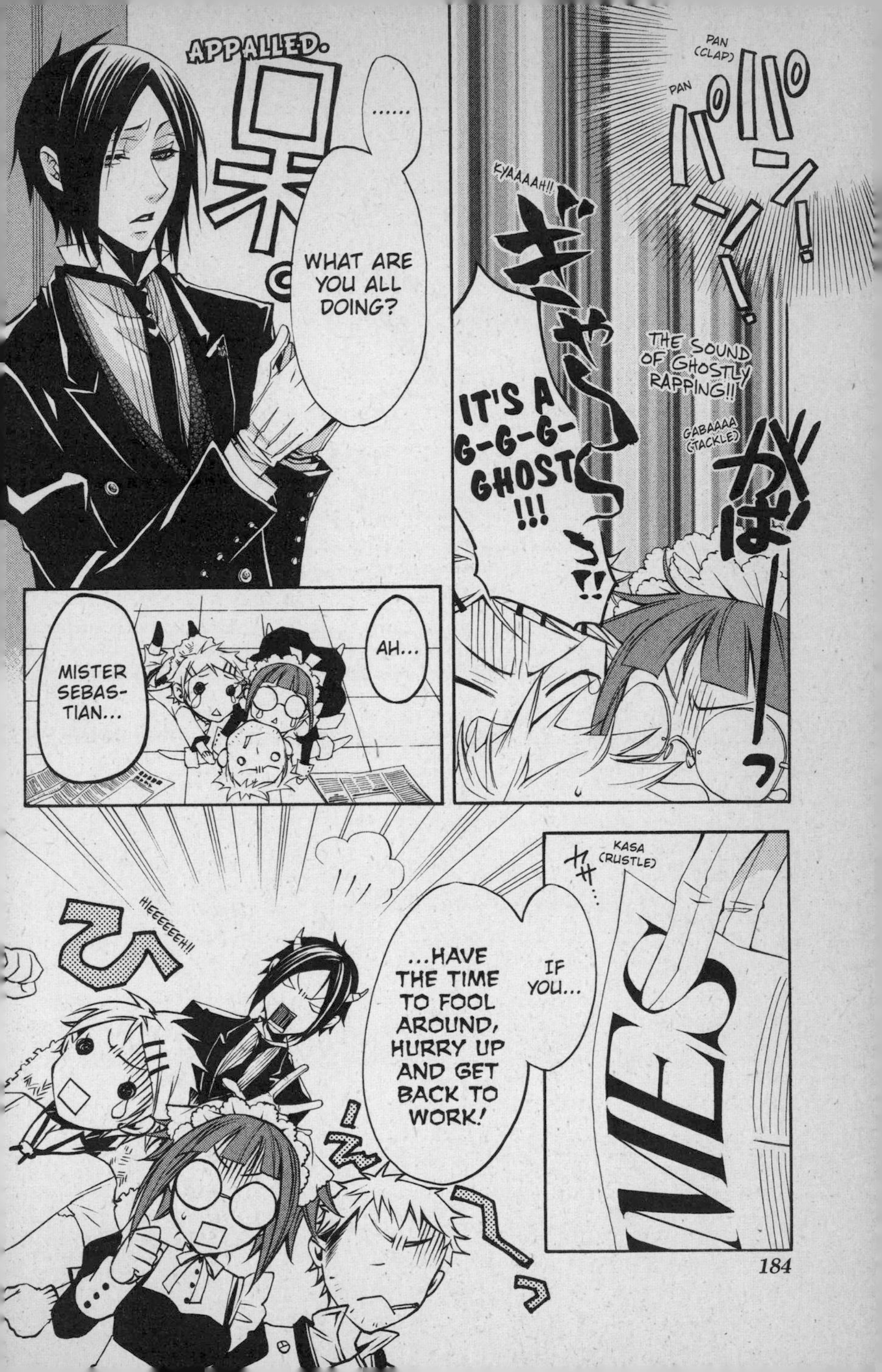
PAN (CLAP)
PAN
KYAAAAAH!!
THE SOUND OF GHOSTLY RAPPING!!
IT'S A G-G-G-GHOST!!!
GABAAAA (TACKLE)
......
APPALLED.
WHAT ARE YOU ALL DOING?
AH...
MISTER SEBASTIAN...
KASA (RUSTLE)
IF YOU...
...HAVE THE TIME TO FOOL AROUND, HURRY UP AND GET BACK TO WORK!
HIEEEEEEH!!

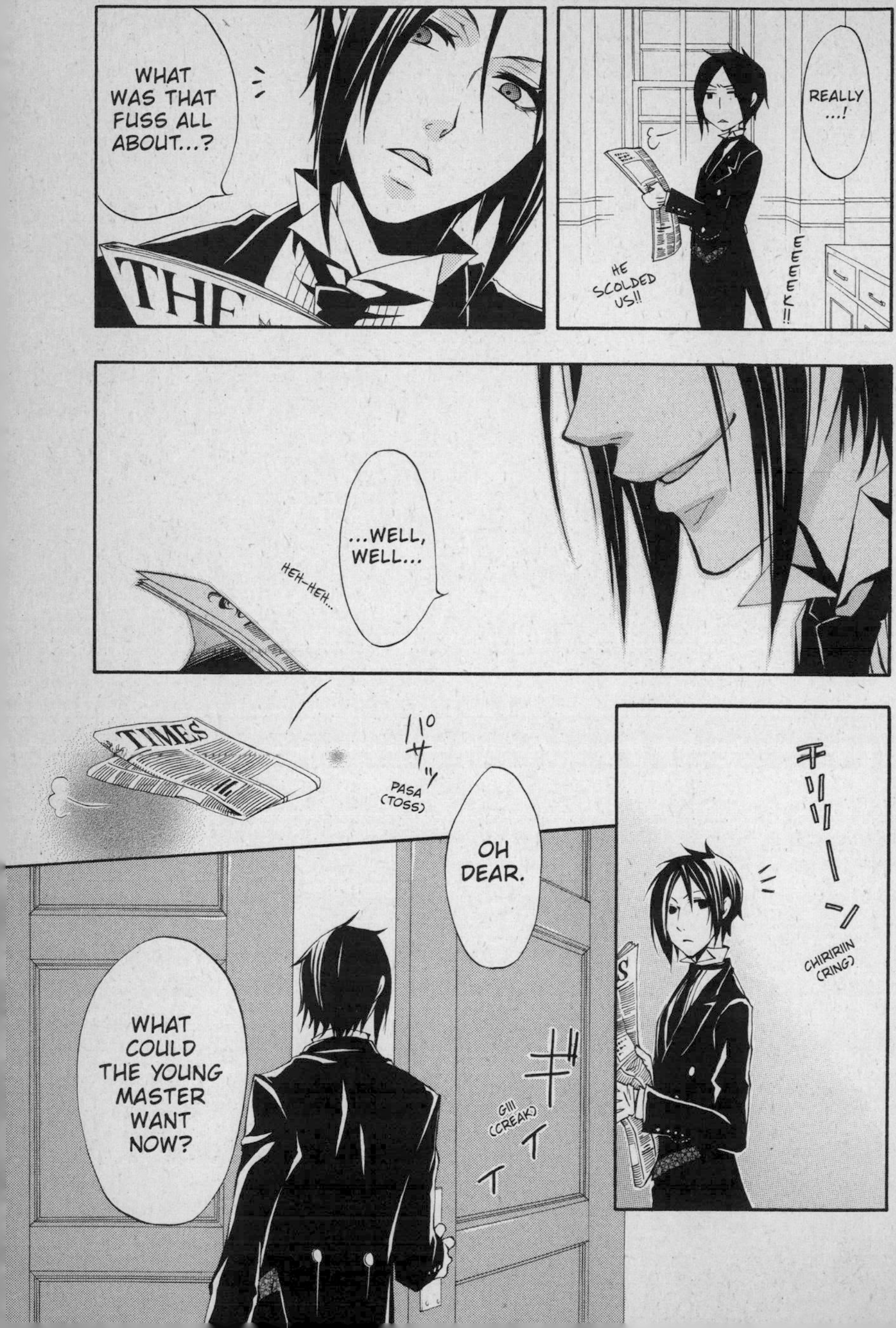
REALLY ...!
EEEEEK!!
HE SCOLDED US!!
WHAT WAS THAT FUSS ALL ABOUT...?
...WELL, WELL...
HEH-HEH...
チリリーン
CHIRIRIIN (RING)
パサッ
PASA (TOSS)
OH DEAR.
WHAT COULD THE YOUNG MASTER WANT NOW?
GIII (CREAK)

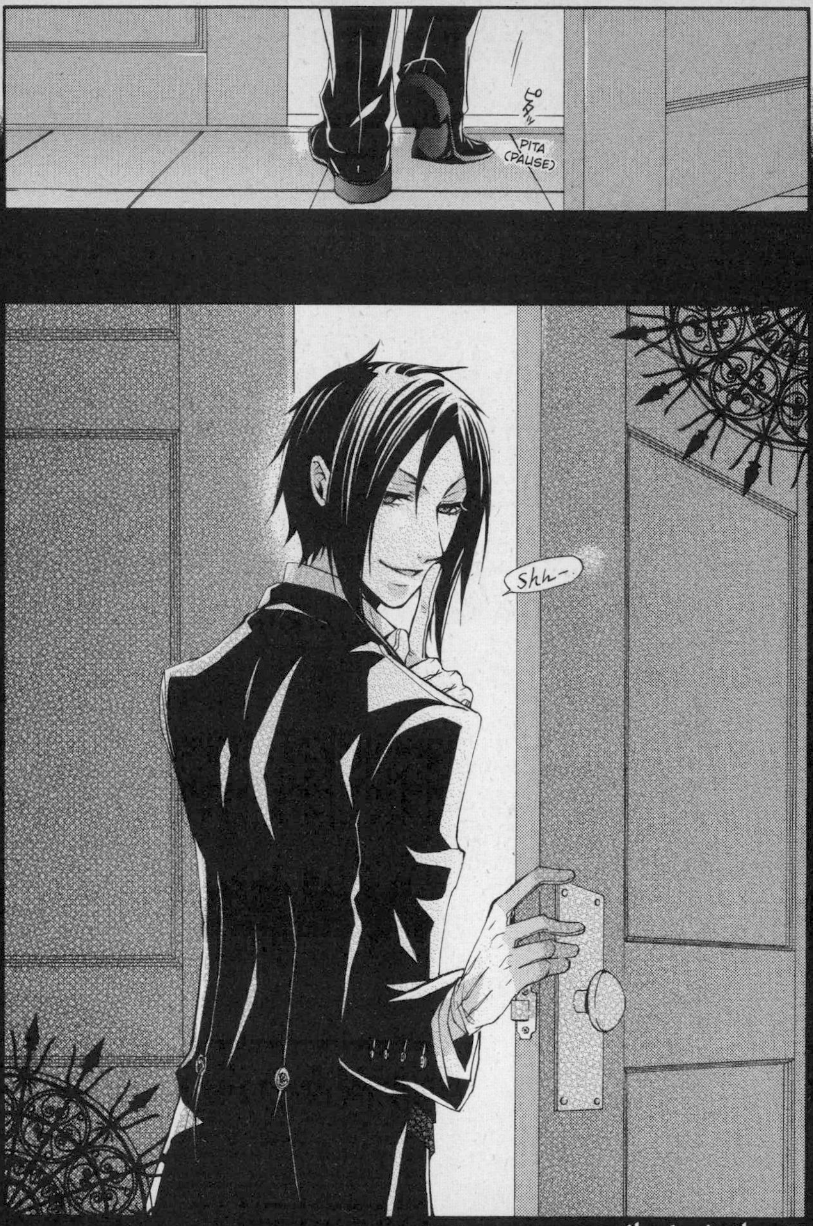
PITA
(PAUSE)
Shh-

*To be continued in* Black Butler 2

# ➤ Black Butler ➤

## 黒執事

⚜

# Downstairs

KiYo

MiNe

Wakana Haduki

Akiyo Satorigi

Yana's Mother

*

Takeshi Kuma

*

Yana Toboso

⚜

# SpecialThanks

Megumi Masuda

YuMe

and You.

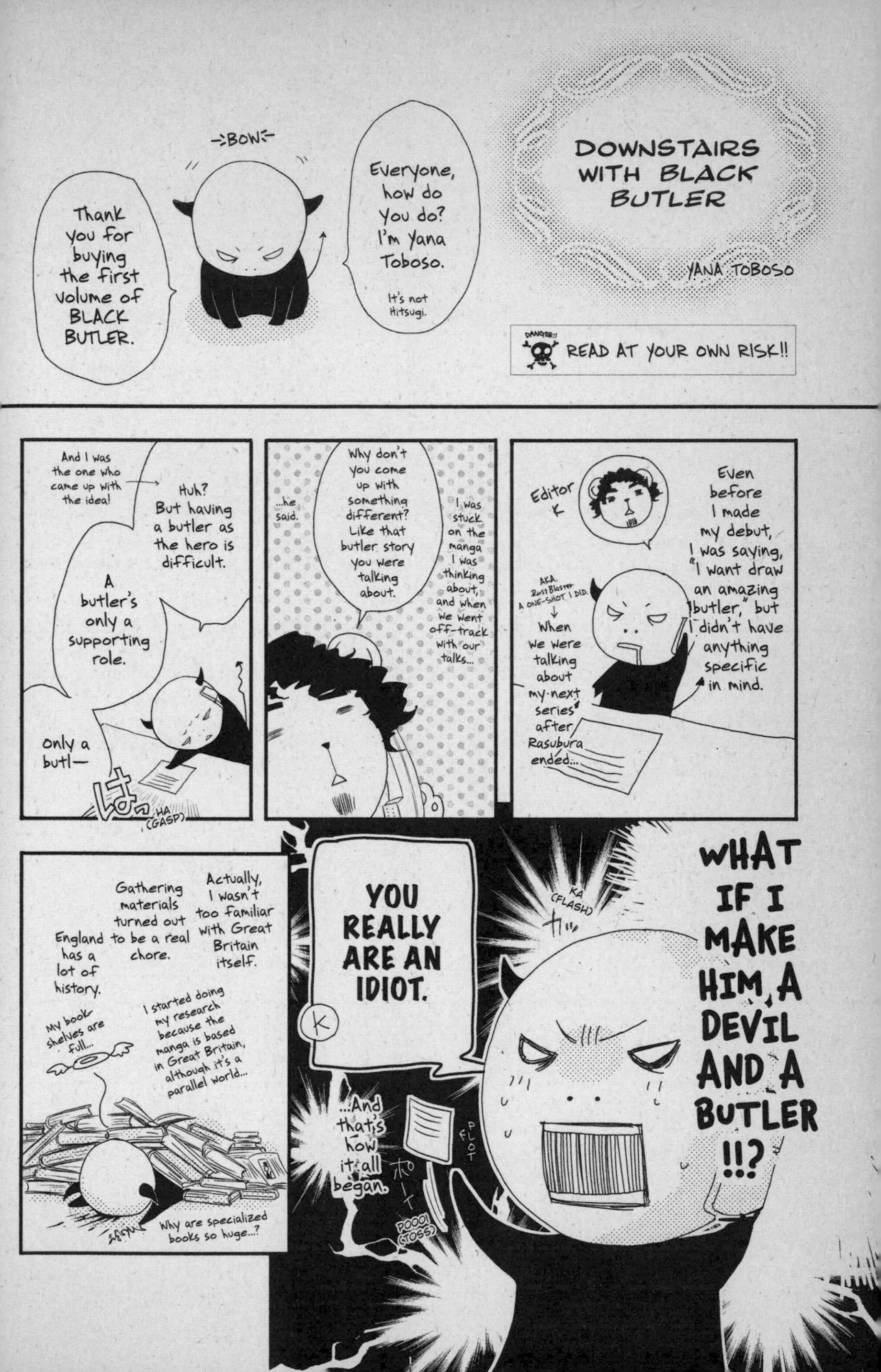
DOWNSTAIRS WITH BLACK BUTLER
YANA TOBOSO
DANGER!!
READ AT YOUR OWN RISK!!
Everyone, how do you do? I'm Yana Toboso.
It's not Hitsugi.
BOW
Thank you for buying the first volume of BLACK BUTLER.
Even before I made my debut, I was saying, "I want draw an amazing butler," but I didn't have anything specific in mind.
Editor K
When we were talking about my next series* after Rasubura ended...
AKA. Rust Blaster A ONE-SHOT I DID.
I was stuck on the manga I was thinking about, and when we went off-track with our talks...
Why don't you come up with something different? Like that butler story you were talking about.
...he said.
Huh? But having a butler as the hero is difficult.
And I was the one who came up with the idea!
A butler's only a supporting role.
Only a butl—
HA (GASP)
WHAT IF I MAKE HIM A DEVIL AND A BUTLER!!?
KA (FLASH)
YOU REALLY ARE AN IDIOT.
K
PLOT
POOOI (TOSS)
...And that's how it all began.
Actually, I wasn't too familiar with Great Britain itself.
Gathering materials turned out to be a real chore.
England has a lot of history.
I started doing my research because the manga is based in Great Britain, although it's a parallel world...
My book shelves are full...
Why are specialized books so huge...?

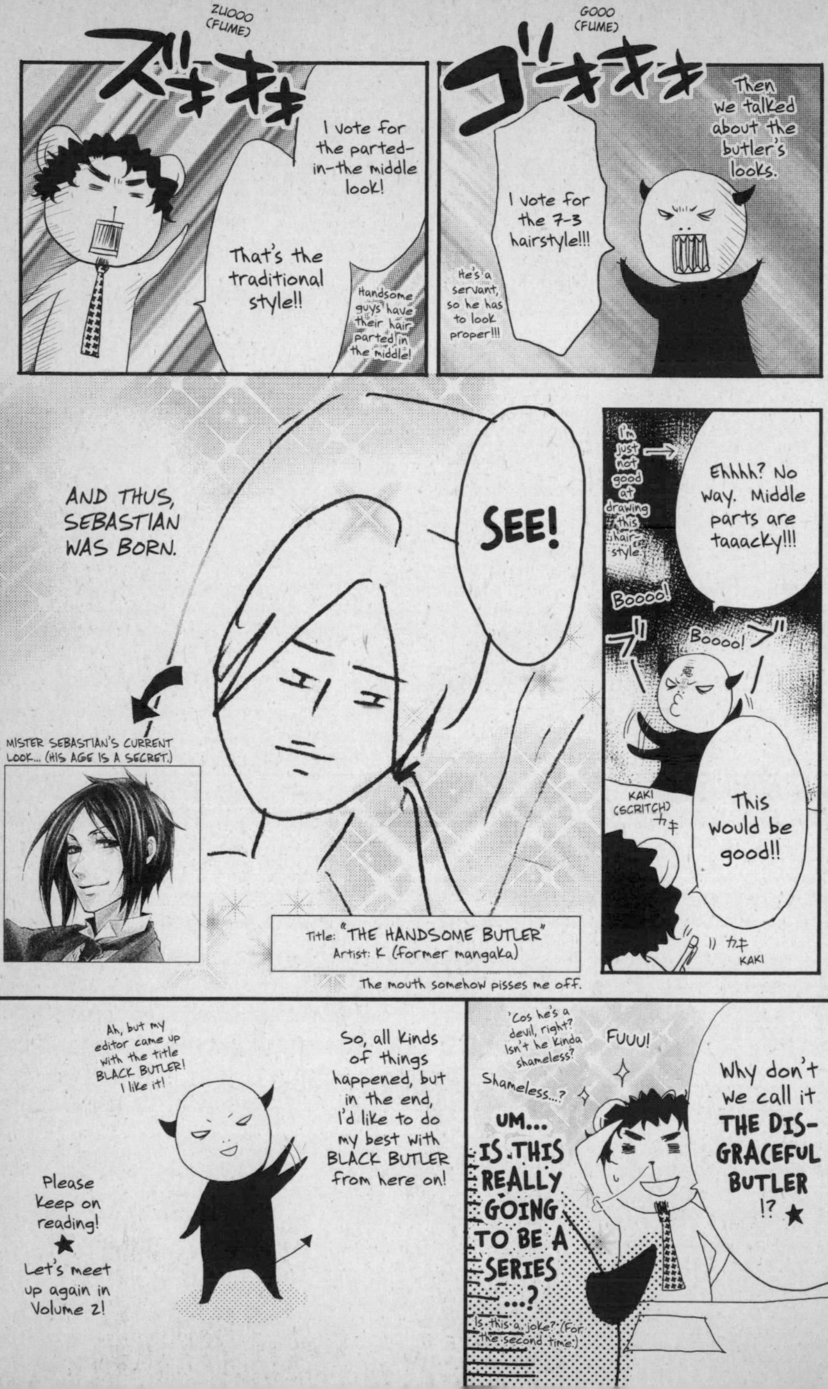
GOOO (FUME)
Then we talked about the butler's looks.
I vote for the 7-3 hairstyle!!!
He's a servant, so he has to look proper!!!
ZUOOO (FUME)
I vote for the parted-in-the middle look!
That's the traditional style!!
Handsome guys have their hair parted in the middle!
Ehhhh? No way. Middle parts are taaacky!!!
I'm just not good at drawing this hair-style.
Boooo!
Boooo!
This would be good!!
KAKI (SCRITCH)
KAKI
SEE!
AND THUS, SEBASTIAN WAS BORN.
MISTER SEBASTIAN'S CURRENT LOOK... (HIS AGE IS A SECRET.)
Title: "THE HANDSOME BUTLER"
Artist: K (former mangaka)
The mouth somehow pisses me off.
Why don't we call it THE DISGRACEFUL BUTLER!? ★
FUUU!
'Cos he's a devil, right? Isn't he kinda shameless?
Shameless...?
UM... IS THIS REALLY GOING TO BE A SERIES...?
Is this a joke? (For the second time.)
So, all kinds of things happened, but in the end, I'd like to do my best with BLACK BUTLER from here on!
Ah, but my editor came up with the title BLACK BUTLER! I like it!
Please keep on reading! ★ Let's meet up again in Volume 2!

# Translation Notes

INSIDE FRONT AND BACK COVERS
**Host / Host Club**
In Japan, there are drinking establishments known as "host clubs" that hire attractive men to cater to a female clientele. A host's job typically includes pouring drinks (as Sebastian is doing here) and lavishing attention on his client, which sometimes includes lighting her cigarette. Poor Sebastian can't seem to figure out which end is up on that lighter though!

PAGE 4
**Pain de campagne**
Literally, "country bread" in French. A rustic French bread with a hard crust and chewy texture that dates back to medieval times and is traditionally vented on the top of the loaf.

PAGE 5
**Ceylon tea**
A black tea grown in Sri Lanka (formerly known as Ceylon) that has a crisp, citrusy aroma.

**Royal Doulton**
An English ceramics and stoneware maker that started up during the Victorian era in London. Royal Doulton is actually better known for its tea sets, not for selling tea.

PAGE 11
**Ajixmoto**
Reference to a brand of MSG (monosodium glutamate), a type of salt that is used as a seasoning.

PAGE 24
***Wabisabi***
A Japanese aesthetic that finds beauty in what is natural, simple, imperfect, and impermanent.

PAGE 27
***Gyuu-tataki-don***
Thinly sliced, marinated beef, lightly seared on the outside, over a bowl of rice. *Don*, or *donburi*, refers to any rice dish served in a large rice bowl.

**Kyoto-style full-course meal**
Chlaus actually expects to be served traditional Kyoto-style tea ceremony dishes. In modern times, tea ceremony dishes are less often used to entertain guests and are more practically served as a light dish or a Japanese meal course so as to avoid drinking strong tea on an empty stomach.

PAGE 28
***Houhan***
Originally a vegetarian dish eaten by Buddhist monks, houhan was a dish in which seasoned trimmings were put on rice.

PAGE 36
**Machaxki**
A reference to Japanese TV personality Masaaki Sakai, one of whose party tricks is to pull the tablecloth off a table with various things on it, just as Sebastian does.

## Page 38
### Mille-feuille
"Thousand leaves" in French, a mille-feuille (also known as a Napoleon) is a classic dessert made of many thin, crispy layers of puff pastry with cream, custard, or preserves spread in between, then dusted on top with powdered sugar.

## Page 47
### Petite bourgeoisie
A Marxist term that refers to the lower middle class, especially shopkeepers and artisans.

## Page 49
### The Wild Earl
A pun on the title of a long-running Japanese televised samurai drama called *The Wild Shogun*, which featured the eighth shogun, Yoshimune Tokugawa.

## Page 54
### Marquess
An aristocratic title second only to "duke" in peerage rank. The Phantomhive family is an earldom and lower in rank than the Midford marquessate, hence Sebastian's aside.

## Page 57
### Peerage
A formal body of British nobility distinguished by ranked titles and the right to sit in the House of Lords in the British Parliament.

### Marquessate
The territory and holdings of a marquess.

## Page 61
### Viennese Waltz
One of the oldest known ballroom dances and the original form of the waltz, originating in Vienna, Austria. The Viennese Waltz is a closed-hold dance (note how Sebastian and Ciel hold each other as they practice) performed at a faster rhythm than the more popular English form of the waltz.

### Schönbrunn Palace
A residence of the Habsburg royal family located in Vienna, Austria, that dates as far back as the fourteenth century, this palace is considered one of the most important cultural monuments in Austria and is now a UNESCO-designated World Cultural Heritage site.

## Page 62
### Natural turn
One of the few moves in the Viennese Waltz, this is the term for a turn to the right.

## Page 94
### Tome and Julie
A pun on *Tom and Jerry*, Hanna-Barbera's classic animation series about a dueling housecat and mouse.

### Mice Hoihoi
A pun on the name of a brand of Japanese cockroach (*gokiburi*) traps called "Gokiburi Hoihoi." *Hoihoi* means "shoo, shoo!"

PAGE 96
**"He always aims for the nine ball."**
It seems that nine-ball is being played at this gathering. The way to instantly win a game of nine-ball is to pocket the nine ball after having struck the lowest numbered ball remaining on the pool table, as Ciel does here.

PAGE 99
**High tea**
Traditionally, an early evening meal for the lower classes during which tea was consumed alongside heartier dinner fare (meats, cheeses, etc.). So if Ciel is using "high tea" in the traditional sense here, he's actually insulting Lord Randall.

PAGE 107
***Inghilterra / Inglesi***
Italian for "England" and "the English," respectively.

PAGE 110
**Dealers and drugs**
In the Japanese edition of *Black Butler*, another reading of "dealers and drugs" is "mice and plague," which is in keeping with the earlier theme of Ciel's mission.

PAGE 119
**Buck's Row**
A street in the Whitechapel area of London's East End, which is sometimes said to be the scene of the serial killer Jack the Ripper's first murder.

PAGE 161
***Perfetto***
Italian for "perfect."

PAGE 176
**"…I am a devil of a butler."**
In Japanese, Sebastian's catchphrase— "I am just a butler"—reads *aku made shitsuji desu*. Here, however, by substituting *akuma de* ("a devil and") for *aku made* ("to the end/merely/ just") in the writing of the phrase, the literal meaning becomes, "I am a devil and a butler," or in this interpretation, "a devil of a butler," even though it is pronounced exactly the same.

PAGE 180
**Bamboo dragonfly**
Tanaka-san is playing with a *taketonbo*, a T-shaped flying toy of bamboo.

# Yana Toboso

AUTHOR'S NOTE

I like black for clothes, small items, and jewelry.

It's a color that can't be violated by any other colors. A color that simply keeps being itself.

A color that sinks more somberly than any other color, yet asserts itself more than all other colors. It's a passionate, gallant color.

Anything is wonderful if it transcends things, rather than being halfway.

I'll be happy if everyone feels such manliness from *Black Butler*.

# BLACK BUTLER ❶

## YANA TOBOSO

**Translation: Tomo Kimura** • **Lettering: Tania Biswas**

KUROSHITSUJI Vol. 1 © 2007 Yana Toboso / SQUARE ENIX CO., LTD.
All rights reserved. First published Japan in 2007 by SQUARE ENIX CO.,
LTD. English translation rights arranged with SQUARE ENIX CO., LTD.
and Hachette Book Group through Tuttle-Mori Agency, Inc. Translation ©
2010 by SQUARE ENIX CO., LTD.

Yen Press
Hachette Book Group
237 Park Avenue, New York, NY 10017

www.HachetteBookGroup.com
www.YenPress.com

Yen Press is an imprint of Hachette Book Group, Inc. The Yen Press name
and logo are trademarks of Hachette Book Group, Inc.

First Yen Press Edition: January 2010

ISBN: 978-0-316-08084-2

10  9  8

BVG

Printed in the United States of America